Public Catholicism

Second Edition

David J. O'Brien

ORBIS BOOKS

Maryknoll, New York 10545

The Catholic Foreign Mission Society of America (Maryknoll) recruits and trains people for overseas missionary service. Through Orbis Books, Maryknoll aims to foster the international dialogue that is essential to mission. The books published, however, reflect the opinions of their authors and are not meant to represent the official position of the society.

Second edition copyright © 1996 by the United States Catholic Conference, Inc. 3211 Fourth Street N.E., Washington, D.C. 20017, U.S.A.
Preface to the Second Edition copyright © 1996 by David J. O'Brien.
Published by Orbis Books, Maryknoll, New York, U.S.A.
Previously published by Macmillan Publishing Company, New York NY 10022, as part of *Makers of the Catholic Community*, the Bicentennial History of the Catholic Church in North America, authorized by the National Conference of Catholic Bishops, General Editor, Christopher J. Kauffman.

ORBIS/ISBN 1-57075-091-2

Contents

To
My Children
Mary, Kenny, Joey, and David

Foreword

"Pilgrims in Their Own Land" is how the French philosopher Jacques Maritain describes the historical condition of religion in America. The statement achieved epigrammatical status when it became the title of one of Martin M. Marty's recent books on American religious history.

"Pilgrimage" is a protean term that can be applied to the continuous movement of peoples in our open-ended society ever in perpetual motion. The term can also serve as an organizing principle for expanding our understanding of the religious story of the American people. David O'Brien has charted the pilgrimage of the Catholic community from a small minority church under John Carroll to its contemporary status as the largest denomination in the United States.

"Denomination" is an American term pregnant with significance in religious and social history. In Europe and in colonial America, established churches possessed specific privileges and a monopoly on the religious influence in the formation of public policy. Denominationalism originated in the development of religious freedom within a pluralistic society. It entailed an unwritten code whereby each religious group agreed that it should not attempt *directly* to influence public policy as had been the custom. To act as a denomination meant that the religious or spiritual bases of one's faith became privatized. Religious groups tended to foster a general morality of democratic behavior, later to be known as *civil religion*. Denominationalism also engendered the development of what John Murray Cuddihy has called the *religion of civility*. In order to get along and dwell in a civility Americans tend to downplay religious differences.

Public Catholicism is the first comprehensive story of the divergent ways in which the Catholic church has defined its role, explicitly and implicitly, in the shaping of public policy in accord with its self-un-

derstanding within democratic pluralism. John Carroll represents the
original accommodation to American denominationalism, with its
strong patriotism and religious privatization. The pilgrimage absorbed many diverse people during nearly a century of continuous
immigration. In the process a Catholic canopy was constructed to
protect the pilgrims from nativism and anti-Catholicism and to nur-
ture religious and ethnic identities. In the twentieth century, new
gospel communities broke down the privatization. Hence, in O'Brien's
cartography of the religious landscape he develops signposts to mark
these various styles of public Catholicism.

Of the many insights included in this book perhaps the most il-
luminating is O'Brien's view that in each of the styles of public Catholicism there is a dialectic between religion and culture. Either religion is privatized and there is an openness to the culture, or religion
is seen as a refuge in a hostile and inherently anti-Christian culture.

Some mainline Protestant communities have also experienced di-
alectical tensions. There are examples of Protestant parishes that
nurtured immigrant subcultures and closed themselves off from cos-
mopolitan American society. In the twentieth century some of these
groups experienced a privatization and an opening to the culture followed by an evangelical "awakening," an anticulture movement that
was a reaction to the specific trends in modern society.

Denominationalism, civil religion, and the religion of civility still
shape the religious behavior in our democratic society. O'Brien's historical analysis concludes with reflections on how and why groups
within the contemporary church shape their identities according to
the three styles of public Catholicism.

Christopher J. Kauffman

Preface to the
First Edition

When Christopher Kauffman asked me to join the team of scholars preparing a series of volumes on American Catholic history marking the bicentennial of the United States hierarchy, I responded both affirmatively and too quickly. Only when I joined Kauffman and the other writers for a meeting did I realize how large an assignment I had accepted. My task, as it turned out, centered on the American Catholic church's relationship with American society, on its public life. In my own work I had gradually come to understand that the public life of the church was an all-embracing concept. All phases of religious activity draw from and in turn influence the larger culture: issues of church and state and of religion and politics reflect deeper problems of the historicity and humanity of those who belong to the church, from its most humble communicants to its most powerful bishops. Unfortunately, neither my own research nor the combined efforts of historians had yet come close to providing adequate information to examine this entire area with confidence.

On the other hand, I also believed that these issues had now moved to center stage because of current developments surrounding the remarkable pastoral letters on peace and economic justice issued by the bishops, and because of well-publicized misunderstandings between the American church and the Vatican. An effort to sort out the ways in which Catholics have understood their church as a public presence seemed to me both timely and potentially useful. What I have tried to do in this book, then, is to survey the history of "public Catholicism," with an eye toward the contemporary scene. I do so without apology, for I believe that the historical project is always anchored both in the past and in the present, that meaning in public events is in part created by the contemporary reappropriation of previous experiences. In this case, in a book prepared as part of the public celebration of the 200th anniversary of the church as an organized presence in the United States, it seems to me quite appropriate to attempt to relate historical developments of its current problems and possibilities.

All efforts at historical generalization are risky at best. Among American historians today the best work is done on small-scale subjects as a new social history, focused on community studies, minorities, women, and the working class. Leading historians regularly praise this work and at the same time worry about the fragmentation of the field, the lack of synthetic and narrative generalization about American history as a whole, and the resulting marginalization of history in public discourse. I am fully aware that the generalizations I have attempted are based on limited research, and that they are drawn heavily upon analysis of contemporary public dialogue about the meaning of contemporary experience. Yet I believe such an effort is needed if Catholics as an organized community of faith are to make sense of their experience, find common ground on which to renew their church, and clarify the terms of their participation in wider public dialogue about their country.

I wish to thank Christopher Kauffman for his confidence in me, for his interest in and support for my work over many years, and for his patience with my procrastination. My distinguished colleagues in this project, the authors of the other volumes in the series, were invariably helpful and supportive in our too-short meetings together. My wife Joanne is still my strongest supporter, my best critic, and my most faithful friend. Finally there are my four children, to whom I have dedicated this book. Mary and Kenny are now out of college—Georgetown and Saint Michael's, respectively—and building lives for themselves. Joseph will soon leave Fordham, while David is half way through Holy Cross. Each in her and his own way has made their own sense of Catholicism as a public faith. They care about the world and about people, they are smart and strong and good-natured, and their parents are very proud of them. If I am hopeful about the future of the things I most revere, especially the hard-won gains of freedom, equality, and justice, it is largely because of them, and because of others of their age I have taught at Holy Cross. They and their generation will build a new church for a new age and in the process fulfill the providential promise of American Catholic history.

Preface to the Second Edition

Public Catholicism appeared in 1988, and the writing took place during the two preceding years, so a decade has intervened since I started the project. Like all authors, I would now welcome a chance to prepare a revised edition, incorporating information from ten years of research by a growing body of scholars in the rich field of American Catholic studies. Perhaps the day for revision will come, but not yet. The text which reappears, now more accessible thanks to Orbis Books, is unchanged.

There are at least three things I would like to say to each generous reader before reading begins.

First, a word about what is here. This book was written at the center of this field of American (read U.S.) Catholic history. It presumes the simple chronology that informs other surveys. First, there was a republican period, centered on the Maryland Catholic community and its leader, John Carroll. This period was marked by grateful Catholic affirmation of the American constitution, confident assertion of a Catholic place at the center of American culture, and cautious, somewhat independent dealings with Rome. All that changed with the arrival in large numbers of additional European immigrants, beginning about 1820. Led by the Irish, they created a distinctive, somewhat militant Catholic subculture composed of immigrant, working-class outsiders. Finally, after World War II, this "immigrant church" was transformed through the acceleration of the complicated process of Americanization. The result is a quite new, still largely undefined Catholic church in the United States.

Thus the center of attention in this book is the life of European immigrant Catholic communities, especially the Irish, who dominated the church's internal life and its public articulation. Other European immigrant groups are discussed, their varying parts in the story reflecting their different relationships with the institutional church and the Catholic mainstream.

A great deal of excellent research and writing is being done on all the elements of this story. We know more than ever about the Carrolls, the converts who continued their tradition, about the working lives and families and neighborhoods where the immigrant churches took shape. We know more about bishops and priests and a great deal more about women, lay and religious. But for the most part this new knowledge comes from specialized monographs. There have been few ventures into broad interpretation, so this basic chronological outline remains intact. It needs revision, I think. I even hinted in this book at some lines of that revision. For example, I began to question the theme of Americanization, which suggests that Catholics only recently became "real Americans," that the immigrant church was a foreign transplant, doomed to wither under the pressure of American modernity. But so far there has been no revision of the basic outline, no new, compelling story which will make sense of the American experience of Catholicism as a whole. I hope that one day I will get a chance to work on a revised version of this book.

Second, a word must be said about those who are not here. Public presence in its obvious forms is shaped by those who have the power of self-projection. That is true even among groups who are poor, as all immigrants were. Here I said far too little about those on the margins of the noisy Catholic subculture, too much about those who presumed to speak for them. The historical literature on these groups was thin when I wrote, but there was enough to justify closer attention on my part. Now we have considerable scholarly research

- on *African-American Catholics*, few in number but stunning in their unique and tenacious fidelity;
- on *Native American Catholics*, treated as objects of missionary outreach even today, rarely understood as subjects with a rich history of their own making;
- on *Spanish-speaking Catholics* in their great numbers and diversity. They were here from from start, which we need to date earlier than we have. They have enriched the church, and by their presence challenge many of its assumptions. Now they stand as central actors shaping the future of American Catholicism.

Each group deserved closer attention when I last wrote; each will need to play a central role in the story yet to be told.

Finally, a word about perspective. A book like this is intended to make a contribution to historical literature, to offer a vision of what has been and how the present has come to be. But I also hoped that this book would help American Catholics sort out their personal and collective public responsibilities. I offered three "models" of public responsibility I saw evident in contemporary Catholic politics. Nothing I have seen since has changed my conclusion that each of these models has both theological and practical justification.

The *republican style*, with its dualism of citizenship and discipleship, remains the best articulated, but still searches for a pastoral and political strategy. The *interest group* or *immigrant style* remains an impulse of institutional self-interest and is always attractive to powerless groups seeking a place at the table. It has a rich history and a relatively clear pastoral and political strategy, but it has yet to find a persuasive theological articulation. The *evangelical style* continues to grow, reflecting the dynamics of American democratic religious and cultural pluralism. It is the approach most affirmative of American individualism and personal freedom, the most open to the pull of the spirit to religious and social renewal movements of all sorts. It is the hardest to contain within institutional boundaries, the least "Catholic" but perhaps most "Christian" of the styles. Among middle class, "postethnic" Americans evangelical piety will most likely be the starting point for evangelization and pastoral planning. The interaction among these three styles will shape the future of public Catholicism in the United States.

One last word. I have always believed, and I am more convinced than ever, that the outcome of the Public Catholicism story is of real significance. Americans seem interested in religious questions, less attached than they once were to doctrinaire slogans about church-state separation, more intense in their search for meaning in their lives as citizens and participants in particular communities. Catholics are strategically well placed for the discussion of public meaning, for some are now well established at the centers of power in American society and culture. Others live on the edge, in new immigrant communities and in Spanish-speaking neighborhoods across the country. Other Catholics are present in service in the midst of every struggle for human dignity in the country. To public work Catholics bring a rich heritage of symbols and experience, and a body of social thought as comprehensive and convincing as any available in the post-Cold–War world. What remains needed is a revival of a sense of mission which will inspire individual Catholics to probe their experience, appropriate their tradition, and commit themselves to building justice and peace in the works of their everyday lives. If they—*if we*—can do some of this, it will make a difference for the country and for a globe-spanning church still unsure how to handle the claims of democracy.

Now, as ten years ago, I pray that this book will make a modest contribution to that work of Catholic renewal.

CHAPTER

1

Public Leadership and American Catholicism

In 1983 the United States Catholic hierarchy published a widely discussed pastoral letter on nuclear weapons, "The Challenge of Peace: God's Promise and Our Response." In preparing the letter, the bishops consulted with experts in science, nuclear strategy, and international relations, as well as with theologians and leaders of the Catholic peace movement. For the first time in history, they distributed draft texts of the letter, encouraging commentary from all interested parties. Naturally enough, those drafts caught the attention of government officials, leaders of other churches, and the media. While Catholics were examining the drafts in parishes, schools, and diocesan offices, the bishops and their letter were being featured on the evening television news and in the Sunday newspaper supplements. As a result, the letter became a public document as well as a church document. It rekindled a national debate on the ethics of nuclear policy and the arms race as well as a church debate on the requirements of Christian discipleship.

Interested Catholic citizens found themselves involved in two types of dialogue. The first took place when they discussed the issues of war and peace with their fellow Christians; then talk centered on what was required of them as followers of Jesus Christ and members of the Roman Catholic communion. The second took place when they discussed the latest reports about the arms race with other people, some not Catholic or Christian, at work, at parties, or in public meetings; here the dialogue revolved around the responsibilities of citizens of the United States living in an interdependent and dangerous world. For some, perhaps, there was little difference between the two experiences. A person might, for example, argue that the conclusions of the civic discussion are binding on the Christian: what is required by the nation sets the parameters for what the church and the believer must do. In its crudest form this means that "religion has nothing to do with politics." In more sophisticated terms, set most clearly by the great Protestant theologian Reinhold Niebuhr, moral persons live in an immoral society, so that Christian moral ideals may be binding on individual conscience but they cannot become normative for collective groups or for the state.

The other way to avoid a problem relating the two conversations is to reverse the priority, arguing that what is binding on the Christian is also binding on society. This was the approach of an older version of the Protestant Social Gospel, which asked simply: "What would Jesus do?" It shows up today in its simplest form in demands that Christian moral obligations regarding sexuality be taught in public schools or even enforced by law. Its more sophisticated form is expressed by theologians as the demand that the church and each Christian witness to the moral demands of the gospel and recognize that, because of the depth of contemporary pluralism, it is simply not possible to shape a public morality, much less live by one, without compromising the integrity of Christian faith. There are other ways to avoid the problem of the two debates. Church people can refuse to take part in the public conversation, or citizens can ignore the religious and moral dimension of the issue. Or an individual can engage in both but simply refuse to relate the two: the gospel makes serious demands, but one must be realistic.

To their very great credit, the bishops recognized the problem. In the 1983 pastoral letter they described "two styles of teaching" in the contemporary church.[1] One, addressed primarily to Christians, begins with shared faith in Christ and explores the demands of discipleship. The other begins with the common moral norms of all citizens, most important, the dignity of the human person, and explores the demands of citizenship. There are two distinct but overlapping audiences addressed, Catholics and all Americans. The letter has two purposes, to help the church and its members form their consciences on war and peace, and to help shape the public morality on the basis of which public decisions about public policy are made. Finally, the letter uses two languages, or types of discourse, one Christian, the other more broadly human. The tension between the two runs through the letter. This tension is exemplified by setting side by side passages that uphold nonviolent love as the better way with passages that define a "strictly conditioned moral acceptance" of deterrence. The striking honesty of the letter, unique in modern Catholic documents, is matched only by its audacity. For the bishops want nothing less than to find a way of dealing with this issue that allows the church and the person to live with integrity, with their actions matching their beliefs and values, and to live responsibly as well, sharing with all other Americans in making decisions about a common life. It is the most direct, forthright encounter with the problem of pluralism in the history of American Catholicism.

This volume deals with the *public* presence of the church in the United States. Of course, all facets of the church's life are public, but this book will be concerned with the conscious aspects of that public presence, how Catholics thought about their responsibilities as participants in wider communities, local, state, and national, and how they acted on those responsibilities. In emphasizing the word *conscious*, we touch the heart of the problem. In the more integrated, traditional societies of Catholic Europe before the nineteenth century, the church had a clear public role because it was an official church; parish and civic birth and marriage records were one and the same; in one way or another the church enjoyed public financial support; it ordinarily controlled education, provided necessary social services, and was the custodian of the community's moral life. The state, for its part, had a religious character. Kingship was surrounded with religious symbolism, political authority was sanctioned by divine mandates, and, in the years prior to the formation of the new church in the United States, the governments of most European Catholic countries effectively chose bishops, controlled publication of papal and episcopal decrees, and even attempted to determine the location of churches and schedules for religious services.

What was reflected here was a traditional society in which participation in the church was not considered distinct from participation in the wider community. By the end of the eighteenth century, however, the spheres of the religious and the secular were beginning to separate. Already struggles were taking place over censorship, finances, ecclesiastical courts, and education, and these would become more severe, culminating in the outbreaks of anticlericalism that punctuated the French revolution. By the nineteenth century, the problems posed by modernization, often accompanying urbanization and industrialization, threatened the hegemony of the Catholic church and posed choices for individual citizens. Religion, like it or not, was becoming more and more a matter of personal decision, which is to say that affiliation with the church, and the quality of that affiliation, were becoming matters of self-conscious decision.

This new consciousness has been well explored by historians of colonial America. Bernard Bailyn, for example, in a seminal essay on education, argued that the transmission of values and disciplines across the generations became a matter of consciousness in the North American colonies; the passage of a child from family to society was no longer automatic and taken for granted, but problematic, in need of definition, guidance, and control.[2] For churches, the new consciousness arose out of the threat that the New World posed to the memory of Jesus and of the Protestant Reformation. If awareness of the struggles over religion in the immediate past was lost, so might be a person's loyalty to one or another brand of Protestantism, to the Reformation, even to Christianity itself. Keeping those memories alive, and persuading people to join and support the church, was complicated by the fact that pluralism became an unavoidable reality within a generation or two; not only were the several brands of Protestant Christianity transplanted to the colonies, but inner disputes could breed new churches as the restraints of bishops and state authority were far weaker in New World conditions. The absence of taken-for-granted tradition and the presence of competitive pluralism insured that churches would become self-conscious projects.

So it was for American Catholicism after John Carroll launched the new church in 1789. As a minority, Catholics found the challenge of pluralism particularly intense. Providing priests and places of worship, educating children and relieving the needy, buying land and building centers of community life, all required people, money, and motivation. When hundreds of thousands of immigrants began to arrive, the organizing, unifying, and educating of Catholics became an even more deliberate process. It is hardly surprising that the American church appeared preoccupied with itself. Non-Catholic Americans worried that the church's success in organizing would divide communities and endanger the precarious experiment in self-government, while European Catholics had the opposite fear, that their American brethren would become too American, too concerned with buildings, money, and quantitative measures of success. Both concerns were justified to some degree but each reflected a lack of appreciation of the dynamics of the American religious environment. Bishops and clergy had little choice but to segregate Catholics to some degree from other Americans if the church was to survive as an identifiable community of faith; they also had little choice but to accommodate to the basic institutional imperatives of the United States if it was to survive as an American church.

American Catholic history, naturally enough, has been focused on the internal life of the church. Even the burgeoning social history of the last generation, emanating from immigrant labor and local community studies, has concentrated on Catholics as Catholics and on the church as an organization. Conscious of the imperatives facing the church and its people in pluralistic America, historians, like Catholics themselves, have been concerned with the church as church, and thus with what makes Catholics different from other Americans. Yet throughout American history individual Catholic leaders have known quite well the need to think about the relationship between Catholic faith and American culture, and thus about the life of Catholics outside church and the church as a public community and institution. They have taken pains to defend the church's pastoral activities as beneficial to the public, and they have undertaken many forms of activity designed to show that the church and its members were serious and responsible citizens.

The purpose of this book is to describe this public thought and action of American Catholics, to examine those Catholics and those organizations and institutions that attempted to mediate between the church and the larger society, perhaps even to find religious meaning in supposedly secular activity. We will see that two distinct strands exist, with a third emerging in the middle of the twentieth century. The first is republican, shaped by the Enlightenment, by the experience of the early Anglo-American Catholics, and by notable converts from Yankee America. It produced a lay style, because it grasped the fact that the individual Catholic was both Catholic and American, that there were tensions between the two, but that on the basis of reason and mutual respect one could be fully responsible to both. The paradigm of this style, to use a modern term, was the relatively successful middle-class Catholic laity, so faithful to the church that they could not understand themselves apart from it, but fully at home, or at least wishing to be fully at home, in their community, their nation, and their world. At times, as when facing persecution or its threat, or when caught up in the heady experience of economic and social advancement, the republican Catholic rigidly segregated religious and civic loyalties, urged the church to stick to religion, and engaged in economic and political life with no direct and little indirect reference to religious faith. At its best, the republican tradition recognized the tension between religious and civic allegiances and attempted to mediate between them, asking what America had to teach the church and what the church could offer to America. In more concrete terms, lay middle-class Catholics helped priests, bishops, and religious build the church by organizing, educating, and disciplining the poor immigrants, and they told their neighbors that this was an obvious contribution to civic welfare. They also took part in civic affairs with broad good will, concern for the commonweal, sincere dedication to American ideals, and occasional suggestions that the church had something important to offer the community.

The other two strands of the public tradition represent a split in the republican inheritance. If the latter mediated between the internal preoccupations of the church and the secular concerns of the public, the immigrant tradition, assisted by the ultramontane movement in Europe, gave church needs and interests the priority. Inside the church, this tradition has always been present, for churchmen, after all, have dedicated their lives to the church and sincerely believe it is the means through which men and women can attain salvation; personal considerations and truth itself demand that priority be given to religious values and interests. In the United States the threats posed by external hostility and internal diversity, in a setting in which money and personnel were always inadequate, reinforced the drift toward a more self-interested form of public presence. Externally, many of the church's own members were poor, working-class immigrants. On both scores of class and nationality, they were at the bottom and outside the dominant culture, exploited to a degree, looked down upon as well. The United States was a nation with very weak public institutions. Local and state governments did little to relieve poverty, even at times of panic and financial dislocation; nor did they do anything to ease the process of adjustment for newcomers to the badly governed, almost anarchic cities. What institutions did exist were for the most part in the hands of native-born non-Catholics. Many of these immigrants were peasants, who had few illusions about public life; they knew that life was hard, that power mattered, and that rewards came to those who were shrewd, tough-minded, and dedicated to their own survival. Thus they adapted well to the marketplace of interest-group politics and to the economic marketplace where power determined rewards. The more ambitious among them took the lead in organizing ethnic associations, often with churches at the center, both to preserve Old World traditions and facilitate advancement in the new, and the organizing skills they exhibited there spilled over into political machines and developing forms of trade unionism. Samuel Gompers's business unionism and the bread-and-butter liberalism of the political machines were expressions of the immigrant style, an American form of interest-group liberalism.

The third Catholic public style reflected the other side of the tension between Catholicity and American pluralism. For some sensitive Catholics the republican style was too secular, the immigrant style too selfish. Neither, it appeared, had much to do with Christianity or with the life and witness of Jesus. They could not be satisfied with the subculture that the church's leaders constructed in order to preserve the faith and insure institutional survival, but neither were they satisfied with the dualism of a republican tradition that, by the time industrial society arrived, tended to segregate religion from the rest of life and to reinforce the modern schism that historians have noted as part of the experience of Christianity in the modern world.[3] Instead they sought a reintegration, personal, communal, and public, by means of a complete commitment to the gospel, expressed in profound religious faith, an interiorization of the spiritual life, and a dedication to serving the poor and healing the wounds besetting society.

Evident first among founders of religious orders and a few idealistic lay people, this strand emerged in the Catholic Worker movement of Dorothy Day and Peter Maurin. Practicing voluntary poverty, experimenting with utopian alternative communities, and, later, offering a witness of Christian nonviolence to war and the arms race, the Catholic Worker represented the appearance of an evangelical style in American Catholicism. Relegated to the margins of a church organized in the interest-group style and a culture dominated by new manifestations of the republican tradition, evangelical Catholicism would begin to spread in the wake of Vatican II, the race crisis, the war in Vietnam, and the deepening specter of nuclear annihilation. While few Catholics would join the Catholic Worker or the various resistance and countercultural movements that sprang up around it, many responded to a spirituality that called for fundamental commitment to the gospel and witness of Jesus and the resulting distance from contemporary culture.

The book concludes with the suggestion that, after two centuries of organized existence in the United States, the American church has not evolved a coherent understanding of its public role and responsibilities. Immigrant styles gave way in the caldron of the 1960s, theology and spirituality moved in an evangelical direction, and church leaders, attracted by evangelical and prophetic appeals, struggled to make the republican style their own. Some used that republican tradition to justify accommodation to the prevailing culture; others, including the majority of bishops, wished to encourage a more dynamic process of bringing Catholic resources to bear on public problems. The majority of Catholics were for the first time in a century politically unmobilized, uncertain of the character of Christian commitment in a Catholic framework, and confused about the relationship between their Catholic inheritance and their public and daily experience. Historical experience enlightens this situation, suggests some degree of modesty, and points a few directions; but it suggests as well that pluralism as an internal experience within the church is here to stay. Making that pluralism constructive, opening up authentic public dialogue within the church as well as with others outside, building open and democratic structures through which all may share responsibility for the church's common life and public presence, setting limits to pluralism by a renewed understanding of authority and the demands of faith and community—these are the challenges that must be met in order to build an authentically public Catholicism, one that takes with full seriousness the idea that Jesus and his church, which is his presence in history, exist for the salvation of all persons. To be the Body of Christ is to be a visible sacrament of God's love for all creation. That is what the church claims to be called to; it is a call to public presence, to faithful discipleship through authentic citizenship.[4]

CHAPTER
2
Republican Catholicism

※

$\mathcal{O}$ur religious system has undergone a revolution, if possible, more extraordinary than our political one," the most important Catholic in the new United States wrote in 1783. In all of the states, John Carroll explained, "free toleration is allowed to Christians of every denomination," while in several "a communication of all civil rights, without distinction or diminution, is extended to those of our religion."[1] Extraordinary the new situation surely was, though hardly more extraordinary than the independence of the former British colonies in North America. John Carroll's exaggeration could be forgiven, however; the conditions under which he and his fellow Catholics now lived had indeed changed profoundly. For the first time since the break of Henry VIII with Rome, English-speaking Catholics were free to worship as they pleased, educate their children, and, in some states, participate on an equal basis in public affairs. Suspicion, even prejudice, remained, of course, sometimes only superficially masked by tolerant good will, but Catholics almost everywhere in the new nationexperienced a new sense of freedom, and now they had the law on their side. They could openly proclaim their ancestral faith, acknowledge their spiritual bond to the Holy See, and join together to build churches and schools, while at the same time participating with their fellow citizens in this new and truly extraordinary experiment in self-government. It was a new situation, not just for Anglo-American Catholics like John Carroll but for all Catholics. For the first time, the church found itself living under a republican regime on an equal basis with other religious groups. Religious freedom, separation of church and state, and religious pluralism, the three basic elements of this new religious culture, were bound to shape a new form of public Catholicism.

Historians have in recent years identified a distinctive republican style in the early experience of the American Catholic church. Originating in the response of Catholics in England to that country's Anglican establishment and Puritan culture, this remarkable set of attitudes and ideas constituted a unique blend of republican and Catholic principles quite different from the defensive posture of post-Reformation Catholicism generally and from the self-interested group consciousness of the immigrant church that would develop later. The Carroll family, their Anglo-American contemporaries, and many of the French clergy who came to assist the new church during its formative years, shared a distinctive sense of the relationship between faith and citizenship; their experience of survival amid disabilities, their participation in the nation-making process, and their intelligent grasp of the dynamics of freedom and pluralism gave them a sturdy feeling of independence and produced high hopes for a new age of progress and civility.

THE CROWN AND ESTABLISHMENT

The Peace of Westphalia (1648), which marked the end of the wars sparked by the Protestant Reformation, left the religious question to be resolved by the crowned heads of Europe. Whatever the religion of the monarch, that would be the religion of the realm. The result was the division of Europe into nations officially Catholic and Protestant, a solution that brought the order required by emerging nation-states, but at the expense of religious minorities. Protestants in Catholic Europe were under the ban; so were Catholics in Protestant Europe. Determined to repress the bitter internal divisions associated with religious differences, governments on both sides would tolerate private dissent but not public contention. Religious uniformity, most agreed, was absolutely essential to political unity and governmental stability. Not surprisingly, religious minorities were not always satisfied with this arrangement and, in the century and a half that followed Westphalia, the more thoughtful among them were attracted by alternative ideas about the role of religion in public affairs. There were, of course, Protestant and Catholic leaders whose only objection to religious establishments was that they were not their own, but a growing number shared with an even smaller minority of nonreligious persons the belief that public life should be based on reason, not religion, that religious professions should be regarded as private preferences, and that the rights of persons and the general welfare should be the guiding norms of public life. Those who were outsiders because of their religious faith might retire to the country, as so many Catholic aristocrats did in England, but others, in more precarious circumstances, might find in the reasonable arguments associated with the Enlightenment the road to religious emancipation, political participation, and personal and family security. Protestants in France naturally enough found the anticlerical diatribes of Voltaire and the social contract arguments of Rousseau attractive; the triumph of Enlightenment principles could not but reduce the power of the Catholic church over political and cultural affairs and leave non-Catholics more free to live with integrity. Similarly, Catholics in England, and even more in England's Puritan-dominated colonies, could be forgiven if they found themselves enchanted by the more moderate but altogether reasonable version of human rights and social contract associated with John Locke and carried on in the eighteenth century by a variety of republican thinkers.

Yet even the most liberal republicans and most indifferent dissenters had little use for Roman Catholics. English-speaking peoples regarded Catholics as superstitious, slavishly subservient to the pope and his Jesuit minions, and treacherous allies of the country's enemies during her hours of supreme crisis. Law reflected these judgments, banning priests, public worship, and political participation. In Ireland these laws were severely enforced. In England itself the latitudinarian Anglican establishment was prepared to leave Catholic aristocrats alone as long as they avoided political intrigues and did not antagonize the sometimes violently anti-Catholic masses. In the colonies, however, things were different. There the more passionate and exclusive Puritans were usually in charge, Catholic France and its Indian allies sat on the frontier, and militant anti-Catholicism remained respectable. A Massachusetts statute of 1647, for example, threatened death to "every Jesuit, seminary priest, missionary or spiritual or ecclesiastical person made or ordained by any authority, power or jurisdiction, derived, challenged or pretended, from the Pope or see of Rome."[2]

In the face of such attitudes, both in England and North America, it was not surprising that, given a chance themselves to found a colony, English Catholics would avoid even the appearance of interest in a Catholic restoration and would instead stand forth boldly for religious toleration. In 1632 Charles I, in gratitude for the loyalty of George Calvert, decided to allow his son, Cecilius Calvert, to found a colony in North America. The undertaking was a family business enterprise, but it did provide Calvert and the small group of English Catholics associated with him an unusual opportunity to shape public institutions for themselves. Earlier, when George Calvert had made an attempt at colonization in Newfoundland, he provided the settlers with Anglican clergy, and visiting Catholic priests were ordered to share a place of worship with them. Cecilius Calvert, as the semifeudal proprietor, could make laws, but he was very much aware of the precariousness of a Catholic company under Protestant auspices and a Catholic-owned colony whose settlers included a majority of non-Catholics. The situation called for caution. Calvert told the original governor and commissioners to

> be very careful to preserve unity and peace amongst all passengers on Shipp-board and . . . suffer no scandal or offense to be given to any of the Protestants, whereby any just complaint may hereafter be made by them, in Virginea or in England, and . . . for that end . . . cause all Acts of Romane Catholique Religion to be done privately and . . . instruct all Romane Catholiques to be silent upon all occasions of discourse concerning matters of Religion; and . . . treat the Protestants with as much mildness and favor as Justice will permit.[3]

Calvert believed, in the words of one historian, that religion was "essentially a private matter and the settlers should overcome their religious differences for the greater good of the colony."[4]

Maryland, then, followed a policy of universal toleration as long as the Calverts were in charge. The original ordinance of 1639 recognized the primacy of conscience, and the famous decree of toleration of 1649 codified what had been the practice. New York, under the short-lived governership of Thomas Dongan, followed a similar policy, but Maryland, founded under Catholic leadership and having a substantial Catholic population, was a unique experiment aimed at demonstrating that there could be civil harmony and political unity without religious uniformity, a sharp break with the Westphalia principle. Having enshrined toleration in the founding legislation, the province's Catholics had to defend it, for Protestants were a majority from the start and regularly clashed with the Proprietor. They took full control after the Glorious Revolution and, in 1702, installed an Anglican establishment that required payment of taxes to support the church and excluded Catholics from voting or holding office, although the Catholic party skillfully prevented enforcement of the harsher of the penal laws. Despite the prosperity of many Catholic families, the situation of the Catholics worsened as conflicts with the French became more intense after 1750. When Catholics were told to pay a double tax to support the military after Braddock's defeat in 1756, they felt betrayed, and the richest among them, Charles Carroll of Carrollton, even considered abandoning Maryland for the more favorable climate of Catholic Louisiana. But the crisis passed, and Catholics continued a normal social life, assured of the security of their property. "The fact is that Maryland Catholics paid no substantial penalty for the faith," historian James Hennesey concludes.[5] This may be an exaggeration, for Catholic families had to send their young men to Europe for a suitable education and they were unable to vote, hold office, practice law, or worship publicly. However, they could worship together on their estates; the Jesuits who had been with them from the beginning held property and slaves; and they lived in relative peace with their neighbors.

Given these favorable circumstances, in comparison with Catholics elsewhere in the English-speaking world, Maryland Catholics were naturally conservative, defending the early legal arrangements and the later customary toleration, and even articulating theories of social contract, private conscience, and personal rights that were quite advanced for the time. They attacked divine right theories of the state and stressed the popular origins of all government. Civil authority came from God through the people, so that all inhabitants, regardless of religion, should enjoy the rights and immunities of English subjects.[6] Accepted socially as the equals of their neighbors, doggedly determined to defend their property rights and their political influence, and hoping eventually to achieve civil equality, Maryland Catholics were conformists, anxious to be seen by their Protestant counterparts as differing from them only in religion. They were no establishment in exile, seeing religious freedom and toleration as useful until papal domination and Catholic control could be restored. They experienced their faith as a voluntary, personal, and family matter; they saw the church as a community bonded together by family tradition and commitment and supported primarily by the laity; and they had little use for extreme claims of exclusive salvation, even less for Catholic claims to control the political, cultural, and religious life of the community. "I am a warm friend to Toleration, I execrate the intollerating spirit of the Church of Rome, and of other churches—for she is not singular in that," young Charles Carroll in 1774 told a friend who had urged him to join the established church to promote a political career. "If my countrymen judge me incapable of serving them in a public station . . . I will serve them in a private capacity notwithstanding." For such Maryland Catholics, religion was a matter of "deliberate decision" and they approached their public life with a tough self-consciousness that stood them in good stead during the period of national construction.[7]

TOWARD THE NEW REPUBLIC

Anti-Catholicism was given a powerful stimulus in the colonies by the Quebec Act of 1765, which recognized the rights of the Catholic church in the newly acquired territory to the north. In Maryland, however, when the conflict with the mother country came, Catholics almost unanimously supported the patriot cause, in part because they calculated that it offered the best chance to bring about a government that would recognize their claim that civil rights should be based on property, a claim that excluded interference by the state with religion.[8]

Charles Carroll of Carrollton became a hero in 1773 by defending the colonists' cause against Tory Daniel Dulaney. In the process he advanced the Catholic cause as well, demonstrating that the long experience of minority status had purged English Catholics of the papalism and intolerance that so worried their neighbors. Writing as "First Citizen," Carroll responded to Dulaney's charge that he, as a Catholic, could not be trusted because of his loyalty to the persecuting church of Rome, by condemning all intolerance, and reminding his readers that he and his fellow Catholics had been victims, not perpetrators, of religious persecution.

Charles Carroll served on the committee of correspondence and in the provincial convention; he was elected to the Continental Congress and was one of two Catholics to sign the Declaration of Independence. With his cousin, John Carroll, recently returned from Europe, he served on a delegation to Canada to seek support for the Revolution. John Adams, no friend of Catholics, was astonished that Charles Carroll would risk his huge fortune, "the largest in America." Other Catholics were equally active. The Brents of Virginia, for example, served on committees of correspondence and public safety. While there were some Catholic Tories in northern New York and in Philadelphia, Catholics generally were ardent patriots. The French became the nation's allies, members of Congress attended Catholic services in honor of French ambassadors, and a mood of toleration swept wartime English America.[9]

Successful rebellion was bound to bring change. Catholics were not the only Christian minority in the colonies; in fact, the mid-century revival known as the Great Awakening had extended an already marked religious pluralism, while influential leaders of the Revolution had concluded that civil peace and prosperity required not uniformity but freedom and the separation of religion from state control. In 1776 Patrick Henry told Virginians that "religion, or the duty we owe our Creator, and the manner of discharging it, can be directed only by reason and conviction and not by force and violence and, therefore, that all men should enjoy the fullest toleration in the exercise of religion according to the dictates of conscience, unpunished and unrestrained by the magistrate." Later James Madison would express the same sentiment: "All men are equally entitled to the full and free exercise of religion according to the dictates of conscience." Madison added that the rights of citizens should be independent of religious considerations: "No man or class of men ought, on account of religion, to be invested with peculiar emoluments or privileges, nor subjected to any penalties and disabilities." Gradually this view found its way into law, first in the Virginia Declaration on Religious Liberty, then in the exclusion of religious tests for office-holding in the new Constitution, and finally into the First Amendment, adopted in 1791. While disestablishment and free exercise covered citizens only in their dealings with the national government, and several states retained forms of establishment well into the nineteenth century, the institutions of the new nation were clearly "extraordinary." As one Maryland Jesuit, speaking of the situation in his state, put it plainly in 1784: "The toleration here granted by the Bill of Rights has put us all on an equal footing and has been of great service to us."[10] For the Catholics of the country, whose endurance and determination had preserved the faith over generations, separation and liberty represented a liberation beyond their fondest hopes.

The heart of the matter, in the words of a major student of the period, was a "movement away from the absolute state . . . coextensive with society and the nation." From Locke and even more from their own colonial experience, Americans had forged an idea of limited government, charged with responsibility for temporal affairs but limited by written constitutions, bills of rights, and federalism. Government had only the specific powers delegated to it by the people; constitutionally guaranteed rights protected the citizen against governmental authority; and large areas of life in society remained outside the jurisdiction of legislatures, magistrates, and courts. Because the United States was a large country, and its people remarkably diverse, all authority was precarious, and all organizations and associations, religious, political, and social, had to depend upon the voluntary support of persons and groups. The vast majority of Americans were Christians, but few attended church. Their culture remained vaguely Christian, but no one brand of Christianity could dominate the rest. As a result the Catholic church "found herself in America confronted with a state that was never before experienced in her centuries long history." From now on Christian influence on public life and on public policy would depend not on "the Church's direct dealing with the state" but on its influence upon the citizens "upon whom the government depends and to whom the church ministers."[11]

SECURING FREEDOM

The extraordinary new situation that confronted John Carroll and his fellow Catholics, dependent as it was on the toleration brought about

by the Revolution, had to be carefully protected. As Carroll told the
same correspondent who received his description of the "extraordinary" situation, Catholics would have to "preserve & improve" their
new-found status "by demeaning ourselves on all occasions as subjects
zealously attached to our government & avoiding to give any jeal-
ousies on account of any dependence on foreign jurisdiction, more
than that, which is essential to our Religion, an acknowledgement of
the Pope's spiritual supremacy over the whole Christian world."[12]
Freedom of worship and enjoyment of civil rights were all they could
wish for, and all they believed necessary. Carroll was astute enough
to recognize that his countrymen were by no means fully secure in
their independence, and that fear and suspicion toward Catholics
could easily revive. They would have to conduct themselves with cir-
cumspection, acting always as good citizens and good neighbors. Furthermore, given the emphasis most non-Catholics placed on the papacy as a foreign institution, possessing power as a state and having
historically allied with other states to crush Protestants, it would be
necessary to minimize the authority of the pope over the new American church.

Carroll and his associates strove to make the new situation permanent, balancing their Catholic convictions with respect for the religious views of others and calling upon their fellow Catholics to
manifest charity and forbearance while avoiding occasions for contention. Carroll himself was far removed from the "rigid Catholic"
so many feared. He had collaborated with Benjamin Franklin during
the war; afterward he joined with other non-Anglicans to defend the
separation clauses of the Maryland constitution. When he responded
to an attack on the church by a former priest, Charles Wharton, he
made it clear that his message was addressed primarily to his own
flock and he refrained from extending the controversy. He professed
to welcome the exchange because "general and equal toleration, by
giving a free circulation to fair argument, is the most effectual method
to bring all denominations of Christians to a unity of faith."[13] But,
six years later, in 1791, he kept one of his priests from engaging in a
similar public debate.

Publicly Carroll stressed again and again the common heritage of
all Christians; privately he urged other Catholic leaders to be aware
of the manner in which their words and actions would be received
by non-Catholics. He told one arriving French priest: "More caution
is required [here] than elsewhere" and another that, while Catholic
positions needed to be stated clearly, he should be alert to the Protestant mentality that would receive them. In one letter, describing
the atmosphere around him, he crossed out the words "violent opposition" and substituted "deep rooted prejudice."[14] But by 1792 he

could tell an English friend of "the decay of religious prejudice here," citing as evidence the election of Thomas Sims Lee, a recent convert, as governor of Maryland.[15]

Not until the influx of massive numbers of Catholic immigrants after 1830 would bitter interreligious hostility revive. In many areas of the country, the small numbers and apparent republicanism of Catholics meant new experiences of interreligious understanding. In Boston, the heart of Puritan America, the first bishop, Jean-Louis Cheverus, enjoyed the admiration and even friendship of local non-Catholic leaders.[16] Regarding the pluralistic character of the frontier, historian Joseph P. Chinnici, O.F.M. describes the opening of a new Catholic church in Lebanon, Pennsylvania, on 23 July 1810. The pastor, John W. Beschter, preached in German and English on Protestant misunderstandings of Catholicism to a mixed congregation that included three Lutheran, three Reformed, and one Moravian minister. Dinner was served at the home of one of the Lutheran ministers.[17]

Avoiding religious controversy meant avoiding political controversy as well. In Europe John Carroll had experienced the problems that arose when the church became too involved in politics. His Jesuit order was suppressed in 1773 in part because Jesuits had intrigued at the courts of Catholic monarchs, and they in turn had intrigued at the papal court. Carroll's fears regarding the political actions of church leaders were confirmed by the events in France during the 1790s, when revolutionary fervor was directed against the clergy, driving many into exile. By depending on the Catholic monarchs in its war against the Reformation, the church had become the handmaiden of the old regime and suffered its fate; it was not surprising that new revolutionary governments should attempt to use the church as the monarchs and aristocrats had for centuries. In the United States, of course, a priest could expect to have little political influence; but even before independence and liberty were assured, Carroll expressed his belief that the church's representatives should keep their distance from political affairs. When he reluctantly agreed to serve on the Quebec mission, he wrote a friend: "I have little regard to my personal safety amidst the present distress of my country, yet I cannot help feeling some for my character and I have observed that when the ministers of religion leave the duties of their profession to take a busy part in political matters, they generally fall into contempt; & sometimes even bring discredit to the cause, in whose service they are engaged."[18]

While priests were to remain aloof from politics, Catholics were to claim their full rights as citizens; indeed, it was for these rights that they had taken the substantial risks of joining with their countrymen. In an address to George Washington, written by John Carroll for the clergy and by Charles and Daniel Carroll, Thomas FitzSimons, and Dominick Lynch of New York for the laity, they made the claim explicit: "Whilst our country preserves her freedom and independence, we shall have a well founded title to claim from her justice equal rights of citizenship, as the price of our blood spilt under your eyes, and of our common exertions for her defence, under your auspicious conduct, rights rendered more dear to us by the remembrance of former hardships. . . . We pray for the preservation of them, where they have been granted; and expect the full extension of them from the justice of those states which still restrict them."[19]

In later years, John Carroll, whose sympathies were conservative and Federalist, kept his political views to himself. He had been repelled by the French Revolution's assault on the church and was incensed by the rising tide of opposition to England during the Napoleonic wars. "Our American Cabinet and a majority of Congress seem to be infatuated with a blind predeliction for France and an unconquerable hostility to England," Carroll wrote his English friend Charles Plowden.[20] Yet when war broke out in 1812, he insisted that his people rally once again to the national cause, arguing that all means had been used to avoid war and the United States had no ambition for territory. Fearful of anti-Catholicism, practiced in "survival tactics," these Catholic leaders inaugurated what historian Gerald Fogarty has called "an American Catholic tradition of making their religion a private matter."[21]

ORGANIZING FOR FREEDOM

Securing the position of the church in the new republic by affirming republican principles and supporting the institutions of the new society were responsibilities that John Carroll fulfilled magnificently. But there was more to the problem, for Catholicism as an organization faced in two directions, either of which could and did cause problems. One direction was toward Europe and Rome, where republican principles were anathema; church–state separation and religious liberty would be condemned in principle throughout the next two centuries. Furthermore, the papacy symbolized all that English-speaking peoples had learned to fear and hate in the Catholic church. It was in the interest of the American church to secure a degree of independence from Roman control and to avoid even the appearance of political subservience to the Holy See.[22] "No pretext should be given the enemies of our religion to accuse us of depending unnecessarily on a foreign jurisdiction," Carroll wrote. The pope was the bishop of Rome, a local church among the others. His spiritual supremacy was an "essential tenet of our religion . . . the bond of our union, which cements and keeps together, in the profession of the same faith, and in the celebration of the same solemn and public worship."[23] However, like most writers of the day, Carroll believed that ecclesiastical authority resided in the body of bishops united with the pope, not in the pope alone. In his debate with Wharton he wrote:

> I will venture to assert that he cannot cite one Catholic divine, who denies infallibility to reside in the body of bishops, united and agreeing with their head, the Bishop of Rome. So that when [he] says that schoolmen have taught the infallibility of the Pope, some place it in a general council and others in the Pope and Council, received by the whole church . . . he is under a great mistake for the last is not the mere belief of schoolmen, but the constant belief of all Catholics, a belief in which there is no variation."[24]

In the nineteenth century the Catholic church would witness a unique effort to strengthen papal authority, but in the period when Carroll was organizing the American church the pope's power over local churches was at an all-time low. In France, Austria, and Spain, kings nominated bishops, who in turn worked closely with the government in administering church affairs. Carroll had spent much of his life in Europe and knew well that national churches operated with little reference to Roman authority; he was determined to secure such privileges for the American church, but without the Gallican association with the state. His determination became even firmer when the papal nuncio in Paris approached Benjamin Franklin to solicit his government's view of the appointment of a bishop. Fortunately, Franklin was told to tell the nuncio that "Congress will always be pleased to testify their respect for his sovereign and state; but that the subject of his application to Doctor F., being purely spiritual, it is without the jurisdiction and powers of Congress, who have no authority to permit or refuse it, these powers being reserved to the general states individually."[25]

In 1784 Carroll was named superior of the American mission, but he was dissatisfied, for that office was directly under the supervision of the Vatican's Congregation of the Propaganda. Carroll was outraged:

> But this you may be assured of: that no authority from the Propaganda will ever be admitted here; that the Catholick Clergy and Laity here know that the only connection they ought to have with Rome is to acknowledge the Pope as the Spiritual head of the Church; that no congregation existing in his states shall be allowed to exercise any share of his Spritual authority here; that no Bishop Vicar Apostolical shall be admitted; and if we are to have a Bishop, he shall [be] . . . an ordinary national Bishop, in whose appointment Rome shall have no share.[26]

In the end, Rome granted the priests in the United States the right to nominate their bishop, Carroll was chosen, and the new church was launched. It should be noted that later, when additional bishops were needed, Carroll acquiesced in direct Roman appointment with minimal consultation, a method that would become normative in the Western church in the nineteenth century. On the other hand, the pastoral and political concerns that led Carroll to contend for the relative autonomy of the American church eventually led his successors to unite in regular councils and to work together to keep Roman intervention under control, at least until the end of the nineteenth century.

In the other direction was the church's own people. The organizing process required establishment of episcopal authority and definition of the Roman connection if the new church was to be in fact Catholic, united in common faith and discipline. But it also required persuading the Catholic people of the new nation to accept the authority of bishops and clergy and to enter into organized forms of Catholic life. This was no small challenge, first because of the size of the country and the scarcity of priests, and second because authority of any kind was not easily established and accepted in the new United States. Both problems would preoccupy Carroll during his lifetime and would explode in the new church's first crisis in the years that followed. The experience would demonstrate the presence of the republican style, and its limits.

TRUSTEEISM

At the start there were about 25,000 Catholics in the United States out of a population of almost three million. In a 1784 report Carroll counted 15,800 Catholics in Maryland, of whom 3,000 were slaves, 7,000 in Pennsylvania, 200 in Virginia, and 1,500 in New York. New Catholics were constantly arriving, but, for lack of priests, few were making their Easter duty, and children and slaves were uninstructed in their faith.[27] In frontier areas the faith persisted through the efforts of lay people beyond the reach of priests. In upstate New York, for example, lay persons from Rochester, Salina, and Utica joined Albany Catholics to establish a parish in the state capital; its pastor spent months on horseback serving his scattered parishioners while, in his absence, more prosperous Catholic families gathered their coreligionists for prayer and catechism until new churches arose as new priests became available. There, most of the Catholics were Irish, drawn to the region by construction and trade along first the rivers, then the Erie Canal, then the plank roads and railroads.[28] In the larger cities, there were already signs of a pluralism that would become the major pastoral challenge of the nineteenth-century church. As one of New York's first priests, the Irish Capuchin Charles Whelan wrote, Catholics were "very poor but very zealous" and the priest had to know "at least the Irish, English, French and Dutch languages, because our congregation is composed of those nationalities, as well also as of Portuguese and Spaniards."[29]

Carroll and his successors argued for a high degree of autonomy from Rome, in part because they worried about the adjustment of Catholic authority to the new situation of religious liberty, but, more important, because they shared republican assumptions about conscience and freedom. When they faced their own people, however, they stood in a position analogous to that of Rome, for American Catholics took these republican assurances seriously at a time when other Americans were constructing a "theology of the people" that emphasized personal conversion and commitment and voluntary community. The language, while evangelical and scriptural, was not entirely outside American Catholic experience. In his response to Charles Wharton, Carroll distinguished between those who were members of the church and those in communion with it. The former included "all those who, with a sincere heart, seek true religion, and are in an unfeigned disposition to embrace the truth wherever they find it." He specifically rejected the doctrine of no salvation outside the church.[30] Like the conscience arguments of the colonial period, this seemed to suggest that men and women were free to decide for themselves what their religion would be. If this were the case, it was a small step to claim the right to define for themselves the terms of their affiliation with any particular church. If such freedom were allowed, how could the unity and integrity of the Catholic church be preserved?

One answer, the dominant one in the early years, was persuasion. What historian Timothy Smith has written of the Protestant churches could be said with equal force of the Catholic: "Persuading men to make and keep the commitment necessary to voluntary associations became the church's central task."[31] It was a task that could command no legal backing. As the Virginia Bill of Religious Liberty expressed it in 1786; "the opinions of men are not the object of civil government nor under its jurisdiction." In fact, by placing ownership of church property in the hands of lay trustees of individual congregations, the law institutionalized lay control. The law gave no formal recognition of the clergy and thus no means whereby priest or bishops could control a recalcitrant congregation. In most places skillful pastors could win their way through their personal qualities and pastoral services, but priests unsympathetic to republicanism or simply bent on resisting episcopal authority could cause as many problems as lay people that were too independent. French-born Stephen Badin, for example, warned Carroll that his scattered western parishioners held "Calvinistical principles" that "bordered on Jacobinism." Fearful that churches would fall into the hands of "haughty and nominal Catholics," Badin kept ownership in his own hands. When Benedict-Joseph Flaget became bishop of Bardstown, Kentucky, he had to battle Badin to gain control of his freehold churches while using his considerable pastoral and political skills to keep parishes unified and disciplined. In one seriously divided parish, Flaget arbitrated the dispute and won control of the property subject to the restriction that it not be sold without the people's consent.[32]

Carroll and others saw many advantages in the trustee system, but increasing ethnocultural tensions, especially between French clergy and Irish congregations, multiplied opportunities for discord, especially when the bishop was distant. The problem was not simply lay control, but congregationalism, a church polity in which each parish could go its own way. When the trustees of Saint Peter's Church in New York were unwilling to accept a pastor sent them by Carroll, the latter remonstrated that their assertion of local control was incompatible with Catholic unity: "If ever the principles there laid down should become predominant, the unity and catholicity of our Church would be at an end; and it would be formed into distinct and independent societies, nearly in the same manner as the congregational presbyterians of our neighboring New England states."[33]

Carroll was able to resolve that dispute, but his successors were plagued by the independence and contentiousness of priests and people, just as Protestant leaders and American politicians had trouble checking the fragmentation occasioned by the popularization of democratic ideals. As Archbishop Ambrose Maréchal wrote to Rome in 1818:

> The American people clings with the most ardent love to the civil liberty it enjoys. Again, it is a primary principle of civil liberty among them, that absolutely all magistrates, whether high or low, at stated times of the year, should be elected by popular vote. Likewise all sects of Protestants, by the same principle and accordingly, elect and dismiss, at their pleasure, their pastors. Now the Catholics living in this society are evidently exposed to the danger of admitting the same principles of ecclesiastical rule, and by the artifice of impious priests, who cater to their pride, are easily led to believe they have the right to elect and dismiss their pastors as they please.[34]

By the time Maréchal became archbishop of Baltimore, the trustee problem had reached crisis proportions in New York, Philadelphia, Norfolk, and Charleston. In Philadelphia the absence of a strong bishop allowed the trustees of Saint Mary's Church, perhaps the nation's wealthiest parish, to assert control, assisted by a talented, unstable Irish priest, William Hogan. Hogan left the city in 1824 but the trustees, aided by other Irish priests, pressured their aged bishop, Henry Conwell, into accepting an agreement that gave them a veto over pastoral appointments. Rome, incensed by the agreement, ordered Conwell to Rome; he refused to go unless his clerical opponents also left. Rome ordered them to do so through the Dominican authorities, but they appealed, first to the unsympathetic archbishop of Baltimore, then to Henry Clay, the American secretary of state. They told the latter that Rome's actions confirmed the charge that Catholics had a divided allegiance, to their own government and to the pope. Worried, the Vatican arranged a meeting between the American ambassador to France and the papal nuncio in Paris; Clay was convinced that it was a purely ecclesiastical matter, and the case was closed, but the incident revealed the distance that existed between the American practice of self-government and the Catholic approach to religious authority.

The Philadelphia conflict dragged on, but it was hardly unique. In Charleston and Norfolk, Irish priests and people resented the authority of Maréchal, a Frenchman, just as later German parishioners would assert their parochial rights against Irish bishops and clergy. Ethnocultural differences complicated matters, but they were far from being the only source of the problem. The trustees were often prominent laymen who in fact strongly supported their church. In Utica, New York, for example, John and Nicholas Devereaux helped build Saint John's Church, financed a new orphanage, and led the trustees who regularly collected money to maintain the parish and pay the pastor. But they also led the trustees in their refusal to meet the pastor's demands when they thought these demands excessive.[35] They and other trustees in fact could make a strong case. Dr. J. F. Oliviera Fernandez of Norfolk, for example, argued that many foreign-born priests did not understand the country. Furthermore, for centuries kings and landlords in other countries had endowed churches and in turn enjoyed the privilege of nominating the priest. In the United States, where the people were sovereign and where the parish depended on popular support, where indeed lay initiative and sacrifice had built the church, the people should have a similar privilege. Frustrated by the seemingly arbitrary action of the archbishop, the Norfolk laymen went so far as to recruit an Irish priest in Rome, seek the backing of the schismatic Jansenist bishop of Utrecht, and appeal to President Thomas Jefferson and members of Congress for protection.

In Charleston the trustees claimed the same prerogatives recently granted by concordat to the government of France. "Your memorialists beg leave to suggest to your Reverence that that part of the sovereign people of the United States in communion with his Holiness the Pope, as their government interferes not in matters of religion think and hold themselves immediately entitled to the same benefits and immunities in their religious concerns as are established between the Court of Rome and Sovereigns of Europe."[36] The Philadelphia trustees, seeing themselves in a situation similar to that of Napoleon or the monarchs of Europe, sent representatives to Rome to negotiate a concordat or treaty to regulate relations between the Vatican and the American church. This action indicated that the trustees were loyal to papal spiritual authority, as Carroll had been, but they also upheld as he did the right of a national church to govern itself. Trustee support always dwindled when a leader denied papal authority, which was the "first great characteristic of Catholicism," as a Philadelphia trustee expressed it in 1824. "I do not ask you, nor do I wish you to disclaim or discard the spiritual supremacy of the Apostolic See— retain it by all means—but retain it as a bond of federal union, not as a yoke of servile dependency."[37]

Matthew Carey, a well-known public figure in Philadelphia, claimed that priests recently arrived from Europe exercised an "extravagently high-handed authority" and expected "servile submission" from a people who would "never submit to the regime of civil and ecclesiastical affairs that prevails in Europe." "A different order of things prevails in this country," wrote Carey. "The extreme freedom of our civil institutions has produced a corresponding independent spirit respecting our church affairs, to which sound sense will never fail to pay attention, and which it would be a manifest impropriety to despise or attempt to control by harsh or violent measures. The opinions and wishes of the people require to be consulted to a degree unknown in Europe."[38]

Trusteeism showed the degree to which Catholic republicanism had spread among the laity, and the limits of such republicanism for the church as an organization. Archbishop Maréchal responded to the Charleston trustees: "In a word, are you willing to be governed by the sacred laws of the Roman Catholic Church of which you signed yourselves members, or are you determined to make use of the liberty which we enjoy under our free and happy government to introduce into the spiritual and temporal administration of your congregation sectarian principles totally subversive of the discipline sanctioned by the whole world Church."[39] Maréchal claimed that the laws of the church did not apply in mission situations; there were technically no canonical parishes in the United States, and therefore no right of patronage. Each parish was a mission, each priest a missionary, subject to the direct authority of the bishop and all responsible to the Congregation of the Propaganda, the Vatican office charged with responsiblity for mission countries, the very situation Carroll had wanted to avoid. Faced with divisive laity and clergy, the bishops were prepared to accept a far higher degree of Roman authority. Lay leaders who had preserved the faith and often built the church with minimal clerical assistance were understandably upset that they were defined as objects of missionary evangelization, placing them under the "high handed authority" of the bishops and demanding a "servile submission" comparable to that expected of converts in mission territories. In the words of the Saint Mary's trustees: "We are, therefore, viewed in the same light as the nation of Cherokees or Choctaws, or the natives on the coast of Africa—our country is termed a missionary colony and for want of a proper understanding with our Holy Father, we are subjected to receive foreigners of every class and description to direct and command us, as if we were incapable of understanding our religion, or protecting our own property."[40]

Throughout the controversy, the Saint Mary's trustees argued for a national church, similar to that demanded by John Carroll, but they also wanted a balance of power within the church comparable to that in their political institutions. The only place where this was achieved was in Charleston, where the newly appointed John England, fresh from battles over the independence of the Irish church, arrived in 1821. An ardent admirer of American republicanism, England developed a full-scale constitution for his diocese. He abolished pew rents, had vestries elected for each congregation, granting them control over finances, and made provision for regular conventions composed of two houses of clergy and lay delegates, all subject to the spiritual authority of the bishop, who promised to follow the advice of such bodies "as far as his conscience will permit." A diocesan board of trustees, composed of the bishop, several diocesan officials, and twelve elected laymen, had responsibility for all funds, to be spent only on order of the convention. England believed that close pastoral attention and mechanisms of consultation could overcome the tensions and legitimize the necessary authority of the bishop. The convention was not to be considered "a portion of the ecclesiastical government of the church," he insisted, but "a body of sage, prudent and religious counsellors to aid the proper ecclesiastical governor in the discharge of his duties." Unfortunately Archbishop Maréchal rejected this plan for general application because he considered it too "democratic." England tried to enlist Roman support to nationalize such a compromise, but he failed.[41]

Historian Patrick Carey has outlined two types of episcopal response to trusteeism. One, associated with Carroll and later with England, recognized the need to incorporate the laity into church administration in some way, and to adopt within the church at least

some of the spirit and form of the surrounding democracy. While insisting that the priest's powers were spiritual, and subject to spiritual
authority, Carroll promised to consult the laity and anticipated some
form of participation. The other approach, which became dominant,
Carey associated with Archbishop Leonard Neale, who argued that
"the Presiterian [sic] system puts the Vestrymen over the clergyman,
but the Catholic system places the clergyman over the vestrymen
whom he appoints and dismisses at will." Eventually strong bishops
like John Hughes of New York abandoned the search for a middle
ground and translated the monarchical position literally into church
policy. "I will suffer no man in my diocese I cannot control," Hughes
thundered, and he bent priests and religious orders as well as lay
people to his will. Even the more scholarly and gentle Francis Patrick
Kenrick, who succeeded Conwell in Philadelphia, commenting on the
liberality of Pittsburgh's Michael O'Connor, said that "he has not yet
learned how hard it is to uphold sacred rights when laymen meddle
in the affairs of the church."[42]

In 1829, meeting for the first time as a council legislating for the
American church, the bishops decided to eliminate, as fast as the law
would allow, all forms of effective lay participation and instead ensure
that the title to church property was placed under the effective control
of the bishop. It took years to find the favorable political climate in
each state to allow for such control in law, but strong bishops now
insisted that title be turned over to them before a new church would
be blessed. Older churches were denied pastoral services, even in some
cases placed under interdict, if they refused to recognize the absolute
control of the bishops over the appointment and transfer of priests.
In later years priests would chafe under the near total control of their
careers by the bishops, while generations of new immigrants would
find such American forms of financial and pastoral control difficult
to accept. The church, it seemed, while affirming republican values
of self-government and individual responsibility in public life, all but
totally rejected those principles in organizing the church's internal
affairs.

On the other hand, episcopal and clerical authority always had to
accommodate popular attitudes, so that benevolence and persuasion
remained indispensable. Furthermore, the bishops faced a serious organizational problem. Short of home-grown priests, they had to rely
upon men whose background was often shrouded and whose relia-
bility was questionable; if they could appeal to popular support there
would always be the danger of schism and, even more worrisome,
constant internal turmoil in the parishes themselves. In addition, the
congregational dynamic was strong in the voluntary setting of the

United States, as the ever-multiplying number of Protestant groups demonstrated. Coupled with increasing ethnic pluralism, this centrifugal tendency made it hard to imagine how the unity and integrity of the church could be preserved if bishops and priests had to engage in constant negotiation with foreign-born priests and people whose customs differed so widely. If there was to be a church at once unified and distinctively Catholic, episcopal authority seemed essential, and alternative methods of grounding that authority on the voluntary principle seemed all but utopian. In addition, Catholic priests had learned from the experience of their Protestant counterparts the spiritual and moral dangers consequent on too great a dependence upon the laity. England, who went further than most in accepting democracy, saw the value of clerical autonomy: "A pastor who feels himself to a certain extent dependent upon the good will of his flock will be frequently urged to reflect upon the best mode of securing their affection, for it is in his interest," while the Catholic priest, secure in his position, "is not the slave of any individual nor of any faction, though he must endeavor to conciliate all."[43]

Still there is no avoiding the fact that the trustee question has exerted enormous influence over the development of the church's public life from that time up to the present. The corollary of clerical control was emphasis on the religious, as distinct from the political or social role of the church. If the church dealt only with religion, and religion was a matter of belief, ritual practice, and personal morality, and if its major and distinctive mission was to offer the sacraments, then the argument that clergy should control the church was obviously more persuasive. If on the other hand the parish was the organizing vehicle for an ethnic community bent on securing political power, or if it was a major vehicle for economic advancement, then the stakes in control of that church were far higher. For this reason it becomes clear why in most ethnic communities the second and third generations generally showed less interest in internal church affairs and accepted clerical and episcopal control more easily; it was less important. Finally, if the church had a responsibility in public life to defend human dignity, promote human rights, help build up the human family, and shed light on human activity, as would be argued after Vatican II, echoing the republican tradition, then the sharp differentiation of clergy and laity, and the reduction of the church's voice to a one-way teaching authority, from the top down, would not only be inappropriate but also positively damaging to its public witness and to the coherence and power of its worship. For non-Catholic critics, clerical control provided evidence of the church's insincerity in professing loyalty to American democracy; internally it caused some to wonder about how the church could encourage public responsibility when it gave no responsibility to its people for their own affairs within the church.

THE CHURCH AND PUBLIC LIFE

The Catholic community in the United States is sometimes pictured as always an outsider church, hidden in out-of-the-way slums and a few rural outposts, only slowly coming into public view. But Maryland Catholics were active in the revolutionary cause and well known throughout the colonies. In many frontier communities, too, Catholic missionaries were there first, and arriving American colonists, sometimes to their alarm, found the church present and waiting for them. Some of these pioneer missionaries had considerable public influence, none more than Gabriel Richard, who arrived in Detroit from Illinois in 1798. He introduced the territory's first printing press, started the first newspaper, helped found the first university, was arrested by the British during the War of 1812, and served as territorial delegate in Congress.[44]

The arrival of settlement meant the incorporation of the area into the new ecclesiastical organization centered in Baltimore, the development of parishes, and the enforcement of a degree of discipline on the Catholic flock. Saint Louis, for example, was a city less Catholic than freethinker during its French colonial phase. The town's leading merchant, René Auguste Chouteau, possessed a large library, one-fourth of whose volumes were on the Index. In 1826 the new diocese was established; two years later the sisters opened a hospital, then schools, and gradually the erstwhile godlessness of the city disappeared.[45] Elsewhere hospitals and schools constituted a major expression of the church's presence. Often they were the first hospitals, orphan asylums, and female academies in the area and were both assisted and patronized by Protestants. In the towns of upstate New York, the famous "burned over district" swept by revivals in the early nineteenth century, local records are filled with land donations to struggling parishes, financial backing for hospitals and orphanages, and even contributions to school fund-raising projects from civic-minded Protestants. In town after town throughout the country, the toleration, good will, and civic-mindedness of the republican period preceded, and sometimes survived, the outbreaks of conflict that punctuated American life after 1830.[46]

Lay Catholics placed a high premium on equal citizenship. It was indeed the embarrassment caused by public conflict with bishops that led some laymen to oppose arbitrary episcopal authority. In dealing with non-Catholics, or with public affairs, they claimed the freedom of opinion they thought their due, and they held to no specifically Catholic view of politics or economics. Robert Walsh, for example, editor of the first United States quarterly, *The American Review of History and Politics,* was a leading defender of laissez-faire. He opposed labor unions and government action on behalf of the poor. Matthew and Henry Carey, in contrast, abhorred Adam Smith and became nationally known champions of protectionism. Disturbed by the growing gap between rich and poor, Matthew Carey wanted the government to provide work at a living wage. "Many citizens entertain an idea that, in the present state of society in this city, every person able and willing to work, may procure employment; that all those who are thus employed, may earn a decent and comfortable support; and that if not the whole, at least the chief part of the distress of the poor, arises from idleness, dissipation and worthlessness. Alas nothing can be further from the truth," Carey wrote.[47] In *Female Wages and Female Oppression* (1835), Carey surveyed the wages of seamstresses, concluding that female vice was due to low wages and lack of suitable employment at a living wage. "Society must assume the care of those reduced to want through no fault of their own," Carey wrote, "and no citizen should be allowed to suffer from want of the necessities of life."[48]

Active if contentious Catholics, the Careys and Walsh in their economic writing made no reference to church teaching beyond general supportive quotes from Scripture. Nor did they see themselves as spokesmen for the church or the body of Catholics. Matthew Carey was an active Irish nationalist but combined that cause with republican civic-mindedness. In 1790 he joined with the local Episcopal bishop and Universalist Benjamin Rush to encourage formation of Sunday schools that became Philadelphia's first free schools.[49] These men expressed the dualism of the republican tradition, regarding religion as a personal and private matter, approaching public issues as reasonable men and dedicated citizens.

The republican position required defense of religious liberty for all, both as a matter of principle and as an advantage to the Catholic minority. In North Carolina, for example, William Gaston led the fight for freedom of religion as a delegate to the state constitutional convention of 1835. A distinguished lawyer and state supreme court justice, he argued for the withdrawal of the state's religious test for office, arguing that the state had no competence to judge religious opinions. Robert Walsh went further, eloquently defending American Masons during an outbreak of antimasonic mania. When demands were made for government investigation of supposed plots, Walsh outlined the danger such investigations would pose for equal rights and worried

that the country had "sufficient materials of ignorance and fanaticism
. . . with which to fashion the implements of proscription and persecution."[50]

It was Bishop John England who gave the clearest expression to
the republican tradition before it gave way to a new and more abrasive
style. In addition to his creative resolution of the trustee crisis in his
diocese, England launched the first successful Catholic journal, the
U.S. Catholic Miscellany, in 1822. In 1825, after a Christmas sermon
at Saint Patrick's in Washington, he was invited to address the House
of Representatives on 8 January 1826. Even before leaving Ireland he
had seen the need for the American Irish to enter fully into the life
of their new country; after his arrival he worried that anti-Catholic
prejudice and a too rigid application of Old World models of authority
within the church would hamper the adjustment of Catholics to the
new nation and their full participation in its public life. Most important, he feared that prejudice and their own deep loyalties would
cause them to turn away from the responsibilities of citizenship and
throw their votes and influence to party politicians "who flatter, or
cajole, or insult them, or denounce them, as it may suit their interest
or their caprice." England believed in the separation of church and
state; earlier he had told the Irish liberator Daniel O'Connell: "I am
convinced that a total separation from the temporal government is
the most natural and safest for the church in any place."[51]

In his speech to Congress he set forth the position associated earlier
with Carroll and the Maryland Catholics: "We desire to see the Catholics as a religious body upon the ground of equality with all other
religious societies. . . . We consider that any who would call upon them
to stand aloof from their brethren in the politics of the country, as
neither a friend to America nor a friend to Catholics." Unfair treatment
of Catholics might force them to stand together in self-defense, but
the ideal of citizenship was quite different: "We repeat our maxim:
Let Catholics in religion stand isolated as a body, and upon as good
ground as their brethren. Let Catholics, as citizens and politicians,
not be distinguishable from their other brethren of the commonwealth."[52]

The corollary of this civic equality was acceptance of religious liberty, which Rome would soon declare a "most pestilential error." In
1829, at the very moment the bishops were declaring war on trusteeism, they set forth directly their commitment to American institutions and republican principles, affirming "a milder, a better, a
more Christian like principle, that of genuine religious liberty which,
though it declares truth is single, that religious indifference is criminal
in the eyes of God, and that religious error wilfully entertained is
destructive of the soul," yet recognizes "that the Savior did not ap-

prove of disseminating the Gospel by force and would allow all Christians to repose securely in the exercise of their civil and political rights even though they were in religious error." They went on to instruct lay Catholics to manifest a spirit of good will "not only in your civil and political, but also in your social relations with your separated brethren." In 1837 they were even stronger, sharply distinguishing between the "religious allegiance" of Catholics and the "civil and political allegiance" that they gave to the "several states" and to "the general government." Echoing Carroll, they insisted they would grant no "civil or political supremacy or power" to any "foreign potentate or power, though that potentate might be the chief pastor of our church."[53] Thus was established the unbroken line of Catholic affirmation of republican institutions that would extend throughout two centuries of church history in the United States, setting a standard against which to measure Catholic practice at home and Catholic teaching abroad.

THE REPUBLICAN HERITAGE

In a memoir written when he was thirty-seven, Italian-born missionary Samuel Mazzuchelli tried to explain the "American system" to his Italian countrymen. "To one who thoroughly understands the political spirit which prevails in a society composed of every nationality and every possible religious belief," he wrote, "it will not be surprising to see a solitary, unlettered Catholic in one of the great cities of the American Union protected in the practice of his religion even though all the other citizens believe it to be false. Faith in its most ostentatious manifestations and most extravagant forms is considered by the public to be the private business of the individual, and protected by the law, not as a belief or form of worship, but in the same way that it protects his house and his choice of food and drink." Explicitly contrasting this arrangement with others where church and state were united, he pointed out that the American Constitution protected "not religion but the citizens in the practice of their religion."[54]

Mazzuchelli recognized that republican Catholicism arose from the "extraordinary" situation that confronted the American church. It was a style suited to a church composed of relatively prosperous, native-born men who remembered the price of bigotry and prejudice, who understood what it meant to be victims of official discrimination and marginalization, and who knew from experience that to gain respect they had to give it, to win their own freedom they had to defend the freedom of others. From their own experience in colonial and early national America, they formulated a defense of equal citizenship that affirmed their aspirations. They risked their fortunes for their province and nation; they claimed the right to share equally in the public life of the country they had helped to build. The good citizen, they argued, was one who cared deeply for his community, thought first of its welfare rather than his own self-interest, and avoided sectarian controversy that could only divide the community, embitter intergroup relations and thus weaken the institutions of self-government. Finally, they could draw upon older scholastic ideas of natural law, different in origin but not in practice from other concepts of natural law common in America, to argue that there was in fact a human and humane common ground of reason on which persons of differing religious views could meet to shape a common life.

Such a style required, however, that the state deal with temporal matters and leave divine matters to the church. It meant dealing with one's fellow citizens in terms of a language of common humanity rather than shared faith. For Catholics, indeed, even the use of biblical symbols and images in discussing public affairs had to be viewed with suspicion, for the same Americans who shared a common biblical heritage also constituted a Protestant majority; if granted the right to define public issues in biblical terms, they might easily move on to exclude those who stood outside the evangelical consensus. A later generation might regard this splitting of religion, private and personal, and public life as secular and segmenting, as purchasing security and acceptance at the price of religious integrity. For Catholic republicans, however, such a division was both necessary and natural, necessary because it was the only way to insure that a sacred state was not turned against them, natural because as long as men differed over matters of religion, uniformity could be purchased only at the price of repression or hypocrisy.

All this had implications for the way in which Catholics viewed their faith and their church. Generally they shared an optimistic understanding of human nature; men and women were sinners, to be sure, but sin had not obliterated the human capacity for reason and at least a minimum of virtue. For those who sought God with a sincere heart, grace was available, and salvation could be secured outside the visible communion of the Catholic church. Furthermore, prayer and sacraments were means by which persons came to a knowledge of God and holiness was an interior, personal matter, requiring no undue separation from the world. While the larger world was filled with dangers and temptations, it was also filled with opportunities to experience God and develop one's gifts. The church was limited in its claims, a spiritual force, just as the pope's authority over each Catholic was spiritual, not political; he could insist on correct doctrine and morality, he could not dictate one's political views or even demand an attitude of intolerance toward non-Catholics. From long experience the founding generation had learned that the distinction between religion and public life offered a way of dealing with the realities of freedom, separation, and voluntarism, while securing the church as an institution within the pluralistic framework of American religion. Most important, it reflected the views of men like the Maryland Catholics, relatively self-sufficient economically, sure of their ability and their right to share in public affairs, and confident that reasonable people should be able to find common ground in their shared humanity, leaving to each person the right to form his own religious views and associations.

Insofar as Catholics wished to talk with others about their religious views, they had to make those views intelligible not on the basis of an authority that others did not accept, but on the basis of reason, which constituted a common bond among human beings. As John Carroll expressed it: "I do not think that Jesus Christ ever empowered his church to recur to the means of force and bloodshed, for the preservation of the faith against error. My idea is . . . that the means be proportionate to the attack: persuasion, argument, coercion by spiritual censures . . ."[55] Finally, as the situation of pluralism commanded adjustment of long-standing Catholic ideas, republican Catholics almost instinctively distinguished between "the substance of the ancient doctrine of the deposit of faith" and "the way in which it is presented," in the words of a later pope, John XXIII.[56] Similarly, republican Catholicism opened the door to distinctive national traditions, to an ecclesiology that allowed local churches to adapt to their unique circumstances, to define a relative independence of Rome and a vision of the universal church as a communion of local churches, to open an apologetics of convergence, one that emphasized what men and women held in common rather than what separated them. It would prove a controversial but enduring legacy.

CHAPTER
3
Immigrant Catholicism

ᗡᖾᓎᒫ

*T*he republican style persisted throughout the nineteenth century, drawn upon from time to time to defend the quality of Catholic citizenship, but advocates of the principles that governed Catholic republicanism came to be regarded as liberals, whose views ran counter to those of the church in Europe and no longer met the needs of the American church or the majority of the Catholic people. This displacement reflected a major shift in Catholic self-understanding expressed in theology, piety, apologetics, and ecclesiology. In Europe this shift was associated with the ultramontane movement, which sought to increase the power of the papacy, to mobilize Catholics into a more organized, disciplined church, and to oppose the basic institutions of modern liberalism. In the United States, where such political reaction would have been suicidal, similar pressures were moving the church toward a degree of separation from the broader society and culture, the enhancement of hierarchical and clerical authority and more self-centered forms of organization. The result was that the immigrant church, less certain of how to integrate its loyalties to an increasingly conservative church and to a nation that offered remarkable freedom, was less respectful of Catholics and all but identified with values the European church rejected. In the end, the American church would achieve its most cherished objectives, preserving the faith and loyalty of its rapidly expanding people while securing a respected place in American society. But it would be a long and arduous struggle.

"John Carroll's grand plan failed," James Hennesey writes. "The Church in the United States did not develop along the lines he envisioned."[1] The major reason for this was the arrival of large numbers of Catholic immigrants in the cities of the Atlantic seaboard. They came from Ireland, first in a steady stream, then, after the outbreak of the potato famine in the mid-1840s, in a flood. They came, too, from Germany, attracted by employment opportunities, refugees from the constant provincial battles in the German states and the turmoil created by the Revolution of 1848. Increasingly, the people the church served were not educated, prosperous Anglo-Americans but Irish and German day laborers, industrial workers, artisans, and shopkeepers.

By the third decade of the nineteenth century, the Catholic population was urban, working-class, and foreign-born. Instead of a minority of English-speaking families who had preserved their faith over long centuries of persecution, the Catholic people were increasingly poor, uneducated, and in large part unchurched. In place of the self-conscious, deliberate Catholicism of the founding generation there was a Catholicism of tradition and memory, inseparable from the national identity of the newcomers. For Carroll the task had been to secure the place of the church in a potentially hostile but at least temporarily benevolent environment while reaching out to the pockets of Catholics without services of a priest. After 1820 the emphasis changed. The task now was to preserve the faith and loyalty of these immigrants, and those who followed, in a society perceived as more threatening, a more complex task for an increasingly heterogeneous community. From the perspective of another century of worldwide experience with problems of pluralism, the American experiment of building a nation from such a large and diverse population seems all the more unique. How to build one nation, how to make one church, these were questions never faced before.

PRACTICING CATHOLICS

A young seminarian who would later become a bishop, James F. Wood, while studying in Rome told the father general of the Franciscans: "Now, it is not a question of converting the Protestants or the Infidels, rather of preserving the children of the Holy Church from the temptations of the devil and his apostles." When he returned to begin work in Cincinnati he wrote Propaganda lamenting "the losses that the Church suffers of many of her children from among those who, poorly instructed in their homeland, come here, forget their own religion, neglect its holy practices and proceed to perish miserably together with their families on the rocks of indifferentism."[2] Wood and his generation struggled to bring these people to the practice of the faith, convinced that this would protect them from the dangers they faced. In the process they were building a new church in a new way. Elsewhere the church might preserve itself by cultivating government favor, negotiating treaties, concordats, guaranteeing its privileges, or by controlling the schools, but in the United States the public influence of any church, like its internal unity and strength, depended upon its members. This meant that the church must meet personal, family and group needs. Alexis de Tocqueville saw the matter clearly: "There is no country in the whole world in which the Christian religion retains a greater influence over the souls of men than America. . . . In the United States religion exercises but little influence upon the laws and upon the details of public opinion, but it directs the manners of the community and by regulating domestic life it regulates the state."[3]

Evangelical Protestants were becoming convinced they could build a Christian America by regulating manners and morals and controlling education. To achieve this goal, religion had to become organized, people had to be persuaded to join a church, to support its minister and its works, and to make its teachings a part of their daily lives. To resist the evangelical project and insure the survival of Catholicism, bishops, priests, and lay leaders had to do the same.

The formation of the immigrant church, then, brought with it a separation of religion from public life different in its sources but similar in its effects to the splitting associated with republican Catholicism. In the Western world, as growing numbers of people moved from country to city, experiencing new forms of religious and political pluralism, they tended to center their religious lives upon their families and distinct national groups, while regarding public life as beyond the reach of traditional religious symbols and church influence. As both ethnic and religious minorities, Irish and German Catholics had little prospect of making their religion normative for public institutions, even if they had wished to do so. Rather, the Catholic project was to draw the immigrants to the regular practice of their religion. Most had come from Catholic countries where attendance at mass and the sacraments was casual and irregular.

While Catholicism informed the culture and the church exercised various public responsibilities, the people often adhered to a variety of devotions that gave them a direct relationship to God, usually through the mediation of Mary or the saints. In a setting of pluralism, however, such casual practice and independent devotion were no longer adequate. In the nineteenth century a "devotional revolution" took place, centered upon the parish church and reception of the sacraments, for which the presence of a priest was essential.[4] This effort to organize Catholics into a regularly practicing membership reflected the new realities of pluralism and secularization, where preservation of the faith and defense of the church both required more organization and discipline than was needed when the church could deal with its problems and enforce orthodoxy through its control of social institutions.

In the United States, the organizational need to persuade Catholics to attend church and contribute to its support was even more pressing than in Europe. Casual practice and lack of instruction might easily lead to defections. Equally important, in many immigrant groups there were other organizations competing for the loyalty of the people, including non-Catholic churches and anticlerical political groups. Independent organizations and movements might also threaten the security of the church by placing a stamp of radicalism on the group as a whole. The same impulse that led Carroll to seek a degree of autonomy from Rome and to work against trustee extremes required that a growing Catholic population be brought into an organized and disciplined relationship with the church, which meant under episcopal and clerical authority.

One instrument was the parish mission, pioneered in the United States by German Redemptorists and brought to other groups by a number of religious congregations, including the Paulists, a small group of English-speaking preachers who broke off from the Redemptorists in 1858. The missions constituted a form of Catholic evangelicalism, as powerful preachers denounced sin and called for conversion, but in this case conversion not just to Christ but to the church. A successful mission resulted in increased reception of the sacraments, more stable financial support, greater respect for clerical authority, and moral changes designed to build a more sober, industrious, and family-centered community. In the process the image of the "good Catholic" changed from the quiet, unobtrusive personal piety of an earlier period to a more demonstrative, emotional, and church-centered faith and loyalty expressed in participation in the rituals and community life of the parish.[5]

The pastoral imperatives facing the leaders of the church had to find a response among the immigrant people themselves. The American Catholic church succeeded magnificently in creating a parish-centered church, by the mid-twentieth century the best organized and most regular in its practice of any church in history. To learn why it was so successful requires examination of the inner life of American immigrant groups. For early nineteenth-century Catholicism, the best work has been done by Jay P. Dolan, in his study of pre–Civil War New York City parishes.[6] Dolan's study was influenced by the pioneering historian of immigration, Oscar Handlin, whose book, *The Uprooted*, pictures the immigrants as peasants, nurtured in pre-industrial rural Europe, who were caught up in a series of shattering changes that drew them against their will from the settled life of Irish villages and Jewish ghettos to the teeming industrial cities of North America. They experienced all at once the massive historical changes associated with urbanization and industrialization, in the context of the radical cultural shift of migration. Their reaction, as Handlin saw it, was profoundly conservative. Unwelcome strangers, they naturally grouped together in neighborhoods where they could live among people familiar to them, where they could construct churches and voluntary associations to support family and communal values, defend themselves in a hostile environment, and preserve some of the old way of life. The result was the American ethnic group, defined by Handlin as "a loose agglomeration of individuals, aware of a common identity and organized to some degree in voluntary associations, which transmit a definable social and cultural heritage from generation to generation."[7]

Like Handlin, Dolan speaks of the "ethnic villages" of the New York neighborhoods, within which the immigrants recreated as best they could the world they had left behind. His central thesis is that the motivation for formation of the church was essentially conservative, to preserve the traditions, customs, and values formed in the old country. The prewar church of New York was a "transplanted church," organized around these national groups: "The patterns of the past provided the guidelines for the Church in the United States. Transplanted from across the ocean, time honored practices outweighed any attempts at improvisation in the new world. . . . A transatlantic voyage did not alter or rearrange the truths of Catholicism. They were packaged and shipped across the ocean to reappear in America."[8]

But there was more than one package. Irish and German Catholicism differed from one another, and both differed from the style of Catholicism known to Maryland's colonial families. John Carroll, bent upon adapting to the new experiment in self-government, disliked the emphasis placed on nationality by many of his fellow Catholics in the seaboard cities. He would strive to form "not Irish nor English nor French congregations and churches, but Catholic and American congregations and churches"; but this was not to be, at least for many generations.[9] In 1815 there were two parishes in New York City; by 1865 there were thirty-two in the diocese, one French, eight German, and the rest predominantly Irish. The latter constituted most of the territorial parishes, embracing a geographic area; the others were "national" parishes, composed of people from distinct language groups, in this case mostly German. These were supposed to provide their parishioners with religious services in their own tongues until they had adjusted to the new society, but they were destined to take on a life of their own.

The Irish parishes were large, embracing from eighty-five hundred to as many as twenty thousand parishioners. While the Irish community as a whole was composed of predominantly unskilled workers, moving often in search of employment and housing, the active members of the parish, those who served as trustees and had their children baptized or themselves married in the church, were disproportionately drawn from the ranks of skilled workers and lower-middle-class shopkeepers and civil servants. The Germans were a "double minority," Catholics in a Protestant country, Germans in an increasingly Irish-dominated church. They brought with them a richer liturgical and devotional tradition than the Irish, and because they were determined to preserve their language and their distinctive tradition, they were even more intensely conservative than their Irish coreligionists.

Germans came to America, Dolan claims, "less to build something new than to regain and conserve something old." The charitable and educational work of the church was similarly conservative, drawing upon Old World models little influenced by American ideas or practices. Poverty was understood as a permanent feature of the human condition; men and women were encouraged to accept their lot while those who were better off were told to assist their less prosperous neighbors through parish-based organizations such as the Saint Vincent de Paul Society and a variety of German mutual benefit societies. In education, whether in sermons, Sunday school classes, or schools, Old World catechisms provided simple instruction in traditional truths. Protective institutions sought to place children in a rural setting, while sermons and Irish and German newspapers held up rural life as preferable to that in the city. Some Irish Catholic leaders attempted to develop colonization projects to remove families to western farms, but they ran into opposition from the strong New York archbishop, John Hughes, who feared that a scattered rural population would be lost to the church.

Hughes gave the New York church strong centralized leadership. With cities expanding so rapidly, the church needed to develop a "new style of government," Dolan argues. "The needs of a changing society had to be met as quickly and effectively as possible and a parochial form of government was not suited to such a task. What ultimately emerged to fill the vacuum was the rule of one man, the church boss."[10] Instead of the decentralized, rather relaxed administration characteristic of Carroll and such Americanized bishops as John Fitzpatrick and John Williams in Boston, the diverse urban church required a more monarchical episcopate that would combine unquestioned authority with centralized administration, what Dolan describes as the ecclesiastical equivalent of "boss rule." Certainly John Hughes, then

bishop of New York, later archbishop, led his church with greater
firmness and control than any of his predecessors, foreshadowing the
great urban bishops of the twentieth century. "Episcopal authority
comes from above and not from below," Hughes pronounced. "Catholics do their duty when they obey their bishop." He regarded himself
as "bishop and chief" and his people were "one dough to be leavened
by the spirit of Catholic faith and of Catholic union."

Theological justification could be found in the increasing cleri-
calism and reformed episcopate in Europe, where bishops and priests
increasingly saw themselves as delegates of the papacy, exercising
under his authority an unquestioned rule within their own jurisdiction. Thus, for Dolan, "boss rule appeared at a time when it was theologically justified and culturally necessary with the happy result that
it effectively united the diverse elements of urban Catholicism."[11]

Ethnic diversity, according to Dolan, was "the achilles heel of the
church." Hughes and other bishops solved the problem by allowing
the development of national parishes, first for the Germans, then for
other groups, and recruiting foreign-born priests, usually from religious orders, to staff them. But internal divisions plagued the nineteenth-century church. In Cleveland, for example, Bishop Louis Ama-
deus Rappe, who presided over that diocese from 1847 to 1870, was
all but destroyed by his strong opposition to nationalism. During his
administration the number of churches and chapels expanded from
33 to 160; but his lack of sympathy toward ethnic separatism aroused
the wrath of the Germans, led by Francis X. Weninger, whose motto
was "language saves faith." Pushed by Rome, Rappe appointed a
German vicar general and granted permission for more national parishes, but he refused to allow the use of German in parochial schools.
The French-born Rappe had little use for the Irish, either; he thought
their excessive drinking "produced quarrels, public battles, the
breakup of families, divorce [and] profanation of the Sabbath." Instead he recruited Belgian and French priests, who knew German and
would learn English. After long disputes with his German- and English-speaking priests, Rappe, in 1870, was finally forced to resign.[12]
This was only one of many incidents that were to demonstrate how
difficult it would be to make one church from many or to present one
public face to the larger society.

This portrait of the immigrant church is far from complete. Newcomers to eastern cities found a well-established Protestant elite, often
with their own educational and charitable agencies, in full control
of government and business. In these cities Catholic educational and
charitable institutions were alternatives to those controlled by native
Americans. The situation was a little different in the Midwest, where
evangelical Protestants were threatened by Catholics in part because

social structures were less stable and Catholics shared in the provision of needed services. Historian Timothy Walch has pointed out that in Chicago and Milwaukee the hospitals, orphanages, and schools established by religious orders received broad community support, from Catholics and non-Catholics alike, because they were seen as meeting community needs. Press reports conveyed respect and gratitude for the "useful" work done by the church, and indicated that a different relationship existed between Catholic and non-Catholic citizens there than in the cities of the East, one that "encouraged Catholics to involve themselves in urban affairs equally with other citizens and not as members of a beleaguered minority." A similar ease of entry into civic affairs could be found in smaller cities and towns in upstate New York and in Michigan. One conclusion to be drawn is that the conflicts that came to these cities and towns, as they did to Boston, New York, and Philadelphia, arose not simply from upper-class prejudice and Catholic exclusion but from the inner need of the various groups to establish their own identity while finding new ways to share in the common affairs of pluralist communities.[13]

THE SCHOOL QUESTION

As contemporary Catholics and most historians saw it, immigrant Catholicism was altogether compatible with republican values. Catholic leaders claimed that they would have been, as in John England's ideal, separate in religion but otherwise indistinguishable from their fellow citizens, had it not been for the bitter, sometimes violent, reaction of many native Americans to the growth of the church and to the people it served. Nativism was nothing new, for concern about foreigners had surfaced regularly throughout the history of the new republic. The American ideal had been set forth in the eighteenth century by Hector Saint Jean de Crèvecoeur. Here, in the United States, he told his European readers, "the idle may be employed, the useless become useful, and the poor become rich." Immigrants "no sooner arrive than they immediately feel the good effects of that plenty of provisions we possess; they feast on our best foods, and are kindly entertained, their talents, character and peculiar industry are immediately inquired into; they find countrymen everywhere disseminated." Yet even Crèvecoeur saw some dark clouds on the horizon, and they were mainly the Irish, who did "not prosper so well." In fact, they were a problem: "They love to drink and to quarrel; they are litigious and soon take to the gun, which is the ruin of everything; they seem besides to labor under a greater degree of ignorance in husbandry than the others; perhaps it is that their industry had less scope and was less exercised at home."[14]

Whatever the cause, Crèvecoeur was a good prophet. The Irish became America's great urban problem as the nation's cities grew rapidly after 1820. By 1860 they constituted 23 percent of the six largest cities in Massachusetts, 23 percent of the seven largest in New York, 16 percent in Philadelphia and San Francisco, and 18 percent in Saint Louis.[15] Everywhere even professedly friendly observers found a range of social problems; throughout the century newspapers were filled with complaints about the Irish, complaints similar to that of Rappe. Later historians would confirm some of these charges. Professor Hasia Diner, for example, studying Irish women, found extremely high rates of drunkenness, desertion, violence, and schizophrenia among Irish males.[16] Another historian found that between 1860 and 1873 in Philadelphia, murder indictments took place among the Irish at a rate of 4.7 per 100,000, far above the city average of 2.9.[17] While German communities in cities like Cincinnati, Cleveland, and Milwaukee were more stable, there were equally vociferous complaints about German clannishness, drinking, picnics, and sabbath customs.

By the third decade of the nineteenth century, intergroup tensions had reached crisis proportions and were now mixed with revival of anti-Catholicism. In colonial America, anti-Catholicism was theological and religious: the church was seen as engaged in a gigantic anti-Protestant conspiracy.[18] Nineteenth-century anti-Catholicism preserved some of these elements, but was now expressed in more political and social terms. Catholics were associated with the growing immigrant population, who seemed to threaten the security of the native-born population and the stability of still fragile republican institutions. Their religion was only one element of the cultural barrier that prevented the immigrants' assimilation into the larger society. Catholics were also a political threat; the supposedly ignorant, uneducated immigrant masses, quickly granted citizenship and voting rights, seemed easy prey for demagogic politicians. Worse, organized into parishes, educated in separate schools, with no experience of self-government, they divided the community and seemed to constitute an easily manipulated, subversive fifth column, slavishly devoted to a church that by its own official papal admission was hostile to church-state separation, religious liberty, and indeed, in the words of the 1863 "Syllabus of Errors," to "progress, liberalism and modern civilization." No wonder native Americans were worried.[19]

Scholars have discovered behind the evident prejudice and fear of nativist movements a complex mixture of status rivalries, real religious differences, class antagonism, and honest cultural discord.[20] On the one hand, there was the folk tradition of anti-Catholicism and its literature of captive nuns, immoral priests, and papal plots; on the other hand, there were understandable anxieties felt by ordinary Americans about the stability of republican government and even more the cohesion of their own communities in a nation where instruments of social control were weak to an unprecedented degree.[21] For earlier historical images of confidence, progress, and unparalleled success, the new social history has substituted a portrait of expansion, mobility, and the accompanying erosion of traditional authority that made it necessary for Americans to self-consciously and actively demonstrate their loyalties. As David Davis expressed it: "with only a loose and often ephemeral attachment to places and institutions, many Americans felt a compelling need to articulate their loyalties, to prove their faith, and to demonstrate their allegiance to certain ideals and institutions. By doing so they acquired a sense of self-identity and personal direction in an otherwise rootless and shifting environment."[22] And, after all, popular democracy was still an experiment, and an uneasy one, and it was not at all clear that it could be reconciled with the claims of the most authoritarian of Christian churches. As Edward Beecher put it starkly, the "systems" of democracy and Catholicism were "diametrically opposed; one must and will exterminate the other."[23]

American government at all levels was weak, in part because Americans felt the need to do few things together. Pluralism, the coexistence of diverse communities in a single polity, depended in part on the willingness of each group to allow others to go their own way. If carried too far, of course, Americans would cease to be one people. By the 1830s a considerable number of American evangelical Protestants had become convinced that matters had in fact gone too far, that unchurched people on the frontier, slaveholders to the south, Catholics and foreigners in the cities, and even those people who had accumulated too much wealth, constituted threats to the American experiment. Through a variety of benevolent societies concerned with distributing Bibles and tracts, improving and extending public education, Sunday schools, and home missions, and working for a broad range of reforms, evangelical Christians reached out to their lay people for aid in combating religious indifference, the abuse of alcohol, and the Catholic church. They were convinced that Protestantism provided the only reliable foundation for the restraint and self-discipline needed for republican self-government. As for Catholics, they were "bone of our bone and flesh of our flesh," but they were also kept in darkness by their church. Immigration, according to the American Home Mission Society, was the "fulfillment of our national destiny." Let "the victims of oppression and error gather to our shores," they argued, but let Protestants meet them "on the beach, with bread in one hand

and the Gospel in the other, and welcome them to the liberty where-
with Christ has made us free."[24]

Unfortunately, it soon became clear that a warm welcome and an
evangelical appeal would not solve the problem. Education offered
more hope, so reformers soon embarked upon crusades to bring
knowledge of American ways and Protestant piety and morality to
the outcasts. All agreed that there could be no education without religion, but diversity required exclusion of sectarian instruction. Instead, "our system earnestly inculcates all Christian morals," wrote
Horace Mann of Massachusetts: "it founds its morals on the basis of
religion; it welcomes the religion of the Bible; and, in receiving the
Bible, it allows it to do what is allowed by no other system—*to speak
for itself.*" Throughout the country Protestant clergy often took the
lead in organizing and supporting the common schools, recruiting
teachers, and naming superintendents. This effort coincided with an
eager turn to education by the leaders of other American institutions,
so that by the 1840s the public school had come to occupy a central
place in the imagination of many Americans in the north and Midwest.
The school would bring morality and self-discipline to the religiously
indifferent and the Catholics alike, teaching civic virtue, personal
morality, and authentic Christianity. But if it did, it would run directly
into the determination of those immigrants to preserve the faith and
loyalty of their children. Thus the school question entered American
life; it would gradually undermine the Americanist assimilation
strategies of early Catholic leaders and force a new set of attitudes
to public affairs.

The first major fight came in New York, whose common school
legislation exempted New York City, where distribution of the school
fund rested with the common council. In 1825 the council excluded
schools attached to denominations; instead a private corporation, the
Public School Society, dominated education in the city. Organized
in 1805 to provide "for the children of such parents as do not belong
to, or are not provided for by, any religious society," the corporation
was open to all upon a donation of ten dollars. By 1840 the society
was educating 20,000 children and virtually monopolizing the school
fund. Periodically churches sought assistance, but the council declared
in 1831 that "if religion be taught in a school, it strips it of one of the
characteristics of a common school. . . . No school can be common
unless the parents of all religious sects . . . can send their children to
it . . . without doing violence to their religious beliefs."[25] Yet Catholic
parents did object when children were required to read the King
James Version of the Bible and many texts were found to contain
prejudicial passages. Moreover, Bishop Hughes described the theory
of nonsectarianism as "equivalent to the practical exclusion of Chris-

tianity itself."[26] As a result, Catholic parishes began establishing their own schools; by 1840, 5,000 Catholic children attended eight schools, but an estimated 12,000 were going without education. In that year the newly elected governor, William H. Seward, called for "establishment of schools in which [immigrant children] may be instructed by teachers speaking the same language with themselves and professing the same faith."[27] Seward, a strong advocate of universal education, was sympathetic to the Irish and irritated by religious prejudice; in his first year in office he had intervened to allow a Catholic priest to visit a condemned convict.[28] Like many Americans nurtured in the republican tradition, he had been raised "content with the general system of religious doctrine held in common by many sects." As for Catholics, he told a friend he was quite aware of "the errors of the Church of Rome", but he would be "an unworthy Protestant and no Christian" if he "forgot that the Catholic holds fast to every article of the Christian faith that I deem essential."[29] At the height of the controversy, Seward asked a question that would echo through the years: "Why should Americans hate foreigners? It is to hate such as his [*sic*] forefathers were."[30] Guided by his Whig political mentor, Thurlow Weed, Seward hoped to crack the Democratic party stranglehold on the Irish Catholic vote, but he drastically underestimated the antipathy to Irish Catholics. His action in the school crisis would later contribute to his losing his bid for the presidency.

Seward's generous strategy found an eager response among Catholic officials. Vicar General John Power praised Seward and denounced the Public School Society in terms that clarified the impossibility of reconciling Catholic claims with public education. On the one hand, Power charged, the public schools did not offer an education "based, as in a Christian community it ought to be, on the Christian religion. Its tendency is to make deists." On the other hand, he also charged that its vaguely Christian programs were "sectarian" because they taught religion not "by authority," as would Catholics, but allowed children "to judge for themselves," a "Protestant principle."[31] A Catholic petition to the city council based on Seward's appeal was turned down. The society tried to conciliate the diocese by removing passages to which the clergy objected, but Hughes, who had been away early in the controversy, rejected such a compromise. Taking charge of the Catholic cause, Hughes prepared to carry the fight to the state legislature, not so much because he thought he could gain money for Catholic schools as because he believed he could destroy the Public School Society, unite his people, and lay the groundwork for parochial school development. In a letter to another bishop, he demonstrated the gap that had opened between the republican tradition and the more self-interested approach of the immigrant church. He was making "an effort . . . to detach the children of our Holy Faith from the dangerous connexion and influence of the Public Schools," he wrote. "Whether we shall succeed . . . in getting our proportion of the public money or not, at all events the effort will cause an entire separation of our children from those schools—and excite greater zeal on the part of our people for Catholic education."[32]

In Albany Bishop Hughes threw his support behind a bill to extend the state's common school system to the city while arousing Catholic opinion against the local schools and the Democratic party, which opposed the bill. He flattered Seward, who became a lifelong friend, and he and Power made clear their Whig sympathies. In 1841, angered by the failure of the city's Whigs and local Democrats to suport his position, Hughes organized his own slate of candidates for the assembly elections.[33] Seven of his ten nominees repudiated his support, but all ten were elected, with the twenty-two hundred votes on the Catholic ticket holding the balance.[34] Hughes had demonstrated that the Democrats could not carry the city without Catholic support; he hoped he had also taught Catholics that an independent stance could gain them more than automatic support for the Democratic party. The bill passed by the legislature extended the common school system to the city, where local elected commissioners could determine curriculum and texts, and specifically excluded aid to schools teaching "religious sectarian doctrine."

The Public School Society turned over its schools to the new districts, but the fight left a bitter legacy among Catholics and their opponents. The fight had reawakened the dormant nativist movement in New York, alienated moderate Protestant opinion, and made achievement of a denominationally based but publicly supported educational system even less likely to win support. Seward had hoped to "break down the partition wall that separated the Native American and the immigrant citizen" and to "reduce uncongenial masses into one intelligent, virtuous, harmonious and happy people."[35] Frustrated in his desire to "let the Catholics have sufficient schools of their own" and share public funds with them, he had settled for a system that abolished the "monopoly" to which Catholics objected and organized education "without reference to religion," giving Catholics "exactly the same rights and privileges as Protestants, no more and no less."[36]

Hughes had helped to drive religion out of the schools, but now he saw these same schools as ruined by secularism; as he told another bishop, they were filled with "Socialism, Red Republicanism, Universalism, Infidelity, Deism, Atheism, and Pantheism, anything, everything, except religionism and patriotism."[37] Hughes had used the episode to break the "wicked monopoly" of the Public School Society and to render the common schools less dangerous by excluding religion altogether, while he worked to establish parochial schools.[38] He was pleased with the way the fight had unified the Catholic people against what they took to be bigoted opposition. That unity led to more parochial schools. In a circular letter in 1850 Hughes announced: "I think the time is almost come when it will be necessary to build the school-house first, and the church afterwards."[39]

The episode had challenged Seward's republican assumptions, and it had also weakened the stance of those republican Catholics who hoped they could separate their religion from their politics. After the city denied funds to the Catholics in 1841, the usually accommodating John England claimed that there was "not a town or city council in the United States that would not have decided in the same way.... We do not think it likely that a public body can be found in the United States which does not ... think or act under the influence of great prejudice aganst Catholics, their claims, their rights, their principles, their religion and their politics."[40] But what Catholics regarded as their rights, others saw as subversion. In Philadelphia Bishop Francis Patrick Kenrick in 1843 asked the local school committee to excuse Catholic children from reading the King James Version of the Bible and from participating in opening and closing religious exercises. To Kenrick, this gesture seemed only fair, but because the Bible was the key to the evangelical educational crusade, nativists were able to gain considerable popular support when it was believed that Catholics were attempting to exclude the Bible from the schools. In the words of one hymn composed during fights over Bible reading in New York school districts: "We'll not give up the Bible/ God's holy book of truth/ The blessed staff of hoary age/ The guide of early youth."[41] The board's decision to allow Catholic students to read their own version of the Bible during school came in an atmosphere already volatile because of labor and political disputes between Protestants and Catholics; rioting broke out, which left thirteen people dead and five churches burned. Kenrick at one point suspended religious services and briefly left the city to avoid antagonizing the rioters; he argued later that it was better that all the city's churches be burned than that blood be shed. In contrast Hughes responded to the threat that the violence would spread to New York with a promise to fight back. In Phildelphia as in New York, the conflict stiffened Catholic cohesiveness and solidarity. From this time on, Catholics tended to separate themselves socially and culturally from the rest of city. In the next twenty years the number of Catholic schools tripled, and parish societies multiplied dramatically.[42]

German-American Catholics were strong supporters of parochial schools; they were convinced, as one put it, that "without a school children become totally ignorant, or what is worse, unbelievers, God-less and immoral."[43] Hughes, Kenrick, and midwestern bishops with large German parishes made school development a high priority, but others were not so sure. In Boston, for example, although Bishops Benedict Fenwick and John Fitzpatrick found money to build large churches, begin two Jesuit colleges, and send famine relief to Ireland, only a minority of their parishes had schools, in part because the locally born Fitzpatrick had attended the prestigious Boston Latin School and admired the local public schools. Fitzpatrick also disliked Irish nationalism and separatism and counseled patience and mod-eration in dealing with disputes.

The issue of parochial schools tested Catholic relations with non-Catholics, but it also became the convergent issue around which gathered conflicting images of republican and immigrant Catholicism. The change could be observed in the pastoral letters of the American bishops, issued at the end of their periodic national councils. In 1837 they took note of discrimination and charged that nondenominational schools promoted religious indifference and unbelief; but they hon-estly recorded the difficulties they faced in securing their own schools. Three years later they noted their own obligation "to provide estab-lishments where [children] may be carefully educated by competent persons in all that is necessary for their prosperity in this life, while they are taught by admonition and example to walk in that path which leads to heaven." They also urged their people to remain calm in the face of nativist attacks and expressed confidence in the ultimate good will of their fellow Americans. In 1843 they were less sure, expressing their alarm at "efforts to poison the fountains of public education by giving it a sectarian hue, and accustoming children to the use of a vernacular version of the Bible made under sectarian bias and placing in their hands books of various kinds replete with offensive and dan-gerous matter. This is plainly opposed to the free genius of our civil institutions." They again urged calm dependence on civic good will, but they told parents to "avail themselves of their natural rights, guaranteed by the laws, and see that no interference with the faith of their children be used in the public schools, and no attempt made to induce conformity in anything contrary to the laws of the Catholic Church." In 1852 they argued that the newer forms of nondenomi-national education amounted to godless education and they warned Catholics not to be "misled by false theories" that left youth without religion and "consequently without anything to control the passions." Now there seemed no alternative to Catholic education:

> Listen not to those who would persuade you that religion can be separated from secular instruction. If your children, while they advance in human

sciences, are not taught the science of the saints, their minds will be filled with every error, their hearts will be receptacles of every vice, and that very learning which they have acquired, in itself so good and so necessary, deprived of all that could be shed on it in the light of heaven, will be an additional means of destroying the happiness of the child, embittering still more the chalice of parental disappointment, and weakening the foundations of social order."[44]

Catholic education for Catholic children meant social segregation and a moral universe dominated by a faith set off against the larger world; it required insistence on the dangers of associations outside the church to justify the sacrifices required to maintain separate schools. It pointed away from the republican ideal of tolerant good will and equal civic responsibility and toward a subculture nourished in conflict. The need of immigrant families to maintain their integrity thus joined with the need of the church to build an organized way of life to insure its unity and prosperity in a pluralistic society, at a time when external pressures seemed to destroy the republican possibility.

POLITICAL NATIVISM AND POLITICAL CATHOLICISM

The school question introduced a conflict between political ideals and political behavior. During the rioting in Philadelphia in 1843, local Catholics, in their public arguments, clung to the republican heritage of equal rights, civic obligation, and the irrelevance of religion. As one pamphlet expressed it:

> We yield to none of our fellow-citizens in attachment to republican institutions, we owe no allegiance whatever to foreign prince or potentate; the obedience which, as children of the church, we render to the chief bishop, regards not the things that appertain to this world. As Catholics, we are free in our political sentiments, uninfluenced by our religious tenets or by our spiritual guides. We belong to different political parties, according to our judgement and choice, and we have political opinions and predilections over which we acknowledge no control, other than the constitutional and legal restrictions.

They denied any wish to exclude the Bible from the schools, or to interfere with the religious rights of others, but "simply asked for their own children permission to use that version of the Bible, which, as a matter of conscience, they prefer."[45]

Hughes also professed to believe that Catholics should be independent, reasonably judging among men and measures, but his actions, sponsoring his own Catholic ticket in the 1841 elections and placing Catholic interests before the public good, contradicted his appeals for what the nonpartisan republican tradition regarded as good citizenship. Hughes had welcomed Governor Seward's efforts to attract Catholics to the Whig party, but his actions aroused the nativist Whigs and ended by strengthening immigrant loyalty to New York state's Locofoco Democrats. Even bishops more sincerely committed to republican values than Hughes could not overcome the increasing identification of their immigrant flocks with the Jacksonian party. They failed to recognize that the same factors that led the immigrants to the church—their need for group solidarity and generational continuity and the conflict with other religious subcultures— also reinforced their tendency toward group-conscious politics.

It has been said that the Irish found an identity waiting for them when they got off the boat. "They were to be Irish-Catholic Democrats," Daniel P. Moynihan has written. "There were times when this identity took on the mysteries of the Trinity; the three were one and the one three."[46] In New York, in particular, the Irish were courted by the workingmen's parties that soon merged into the Jacksonian Democracy, forming the left wing of the long-established Tammany Hall political organization of the Democratic party. The school question was only one of a series of cultural disputes that had the effect of sharpening party divisions as the Whigs, despite the efforts of Seward and Weed, sympathized with native Americanism while the Democrats avoided antagonizing their immigrant adherents. The cultural basis of party divisions was typical.

In recent years historians have developed a social history of American voting behavior in which ethnocultural issues are found to have played a major role.[47] Lee Benson, who pioneered in this field, found that in New York during the Jacksonian era Yankee evangelicals were attracted to state-guided moral reform through temperance and public education, which led them, and a small number of native-born or well-established Catholics like Hughes and Power, to support the Whigs. The same considerations drew the support of Northern Irish, English, Scotch, and Welsh immigrants. Non-British immigrants, whose ranks included the French and Germans as well as the Irish, resented the elitism of such policies and flocked to the open arms of the Democrats. In the 1830s enough voted Whig (or for the Anti-Masons, who preceded the Whigs) to raise Seward's hopes, but in 1844 95 percent of the Irish and 80 percent of the Germans supported the Democrats.[48] In a later period, in the Midwest, Paul Kleppner and Richard Jensen found political polarization between native-born and immigrant evangelicals and foreign-born Catholics and Lutherans around similar issues.[49] Throughout the century, the tendency of evangelical Protestants to back the Whigs and later the Republicans, while "ritualistic" immigrant Catholics and Lutherans support the

Democrats holds firm. Issues such as Sunday observance, prohibition and licensing of saloons, and use of foreign-language instruction in schools had more to do with party loyalties than such national issues as the tariff and even slavery.

The politics of nativism were complex. John Hughes was pleased that the battle with the nativists had strengthened Catholic unity and solidarity but he and other bishops knew that if they tried to mobilize the Catholic community as a voting bloc they would risk the security of the church in an overwhelmingly Protestant society. Hughes was also sympathetic to the Whigs, despite that party's association with nativists. He regularly urged Seward and Weed to "try to make the difference between the two parties less unequal; do not allow the scale to kick the beam to one end."[50] Upset by public reports of his friendship with the Whig leaders during the campaign of 1841, he had a card inserted in the newspapers: "Bishop Hughes, unable to reply to the many misrepresentations of the public press in any other way . . . respectfully begs leave to assure the community that he is neither a Whig nor a Loco-Foco, nor a politician of any description. He does not permit himself or any of the Clergy to meddle in the business of politics." Hughes only voted once—for Henry Clay, in 1832.

When the Whigs nominated an anti-Catholic vice-presidential candidate, Theodore Frelinghuysen of New Jersey, in 1844, the Democrats naturally made much of this fact in appealing to Catholic voters, and Hughes was furious. Reflecting his views, the *Freeman's Journal* editorialized in September: "We say then, and in this we know we speak for our entire body throughout this country—the politicians must let us alone. They must not profane our religion by mixing it up with their intemperate and often unprincipled strife, nor must they drag it and us, singled out from the nation, into the arena to become targets for mob fury." At the same time, appealing to the older republican ideal, the Whiggish New York *Tribune* urged Catholics to entrust their "rights, if they shall be menaced, to the whole American people and not to the worse than questionable protection of any mere Party." They should "vote with an eye directed solely to the public good, as you may think the welfare of the Republic may demand."[51] Hughes nevertheless favored the Whigs, referring to Frelinghuysen in a private letter as "a sincere, honest, and so far as the two ideas can be associated, honorable bigot."[52]

In the mid-1840s the nativist tide receded temporarily. In December 1847, Democratic President James K. Polk even recommended establishment of formal relations with the papal states, in part to expand American commercial activity in central Italy, in part to improve relations with other Catholic countries while consolidating Catholic support for the Democratic party at home.[53] When the United

States invaded Mexico, the government paid special attention to Catholics, inviting Hughes and Bishop Mathias Loras of Dubuque to Washington to arrange for Catholic chaplains. Hughes even discussed a diplomatic assigment with President Polk and Secretary of State James Buchanan.[54] In the end two Jesuit chaplains were appointed as "employees" to serve Catholic troops and help offset Mexican fears of American anti-Catholicism. The Catholic press, wary of nativist suspicions, made it clear that Catholics must respond to the government's decision. A writer in the *Freeman's Journal*, now the most widely circulated Catholic paper, insisted that "there can be no just ground for the Catholic to oppose the call of his country." The *Catholic Telegraph* of Cincinnati agreed: "It is not a question of Religion but of war which we are now called upon to determine, and though we believe that many and great evils may befall our Church by the prosecution of this war, yet this would not justify our withholding from the 'powers that be' that subjection and ready obedience which is due from every citizen to the government entitled to his allegiance." Thereafter there was surprisingly little Catholic interest in the conduct of the war or in the negotiations that led to the transfer of vast territories, many Mexican Catholics, and much church property to the United States.

While some attention was given by nativists to an Irish regiment serving with the Mexican army, there were many Irish-American volunteers and very few deserters.[55] Nor was there a significant revival of anti-Catholicism. An Ohio Presbyterian denounced nativist fears of a "foreign conspiracy": "Our country is safe enough if we instruct the whole people, and especially the immigrant portion of them . . . in the true principles of government, teach them the difference between intelligent liberty and mere licentiousness, [and] place in their hands the Bible and Constitution of the Republic." The condition placed on the nation's safety, however, once again indicated how important the school question remained in determining the course of relations between Catholics and their fellow Americans.[56]

Anti-Catholicism revived in the 1850s, sparked by the visit of a papal representative, Archbishop Bedini, who came to the United States in June 1853. Three months earlier Alessandro Gavazzi, an anticlerical former priest, had arrived in New York and begun lecturing along the East Coast, denouncing Bedini for his role in suppressing the republican rebellion in Italy in 1848. Later he followed Bedini around the country, stirring up crowds and sparking anti-Catholic demonstrations that led, in some cities, to rioting.[57] All this was a prelude to a major revival of nativist and anti-Catholic activity centered on a secret society that eventually became the Know-Nothing party. By 1856 the party had threatened to succeed the Whigs as the leading opponents of the Democrats, and local fights would erupt into bloody rioting in New Orleans, Saint Louis, and Louisville. Once again some bishops attempted to ride out the storm, depending on the ultimate good will of civic leaders, while Hughes in a pastoral letter told his people to take up "a noble defense of your property" should "a conspiracy against the civil and religious rights" go "unrebuked by the public authorities".[58]

In the 1850s, a resurgent nativism claimed to be reacting to increasing Catholic power while immigrant spokesmen argued that they were simply reacting to the attacks of their enemies. In Massachusetts, for example, Irish nationalism and support for the Democrats was consistently opposed by Bishop Fitzpatrick and the priest-editor of the *Pilot*, who in 1852 declared: "We are . . . a Whig."[59] A short time later, however, Boston's Irish voters joined with the Whigs to defeat a new state constitution that would have shifted the balance of political power in the state to western and rural districts. Nativists charged that a deal had been struck between Fitzpatrick and leading industrialists to get jobs and patronage for Catholics in exchange for their votes. "For the first time in the history of the state the Catholic Church has taken the field as a power," one paper charged.[60] At almost the same time revulsion against the Democratic-sponsored Kansas-Nebraska Act overwhelmed local Democrats.

In 1855 a populist surge found expression in the Know-Nothing party, which campaigned on a platform that combined nativism and anti-Catholicism with antislavery, temperance, and political reform. The Know-Nothings elected the governor, all members of the state senate, and all but eight members of the state's house of representatives. The new government ended imprisonment for debt; established the first state insurance board; included women within the mechanics lien law and exempted them from responsibility for their husband's debts; tightened the state's child labor laws; increased state support for public schools while banning aid to sectarian schools; required prayer and Bible reading in the schools; and passed a number of democratizing amendments to the state constitution. They also disbanded Irish militia companies, dismissed foreigners from police and state agencies, deported several hundred alien paupers, and established a committee to investigate institutions directed by religious orders. This latter group, the infamous "nunnery committee," brought the party to ruin, but its heavy-handed behavior has obscured the achievements of this short-lived alliance of anti-Catholicism with popular democratic reform and antislavery. As the foremost historian of Massachusetts politics in the period writes: "Given the frequent conservatism of the Roman church in opposing nationalism and liberalism in nineteenth century Europe, given the perception of 'popery' among liberals in the Anglo-American world, and given the conservative ideology of Boston Catholics and their support of the national Democratic party and its prosouthern policies, the temporary alliance of anti-Catholicism and democratization was hardly accidental."[61]

The reaction of the Boston church reflected the consistently conciliatory stance of Bishop Fitzpatrick, who had long discouraged the development of separate Catholic educational and charitable institutions. When city officials limited the right of a priest to visit a pubic hospital on Deer Island, Fitzpatrick confined his anger to his diary, in which he once referred to the state legislature as "a vast majority of persecuting bigots," while he worked quietly and successfully to overturn the decision. Incensed by efforts to subvert the faith of Catholic orphans in public institutions, he reluctantly allowed the formation of a Catholic orphanage, but he preferred to win Catholic rights to public services by appealing to fair-minded officials and legislators. He nevertheless insisted on the absolute right of children in public schools to be free from sectarian teaching. When the Know-Nothings required daily reading of the "common English version" of the Bible, along with the reciting of the Lord's Prayer and the Ten Commandments, Fitzpatrick called for passive resistance; parents should have their children attend school but refuse to participate. In March 1859, a teacher at Boston's Eliot School beat a student who refused to recite the Ten Commandments from the King James Version. The bishop filed suit, but the judge dismissed the case because the beating had stopped when the child complied with the order. Nevertheless the school department cracked down on Eliot's administration and in 1859 Father Haskins of the House of the Angel Guardian orphanage was elected a member of the Boston School Committee.[62] For the moment Fitzpatrick's approach seemed successful.

The Know-Nothing party was founded in Chicago in 1854 as part of an effort to develop a coalition of political groups opposed to Democrat Stephen A. Douglas. The Chicago *Tribune*, formerly a Whig paper, charged that Douglas was the tool of Irish Catholics; it denounced the church as the "main support of despotism and arrayed against the republican people in their endeavors to secure political and religious liberty." After the Douglas-sponsored Kansas-Nebraska Act shattered the political truce that followed the compromise of 1850, the Douglas Democrats were portrayed in Illinois and elsewhere as the party of whiskey, slavery, and Catholicism. In 1855 the Know-Nothings swept to victory in Chicago behind an alliance of nativists, prohibitionists, abolitionists, and anti-Douglas forces. Like all Know-Nothings, the new mayor distinguished between the immigrants themselves, who could be educated for citizenship, and the church, which he denounced in his inaugural address: "I cannot be blind to the existence in our midst of a powerful politico-religious organization, all its members owning, and its chief officers bound under an oath of allegiance to, the temporal as well as spiritual supremacy of a foreign despot, boldly avowing the purpose of universal dominion over this land, and asserting the monstrous doctrine that this is an end to be gained, if not by other means, by coercion and at the cost of blood itself." After rioting between Germans and nativists, the antislavery wing shifted to the new Republican party; knowing the nativist party was dead, the local nativists ignored the Know-Nothing candidacy of Millard Fillmore in 1856.[63]

Nativism was not confined to the East. In 1856 there were 6,000 Irish in San Francisco, 80 percent of them males under the age of thirty-five. An educated minority mingled with the city's native-born elite, but the majority were viewed as roughnecks, whose class-conscious defiance of authority laid the seeds for conflict. Under a brilliant second-generation organizer, David C. Broderick, the Irish rallied to the Democratic party, whose increasing local power outraged the Protestant elite. A shooting incident involving an Italian gambler and a local madam, followed by the murder of a local editor by an Irish politican, led to the establishment in 1856 of a vigilante committee composed of Protestant merchants. It ruled the city for months, overlooking murders and banishing from the city persons charged with such crimes as drunkenness, disorderly conduct, and insulting behavior. Seventy-five percent of those banished were Irish. The episode was to leave a bitter legacy of Irish-Protestant conflict that would shape the city's politics for years to come.[64]

THE IMMIGRANT STYLE

The sources of the immigrant style—group consciousness, defensiveness, willingness to use power to achieve concrete results—were complex. On the one hand, the church, associated in the public mind with antidemocratic teachings and activities, was compelled to affirm American republican values and to uphold the virtues of reasonable discourse and unselfish public-spiritedness considered necessary for the success of the democratic experiment. The bishops themselves generally avoided partisan politics, and those who expressed their sympathies rarely favored the Democrats before the mid-1850s. Bishop Martin John Spalding of Louisville, for example, believed bishops should not vote, although his private sympathies were with the Whigs; later, on the eve of the Civil War, his almost violent hatred of the Republicans was to drive him toward the Democrats.[65] On the other hand, the church as an institution had interests to protect, as a religious body it had its own moral values to defend, and as a community composed increasingly of immigrant outsiders, it had to face the realities of culturally defined political conflicts. Part of the problem was politics itself. The American republican tradition had difficulty accommodating to political parties.

Madison, in his realism, had recognized the existence of factions and thought that a large republic could render them so diverse that it would be all but impossible to form a majority united enough to suppress minorities. But factions were a problem, defined as dangerous to liberty and political stability. When such factions and coalitions actually appeared, they seemed to violate republican ideals of dedication to the public good and independent, disinterested use of the franchise, as the public statements of both Hughes and the *Tribune* had indicated. Catholics, whose church repudiated republican and democratic institutions elsewhere, held to theories of natural law, social harmony, and ecclesiastical authority that, in theory at least, made disagreement about principles unnecessary and divisions over interests immoral. Partisanship seemed equally abhorrent to American ideals and Catholic teaching. Even more important, partisan political behavior risked dividing Catholics, weakening their potential influence, and arousing the wrath of the nation's best people. The bishops, worried by the tendency of some urban Catholics to flock to the Democratic party, and stung by charges that Irish Catholics in particular were selling their votes, warned their people in 1840 to "flee this contamination, keep aloof from these crimes," and reflect that they were "accountable not only to society but to God for the honest, independent and fearless" use of the franchise. It was, they said "a trust confided to you not for your private gain but for the public good." They deplored "the havoc and the wreck of religion which political excitement has produced" and urged Catholics to "avoid the contaminating influence of political strife, [and] keep aloof from the pestilential atmosphere in which honor, virtue, patriotism and religion perish." Three years later they returned to the subject, emphasizing again the sacred obligation of the ballot. Disclaiming any "right to interfere with your judgement in the political affairs of our common country" or any "wish to control you in the constitutional exercises of your freedom," they nevertheless pleaded again for a disinterested and honest exercise of the franchise.[66]

Yet even John England recognized that conditions might force Catholics to use the political system to protect themselves. To his demand that Catholics be united in religion but indistinguishable from their fellow citizens in politics, he admitted one exception: "If any candidate for public office, or his supporters, shall single them out from their fellow citizens as objects for insult or for inquiry, we cannot in such a case look upon it as a dereliction of duty to the republic on their part to prefer a capable friend to a capable enemy." Of course defensive reaction against nativist hostility had something to do with the coalescing of immigrants, especially the Irish, around the Democratic party. Condemned as potential agents of an oppressive Catholic regime, they saw themselves as victims of religious persecution at home and in danger of the same Protestant domination in the United States.[67]

But the Irish, like other and later immigrants, were never simply passive victims of injustice. For one thing they had little experience to justify the republican approach advocated by their leaders. In Ireland, they had never had full citizenship and those who spoke in the name of public order and morality were seen to be, and were, their oppressors. Claims made by English politicians and their Irish backers to reasonableness and morality could only seem hypocritical to the Irish. When they did gain rights to political participation, they did so not through reasonable discussion but by the development of their own organized power. Daniel O'Connell "taught the Catholic people of Ireland the value of pride and even of arrogance, encouraging them to abandon the craven slouch of penal times and to combine in order to gain for themselves political power and social reform." O'Connell's Catholic Association had enjoyed considerable support in the United States and the Irish who arrived after emancipation had learned the value of organization, discipline, and loyalty; these values soon found their way into the dynamics of the American political machine.[68]

For Irish Catholics of a political bent, republican values of citizenship expressed an ideal far removed from the reality of their experience. Hughes appealed to that language to break the stranglehold of the Democrats on the Irish vote, but he did so in order to increase their leverage through independent political action. Irish nationalist exile John Mitchell, like Hughes, preferred to see the Irish use their political power independently. They should make an "individual judgement of men and measures," avoid voting as a bloc, and be open to all parties "except Garrisonian abolitionists." But, if nativists isolated the foreign-born, forcing them to act together, they should respond as a body, defeating anyone who sought Know-Nothing support. Responding to the disbanding of Irish militia companies in Boston, Philadelphia, and other cities, Mitchell insisted the Irish would not submit. If forced to turn in their weapons, they should do so, but then buy three more to use if needed. The Irish were here as citizens, Mitchell warned, but if not accepted as citizens, they would be here as enemies.[69]

O'Connell himself pulled back from such assertiveness in the Young Ireland movement, and the American bishops were determined to break radical Irish nationalism in the United States as well. Not only did it threaten to develop beyond episcopal control and risk arousing further nativist fears, but its proponents favored a secular nationalism and welcomed alliances with Protestant Irishmen. To compete with nationalist leaders, bishops like Hughes had to be militant enough to persuade their people of their dedication to the national cause. At the same time they used the fear of nativism and the attraction of republican ideology to make radical nationalism and overly partisan politics seem not quite respectable and vaguely un-American. Thus Hughes, who seemed to non-Catholics the epitome of Catholic power, attacked the Young Ireland exiles for perpetuating Irish separatism. He wanted to have it both ways, a united Irish Catholic bloc loyal to the church and prepared to defend its interests, and a respectable nonpartisanship that would demonstrate to the dominant classes Catholic loyalty to American values and the church's conservative influence over its potentially restive flock.

Perhaps the problem was best expressed in the confused writings of Orestes Augustus Brownson, the nation's best-known Catholic writer. In the 1850s Brownson wrote on all sides and managed to alienate everybody. He agreed with orthodox Protestants that religion was the basis of sound morality but thought that Protestantism could not provide that basis because, like democracy, it followed rather than controlled people's "passions, interests and caprices." Only "the Roman Catholic religion" could "sustain popular liberty, because popular liberty can be sustained only by a religion free from popular control, above the people, speaking from above and able to command them." Liberty was "not possible without Religion" because "you cannot have a state without submission and obedience" and "could not hold people together" save by "the consent of those who are governed." Thus religion, which made people virtuous, also sustained the state, and "therefore Catholicity alone, which is true Religion, can make us free."[70] If this was true, then Catholics had an obligation to claim their full democratic rights and become law-abiding citizens capable of persuading other Americans of the value of their faith and their church.

Brownson urged his fellow Catholics to abstain from political partisanship because "a certain moderation, a prudent reserve, in the exercise of their franchise is expected of them."[71] But this was precisely what Catholics, particularly Irish Catholics, were not doing. While most were "quiet, modest, peaceful and loyal citizens," there were also, "hanging loosely onto their skirts . . . a miserable rabble, unlike anything which the country has ever known of native growth—a noisy, drinking, and brawling rabble."[72] Worse, many Irish did not understand American institutions, showed no respect for law and social order, ignored the balance of liberty and authority, and were "animated with the ultrademocratic spirit."[73]

Claiming to defend Catholic immigrants against nativist attacks, Brownson's effort at honest self-criticism must have grated on Irish ears. "They lack practical republican training," Brownson wrote. "You feel it the moment you begin to converse with them, and it is the want of this interior republican discipline in uneducated Catholic immigrants that strengthens the suspicion that Catholicity is incompatible with republicanism—a suspicion both unjust and ridiculous, for the defect . . . is the result of their previous political, not of their religious, life." Unwilling to forget their past grievances, they clung to their national identity: "They are willing to be treated as Americans certainly, but it must be as Irish Americans."[74] Nativists transferred their sometimes justified suspicion of the Irish to all Catholics, seeing them as foreign, opposed to American nationality, antirepublican, and resistant to progress.[75] While he would defend their basic rights, "insofar as they are foreigners, and insist on remaining foreigners, they have no claim upon me or any other American Catholic." Brownson did denounce the Know-Nothings, but tempered his defense by insisting that Catholics accept the premise that Americans should govern America; as the franchise was not a right but a privilege, the period of naturalization might be extended. Years later Brownson's son Henry wrote that his patriotic convert father "fought almost single-handed to defend against Catholics his right to be an American and against Americans his right to be a Catholic."[76]

Until the Civil War all but destroyed his confidence in the American people and their institutions, Brownson still held to many tenets of the republican tradition, but these values were becoming more difficult to sustain. Nativist prejudice and what Brownson regarded as extreme liberalism undermined his confidence in his fellow citizens. As a Catholic, he professed a strong faith in the teaching authority of the church, a respect for the disciplinary authority of the hierarchy, and a loyalty to his fellow Catholics and to the church that were bound to isolate him from non-Catholics. It was not surprising then that Brownson's voice was not heard by other Americans, who regarded Hughes as a far more representative spokesman for the church, nor that his increasingly militant fellow Catholics should regard him as at best an unreliable ally. When Brownson's unusual response to the Know-Nothings appeared in 1854, the Irish press responded angrily; Hughes publicly reprimanded the fiery editor, and even his old friend Bishop Fitzpatrick, who had guided his entry into the church, insisted to the archbishop of Baltimore that the hierarchy's endorsement of Brownson's journal be withdrawn.[77] Stung, Brownson moved quickly to conciliate the Irish-American clergy and hierarchy, and in the process alienated some native-born allies. When Isaac Thomas Hecker, his oldest Catholic friend, wrote a book in 1853 describing Americans as "earnest seekers" who would find the answer to their search for God in the Catholic church if only the Catholic message was presented to them without its foreign baggage, Brownson gave him a warm endorsement. But, a few years later, when Hecker's second book made a similar argument about the possibility of converting Americans on the basis of reasonable arguments, Brownson severely attacked his friend's optimistic assessment of Americans and his implied criticism of the defensiveness and lack of missionary zeal of the hierarchy. Hughes was not conciliated and Hecker, who was at the time in Rome attempting to win endorsement of his plan to evangelize non-Catholics, was deeply hurt.[78] Henry Brownson was right: his father wanted to be fully Catholic, and he wanted to remain fully American, and it was becoming more and more difficult to be both.

Brownson's ambivalence was not unique, but others were finding a more conservative strategy with which to win non-Catholic respect while not alienating Catholic immigrants. Martin John Spalding, the native-born son of an old Maryland family, called attention to the contrast between the divisive behavior of the Protestant clergy and the conservative influence of Catholic priests, who "are not and have never been either abolitionists or free-soilers, ultraists or politico-religious alarmists." Far from dividing the American people, the Catholic church broke down barriers between people and united them on a common ground and under a common authority. He, too, was worried about some immigrants, not Catholics but the "infidels" and "red republicans" flooding the country in the wake of the 1848 revolutions. "The greatest, and in fact the only real danger to the permanency of our republican institutions is to be apprehended from this fast increasing class of foreigners, composed in general of men of desperate character and fortune, of outlaws from society, with the brand of infidelity upon their brow," Spalding wrote. In dealing with such people native Americans sincerely concerned about their country had no better ally than the Catholic church, which took "open ground" against their "anarchical principles" and felt "honored by their bitter hostility." In fact, he insisted, in words that echoed Brownson's, the church's "principles are eminently conservative in all questions of religion and civil polity." If the Know-Nothings, the "lately organized secret political association," only fought "against the pernicious principles maintained by such foreigners as these," Catholics "would not only have no cause to complain, but . . . would rather applaud their patriotic efforts in the cause of true freedom." Turning the argument back against the church's tormentors, Spalding expressed shock at what the Know-Nothings were in fact doing: "Our boasted advocates of 'American principles' instead of opposing, secretly or openly sympathize with these sworn enemies of all religion and of all social order, of God and man.''[79]

By the time of the Civil War, then, the position of the Catholic church in American public life had changed dramatically. The tiny minority of 25,000 Catholics at the start of Carroll's episcopate had become the largest denomination in the country, with over three million adherents. Rather than settle in as a religious minority well integrated into social and civic life, Catholics had become a well-organized, militant minority, insistent on their loyalty to their church, suspicious of the intentions of others, capable of defending their rights, and no longer certain that the separation of religious loyalties from public affairs would meet their needs or serve the interests of the nation. They expected their leaders, clerical and lay, to defend the church, resist both Protestant aggression and creeping secularism, and confirm their desire to be accepted as equal participants in national life. The only problem was how to reconcile this emphasis on primary loyalty to the church with civic obligation in a pluralistic society. The answer was to claim that Catholics were better citizens, more ardent patriots, and more moral people precisely because they were Catholics. The church's pastoral work moderated immigrant alienation and channeled immigrant energies into acceptable behavior. In fact, the nation should, in its own interest, become Catholic, but this claim had less to do in practice with converting the nation than with enhancing Catholic morale and providing Catholics with a point of view that allowed them to remain Catholic while engaging in the process of personal, family, and group self-development in their social and economic life. If the group conscious, communal loyalties of Catholics could be confined in an alternative culture centered on the church and the school, and if the church could avoid association with radical movements and power politics, it might be possible both to keep Catholics catholic and persuade others that the church was indeed American.

CHAPTER
4
Industrial Catholicism

❧

*I*n worn out, king ridden Europe, men must stay where they are born, but in America, a man is accounted a failure, and ought to be, who has not risen above his father's station in life."[1] Rarely has the American dream, and obligation, of success been stated more clearly than it was by Charles O'Connor, a faithful Irish-American Catholic who became famous as prosecutor of New York's last Protestant political boss, William Marcy Tweed. Another successful Catholic New Yorker, handsome, eloquent Father Edward McGlynn, had some questions about such notions of readily available opportunity and morally condemned failure. After several years as pastor of the city's largest parish, McGlynn recalled, "I began to feel life made a burden by the never ending procession of men, women and little children coming to my door begging not so much for alms as for employment, not asking for food but asking for influence and letters of recommendation and personally appealing to me to obtain for them an opportunity of working for their daily bread." The experience opened his eyes: "I began to ask myself 'Is there no remedy? Is this God's order, that the poor shall be constantly becoming poorer in all our large cities the world over'?"[2] McGlynn experienced the contrast between progress and poverty that stirred a generation of reformers in the age of America's most dramatic industrial expansion. Railroads bound the nation together, new factories achieved undreamed-of productivity, new wealth appeared everywhere, but at the same time farmers cried for relief from debt, the appearance of tramps signaled recurrent depressions, and slums as crowded and unhealthy as any in the world sprawled across the urban landscape. In Henry

George's words: "as liveried carriages appeared, so did barefoot children."[3]

American Catholicism, with its ever-multiplying urban churches and schools, its working-class and lower-middle-class parishioners, its polyglot language groups, stood at the very heart of industrial America. Amid pre-Civil War optimism Ralph Waldo Emerson spoke of the "party of hope" and the "party of memory." Immigrant Catholics, bent as they were on preserving a historical faith and their own sense of the meaning of things, at first glance seemed solidly aligned with memory. But there was hope among them as well, hope for economic security, for personal and political freedom, and for a share of America's new possibilities. As foreigners they were pushed by the Emersons to make a choice between Catholic memories and American dreams. Industrial capitalism posed another, related set of choices. To industrialists they were "operatives," "hands," their religion, their nationality, even their names irrelevant to the deeper reality of their function. Perhaps, then, they were a class and should act like one. Ethnic separatism was a reasonable response to enforced outsiderness; perhaps labor solidarity was another. Yet, as workers and as immigrants, there was that other voice, calling them inside, insisting that they take their place at the center of American life, by striving for success, as O'Connor would have it, or by sharing in solving America's social problem with Edward McGlynn and Henry George. Once again, they were told, they would have to choose. They could no more be loyal to their class and responsible citizens than they could be foreign and American.

In 1904, W. E. B. DuBois posed the same question for black Americans. Ever conscious of their "twoness," they were torn between being black and not really Americans, or being Americans and not really black, alternatives defined for them by others. In a hostile environment, DuBois argued, they could affirm their existence by striking out in anger, they could conform to the expectations of the majority, or they could make a "determined effort at self-realization despite environing opinion." DuBois gave himself to a lifetime struggle for his own and his people's consciousness of themselves, and thus for their self-determination, a struggle authentically American while deeply rooted in the experience of black people in the United States.[4] In their own, and far less painful way, America's immigrants, many Catholic, most industrial laborers, faced similar demands. Some indeed struck back in anger at the violence inflicted on them, others did their best to conform to majority demands, others, like DuBois, sought authentic self-development. To be free and equal, while remaining themselves, was for Catholic immigrants another of the nation's noble if unending struggles.

THE CIVIL WAR

The American Catholic church, as it began to wrestle with the problems of industrial society, lacked the experience of dealing with the moral dimension of social issues that other Christian churches painfully aquired during the conflict over slavery. The issue posed for the Protestant churches all the problems that confront Christianity in a free society. Should churchmen endanger the unity of the nation by demanding the freedom of the slave? At what point should the solidarity of the Christian church be risked in order to offer a clear witness against human bondage? Was it the church's responsibility in a democratic and pluralistic society to guide the conduct of individuals alone, or did it have a responsibility as well to promote Christian principles in public life? If an individual church member violated church teaching, should that individual be disciplined? Could the Christian do violence to achieve loving objectives? What would happen if Americans responded to Edward Beecher's 1835 appeal "not merely to preach the Gospel to every creature, but to reorganize human society in accordance with the law of God, to abolish all corruption in religion and all abuses in the social system and, so far as it has been erected on false principles, to take it down and erect it anew?"[5]

Catholic leaders had little use for such appeals; they thought reform a ruse to impose Protestantism on the nation, or an American version of the "Red Republicanism" threatening the church in Europe, and they would have none of it. When the Irish temperance reformer Father Theobald Mathew toured the country in the 1840s, he found a less than hearty reception from bishops because he was welcomed so eagerly by what the Boston *Pilot* called "ultra reformers" and "pseudo philanthropists" and was joined on the platform by those whom Boston's bishop called "sectarian fanatics, calvinist preachers, idolators and other such."[6] Church leaders north and south believed that antislavery, nativism, and anti-Catholicism were parts of a reform package at once utopian and hypocritical, threatening the church but also offering it an opportunity to contrast such unstable radicalism with its own sound conservativism. According to Hughes, the church had "little confidence in theoretical systems which assume that great or enduring benefit is to result from the sudden or unexpected excitements. . . . Having witnessed so many experiments tried on poor credulous humanity by new doctors who turned out to have been only quacks . . . she is inclined to suspect and distrust all those crudely conceived political changes which disturb the peace of communities and nations, without improving their conditions."[7]

Reformers recognized and denounced reactionary ideas like this, but they hoped to break through clerical barriers and reach the Catholic people, especially the Irish. Contrary to popular belief grounded in Hughes's regular denunciations, the New England abolitionists overcame their instinctive anti-Catholicism to consistently oppose nativism, and they regularly expressed sympathy both for the suffering of Irish-American workers and the cause of Ireland's freedom. They revered and received the unequivocal support of the greatest Irish leader, Daniel O'Connell, a fiery, outspoken opponent of black slavery. O'Connell never wavered, telling American abolitionists he was sorry "there were Irishmen in America who had taken the wrong side with regards to the liberties of the human race." To his fellow Irish he was even sharper: "No man shall dare say that such human beings shall be made the property of their fellowman, and treated, not as human beings, but as the brute beast. . . . The man who will do so belongs not to my kind. Over the broad Atlantic I pour forth my voice, saying— Come out of such a land, you Irishmen, or if you remain, and dare countenance the system of slavery . . . we will recognize you as Irishmen no longer." Using O'Connell's prestige and a petition from leading figures in Ireland, the abolitionists campaigned for two years in the 1840s to win Irish support, but they failed. Church leaders blasted O'Connell and insisted that American Catholics would accept no foreign dictation. A mass repeal meeting of Irish miners in Pennsylvania denounced the abolitionist petition because it was addressed to them as a faction: "We do not form a distinct class of the community, but consider ourselves in every respect as CITIZENS of this great and glorious republic—that we look upon every attempt to address us otherwise than as CITIZENS upon the subject of abolition of slavery . . . as base and iniquitous." The American-Irish, under attack by nativists for lack of loyalty to American institutions, could hardly take the risk of joining a movement widely regarded as disloyal. The historian of this episode concludes: "The Garrisonians were asking these immigrants to join a movement popularly known for its fanaticism, one that was ever ready to denounce the American Union as an abortion and that regularly attacked the traditional Irish political and clerical leadership in America for leading the masses astray and hindering social progress." As the Boston *Pilot* expressed it: "the high admiration [Catholics] feel for the essential characteristics of the American Constitution is too deep and controlling to allow them to engage in a question which imperils the only free government in the world." The Irish remained wedded to the conservative hierarchy and to the Democratic party, which, in abolitionist eyes, was the tool of slaveholders.[8]

O'Connell's passionate advocacy of human rights was not then orthodox Catholic teaching, which had yet to conclude that slavery in itself was a moral evil. Francis Kenrick, whose theological manual was widely used in American seminaries, drew on classical Catholic sources to argue that, although American slaves had been taken by force, which was sinful, that "defect of title" had been "healed by the lapse of a very long time." He condemned the mistreatment of slaves, who had a right to marry, raise children, and receive religious instruction, but also argued that nothing should be done to make slaves discontented with their lot. Priests should instruct slaves to obey their masters and worship God, while admonishing masters regarding their duty to treat their slaves humanely.[9] Hughes agreed. Returning from a trip to Cuba in 1854 he told his flock: "We all know that this condition of slavery is an evil, yet it is not an absolute and unmitigated evil and even if it were anything more than what it is—a comparative evil—there is one thing, that it is infinitely better than the condition in which this people would have been had they not been seized to gratify the avarice and cupidity of the white man."[10]

These opinions were echoed in the Irish-dominated Catholic press. Despite O'Connell's appeals, the Boston *Pilot*, for example, consistently described the abolitionists as nativists in disguise, denounced their "insane radicalism," and charged that they ignored "worse slavery" in Ireland.[11] The clerically controlled paper professed to abhor slavery but, with Kenrick and Hughes, argued that nothing could be done about it, spelling out in detail a pessimistic vision of what would happen if slaves were emancipated in the face of southern economic interests and northern prejudice. The paper defended the Dred Scott decision because it was the responsibility of the courts to declare the law, "whether it squares with the Gospel or not."[12] Political considerations also had their effect. Most Irish Catholics were Democrats. Many bishops had been Whig in their sympathies but, after that party collapsed in the mid-1850s, they tended to align with the Democrats out of revulsion at the "Black Republicans."

There were some 100,000 black Catholics in the South in 1860. Most students of the subject agree that the masters of these Catholic blacks in Louisiana and elsewhere were no better or worse than others, although in New Orleans Irish draymen who owned slaves were known to be particularly harsh. In the lower south, trustees still often controlled parish finances, churches were poorly organized and understaffed, and almost everywhere Catholics were a scattered minority, so that priests constantly complained of defections and laxity among the laity.[13] The result, as Bishop William Henry Elder told Rome in 1858, was that slaves received little spiritual instruction. Rarely were they allowed to leave the plantation for services. A few non-Catholic masters paid a minister to preach or allowed a slave to do so, but in both cases that usually excluded Catholicism; there is only one known case of a black Catholic slave preacher. Priests could visit plantations and urge Catholic masters to do their duty, but there were few priests and those who did so were rarely welcome. On the rare occasions when priests were allowed to minister to the slaves, they found them suspicious, looking on the priest as an "extension" of the master. Blacks themselves generally regarded Catholicism as dull and aloof, in contrast with the emotionalism of evangelical Protestantism. Moreover, blacks who responded to evangelical Christianity tried to shape their own religious affairs and such independence was not encouraged among Catholics. Understandably, then, southern Catholicism produced no antislavery prophet and, nationally, Catholic opinion was more uniform than that of any other religious denomination.[14]

On this issue the best of the Catholic hierarchy deferred to majority opinion. In 1835 John England opened a school for free blacks. The following year, however, a "respectable committee of citizens" asked him to discontinue the school. As he told an Irish friend, he responded that he would do so provided others conducting similar schools did the same, although he "disapproved of the proceeding." The schools were closed. The request was part of concerted measures "taken to guard against the efforts of the Abolitionists"; when a meeting of prominent citizens was held to discuss these actions, England attended and "sat with the presiding magistrate in the most conspicuous place by the courtesy of the Sheriff, who is an Irish Catholic."[15] In 1840 Secretary of State John Forsyth charged that the Catholic church supported abolition; England responded by demonstrating that the pope had only condemned the slave trade, not slavery itself.[16] When the bishops met as a body in 1854, the nation was in the midst of bitter conflict; the bishops said nothing about slavery, but, amid rising opposition to the fugitive slave law and the extension of slavery to the territories, they emphasized the sacredness of law and the duty of obedience to duly constituted authority. While other Christian denominations were splitting apart, they remained united by abstaining from direct comment on what had become for them a "political" issue. In the words of the Provincial Council of Cincinnati in 1859: "Our clergy have wisely abstained from all interference with the judgement of the faithful which should be free on all questions of polity and social order, within the limits of the doctrine and laws of Christ."[17]

When the war came, the bishops lined up loyally, north and south. On Saint Patrick's day of 1861, Hughes told his followers that "there is but one rule for a Catholic, wherever he is, and that is, to do his duty there as a citizen."[18] John Timon, bishop of Buffalo, went further: "Our country it is our duty not to question, but to obey. So much the more holy will be the war, as it is not one of passion, but of duty."[19] Timon, Hughes, and other bishops raised the flag over their cathedrals or episcopal residences to demonstrate their loyalty. William Seward, now secretary of state, asked Hughes to accompany Thurlow Weed to Europe where he could help offset pro-Southern propaganda. Hughes was delighted, telling Rome the government was undercutting the Know-Nothings and honoring the church by the request. Hughes saw the war in the same terms as did conservative Whigs; it was a struggle to preserve the Union, not free the slaves. In a letter to Secretary of War Simon Cameron in October 1861, Hughes warned that if rumors of turning the war into an abolitionist crusade were true, it would make recruiting difficult: "The Catholics, so far as I know, whether of native or foreign birth, are willing to fight to the death for the support of the constitution, the Government and the laws of the country. But if it should be understood that, with or without knowing it, they are to fight for the abolition of slavery, then, indeed they will turn away in disgust from the discharge of what would otherwise be a patriotic duty."[20]

The war seemed to mute nativist and anti-Catholic agitation. In Boston, Bishop John Fitzpatrick encouraged the raising of Irish regiments, while non-Catholic civic leaders went out of their way to conciliate the bishop. Harvard University granted Fitzpatrick an honorary degree and named him to the board of overseers; in 1862 he was elected to the American Academy of Arts and Sciences. A new state law passed during the war provided that Bible reading in schools should be done without note or comment, and none were to be punished for refusal to participate. Fitzpatrick, in ill health, spent the later years of the war in Europe, where he quietly aided the Union cause. Back home, his people were angered by the Emancipation Proclamation; the *Pilot* said that it would lengthen the war and unleash a flood of black workers on the North, where they would not be accepted.

Irish anger found expression in the New York City draft riots of 1863, during which Irish workers murdered blacks and burned their homes; in Boston the militia was mobilized in anticipation of similar outbreaks. The *Pilot* then moved beyond abolitionist baiting to rabid attacks on the blacks themselves. "Servile plantation life is the life nature intended for them," the editors argued, launching a tirade against "negrophilists" and "nigger-worshippers," who thought blacks and whites were equal. In 1864 the *Pilot*, led by Father Tucker, a peace Democrat, denounced Lincoln as a "boob" and backed George McClellan.[21] He was not alone; James McMaster, editor of the *Freeman's Journal*, was jailed for his Copperhead sympathies, sympathies that were widespread among Catholic leaders throughout the North.

Martin Spalding began the war as bishop of Louisville, in the slaveholding border state of Kentucky. Like so many others, he thought slavery neither good nor evil in itself and counseled submission for slaves and benevolence for slaveholders. He had been a Whig, but during the war, in his private correspondence, he regularly denounced the Republicans and praised the peace Democrats. When Rome made inquiries because of complaints occasioned by the *Catholic Telegraph* of Cincinnati's outspoken support of the Republicans and emancipation, Spalding wrote a long report in which he blamed the war on northern ministers and agitators, described slavery as a legacy of Protestantism and the Enlightenment, claimed that blacks would be worse off if free, and denounced the Republican administration for changing the war from one for the Union to one of "confiscation and extermination of the South."[22]

Southern bishops rallied to the cause of the Confederacy with varying degree of enthusiasm. Bishop John Quinlan of Mobile, who in an 1860 pastoral had defended the right of states to secede, told Bishop Lynch of Charleston a month after the fall of Fort Sumter: "We must cut adrift from the North in many things. . . . We of the South have been too long on leading strings." His friend Father William J. Barry wrote from Virginia that he was "heart and soul with the South and the Right," especially as the North intended to make the war "an anti-slavery crusade, a war of total subjugation." Lynch must have agreed; later he toured Europe on behalf of the South. On the slavery issue southern bishops were divided between those who argued strongly in its defense, like Bishop Augustine M. Martin of Natchitoches, and those who had long warned the South of the dangers of improper treatment of the slaves, a warning repeated by Bishop Augustin Verot of Florida after the war broke out.[23]

Most rare were Catholic comments on the suffering caused by the war. Called to give a sermon of thanksgiving for victories of Union armies, Father Samuel Mazzuchelli turned prophet. "Your orators, your statesmen, your writers, have on all occasions, but particularly on the celebration of our national festivals, given way to self-praise, and the words 'American people' made to sound as something above the level of all other nations. . . . We were to be the model to be copied by all nations, we the perfect government, we only had true liberty," the immigrant priest told his Illinois listeners. But now, in the midst of war, with its evidence of "evil and suffering," the United States was no longer a "beautiful and delicate woman." "She has lost her delicacy and beauty, her new children land with a trembling step, she is restless, despised by the nations . . . her seas are stained by the blood of her strong ones and her flourishing lands laid waste and show to the passerby the heap of her slain . . . all seems to be terror, uncertitude and fear. Tears cover her cheeks and the blood of her children has soiled her rich garments."[24] Such reflection was all too rare. Most Catholics, as well as the bishops, found another message in the war. Despite their anger at emancipation, many Catholic leaders agreed with Hughes that the war experience was improving the image of the church precisely because of its conservative qualities. Throughout the war Catholic leaders argued that only the church, with its clear moral principles and divine authority, could heal the breach and mold the nation into one people.

Contrasting the silence of their clergy and bishops on the slavery question with the political meddling of Protestant ministers, Catholic leaders felt they could honestly claim to have no responsibility for the nation's divisions. When they came together again in 1866, this was the message the bishops attempted to convey, turning the anti-Catholic argument about Catholic authority to their advantage. "The enemies of the church fail not to represent her claims as incompatible with the independence of the civil power," they pointed out. "So far from this being the case, the authority and influence of the Church will be found to be the most efficacious support of the temporal authority." The church taught that all power came from God and that the coercive authority of the state was of divine origin. For Catholics, obedience was not submission to force "but a religious duty founded on obedience to God." Among Protestants the individual was "the ultimate judge of what the law of God commands and forbids"; as a result, they often fell victim to "an undisciplined mind and an overheated imagination." But the Catholic had "a guide in his Church, as a divine institution, which enables him to discriminate between what the law of God forbids and allows."[25] Thus, as the nation entered an era of vast industrial expansion, labor and urban unrest, and renewed immigration, Catholic leaders for the most part shared none of the legacy of idealism and moral fervor associated with abolitionism. Rather they believed that it was precisely such moral fervor that had caused the war, and that Americans of substance would welcome a message of discipline, order, and authority.

THE ECONOMICS OF CATHOLICISM

The most important economic reality in the American church was its dependence upon popular support. In much of Europe the church was richly endowed with lands and enjoyed a variety of tax subsidies and exemptions; when its own sources of income were destroyed, as they were by nineteenth-century anticlerical governments, subsequent church-state relations were shaped by efforts to guarantee state support. In the United States such support was out of the question. Nor did the American church enjoy the patronage of wealthy aristocrats and merchants. Instead, it was forced by necessity to depend upon the people. In many places, where priests visited only occasionally when riding a mission circuit, maintenance of the community was a lay responsibility. Elsewhere, among foreign-language-speaking immigrants, it was often lay associations and mutual benefit societies that were the first step toward building a community. In both cases lay leaders, sometimes with the help of a visiting missionary, began raising funds, first for land, then for a church, and only then invited a priest to take up residence. When a priest arrived and the mission became a parish, the continued financial backing of the laity could not be taken for granted. The duty to provide such support was a recurrent theme, for there were few parishes that were not building a new church, school, convent, or rectory, or renovating a facility that had become too small for a burgeoning congregation.

As early as 1792 John Carroll, in his first pastoral letter, insisted on the laity's duty to support the church. Those who refused "to contribute for the ministry of salvation, according to the measure of worldly fortune given to them by a beneficent God," Carroll wrote, violated "divine and ecclesiastical laws" and were "in a state of sin, unworthy of obtaining forgiveness in the tribunal of confession." To the stick Carroll added a carrot, one addressed then to aristocratic, slaveholding planters, later available for use with the non-Catholic employers of Catholic immigrants. "You will find it to be no loss to concur toward the regular support of the ministry," Carroll wrote, for "habits of temperance and frugality are generally the effects of religious instruction," children and servants were "admonished perpetually to shun idleness, dishonesty, [and] dissipation," and the "lessons and duty of industry [were] frequently inculcated by virtuous and careful pastors." All these, "by their effect on domestic economy," made "abundant compensation for the charges in support of religion."[26]

From the start, therefore, the church itself was a self-help project, arising from the commitment and deliberate, disciplined, purposeful action of the congregation. However conservative their motivation, however tied they were to Old World ways, immigrants old and new were doing something unique: forming their own church. Early parish records are filled with stories of lay people raising funds and lending their hands, their tools, or their horses to excavation and construction. Legends grew of priests who visited their people in crowded, steamy tenements, in scattered labor camps, even in saloons, to solicit support for the new church. Later a never-ending series of fairs, bazaars, entertainments, lectures, and door-to-door solicitations seemed to overwhelm parish life. Almost always these were for a building project; day-to-day support came from pew rents and special collections. The annual auction of pews was all but universal in the nineteenth century, despite frequent complaints at this introduction of class divisions into the church. Pastors regularly reminded pewholders to pay their quarterly fee, they berated those who could rent and did not do so, but they insisted that those who could not would be provided for. Door offerings, expected from those who visited or did not rent pews, were sometimes presented as an alternative to pewholding, but such proposals aroused complaints about charging admission to religious services. As for the priests, their salaries, quite substantial in contemporary terms, had to come out of normal parish revenues. In addition, the pastor was entitled to stipends for special sacramental services: baptisms, weddings, funerals, and memorial masses. He was also allowed to keep the Christmas and Easter collections, the size of which provided a measure of clerical popularity and of relative standing among the diocesan priesthood. John Hughes lamented that he was forced to become a builder and a banker rather than a pastor, and Archbishop Bedini complained in his report to Rome after his stormy visit that the American clergy were preoccupied with buildings and money. But with the combination of rapid growth, voluntary support, and opposition to trusteeism, this development was almost inevitable.

The need for voluntary popular support naturally compelled the church to adjust to the prevailing economic order. In Europe aristocratic and landlord support allowed many priests to cling to the economic ideas and practices of the feudal age, while dependence on the state drew them into politics. But in the United States, the church would grow with the country and with its people, and accommodation to prevailing economic values and practices was inevitable, while economic conflicts in society were bound to affect the church in ways that reflected its own economic needs and those of people on whom it depended. John England thought it good that the American church depended upon the "zeal of the people" as a whole, "not upon one or two powerful persons, but upon the body of the people at large." In this situation, pastoral life should be free of the elitism that marked it in Europe, England felt. In the United States the relation between priest and people "ought to be one of friendship. . . . A pastor who feels himself to a certain extent dependent upon the good will of his flock, will be frequently urged to reflect upon the best mode of securing their affection, for it is in his interest," he wrote.

This dependence could undercut the freedom of the clergy to preach the gospel and instruct their congregations—one reason for the rejection of trusteeism. But diocesan and parish histories suggest that priests resented the dependence of which England spoke, especially if they were better educated and from more socially respectable families than the people of their parish, and they welcomed any opportunity to secure their control of finances and put some distance between themselves and their parishioners. Archbishop Hughes, explaining to Rome the relative affluence of American bishops, and by implication the clergy, argued that it was the role of the bishop to give "the Catholic body a social status that will entitle them to the respect of a people who entertain nothing but contempt for poverty."[27]

In advising their congregation, pastors walked a tightrope. Many of their people were in fact poor, although it was the somewhat more prosperous who took an active part in parish affairs. Many more poor remained only casually related to the church. Nothing in Catholic tradition or experience could justify telling such people that they "were accounted a failure and ought to be." Historically Catholic peasants and outcasts had found in the gospel and the ministry of the church a comforting message of compassion, a promise of salvation, a statement that all were equal before God and, as the 1791 synod suggested, an insistence that the poor had a claim upon the rich. Such themes, with their moral thrust toward resignation, dominated parish homilies and mission sermons in early nineteenth-century New York, accordng to Jay P. Dolan. A poem in a child's reader expresses it thus:

> For we all have our proper spheres below
> And 'tis a truth worth knowing
> You will come to grief if you try to go
> Where you were never made for going.[28]

In *The Orphan's Friend,* Father A. A. Lambing told needy young men they had two tasks in life, to make a living and to save their souls. They could accomplish the former "by faithfully fulfilling the duties of our state of life, obeying those who have charge of us, dealing honestly with everyone, and trying to become useful in the trade or work we are set at." Yet success had little to do with salvation; indeed, "riches will hinder those that have them, and love them too much, from saving their souls." That objective was secured in a different realm: "Our life is like a passage in a stormy sea. No one who is not a child of the church can go safely across it; and if he is in the church and is so unfortunate as to leave her, he will certainly be lost. To belong to the Church is to belong to Christ; to be separated from her is to be separated from Him." And within the church, the duty was to follow its teaching and its rules: "there is no greater misfortune than to disobey the Church."[29]

Yet things are rarely as they appear, and the supposedly conservative social message of the immigrant church was not in fact very conservative. The significance of the church's social message, addressed as it was to so many urban, working-class Americans, can hardly be overestimated. Industrialist Abram S. Hewitt, after the railroad strikes of 1877, argued that "the problem presented to systems of religion and schemes of government is to make men who are equal in liberty, that is in political rights and therefore entitled to the ownership of property, content with that inequality which must inevitably result from the law of justice."[30] Toward that end the church could be helpful. As early as 1827 Kirke Boott, the manager of the new, planned industrial town of Lowell, was disturbed by the presence of a boisterous Irish population drawn to the area to work on the town's construction. He asked Bishop Benedict Fenwick of Boston to send "a priest to steady them" and the bishop did so, after securing a grant of land from Boott.[31] Historian Stephen Thernstrom, who studied late-nineteenth-century Newburyport, concluded that priests and employers both needed "thrifty, hard working" people. With Protestant assistance Catholics constructed churches and church-related institutions "dominated by a priest and lay elite firmly committed to the prevailing American idea of enterprise and success."[32]

Catholic priests well knew the declension that accompanied immigration everywhere in the world. Weakened and broken bonds of family life, the absence of parents, the predominance of single males, the pathology of alcoholism, crime, and dependency, all these were realities. As Timothy Smith argues, "uprooted persons seeking a new community needed both a principle of authority and a dynamic and 'progressive' use of it"[33] Catholic clergy had no use for an ethic that identified the poor with the sinful or the unfit. But they did, almost without knowing it, preach a message of personal responsibility. The whole evangelical task was to persuade men and women to decide to attend church, receive the sacraments, contribute to the church's support, and follow its moral teaching, especially by avoiding vice and supporting their families. Those who did not attend church, did not support the pastor, or did not care for their families were condemned in sermons, newpapers, and books. The whole experience, then, was one of personal responsibility for the outcome of life, even for salvation. These priest did not need to remind people close to their peasant roots that there was unfairness and injustice in the world, so that being a good Catholic did not guarantee economic success. Nevertheless, things did not have to be as they had been. The very experience of building a church, as large and as beautiful as any in the town or city, was evidence that things could be different, that with commitment, discipline, and cooperation a new future could be created, if not now then for the children.

The experience of migration, Timothy Smith contends, expanded the sense of peoplehood, "as folk memories were brought to bear on new aspirations." The immigrant church was not transplanted, Smith claims in an argument sharply different from that which informed Dolan's study of earlier groups; instead it was a "reasoned effort to deal with new challenges." It provided a more intense sense of religious identity because "affiliation turned on personal choice." The experience of forming new communities embodied modern ideas of "autonomy, self-realization and mobility" and thus fashioned "new persons, involving new perceptions of individual worth, enlarged hopes for both this life and the next, and the internalization of moral constraints calculated to help realize these hopes."[34] The historian of the American success ethic has argued that in its early stages it encouraged the poor to defy caste and custom and make their own way in the world; only later did it serve to maintain social control and justify economic inequality. Forced by the circumstances of voluntarism to offer similar encouragement to a people only beginning their experience of industrial capitalism, Catholic leaders affirmed their hopes while easing their disappointments. If it had the effect of pacifying a potentially militant Catholic working class, it also had the beneficial effect of sanctioning personal dignity and responsibility. Before men and women could take responsibility for making the world a better place for everyone, perhaps they had to make a place for themselves. In some sense at least, democratic empowerment might be the prerequisite for public social responsibility.

There is no denying the strength of the conservative impulse among Irish immigrants who had settled in the large cities of the Northeast before the Civil War. Ireland had pushed many out; so had Germany. Newcomers did face a well-established Protestant elite who had little interest in assisting them or allowing them to claim a full share of public life. But more Irish came after the Civil War than before, and many settled in the newer cities of the West. Professor Hasia Diner has found that even among the famine Irish the women were deliberate, purposeful, and optimistic about the future. They entered domestic service to earn money to bring over brothers and sisters, they entered marriage reluctantly, and were often left alone with small children, yet they remained determined to build better lives for themselves and their families. Faithful to the church, they were also willing to pursue careers and join organizations that the church did not favor.

For many later groups, the pressure to leave the homeland was much less severe. Timothy Smith has found that in many cases those young eastern Europeans who emigrated were better educated than those of their age group who stayed home. They felt a wrenching sense of loss as they left family and familiar scenes behind, but some at least were filled with hope for economic advancement, education, and freedom. Smith claims that the whole process of migration was one of "self-selection [which] turned upon ambition, upon a wish and a will to believe that the future was more real than the past, and upon a readiness to accept changes and make adjustments." In Smith's view, "the ethnic community was not a room but a corridor. [The immigrant's] ultimate objective was the fulfillment of a dream of success that owed nothing to Horatio Alger. If it was too late for him to make more than a start, it was not too late for his children. And for them, he knew, schooling was the key that unlocked the corridor door."[35]

At the same time the parish nurtured values at odds with American individualism. One study of a Polish parish found that people belonged as family members, unmarried individuals being listed with their families even after the death of their parents. Concerned with "the survival of their families in a hostile new environment and the affirmation of their family's place in a larger spiritual world," the parishioners found that their parish served family needs: "financial help from the building and loan associations, security from the insurance societies and sacramental ceremonies to mark important occasions in the life of the family." Parish organizations could function as surrogate families for immigrants separated from the extended family that had offered help and support in the Old World village. In the mutual benefit societies people were struck from the rolls if they missed their dues payments, they received communion as a group, and reception of the sacraments was a condition for membership. For the Redemptorist priests, "salvation was not an individual affair but the consequence of a way of life that could only be lived in a community organizing existence on earth to ensure salvation in the next world." It thus exerted a counterforce to the pressures of mobility and poverty to divide families and, as John Bodnar writes, suggests "the possibility that urban-industrial society also positively nurtured behavioral patterns such as limited horizons, familial cooperation, fatalism and anti-materialism which were as functional for proletarians as for peasants."[36] Thus, whatever the motivation, participation in the parish constituted a reconstruction of family and group life and could not help but serve the adjustment of immigrants to New World urban-industrial conditions. As two pioneer social workers expressed it: "Any type of organization which succeeds in regulating the lives of its members is beneficial. If you can induce a man to belong to something, to cooperate with any group whatever, where something is expected of him, where he has responsibility, dignity, recognition, economic security, you have at least regulated his life" and in the process promoted rather than retarded assimilation.[37]

By no means did all this suggest opposition to economic ambition and social mobility. As Carroll's words in 1792 indicated, the church depended on its more prosperous members. The church's need for money and desire for security, the quest for acceptance and respectability of many lay leaders, and the clergy's own status as self-made men insured that doing well would not be frowned upon. As the number of business and professional men and aspiring young men and women grew, so too did a Catholic gospel of wealth, found most clearly in temperance societies and sermons. Class divisions appeared within the church, and so did a deep ambivalence about American ideals of success through self-help. By the late nineteenth century there was, as we shall see, a substantial Catholic middle class drawing the church more deeply toward conservative social attitudes; that this was not the only or even the major development of the period was due to the fact that at the same time there were new and unfamiliar arrivals entering the church and the nation at the bottom of the social ladder.

THE NEW IMMIGRANTS

The American Catholic church experienced enormous growth in the years between the end of the Civil War and the First World War. Between 1865 and 1890 Germany, Great Britain, Ireland, and the Scandinavian countries supplied the largest numbers of immigrants to the United States, but, after 1890, the major groups came from Italy, Austria-Hungary, and Russia. In 1907, 81 percent of newcomers came from eastern and southern Europe. As a result, America, and the American church, became even more diverse. By 1917 the church in Chicago, for example, ministered to twenty-eight different nationalities.[38] In Massachusetts, the Boston diocese had 109 churches when John Williams became archbishop in 1866. There was only one national parish. At Williams's death in 1907, there were 248 parishes, 42 of them national, and 598 priests. Jay P. Dolan calculates that by 1916 there were 4,765 foreign-language parishes in the United States, 47 percent of the total. Another study for the same year counted 2,230 parishes in which a foreign language was used exclusively, and another 2,535, many of them German, where both English and a foreign language were spoken.[39]

The church remained a self-help project. Whether through lack of interest or lack of resources, the bishops made almost no conscious effort to directly assist immigrants. There were few settlement houses, and few dioceses had funds to provide seed money for new parishes. In addition, the now well-established Irish leadership resented the claims of those newer immigrants, especially the Italians, who showed many of the signs of social declension the Irish had shown earlier. In

1907 the archbishop of New York complained to another bishop about the burden of "other people's poor, illiterate and unregenerate of all states and nations" leaving the diocese with "only one class of people [the Irish-American] to draw upon for the support of their own churches and schools as well as of so many others."[40]

The Irish-dominated hierarchy found itself caught between increasingly militant demands of ethnic minorities and continuing charges that the church was a foreign presence in American life. In the 1880s German Catholics in Germany and the United States complained to Rome about attempts to force second-generation families into territorial parishes and called for the appointment of German bishops to serve their congregations. The bishops succeeded in beating back the German challenge, in part by claiming that the government was concerned about the perpetuation of such national divisions. In the aftermath, however, bishops were less inclined to challenge German efforts to hold onto their Americanized members by offering English-language services, thus perpetuating the theoretically transitional national parishes; German bishops were in fact appointed to sees in the so-called German triangle of Cincinnati, Saint Louis, and Milwaukee. Similar tensions would later mark relations between Irish and German bishops and restive Polish clergy and people.[41]

Urban parishes were social institutions that by serving immigrant needs served the community at large. Invariably they were far more than places of worship and religious instruction. The Church of Saint James in New York City in the 1880s, for example, conducted a tuition-free school for 1,700 children, an industrial school for older boys, complete with free lunch, clothing, and instruction for 200 destitute adolescents, and a twenty-one-room mission house for the homeless; forty parishioners through the Saint Vincent de Paul Society distributed $5,000 in aid each year to people in need, and another 900 men were enrolled in a temperance league.[42] The Parish of Saint Stanislaus Kostka in Chicago encompassed some seventy-four organizations; while the parish may not have controlled the behavior of its members to the extent the village church did at home, its services to its members were far broader. And always the context was one of cultural declension. When Father Lucyan Bojnowski came to New Britain in 1894, his first task, according to the parish history, was "to turn the people from drink, from getting married in court, from indecent dress, from holding balls on Saturdays and nightly revelries, from playing cards, loafing in saloons, fighting in their homes, immoral life, conjugal infidelity, theft, bad education of children, indecent behavior on the street, and disorderly conduct at weddings and christenings." He encouraged them to go to confession and communion, to participate in various novenas and devotions, and to belong to one of a host of parish societies. Eventually his parish would build and pay for a new church, a cemetery, a convent, and a school (during World War I thirty-five teachers taught 1,700 students), an orphanage, a print shop, a co-operative bakery, a credit union, a clothing shop, and a cutlery firm.[43]

Most remarkable in regard to parish formation among new immigrants, especially the Poles, is the relative absence of even somewhat more prosperous lay people. Ethnic historian Joseph Parot found almost no professionals and very few semi skilled or skilled workers in Chicago Polonia, where the huge 40,000-member parish of Saint Stanislaus Kostka was developed, along with a network of only slightly smaller parishes. What the new immigrants demanded, Timothy Smith argues, "was the right to do what their predecessors had done—to fashion religious communities suited to their own needs." And they "conceived those needs in new as well as in traditional terms, with earthly as well as heavenly ends in view."[44]

One function of parish organization was to preserve and deepen commitment to the particular national group, and that function required organization beyond the parish level. With the hierarchy firmly in the control of the Irish, or in some areas the Germans, the diocese could not serve that need. Instead, many groups organized their own independent national associations, which played something of a denominational role, serving local communities and at the same time broadening ethnic identity. However, the bishops worked hard to break independent Irish nationalist organizations, In the words of one bishop: "Our wisest course here is to break up national distinctions and combine all under one flag. . . . We are enlisted in the cause of the Church, not that of any distant nation."[45] What these words ignored was that in even the most faithfully Catholic community, including the Irish and the Polish, there was a real struggle, sometimes violent, between the church and nonreligious associations to dominate immigrant life. Each group of clerical leaders had to manifest their devotion to the national cause if they were to defeat coalitions of "anticlericals and secular nationalists" such as the one that confronted Polish clergy in Chicago in the formative years.[46]

Some national organizations were more Catholic, some more nationalist, and the battles between them often helped shape community identity. They offered opportunities for public life and advancement for individuals who held office, attended conventions, passed resolutions, and at times used their popularity for political purposes. They were a means of defending the national cause, in the United States and the homeland, deepening and extending national pride, resisting nativist efforts to force assimilation, in the church as well as in society, and later for controlling the programs of Americanization that came with World War I. Like the ethnic churches, they seemed at first glance separatist and divisive, but it became apparent to those who looked carefully that they had precisely the opposite effect. As two pioneer social workers put it: "The nationalistic organizations are the means by which certain men make their living and get their distinction; they assist the home countries materially in their struggle for freedom, they stimulate some older people to return to Europe, but they have almost no effect in keeping the immigrants, especially the younger generation, estranged from American life."[47] On the other hand, unlike the secular national organizations, the religious bodies, with the exception of the now more middle-class-oriented Central Verein of the Germans, showed almost no interest in the economic and social problems of their communities. Clerical and lay elites left the unskilled and powerless laity behind.[48]

Not all immigrants settled in cities. In Minnesota iron range towns there were many nationalities but few separate churches; many children attended public, not parochial schools; and unbalanced sex ratios led to marriage outside ethnic ranks. There as elsewhere, however, voluntary national organizations did appear, often led by small businessmen who found in such organizations a means of improving the group's image in the community, thus easing their own passage to commercial equality with their neighbors. This leadership role of the community's elite was common, as seen in Jay P. Dolan's data on New York parish membership and trustee lists, and in the role played by Italian business and political leaders as mediators with the non-Italian institutions in upstate New York.[49]

Among Italians in Chicago's seventeen "colonies" the padrone was "banker, saloonkeeper, grocer, steamship agent, lodging-house keeper and politician" but, most important, "employment agent."[50] It was these men, and the organizations they led, who shaped the public role of Italian immigrant communities. The Irish, French Canadians, and Poles, and to a lesser extent the Germans, had united around the church at home as a center for cultural survival against external oppression or, in the case of the Germans, against Prussian efforts to define and control German national destiny. Italians, like Spanish-speaking and Portuguese immigrants, came from countries where the church was less identified with the national cause; these groups were apt to find in ethnic social clubs or in mutual benefit societies loosely attached to the parish, more than in the church itself, centers for social life in the United States, at least during the first generation.[51]

In either case, whether in church or social club, the ethnic community maintained a distinct way of life, at times standing at some distance from that of other Americans, at times appropriating American values and symbols in ways that reflected a determined effort at "self-development," denying the need to choose between the Old

World and the New World, between being part of a particular people and part of the American people. It was an alternative, not necessarily an oppositional, community; its members resisted aggression and affirmed their culture, but they did not seek to impose their values or styles on others. They wanted success, but not at the cost of traditional family and communal values; they wanted respect, but not if it required passive accommodation to unfair economic practices or unequal political representation. Nativism accentuated the pressure toward internal unity and conformity, but it did not create the immigrant church or community. That was a conscious and creative response of newcomers who were already American.

THE CHURCH AND THE WORKING CLASS

In 1837 the bishops said of Catholics: "We are indeed comparatively few amongst the millions of our fellow citizens; the greater portion of our flock are in humble, laborious but useful occupations of life."[52] Irish laborers built canals and railroads and worked the mines. French Canadians harvested crops and filled textile mills. Polish and Slavic laborers joined Irish and German workers in steel mills and slaughterhouses. Within the factories the working class was divided into skilled, semiskilled, and unskilled; outside they were divided by race, religion, and nationality. In the workplace and in the neighborhood American workers experienced exploitation; they fell victim to the depressions that punctuated every decade after the Civil War, and they were participants in the bitter strikes that made American labor history particularly violent.

It is a commonplace that the racial, ethnic, and religious divisions of these laborers made working-class labor and political organization particularly difficult. There was the danger that ethnic and religious conflicts in politics might weaken working-class solidarity in the factory. Workers who returned to segregated neighborhoods, to their own churches, clubs, and saloons, who competed with each other for political power and social status, might come together as workers at times of crisis, but they would rarely experience the personal interactions and shared cultural experiences that could move them beyond "pure and simple" trade unionism of wages, hours, and working conditions to more class-conscious forms of economic or political action.[53] Yet internal divisions and religious conservatism had far less to do with the failure of socialism and industrial unionism than the solidarity of the American industrial and governmental leadership: organizers faced a solid wall of opposition, indeed ruthless opposition, from owners, government officials, and the courts.

If ethnic diversity made class politics and socialist organization difficult, it did not hamper labor organization directed at concrete problems. A remarkable number of Irish Catholics led militant labor organizations after the Civil War, among them William McLaughlin of the Shoemakers, John Sidey, the "guiding light" of anthracite coal miners, and Hugh McLaughlin of Chicago, leader of the Iron Puddlers. Historian David Montgomery contends that by the mid-1880s a majority of American unions were headed by Irish Catholics.[54] Indeed, the family and communal values of working-class immigrants helped give American trade unionism its distinctive form. Historian Victor Green discovered that the success of the United Mine Workers in establishing permanent union organization among Pennsylvania anthracite coal miners at the turn of the century resulted from the militance of Polish, Lithuanian, Slovak, and Ukrainian immigrants. Generally literate, these immigrant miners were determined to earn enough to make their families economically secure and, in some cases, enough to return to the old country. Despite the hostility of the majority of their clergy, they backed the union, especially after the Lattimer massacre of 1897 in which twenty Slavic miners were killed in clashes with police. Far from "the naive rustic often pictured by fileopietists or sympathetic social workers," Greene found the eastern European immigrant miner "a man with a definite purpose in coming, with knowledge, some intelligence and a determination to succeed . . . he would challenge any obstacles, even the combination of anthracite operators, to realize his goal."[55]

The fact of its intimate association with the working class posed severe problems for the American Catholic church. On the one hand priests and bishops were pastors, concerned about their people, and on the other they were builders, in need of their people's contributions. Unlike church leaders in much of Europe, they were in fact bringing working-class Catholics to the church. In addition, their church strenuously opposed liberal capitalism; Catholic teaching consistently condemned individualism, laissez-faire, and the separation of economic life from moral law. On the other hand, just as religious differences divided labor organizations, class differences divided the church. While there were few Catholic industrialists, there was a small but influential middle class, and an even larger class of skilled workers bent on rising above their father's station in life. The same teaching that condemned liberalism also condemned socialism and affirmed private property. Priests and bishops were themselves successful men, and their status in the community could be jeopardized by radicalism; thus they consistently distanced themselves from the more militant ethnic nationalists. Moreover, the clergy were bent upon securing the church's place in the larger society; too close association with labor radicalism, or even union organization, could once again arouse the wrath of the establishment. The church's major spokesmen argued that it exerted a conservative influence in a too individualistic and undisciplined society; they therefore felt compelled to demonstrate their capacity to persuade Catholic workers to be patient and orderly in the pursuit of their legitimate rights. Pastoral and ecclesiastical considerations, therefore, suggested the need to affirm the aspirations and recognize the grievances of Catholic workers while at the same time leading them away from radicalism into acceptable channels of social and political action.

One of the few Catholics to offer a positive defense of labor unions was New Orleans lawyer T. Wharton Collens, who supported the National Labor Union, joined with a group of Protestant socialists in the Christian Labor Union, and published a utopian blueprint for a communist society based on the Jesuit reductions in Paraguay.[56] Most Catholic commentators, however, were suspicious of labor organizations, some from fear of socialism, others out of dislike for secret societies, which had undercut clerical authority in Ireland. In 1874 Archbishop James R. Bayley endorsed the Irish Catholic Benevolent Union because it protected Catholics "from what is worse than secret societies–that is, the miserable associations called labor-unions."[57] Bayley and others adhered to a view of the world in which inequality was inevitable and poverty was resolved through charity. Poet and editor John Boyle O'Reilly, for example, condemned strikes and argued through the 1870s that only the influence of religion could overcome employer greed and labor discontent, while Father Augustine Hewit, editor of the *Catholic World*, came dangerously close to arguing that employers should support the church because it kept workers under control.[58]

Yet, as class strife intensified from the great railroad strikes of 1877 through the Haymarket riot of 1886 to the Homestead and Pullman strikes of the 1890s, even conservative Catholics were appalled by the behavior of American industrialists, who seemed to lack the paternalistic concern for their dependents that Old World morality demanded. "It is easier and *more common* for employers to commit injuries upon the workers than the contrary," Archbishop Martin Spalding, then in Baltimore, wrote the Prefect of Propaganda in 1869. "Here, especially, whoever has money believes he can freely oppress the poor, and he does it whenever he can. In all commercial countries, especially Protestant ones, *capital* (money) is the *despotic ruler*, and the worker is its slave. This being the case, I say, leaves the poor workers alone—there being little danger that they can do injustice to the tyrannical employers.[59] John Gilmary Shea in 1882 issued a typical warning that the ranks of discontented Catholic workers were rising rapidly, and they might be attracted to radicalism. "The Church, if she is to retain her hold on them, must show them these dangers and aid them in their lawful struggle and sustain them in their trial."[60]

Shea's warning struck home when Pinkerton detectives, aided by some church officials, exposed the violent activities of the Molly Maguires in the Pennsylvania coal fields. John O'Reilly and Patrick Ford, editor of the *Irish World*, denounced the tyrannical behavior of the mine operators. Earlier, in 1882, western Pennsylvania mine operators had sought church help in combating unions and asked that priests be withdrawn who they suspected were sympathetic.[61] Some bishops must have responded, for Terence Powderly, one of the organizers, recalled anti-union pamphlets circulated by one pastor, who also denounced the union from the altar.[62] One local priest blamed the rise of the Mollies on the suppression of these earlier unionizing efforts; in the aftermath of the trial some parishes organized workingmen's associations to help avoid strikes and promote better labor management relations.[63] At this point the church was confused about how to respond to the labor problem. In 1886 two incidents highlighted this confusion and raised a new set of questions about the public role of the church.

THE MCGLYNN CASE

Nothing serves better to illustrate the conflict between ecclesiastical interests and social responsibility than the case of Edward McGlynn. McGlynn was born in New York in 1837. His father died ten years later and his mother was left to raise eleven children. After studying in public schools, he left at the age of thirteen to study for the priesthood at the Urban College of the Propaganda in Rome. He spent ten years there and was ordained in 1860. On his return he was assigned as assistant to Father Thomas Farrell, an unusual priest who had been a supporter of abolition; he would later leave a legacy to endow the city's first black parish. In 1865 McGlynn went to Saint Stephen's, with some 25,000 members the city's largest parish; a year later he became pastor. He soon became one of the leaders of a controversial group of younger New York clergy who were questioning the conservativism of the local church. He drew some criticism by his championing of public schools and refusal to build a parochial school in his parish. An eloquent preacher and a charming man, McGlynn's sermons drew large and fashionable crowds. But, goaded by Farrell, McGlynn had developed a social conscience. Turning to political economy to understand the problems that surrounded him, he was deeply moved by Henry George's *Progress and Poverty*, finding there "the economic expression of the Gospel."[64] George painted a powerful portrait of the growing gap between the rich and the poor, tracing its cause to unearned increment in land, the increase in land values that came about not through improvements made by the owner but because of the growth of population and economic activity around him. Here was speculative wealth, made without labor, derived from the work of others. George was convinced that injustice could be rectified by the simple expedient of a "single tax" on land.

Irish nationalists in the Irish Land League, which McGlynn supported, were among George's earliest and most enthusiastic supporters. The two men met at a league rally in 1882, when McGlynn called George's teaching "the gospel in its purity [and] a good gospel, not only for Ireland . . . but for America too."[65] McGlynn was then ordered to cease delivering political speeches. McGlynn complied until in 1884 New York's Central Labor Union asked George to come to the city and run for mayor. George agreed and McGlynn actively joined in the campaign, which was the centerpiece of a national political effort of labor groups around the country. Alarmed, New York's conservative archbishop, Michael Augustine Corrigan, ordered McGlynn to stop. At the same time Father Thomas Preston, the vicar general, wrote a public letter to the leader of Tammany Hall condemning George's theories. "I can state with confidence that the great majority of the Catholic clergy in this city are opposed to the candidacy of Mr. George," Preston wrote. "There is no question as to the position of the Catholic clergy. And although we never interfere directly in elections, we would not wish now to be misunderstood at a time when the best interests of society may be in danger.[66]

McGlynn appeared with George and was suspended from exercising his priestly faculties. George was defeated, although he ran a strong second. After the election, Corrigan issued a pastoral letter defending private property. McGlynn was ordered to go to Rome to answer the charges made against him. He refused to do so on the grounds that his superiors had no right to question his political activity. As a result he was excommunicated for disobedience. In June 1887, 70,000 paraded in McGlynn's support, but Corrigan's friends were delighted. Bishop Bernard McQuaid of Rochester wrote the archbishop: "You can scarcely imagine the excellent effect on the non-Catholic community of this action of the church in setting aside a man of McGlynn's prominence."[67]

Efforts were made to place George's work on the Index but Cardinal James Gibbons of Baltimore, alarmed at such interference in American domestic affairs, intervened. Gibbons was not alone. Bishop Richard Gilmour of Cleveland told another bishop that a condemnation would "create bitter hostility towards the Church by the workingmen and the poor who are getting edged enough as it is [and] will soon be looking for a victim to assail."[68] In the end the step was taken but with agreement that it be kept secret.[69]

For six years McGlynn continued to campaign for reform by lecturing throughout the country. Radical as his position appeared to his enemies, he was really quite moderate, his views reflecting those of other middle-class reformers of the day. In responding to an appeal for help from an advocate of tenement house reform, McGlynn described his own experience of the misery caused by slum housing and argued that the community had the right to insure that the landlords did "not injure public health and decency while pursuing their selfish gains." He continued to believe that such evils would not be fully remedied until "the restoration of the land and other natural bounties to the people, and that this will not merely correct the evil of the system but abolish the system itself."[70]

In his most famous address, "The Cross of the New Crusade," he described the struggle for justice as "a religious movement." As a priest he had faced the realities of povery, inequality, and injustice and attempted to apply to those conditions the truths of religion. "I felt it was not amiss to take reverently, as if from the very ark of God, the precious truth and bring it out and scatter it broadcast among men, fearing not that it should ever be soiled or contaminated by coming into closer contact with the minds and hearts of any of God's children," McGlynn said. God had, "by beautiful laws of justice," provided enough for all. The equality of all people before God led to equal rights, most notably the right of access to the bounty that God provided. "All men, inalienably, always, everywhere, have a common right to all the general bounties of nature and this is in perfect and beautiful keeping with the other law of labor that every mouth has two hands with which to feed itself, a necessary corollary of which is that these hands must have equal, direct and indirect access to the general bounties of nature out of which to make a living."[71] Aside from the single-tax panacea, which seemed to some observers, though not all, to mean the end of private ownership of land, McGlynn's arguments about the priority of the right to life and the means to sustain it would eventually underpin a Catholic version of the social gospel, but few were ready yet to move out of the isolation of religion from public life to which the older republican and later immigrant ideologies had confined it.

In 1893, the newly appointed apostolic delegate, Francesco Satolli, after a study of McGlynn's ideas by a team of professors at the Catholic University of America, removed his excommunication. Satolli did not demand that McGlynn recant his views, and he did not, attending a single-tax convention in Chicago a short time later. McQuaid reported the reaction to Corrigan: "Our people are terribly worked up, particularly the better classes. Many say they will go to church no more." Referring to the Catholic leader of Tammany Hall, he added that "[Richard] Croker says it was 'the greatest blow the church in this country has ever received.' "[72] Not everyone would include Croker among the "better classes" but the point had been sharpened; class differences existed and McGlynn and Corrigan had defined a choice that would be difficult to avoid.

THE KNIGHTS OF LABOR

The union issue finally confronted the church directly when the Knights of Labor, originally a secret society founded in 1879, spread rapidly across the country in the mid-1880s. Headed by a Catholic, Terence Powderly, the Knights attempted to embrace all producing classes, employers and employees alike, and favored the eventual creation of producer cooperatives to replace the emerging industrial corporations. Nevertheless, their ranks filled quickly with skilled and unskilled laborers, especially after they conducted a successful railroad strike in the Midwest in 1885. Earlier, alarmed by the growth of the organization in Quebec, the local archbishop issued a stern condemnation and asked Rome to do the same. The United States bishops discussed the matter at the Third Plenary Council in 1884; several, including Archbishop Corrigan and Bishop James Healy of Portland, thought that the condemnation applied in the United States.[73] Nevertheless, when he received word that the Vatican was considering issuing a blanket condemnation, Cardinal Gibbons of Baltimore wrote Rome defending the Knights. Gibbons argued that workers had serious grievances and the right to organize to protect their rights, that American workers were genuinely conservative and the Catholics among them were loyal to the church, and that Powderly had agreed to remove the remnants of secret practice in order to meet church concerns. He added that Vatican action would be viewed as interference in American domestic affairs and might arouse an anti-Catholic backlash. Gibbons's letter was leaked to the press, the Vatican condemnation was avoided, and the church emerged with a reputation as a friend of the labor movement that it would never lose.

Yet the action regarding the Knights was far from unambiguous. Gibbons had established the right of workers to organize and to do so in nonconfessional unions, in contrast to the Catholic unions that developed in other industrial countries. That right to organize, endorsed in 1891 in Pope Leo XIII's *Rerum Novarum*, would no longer be questioned. On the other hand, Gibbons wrote without consulting his fellow bishops; he admitted that in 1884 a majority of the archbishops would have favored banning the Knights. He correctly judged that the Knights would not last; in fact within five years they had faded to a minor organization on the labor scene. The American Federation of Labor (AFL), organized in 1886, became the first permanent national labor body behind the more conservative philosophy of "business unionism" of its founder, Samuel Gompers. Catholic bishops and priests paid little attention to the AFL until concern arose over the rise of socialism after the turn of the century.

Powderly himself had many problems with unfriendly bishops and priests in later years. There was a great deal of interest in arbitration as a solution to labor strife.[74] Archbishop John Ireland told Gibbons after the Pullman strike of 1894: "We have been siding with labor in its grievances and the unthinking ones transgress the golden mean and rush into war against property." Instead, the church should appear before the American people as "the great prop of social order and law."[75] Gibbons agreed, writing in the *North American Review* in 1901 that not strikes or boycotts but "law and public opinion are the natural remedies for social grievances."[76] "Experience hàs shown that strikes are a disaster and at best a very questionable remedy for the redress of the laborer's grievances," he wrote elsewhere. "They paralyze industry, they often foment fierce passions and lead to the destruction of property, and above all they result in inflicting grievous injury on the laborer himself, keeping him in forced idleness."[77]

Most bishops continued to believe that hard work, thrift, and sacrifice could bring economic success and that the social problem could only be cured by moral reform, itself unlikely unless owners and workers alike turned to the church. "The bishop must . . . show the impossibility of a panacea for the ills of life." Bishop James A. McFaul of Trenton wrote in 1903 that "Most modern evils spring from 'man's inhumanity to man.' They can be remedied only by a return to the principles of Christianity."[78]

POLITICS

William Onahan, a Catholic lay leader of the late nineteenth century who was active in Illinois politics, at the end of his life claimed that in over sixty years he had "never once heard a political sermon from a Catholic pulpit; no, nor even a political allusion in a sermon to local or national politics; or to candidates for any public office."[79] He thought that was as it should be, and most Catholics agreed with him. From the time of John Carroll's uneasiness with his Quebec mission, Catholic bishops and priests, with few exceptions, had insisted on staying out of politics, many even refraining from voting. Of course they had their political preferences, usually based on what they considered the good of the church, and from time to time they let those preferences be known—but carefully. As for their people, the bishops regularly announced that they were free to make up their own minds. When they did so, however, the hierarchy was not always pleased. This was particularly true when Catholic political activity seemed to violate the republican ideals of citizenship, thus antagonizing those whom McQuaid called "the best people." In the late nineteenth century this conflict remained a problem as Catholics, who had worried the bishops when they seemed to be tools of local politicians, began to take control of local politics in major cities. As they did so Americans of the better sort began to attack political corruption; the machine became a symbol of all the problems of American urban areas, the source of what Lincoln Steffens called "the shame of the cities." If things were as bad as Steffens claimed, and if the clergy were as silent as Onahan said they were, then the separation of religion and politics might not be a virtue after all.

The Irish, as we have seen, became strong supporters of the Democratic party in the Northeast during the age of Jackson. However, it was not until after the Civil War that they began to take a leading role in the party. The Irish era in New York politics began in the early 1870s when Charles O'Connor began the successful prosecution of William Marcy Tweed, the last Protestant boss of Tammany Hall. The Irish then took charge of Tammany under "Honest John" Kelly and in 1880 elected the city's first Catholic mayor, William R. Grace, a wealthy shipping magnate. By then Tammany Hall was the very model of an urban machine, a bureaucratic organization of precinct workers, ward leaders, a citywide committee, and an overall boss that brought order to city government, selected candidates for office, distributed patronage, and mediated between the city's many ethnic groups, its businesses, and its government. Steffens once asked Tammany boss Richard Croker why the city needed a boss when there was a mayor and city council; Croker answered "that's why, because there's a mayor and a council and a hundred other men to deal with." As Jay P. Dolan said of Bishop John Hughes, the boss brought order to the chaos created by rapid growth and inadequate institutions to deal with it. In the words of a later scholar: "The principle of boss rule was not tyranny but order."[80]

"All politics is local," a future politician of Irish extraction would claim; the machine rested on this premise. The heart of its power lay in the precincts and wards, where political leaders built personal bonds with their people, helping them when they were in trouble, celebrating with them and mourning with them, and expecting their loyalty in return. As in Ireland people and politicians alike were relatively indifferent to the proprieties; in Ireland the formal, legal institutions of government were, after all, illegitimate, the informal networks legitimate, the difference being the quite democratic idea of consent. In the United States the systematic organization of power brought stability: "Honest John" Kelly and his successors, Richard Croker and Charles Murphy, ran Tammany for fifty years. Hugh McLaughlin ran Brooklyn for forty years and John McCooey, for another twenty-five; Ed Flynn ran the Bronx for over thirty years. Contrary to the popular image, none of these men was particularly affable; rather, they administered the political bureaucracy with firmness, predictability, and, by their own lights, fairness. That was their strength; the organization of power for predictable uses. Their weakness, as Daniel Patrick Moynihan noted, was that "the Irish didn't know what to do with power once they got it. . . . They never thought of politics as an instrument of social change—their kind of politics involved the processes of a society that was not changing."[81]

In Boston, Catholics constituted 40 percent of the population by the 1850s but did not elect their first common council member until 1857, their first alderman until 1870, their first congressman until 1882. In 1878, led by Benjamin Butler, the Irish captured control of the state Democratic organization and substantial political gains followed. Lawrence elected its first Catholic mayor in 1881, Lowell in 1882 and, in 1883, Hugh O'Brien was nominated for mayor of Boston. He was defeated but then elected in a close race in 1884. By 1887 Irish Catholics were serving as mayor, chairman of the board of aldermen, president of the common council, city clerk, and chairman of the school committee.[82] But unlike New York, Boston's machine was fragmented into a number of regional fiefdoms, and therefore vulnerable. In the mid-1880s anti-Catholic feeling led to a coalition that took control of the school committee, and in 1888 the Republicans swept the Irish from city hall. But here as elsewhere the machine persisted and returned to power in the 1890s.

In Chicago the chief Irish boss was John Powers of the city's nineteenth ward, the recognized leader of the "Grey Wolves" and known as "Prince of the Boodlers." Typically his strength rested on his personal aid to people who had problems with the police, the courts, and the licensing boards, and who were in need of employment. He was said to have scribbled thousands of notes with the same message: "This is a neighbor and a friend of mine. Please give him work." Powers was very good at this, and he held firm from 1888 until the 1920s as his ward shifted from Irish and German to Italian and Slavic. Jane Addams, the revered founder of Hull House, fought Powers in three aldermanic elections in the 1890s and was badly defeated. She came to have a grudging respect for the boss and to understand the sources of his strength. "The successful candidate must be a good man according to the standards of his constituents," she wrote. "He must not attempt to hold up a morality beyond them, nor must he attempt to reform or change the standard. If he believes what they believe, and does what they are all cherishing a secret ambition to do, he will dazzle them with his success and win their confidence" and their votes.[83]

Obviously not all Catholics in politics were Irish or participants in the machine. In the cities the machine's candidates for mayor and higher offices were often drawn from more respectable Catholic circles, men such as William Grace. In fact, as Bishop McQuaid's reference to Richard Croker indicates, political careers could be avenues to enhanced social status. Patrick Collins, for example, was an organizer for the radical Irish Fenians, then for the upholsterers' union, before embarking on a successful political career that carried him not only to the state legislature and the Boston mayor's office but also to bank directorships and membership in exclusive clubs.[84] In some cases, as in Albany in 1876, the first Irish mayoralty candidates were selected precisely to offset the appeal of a radical labor political movement.[85] William Onahan enjoyed a successful political career as a Democrat in Chicago, serving as a member of the board of education, city collector, and comptroller before joining the Republicans in 1887 to help defeat the United Labor Party, whose members he described as "socialists, anarchists and other undesirable elements."

Historian Alan Dawley has argued that in early nineteenth-century Lynn, Massachusetts, political recognition of labor-oriented candidates served as a safety valve for working-class discontent, as elected officials were able to do less to challenge employer control of production than would a more class-conscious labor movement.[86] In a similar way, ethnic fragmentation, more notable in politics than in union organization, may have served to divert the quite realistic consciousness of exploitation in the workplace. And outside the areas where Catholics were a large majority of the population there were many successful Catholic political leaders. Anthony M. Keiley, for example, played a key role in Virginia politics before the Civil War and during Reconstruction and in 1870 was elected mayor of Richmond, a city that had been won by the Know-Nothings in 1855. He was an active Catholic; his participation in a public demonstration protesting the seizure of Rome from the pope in 1870 later cost him an appointment as ambassador to Italy. He also served several terms as president of the Irish Catholic Benevolent Union. There he opposed the effort of some members to pass resolutions condemning public schools, actions that caused some to accuse him publicly of disloyalty to the church.[87]

It is a mark of the problems that faced the church as a public presence in American society that its leaders had little to say either to the machine politicians who were becoming increasingly responsible for government in urban areas or to reformers like O'Connor and Keiley. Indeed, beyond ritual denunciations of parties and politicians, the American hierarchy all but ignored the moral dimensions of politics. The defensive interpretation of the republican tradition that had begun with Carroll placed politics outside the realm of religious concern, as when the Philadelphia Catholics declared that neither their church nor their religious convictions influenced their political actions. The immigrant style meant that the church as an interest group was attentive to government policy in areas of church concern, such as education and charities, but as an interest group like any other. Its bootstraps experience of parish formation and its pastoral bond with immigrant peoples nurtured the group-centered approach to politics and trade unionism that its people practiced, but so far both had taken place with little reference to faith or church and with little comment from priests and bishops.

SOCIAL THOUGHT AND CATHOLIC EXPERIENCE

Toward the end of his life Terence Powderly wrote a long letter to his niece, a nun in New Jersey. The sister had sent him a religious medal and he wanted to explain why he did not wear such things. He told her that, when he was a child, an aunt who had arrived from Ireland had tied such a medal around his neck, promising that it would protect him from danger. A short time later he lost his balance while swimming and was rescued by a passing friend. His aunt claimed that God had sent the friend, but Powderly was skeptical and never put his faith in such objects again. Nevertheless, he insisted, "I have never gone so far from God as to forget him." But by this time Powderly, stung by the indifference of many of the clergy and the arrogance of others, had drifted away from the church. He did not believe that God "singles out any of His children as favorites to influence him on behalf of others." He made his own faith clear:

> My belief is and always has been to live honestly, injure no person or thing knowingly, give every one of God's creatures kind treatment. If I owe a dollar I pay it; if I owe a grudge I forget it. I have never resented a personal injury through revenge in the whole course of my life. I have never listened to a friend maligned without defending him. I cannot be-

lieve that God is like a politician and must be approached through some person of pull or influence. I go direct to Him as I do to my fellow man. . . . Just two can adjust my destiny, here or hereafter, God and I.

It was a sign of how wary he had become that he wrote at the bottom of this letter that he had made a copy "in order to be able to testify to the exact contents if it should go astray or fall into other hands."[88]

There is a tendency to take at face value the sociological contention that religion in modern society occupies a place distinct and separate from that of economics and politics. It has become a commonplace that, for most people, religion is a matter of private preference and personal choice, with only an indirect bearing, if any, on public life. Powderly had learned that things were more complicated than that, for the neutrality the church claimed was not neutrality at all, but a choice made for the sake of the church. The church contended that it cared for religion and left public life alone; but there were people not overtly very religious, whose lives testified to the love of God; his niece's father was one. By the end of his life Powderly's experience had confirmed what so many historians would discover. Catholicism exerted a "moderating influence on strikers and labor agitators";[89] it fostered a "doctrine of class collaboration";[90] and it was a "basically conservative influence . . . sponsoring attitudes that conflicted with economic values."[91] He knew that behind this there were people who made choices and expressed ideas that reflected their interests. Irish support for the Democrats and reluctance to back third parties was due to "the strategic position of hundreds of socially important saloon keepers, policemen and firemen" and, Edward McGlynn would add, priests and politicians.[92] In 1884 a pastor from Amsterdam, New York, when asked about working conditions in local mills, responded: "I never examined that much; my chief interest is in a moral sense; we have control of the Catholic portion; we have been able to do this; we have been able, as far as they are concerned, to suppress in the mills bawdy songs and bawdy jokes."[93] Unions in fact competed with churches, mutual benefit societies, and other voluntary associations for the time, energy, and commitment of working people; it was many years before most clergy would regard unions as anything other than competitors.

Committed to a lifetime of service to the church, confirming that commitment with vows of obedience and celibacy, priests were bound to regard the church as the most important institution in the community. It was no accident that they developed a theology and a piety that confirmed that judgment and tended to make of the church the center of meaning in modern society, so that professions of political neutrality and economic even-handedness in fact masked a deeper statement of religious and ecclesiastical superiority. Leslie Tentler, the historian of Catholicism in Detroit, describes parish piety at the end of the nineteenth century:

> The devotional life gave the most unlettered Catholic the opportunity to imagine God in terms that were close to his own experience; to see himself as an actor in a spiritual universe peopled with heavenly friends, all of them deeply interested in the affairs of what the world regarded as unimportant lives. It provided the faithful with a plethora of material testimony to the presence of God in the midst of his people, for its paraphernalia were everywhere—rosaries, scapulars, medals, statues. And depending as it did on a world of intercessors, the devotional life indirectly gave enormous support to the hierarchical model of the Church. The devotional life, in short, emphasized just those aspects of Catholic belief and practice which have always most offended Protestants—the disposition to express the mysteries of God in human and material images and to stress the importance of mediators—both human and divine—as the believer approaches his God.[94]

There can be little doubt that this was a comforting piety, and one that could enable poor men and women to maintain a sense of dignity and meaning in hard times. But what Powderly had learned was that it also had the effect of depriving daily life, the interaction of people at work and in the community, of authentic religious meaning. It was profoundly undemocratic because it made the highest goals of life dependent upon human mediators, upon priests and an institution they controlled. He knew, if dimly, that the simple morality he described depended somehow on a personal relationship with God. If the letter had strayed into the hands of his clerical critics, they would have charged him with the Protestant principle of private judgment, and they would have been right. The church grudgingly sanctioned membership in the Knights of Labor, there were priests who were friends of Powderly who understood the connection between religion and what he had tried to do with his life, and eventually the church would develop a social philosophy that would give stronger backing to labor unions and social reform. But, preoccupied with its own internal development, and ministering to people who had not yet made their own the democratic message of personal responsibility for public life, as distinct from personal life, it had failed to give meaning to the experience of industrialization or of democracy.

CHAPTER
5
Liberal Catholicism

◈

$\mathcal{T}$he republican tradition had not died in the nineteenth century, although the pastoral and social problems posed by the massive numbers of immigrants and the conflict they occasioned with the host society had obscured the ideals of equal citizenship, active participation in public affairs, and positive adaptation to American culture. Converts such as Orestes Brownson, at certain points in his career, and Isaac Hecker, founder of the Paulist Fathers, as well as native-born Catholics like Martin John Spalding and his brilliant, Louvain-educated nephew, John Lancaster Spalding, at times felt uncomfortable with the increasing conservatism of the European church and the internal preoccupations, social isolation, and political defensiveness of their fellow Catholics in the United States. When Hecker decided to become a Catholic, he told Brownson that the church needed a "new generation" of leaders familiar with American ways and at ease in the modern world.[1] Even when new leadership of that type did not appear and his own views clashed with those of many bishops, Hecker held fast to his conviction that the American church, if it would put aside its preoccupation with the past and pay heed to the needs and aspirations of the American people, could reap a harvest of souls and eventually bring the universal truths of Catholicism to unity with the ideals and historic destiny of the American nation. He tried to dedicate his new Paulists to this American apostolate, he founded a magazine, the *Catholic World*, to encourage dialogue on contemporary problems, and he launched a publishing house to improve the quality of Catholic education and intellectual life.

During the Civil War, as the nation tore itself apart, Hecker thought he discerned an approaching providential moment when Americans would be more receptive to the Catholic message. Invited to address the bishops at the plenary council of 1866, Hecker set forth a vision of the mission of the American church that went beyond the republicanism of an earlier era. The signs of the times, including the decay of orthodox Protestantism, the yearning of the American people for unity, the new respect for the church resulting from its patriotic support for the Union, all signaled the possibility of winning the nation to Catholicism and bringing about "the future triumph of the church." He hoped this prospect would draw Catholic leaders away from concern with the church itself to a missionary effort to convert their fellow Americans. "Nowhere is there a promise of a brighter future for the Church than in our own country," Hecker told the bishops.

> Here, thanks to the American Constitution, the Church is free to do her divine work. Here, she finds a civilization in harmony with her divine teachings. Here, Christianity is promised a reception from an intelligent and free people, that will give forth a development of unprecedented glory. For religion is never so beautiful as when in connection with knowledge and freedom. Let us therefore arise and open our eyes to the bright future that is before us! Let us labor with a lively faith, a firm hope and a charity that knows no bounds, by every good work and good example, for the reign of God's kingdom on earth.[2]

Hecker hoped to draw the church to an active, passionate engagement with the larger world of politics and culture, to awaken a missionary sense of responsibility for the outcome of the American experiment. Openly and behind the scenes he campaigned for a more vigorous Catholic press, including a daily newspaper; for missions to non-Catholics; for a national Catholic congress; and for the organization of the laity to support evangelical work and develop a sense of their own power to promote Catholic answers to the problems of contemporary society. Partly under his inspiration, a new generation of episcopal, clerical, and lay leadership did emerge, led by Bishop John Ireland of Saint Paul. Few of them understood the spiritual foundations of Hecker's Americanism, but they shared his love for church and country and his passionate desire to bring Catholics to a more constructive engagement with the age. In the end their effort to change the direction of the American church was defeated, but they helped to keep alive an alternative sense of American Catholic possibilities that would continue to challenge Catholic complacency and self-righteousness in the twentieth century.

REPUBLICAN IDEALS

Nineteenth-century American Catholics were caught between the conservatism of the European church and the all but consensual liberalism of American culture. The focus of this problem was, and would remain, the conflict over church–state separation and religious liberty, authoritatively rejected by Rome but essential to American citizenship. All American Catholics accepted the First Amendment as sincerely as had John Carroll, both because they believed in freedom of religion and because it worked: the church flourished in the United States while it was in deep trouble elsewhere. Unfortunately Catholics had to constantly reaffirm their commitment to American institutions. In an 1888 speech at the dedication of the new Catholic University of America, in the presence of the president of the United States, John Lancaster Spalding made the case for the American arrangement: "We have shown that respect for law is compatible with civil and religious liberty; that a free people can become prosperous and strong . . . that the State and the Church can move in separate orbits and still cooperate for the common welfare; that men of different races and beliefs may live together in peace . . . that the government of the majority, where men put their trust in God and in knowledge, is in the end the government of the good and the wise." The American experience demonstrated that "the Church can thrive where it is neither protected nor persecuted, but is simply left to manage its own affairs and to do its work." Spalding, like Hecker, was convinced that this was "the position toward the Church which all the nations will sooner or later assume; just as they will be forced finally to accept popular rule, since the underlying principle of democracy—that all men are brothers and have equal rights . . . is a truth taught by Christ, is a truth proclaimed by the Church."[3]

This position was bound to arouse suspicion abroad, for what it implied then as it did a century earlier was the limitation of the church's and the pope's authority to spiritual matters. "Our obedience to the Pope is confined to the domain of religious faith, morals and discipline; and since the state, with us at least, claims no jurisdiction over such matters, there can be no question of conflict," Spalding said. "If it is urged that to draw the line of demarcation is difficult, I reply that in the general course of things this difficulty presents itself hardly at all. That it may arise, all confess, but it arises just as easily for Protestants as for Catholics. All men in our age . . . hold a double allegiance and are prepared, if needs be, to appeal from men to God, from laws to conscience, from authority to reason, from numbers to justice."[4] Spalding admitted the possibility that any serious Christian might experience "double allegiance," but other liberals were convinced that such a conflict was all but impossible.

Baltimore's Cardinal James Gibbons was America's best-known Catholic leader for almost half a century, and no one was more persistent in affirming Catholic loyalty to the nation. Catholics "accept the constitution without reserve and with no desire as Catholics to see it changed," Gibbons wrote in the *North American Review*. Separation "seems to them the natural, inevitable, and best conceivable plan, the one that would work best among us, both for the good of religion and of the State."[5] If Catholics at times seemed exclusive and aggressive, the reason lay in the bigotry they had experienced. "Religious tolerance is not the easy, superficial virtue it seems," Gibbons wrote. "Intolerance in the dominating party tends to produce intolerance in the injured party." But Gibbons, like Carroll and Hecker, preferred to appeal to the better nature of his countrymen on the basis of their common citizenship: "We are strong, not only in our own union and strength, but in the broad American spirit of fair play and love of liberty."[6]

This liberal position carried with it the implication that the church could and should adapt to some degree to the conditions in which it found itself, even if that meant risking its unity and making the preservation of orthodoxy difficult. "The conservatism which wishes to be safe is dryrot," exclaimed John Ireland. "The Church in America must be, of course, as Catholic as in Jerusalem or Rome, but so far as her garments may be colored to suit the environment, she must be American." Gibbons agreed: "The Catholic religion subsists and expands under all forms of government and adapts itself to all times and places and circumstances. . . . For while the truths of faith are eternal and immutable, the discipline of the church is changeable, just as man himself is ever the same in his essential characteristics, while his dress varies according to the fashions of the times." To explain the difference between papal teaching and American practice, Gibbons wrote: "Other countries, other manners; we do not believe our system adapted to all conditions. We leave it to church and state in other lands to solve their problems for their own best interests."[7]

From there it was a short step to reasserting the demand for Americanization that had been evident as early as Carroll's cry for "Catholic and American" parishes. Ireland became identified as an Americanizer, one who would exert pressure upon national groups to conform in both church and society. "There is danger," he stated at the centennial celebration of the American hierarchy. "We receive large accessions of Catholics from foreign countries. God witnesses that they are welcome. I will not intrude on their personal affections or tastes, but these, if foreign, shall not encrust themselves upon the church."[8] Confronting German separatism directly, Ireland spelled out the relationship between the liberal desire for active enagement with the times through an active laity and the pastoral strategies of the immigrant church aimed at perpetuating a high degree of segregation:

the Church will never be strong in America, she will never be sure of keeping within her fold the descendents of immigrants, until she has gained a decided ascendancy among the Americans themselves. She must be presented in a form attractive to Americans. The great objection which they have until now urged against her . . . is that the Catholic Church is composed of foreigners, that it exists in America as an alien institution, and thus it is consequently a menace to the existence of the Republic.[9]

Accordingly he urged the church "to speak without ceasing in a language understood by those around us and in ways that circumstances in which Providence has placed us have opened to us to make the spirit of the Gospel effectively enter human life." To do so they must put aside, or at least minimize, their loyalty to other lands and give their love to their new homeland. As Gibbons put it: "Next to God, our country should hold the strongest place in our affections."[10]

These ideas were often directed at non-Catholic Americans, designed to convince them that they need not fear the church but instead should appreciate its conservative influence on Catholic immigrants and workers and welcome its patriotic defense of American ideals and institutions. The need for this defensive articulation of "Americanism" seemed stronger than ever as anti-Catholicism revived in the post–Civil War years. Yet the most serious problems facing those who most ardently championed these ideas came from Rome, where liberal Catholicism had been all but destroyed at the First Vatican Council. Revived briefly during the early years of the long reign of Pope Leo XIII, republican teaching still aroused passionate opposition and would once again be decisively repudiated at the end of the century. One moment in that repudiation would be the condemnation of a supposed heresy of Americanism, associated with the ideas of Isaac Hecker but aimed more directly at a liberal party in the American church headed by John Ireland. That rebuke would stifle creative efforts to develop the republican tradition for many decades, leaving the American church without an intellectual basis for engaging the deepest problems of modern culture during the tragic events of the twentieth century.

MIDDLE-CLASS CATHOLICISM

In retrospect it is clear that mass support for such a position required the presence of a large middle class, anxious to find meaning in its experience of social mobility, to find a basis for its participation in a common life with non-Catholics, and to define an understanding of Catholicism that minimized conflict with national values. In the United States, where a high premium was placed on economic success, this implied a religious affirmation of upward mobility. Hecker rarely emphasized economic progress, but he did insist that the middle-class Catholic had special opportunities and responsibilities to bring Catholic influence to bear on the dominant institutions of American society. He developed a spirituality aimed at assisting the pursuit of holiness by active, busy people engaged in the world. Moreover, he explicitly emphasized his own vocation to the Americanized children of the immigrants, insisting that the day-to-day needs of their parents were well provided for in the parishes by the secular clergy.

Ireland and other liberal Catholics, enchanted as they were by American economic progress, felt little restraint in affirming the American success ideal. As Ireland told the 1901 convention of the Catholic Total Abstinence Union of America, there were too many Catholics who, because of intemperance, did "not appreciate money and have not in the past accumulated wealth." Yet, he insisted,

> money well understood is desireable and it is all nonsense to say that money is not to be thought of, poverty is all honorable. . . . If our people had saved up for the last fifty years and their money had not all gone into saloons . . . how different socially would they not be, how much more influence they would have. . . . I am considering the fact that in business we have not our proper representation, nor in the State or national Governments and in the intellectual life of the country. . . . It is a fact; I mention it so that it will not [remain] a fact."[11]

It was no accident that he spoke these words at a temperance convention; almost all the liberal leaders of the hierarchy made temperance work a central feature of their early ministry. In most places temperance organizations attracted ambitious young priests and lay people (one historian refers to them as "middle class mobiles" and "working class respectables") and their leaders often championed the policies advocated by Ireland and his friends.[12]

Irish-American Catholics were experiencing a degree of upward mobility in these years; the middle class was growing slowly, providing at least a potential audience for the liberal message. More and more Irish women were moving into school teaching; in New York and on the West Coast there was evident ascent into the managerial and professional classes. In a study of Irish Americans who appear in the *Dictionary of American Biography*, Dorothy Ross found that those who achieved their greatest success between 1880 and 1900 did so in the following areas: 8.6 percent in politics, 14 percent in law, 10 percent in journalism, 32.9 percent in religion, 5.7 percent in letters, 8.6 percent in fine arts, and 27.1 percent in business. Irish Catholics in the first generation were overrepresented in occupational scales only in government; in the second generation they were overrepresented in law, acting, journalism, sales, and literary and scientific pursuits.[13]

The other factor that encouraged liberal hopes was the impact of the Civil War on a small but talented number of priests. Ireland himself had served as a chaplain and was to become an enthusiastic member of the Grand Army of the Republic. In New York a small but influential group of priests, led by Edward McGlynn, emerged from the war with a new sense of patriotic obligation. One of the group, Richard Burtsell, expressed the change from the internally preoccupied immigrant church. He recalled that, when he and McGlynn were in the seminary, they had been forced by the Civil War to confront for the first time an issue that was not directly Catholic; in doing so they came to appreciate the need for a more open and democratic church. When another New York priest praised Catholic abstention from the slavery controversy and blamed the Civil War on Protestantism, Burtsell said he did so "through cowardice because he ought to have spoken for the Union and against slavery." When that same priest noted the change in Burtsell's view, the latter explained: "I once thought rulers ought to take care of the people; in America I have learned that the people know how to take care of itself."[14]

Burtsell, McGlynn, and their friends championed radical reconstruction and they were drawn to the Republican party, which seemed to represent Civil War idealism. They were sympathetic to the Irish Fenians, who threatened to liberate Ireland by force, and to the Irish Land League, when radical nationalists were being rebuked by the hierarchy for their refusal to accept clerical dictation. They challenged prevailing policies favoring parochial schools and the temporal power of the pope; they even questioned, privately, papal infallibility and clerical celibacy. Like Hecker, they believed there was no limit to the beneficial influence the church could have if it would only open up to the realities of American life rather than confine itself to the cloister.[15]

Their hopes, however, were constantly dampened by the conservatism of most American bishops, who could look to Rome for support, for the Vatican was fighting bitterly against a similar liberalism in Europe. Thomas Preston, an influential New York diocesan official, told Roman authorities that the group led by McGlynn and Burtsell were

> a few priests who are really disloyal to the Holy See. They minimize all the declarations of His Holiness. They were opposed to the infallibility until its definition, and now are disposed to make it as little as possible consistent with a declaration of faith. They are opposed to parochial schools. . . . They have spoken in favor of saying Mass in the English language, of doing away with the vestments and ceremonies prescribed by the Church, of getting rid of what they call medieval and obsolete prac-

tices, and of Americanizing the Catholic Church here, and adapting it to our liberal and republican institutions.[16]

As Preston's charges indicated, the climate in Rome was turning even further right just as this revival of republican ideals was occurring in the United States.

In 1863 Pope Pius IX had published the encyclical *Quanta Cura* with its attached "Syllabus of Errors," condemning religious liberty, church-state separation, freedom of speech and of the press, indeed insisting that the church could never reconcile itself to "progress, liberalism and modern civilization." Even conservative American churchmen were worried, for the syllabus, if taken literally, would place them in an untenable position. Bishop William McCloskey of Louisville expressed his dismay to Martin Spalding, then archbishop of Baltimore: "It is consoling to think that Our Holy Father has in all his official acts a light of guidance from on High, for according to all the rules of mere human prudence and wisdom the encyclical *with its annex* of condemned propositions would be considered ill-timed. It can hardly be doubted that it places us in a state of apparent antagonism, at least as far as our principles are concerned, to the institutions under which we live—and affords a great pretext to the fanatics who are eager to get up a crusade against us. God knows best what is good for His Church."[17] Spalding agreed and had his nephew make inquiries in Rome regarding some points that "will be construed here as condemning our system of religious toleration" and "furnish a pretext to the fanatics to persecute us."[18] Spalding then wrote a pastoral letter making the republican argument that the church's teachings could be tailored to local conditions: "to stretch the words of the Pontiff, evidently intended for the stand-point of European radicals and infidels, so as to make them include the state of things established in this country by our noble constitution, in regard to liberty of conscience, of worship, and of the press [is] manifestly unfair and unjust."[19] There were no complaints from Rome about Spalding's effort to divert the syllabus, but as Preston's reference to infallibility indicated, pressure to conform to Roman teaching was growing. After the Vatican Council's declaration of papal infallibility in 1870, American opponents, including bishops, knew they had to make official declarations of acceptance.[20]

The Roman question, Italy's seizure of the last of the papal states, also became a matter of loyalty. When Orestes Brownson questioned the pope's temporal jurisdiction in the 1860s, he was forced to recant. In 1889 the *Catholic Mirror* of Baltimore said that the pope did not need "extensive territory wherein to wield the power and exercise the rule of an earthly kingdom," Gibbons was forced by Rome to rebuke the editor, who then reversed his position.[21] By that time the American hierarchy, however, was no longer prepared to offer a united front against Roman conservatism, for severe internal divisions had created a situation that opened the door to more direct Roman supervision of American church affairs.

THE SCHOOL QUESTION

Throughout the nineteenth century the school question plagued Catholic efforts to integrate into American culture. Given their commitment to bring Catholicism into the center of American life, it was inevitable that liberal Catholics would confront the problem. Burtsell, McGlynn, and their friends questioned the wisdom of parochial schools in the middle of New York City, where John Hughes had long ago committed the diocese to Catholic education. But that commitment was far from universal. In areas where there were many German Catholics, such as Cincinnati and Milwaukee, support for parochial schools was strong; but in many localities the costs involved, the quality of public schools and the attitudes of bishops and clergy kept the development of Catholic education limited. It was a layman, James McMaster, editor of the *Freeman's Journal*, who launched an all-out campaign to pressure the American bishops into backing parochial schools. Frightened by the Paris Commune of 1870, McMaster became convinced that secular, irreligious education threatened the stability of American institutions and the security of the American church. He accused the bishops of violating the laws of the church, which required that Catholic children be taught by Catholic teachers in schools under church control. The remedy was "not in the lax pastors' soothing plasters called Sunday Schools" nor in compromise arrangements made in some places where the public school board leased a Catholic school building and offered instruction in secular subjects during regular school hours. In 1873 David Phelan of the *Western Watchman* joined the campaign, introducing a resolution before the Irish Catholic Benevolent Union charging that "the present system of public schools, ignoring all supernatural authority and making knowledge the first, and God the last thing to be learned, is a curse to our country, and a floodgate of atheism, sensuality and of civil, social, and national corruption." Through the efforts of Mayor Anthony Keiley of Richmond, the resolution was defeated, but McMaster and his allies carried the battle to Rome, which proceeded to make inquiries among the bishops. Ignoring the practical problems that the bishops emphasized in their reply, the Vatican in 1876 concluded that the public schools were "most dangerous and very much opposed to Catholicity." Parents were bound to protect Catholic children "from familiarity with other school children whose company might be dangerous to their faith or morals," and this could only be done by sending them to Catholic schools.[22]

Even bishops committed to Catholic schools saw little to be gained by prohibiting Catholic attendance at public schools. The instruction was ignored until the Plenary Council of 1884, when the issue was debated by the bishops and resolved through a series of close votes. The bishops decreed that there should be a Catholic school in every parish within two years, and they warned of spiritual penalties against those who did not support them. In their pastoral letter at the end of the council, the bishops charged that "teachers of skepticism and irreligion" had "crept into the leading educational institutions of our non-Catholic fellow citizens." Catholics could no longer "rely fully on the innate good sense of the American people and on that habitual reverence for God and religion which has so far been their just pride and glory" because of "daily signs of growing unbelief" and "materialism." Unfortunately this new philosophy of secularism was infecting education:

> To shut religion out of the school, and keep it for home and the Church is, logically, to train up a generation that will consider religion good for home and Church, but not for the practical business of real life. But a more false and pernicious notion could not be imagined. Religion, in order to elevate a people, should inspire their whole life and rule their relations with one another. . . . Therefore the school, which principally gives the knowledge fitting for practical life, ought to be preeminently under the holy influence of religion. From the shelter of home and school, the youth must soon go out into the busy ways of trade or traffic or professional practice. In all these, the principles of religion should animate him and direct him. But he cannot be expected to learn these principles in the work-shop or the office or the counting room. Therefore let him be well and thoroughly imbued with them by the joint influence of home and school, before he is launched out on the dangerous sea of life.

They then concluded by issuing a "command" to Catholic parents to provide a religious education for their children, "to defend and secure all of them from the dangers of secular education during the whole term of their infancy and childhood and, finally, to send them to Catholic, and especially parochial schools, unless, indeed, the bishop of the diocese judges that in a particular case other provision may be permitted."[23] As these last words indicated, the legislation left loopholes, reflecting continued division among the bishops and in the country at large.

The bishops did not notice any more in 1884 than they had in 1840 that their own actions in local school politics were producing the very godless schools they decried. The battle of the Bible was far from over. In 1869, in Cincinnati, to take but one example, the school board decided to end Bible reading in the schools. After a bitter fight, a new board, now with ten Catholic members, implemented that decision.[24] But few were satisfied. Common school crusaders had long claimed that education was necessary for the preservation of public and private morality; believing with most Americans, including Catholics, that religion and morality were inseparable, they fought to preserve some religious presence in the schools. In the late nineteenth century rapid growth, immigration, public corruption, and periodic outbreaks of labor and urban violence made nervous Americans insist even more strongly on the need for common education to Americanize immigrants and instill some common values.

A speaker at the 1880 National Educational Association Convention put it in the starkest terms:

> The terrible revelations of public dishonesty, the growing curse of youthful depravity in the great cities, the ominous rumblings of communism under the very foundations of society, the wild and reckless theories of social and private obligation blurted out in thousands of platforms by the new lights of the 'new morality,' the corruption of parties and politics which always holds the country on the edge of a new civil war, the conditions of several millions of utterly unschooled children and youth, the appearance of another million of school children in the south, all born in a revolution that laid society in eighteen states in ruins, half a million of them children of emancipated slaves, has thoroughly aroused the country till everywhere we hear the call for the more thorough moral instruction and discipline of children, especially in the public schools.

It was "absurd," he argued, to deny that the public school was "in the most pronounced and thorough sense a school of instruction and discipline in . . . Christian morality."[25]

A decade earlier the National Teachers Association, predecessor of the National Educational Association, had resolved that "the bible should not only be studied, venerated and honored as a classic for all ages, people and languages . . . but devoutly read and its precepts inculcated in the common schools of the land." Yet, the resolution continued, "the teaching of partisan or sectarian principles in our public schools, or the appropriation of public funds for the support of sectarian schools, is a violation of the fundamental principles of our American system of education."[26] If one speaker argued that Bible reading and nondenominatinal instruction violated the rights of conscience, another answered that no right was as sacred as the "self preservation of a body politic." One 1887 estimate claimed that there was prayer and Bible reading in 80 percent of the nation's public schools. Catholic actions to either introduce a "sectarian" Bible or ban it altogether thus appeared as an assault on the very foundations of America's public life. Catholics could only regard this approach with fear, if not anger. Elihu Burritt, a New England reformer in the Garrison tradition, put the situation clearly as Catholics saw it: "ninety nine common school teachers in one hundred in all the Northern states are Protestant . . . the literature of all our reading books and the atmosphere of our schools and even their out-door sports are Protestant in their influence. . . . We ask and require [Catholics] to yield some of their scruples in sending their children to schools which are effectively Protestant and which they have considerable reason to expect will influence their young minds."[27]

So the old problem of how to have moral education in a pluralistic society would not down. It was natural that politicians should pick up these concerns. In 1871 Senator Henry Wilson, known for his hostility to Catholics and immigrants, proposed a national educational system as part of a "New Departure" for the Republican party. President Ulysses Grant warned: "If we are to have another contest in the near future of our national existence the dividing line will not be Mason and Dixon's but it will be between patriotism and intelligence on one side and superstition, ambition and ignorance on the other." He then called for a common school education for everyone, "unmixed with atheistic, pagan or sectarian teaching." This proposal was incorporated into a constitutional amendment sponsored by Senator James G. Blaine of Maine: "No state shall make any law respecting an establishment of religion or prohibiting the free exercise thereof; no money raised by taxation in any State for the support of public schools, or derived from any public source, nor any public lands devoted thereto, shall ever be under the control of any religious sect, nor shall any money so raised or land so devoted be divided between religious sects or denominations."[28]

The amendment was defeated in Congress in 1875, but a similar proposal found its way into the 1876 Republican platform, and again in 1880, when the famous charge of "rum, Romanism and rebellion" against the Democrats boomeranged, costing Blaine the presidency. In 1882 Senator Henry Blair proposed a ten-year plan of federal financial aid to states for support of education. Republican papers described the bill as a response to the need for modern states to control education, while most pointed out the danger to the republic of divisive, backward-looking Catholic schools. The Blair bill was considered several times during the next decade. Although it, like the Blaine amendment, was defeated, thirty-four states considered and passed Blaine-type amendments during the next several decades. The outcome of the great Bible war, then, was that forecast in the New York fight four decades earlier: the secularization of public education and the ban on aid to church-sponsored schools.[29]

If nondenominational or, worse, purely secular education was as bad as Catholics said it was, they were obligated to persuade other Americans of that fact and to present an alternative. When John Keane, a close friend of James Gibbons, disciple of Isaac Hecker, and ally of John Ireland, became bishop of Richmond in 1878, he made that clear. "Our country may think us unfriendly because we tell her of her mistakes, because we warn her that, by the system of Godless education, she is training generations that, for want of proper religious moulding and principles, will be as unfit to be good citizens as to be good Christians." "The only way to make a prosperous and happy state is to mould the individual and the family in the mould of Christain principle and virtue, for such as are the individual and the family, so must also be the nation."[30]

Keane, Hecker, and Bernard McQuaid contended for a denominational system similar to that developing in other countries. Father Patrick McSweeney of Poughkeepsie, New York, who presided over a publicly supported school where he selected sister teachers and where catechism was taught after school hours, pleaded for release "from this cast iron school system" and for its replacement with "a more elastic and more truly American one" in order "to save the free institutions of the land which depend upon religion for their permanancy," arguing that it was "better to have a little rivalry among sects than to let Christianity die out."[31] This approach alone had any prospect of resolving the school question as a public problem centered on the commonly shared concern for personal and public morality. The obvious need was to bring Catholics and Protestants together to support a denominational system. Unfortunately, such cooperation proved impossible. For Catholics the morality-in-education question could only be resolved by parental control delegated to ecclesiastical authority; such a system not only awakened anti-Catholic prejudice but it seemed to Protestants to surrender the ideal of making Americans one people. They preferred a public system that instilled Christian morality, which Bernard McQuaid, bishop of Rochester, described as "mongrel morality, this code of compromises and concessions, a bit from Tom Paine, another from Jesus of Nazareth, some sentences from Benjamin Franklin, then Saul of Tarsus, something too from atheist Frenchmen, all sifted and sorted by a school board nominated at a ward caucus and elected amid the turbulence of party strife."[32]

Given the choice, local school boards such as those in Cincinnati and McQuaid's own Rochester preferred to jettison prayer and Bible reading altogether, leaving what Hecker called "the worst sect of all—

secularism"; they further forced Catholics to pay taxes for public schools while financing their own as well. Hecker had argued the school question from the viewpoint of public interest, making education a "test question" with Catholics, and when he failed to gain a hearing for a denominational system, he fell back on the defense of Catholic rights, moving toward an interest group approach reflective of the immigrant style.[33]

McQuaid, at the beginning of his career as bishop, agreed with the Protestants that religion was absolutely necessary for sound education. If Catholics insisted "on the letter of the law," they were merely depriving Protestants "of what is a great advantage for their children and gain nothing for ourselves." But when Protestants refused to back a denominational system, or to even endorse a system of shared responsibility between churches and the school board, preferring the secularization implied in the Blaine and Blair measures, McQuaid redefined the question as one of Catholic rights.[34]

In 1890 Archbishop Ireland reopened the question and launched a bitter fight within the American church. Ireland, who had emigrated with his family to the United States at the age of twelve, was ordained in 1861. After service with the Minnesota volunteers he became rector of the diocesan cathedral, where he unsuccessfully proposed that the parish school be given free of rent to the local school board, allowing religious instruction to be offered after school hours. Like so many other Catholics, Ireland denounced the Protestant atmosphere in most public schools and denied the possibility of basing instruction on a nondenominational Christianity. Instruction without religion was worse; it would foster atheism and materialism, which would undermine American institutions. So there was a national problem as well as a Catholic problem. In a widely reported speech to the National Educational Association, Ireland praised the American public school in glowing terms, acknowledged the state's right and obligation to provide universal education for its citizens, and lamented the necessity for Catholics to provide their own schools. He called for compromises, one that would allow the state to take responsibility for instruction in nonreligious subjects, with religion provided by the church after school hours. In his own diocese he had already begun an experiment similar to that proposed for the cathedral earlier. In Faribault-Stillwater, the school board leased the school, paid salaries to the sisters, and allowed them to provide Catholic children with religious instruction at the end of the normal school day.[35]

Understandably, Ireland's speech caused an uproar. Ethnic groups, such as the Germans, who had long supported their own schools, were upset, all the more so since Ireland had supported laws that would require English-language teaching in all schools. The security of their schools, they believed, required independence of government control. Those bishops and pastors who had begun schools and who were demanding financial sacrifices from their people to support them, were bound to be angered by newspaper reports of a highly regarded prelate praising public schools and indicating that parochial schools were at best a regrettable necessity. New York's Archbishop Corrigan, who led a diocese long committed to Catholic education and had personal reasons to dislike Ireland, and his friend Bernard McQuaid led the assault on the Ireland scheme, which McQuaid regarded as tantamount to turning the Catholic schools over to the government. As for the Catholic public, there were obvious divisions. One vicar general reported that when a pastor began a school he faced the upper class, who could not be forced to support it; the middle class, who could be forced, and the poor, who were strongly in favor of supporting it.

In 1893, in order to resolve this and other controversies dividing the hierarchy, the pope sent an apostolic delegate, Francesco Satolli, to the United States. Taken in hand by Ireland and his friends, Satolli issued a report allowing Ireland's experiment to continue, while affirming the 1884 legislation. Ireland and the liberals were exuberent, convinced they had won a major victory. In 1894, when a vacancy occurred on the New York State Board of Regents, Bishop McQuaid allowed the Democrats to place his name in nomination, while the Republicans named Sylvester Malone, a Brooklyn priest and Ireland supporter. Ireland campaigned for Malone, who was elected, leading McQuaid to denounce the Minnesota bishop from the pulpit.[37] Meanwhile, Corrigan, who was threatened for criticizing the Roman decision, was able to win support in Rome and, in 1895, Satolli came out strongly in favor of parochial schools. By the end of the decade Rome had clearly come down on the conservative side, the commitment to parochial schools was finalized, and for over half a century there would be no public criticism of the commitment.

There were several factors at the heart of the dispute. All the contending prelates agreed that the best system for the United States would be a denominational system, similar to those developing in other Western countries, with tax support provided for all groups. Ireland believed that, in the absence of a denominational system, there should be some compromise between the church's obligation to provide religious instruction and the state's right to educate for citizenship. Catholic University philosopher Thomas Bouquillon, an Ireland supporter, published a pamphlet setting forth the rights of the state in education.[38] This initiated a pamphlet war in which opponents denied state responsibility, insisting instead on parental control. McQuaid believed that Bouquillon and other "imported Europeans" were propounding Old World notions of the state; if they "would keep quiet, until they found out where they were, it would conduce greatly to their comfort." To grant the state an educational mandate was to open the door to a monolithic system, or, even worse, to allow the state to supervise what went on in Catholic schools. He told Rome that "in a country like ours, whose form of government depends on the people, the less interference with our natural rights we concede to what is called the State the better." As he saw it, Ireland was merely turning Catholic schools into state schools. Until Americans were prepared to accept a denominational system, "it is better for us to bear with injustice and wrong and preserve our virility and independence." As one bishop asked, why should they "fall down before the state in abject slavery" for the sake of "a few dollars?"[39]

Perhaps the decisive factor, however, was the conviction that public school education, even when supplemented by Sunday school or after-hours instruction, would endanger the continued loyalty of Catholic children. McQuaid and many others had been converted to the widely held belief in the malleability of the child: environment determined character. The Germans had long held the view expressed by Father Michael Mueller: "I assert that a Catholic boy of tender years, and perhaps careless training, can be preserved from moral contamination, in public and mixed schools, by nothing less than a miracle."[40]

In nondenominational schools, as McQuaid saw it, students would be trained in an atmosphere of neutrality and indifference, and therefore be less inclined to accept the demands of the church, more likely to intermarry and drift away. In the bishop's words to Rome: "What we have most to dread is not the direct teaching of the state schools, it is the indirect teaching which is the most insidious and most dangerous. It is the moral atmosphere, the tone of thought permeating these schools that gives cause for alarm. It is the indifferentism with regard to all religious belief we most of all fear. This is the dominant heresy that, once imbibed in youth, can scarcely be eradicated." Of course it was the church's chief mission to preach the gospel, but "there is little likelihood of that gospel reaching and abiding in the hearts of the children except through the institution of the schoolhouse."[41] The nondenominational approach had already all but destroyed the Protestant churches and "will decimate our churches unless checked in time."[42] At the Plenary Council of 1884 he told the bishops: "Without these schools, in a few generations our magnificent churches and cathedrals would remain as monuments to human folly."[43] Later he told the pope: "It will be useless to build churches that in one or two generations hence will be vacant because children or grandchildren of European parents no longer follow the religion of their ancestors." Add to this the fact that by the 1890s some 60 percent of the parishes had a school of some sort. The eastern European immigrants beginning to arrive in large numbers generally adopted the German position that independent schools were essential for the preservation of faith and culture, and for generational continuity and family stability as well. Moreover, in the major urban areas reformers were successfully campaigning for city-wide school boards, professionalization of the teaching staff, and improvement in educational facilities, all under the progressive argument that education was the major means by which this diverse and increasingly class-conscious people could be bound together by shared values and loyalties. These new professional educators were even less inclined than their more political predecessors to consider compromises, not only with religious groups but with ethnic communities as well.

Few decisions so decisively effected the public witness of the church. In the twentieth century it was separate education more than anything else that shaped the public image of the church and influenced Catholic understanding of the relationship between the church and public life. Catholics defended their right to conduct such schools; they complained of the injustice of double taxation, and they denounced the supposed secularism of the public school as a threat to the religious and moral life of the students and a danger to American society as a whole. In sharp contrast to the development of Catholic charitable and social welfare work, there was little talk of the common concerns of the community, less consideration of cooperation with public institutions, and no further consideration of compromise. The battle was so bitter because its major actors, Ireland and McQuaid, understood that the future of the American church was at stake. For Ireland the very possibility of a Catholicism at the center of national life would be destroyed if Catholic children attended separate schools, imbibing a sense of isolation from, and irresponsibility for, the common life of the nation. For McQuaid, a public school education would mean the ruin of the church, its people lapsing into indifference, doctrinal incoherence, moral laxity, all eventually resulting in empty churches. As one bishop told McQuaid, lamenting the damage Ireland had done to lay support, "we must . . . have it accepted by Catholics, lay or clerical . . . that in our day the schoolroom is the battleground of the faith and the hope of the Church."[44]

From McQuaid's point of view, Ireland's republican position meant surrendering the integration of life and adopting a Catholic form of secularism that would render religion irrelevant to the daily affairs of the people. From Ireland's point of view, McQuaid's separatism would have the same effect, draining public life of meaning, turning Catholics in on themselves, and abandoning the hope of fulfilling the American promise by ultimately uniting it with Catholic faith. The tension between the republican and immigrant styles could not have been more complete. Ironically, in retrospect, both were right. Neither separate schools, under the auspices of a church committed primarily to its own survival, nor public schools deliberately excluding religion in any form and leaving religious instruction to home and church, could of themselves overcome the problem stated in the 1884 pastoral letter: people would "consider religion good for home and church but not for the practical business of real life." To a larger degree than anyone anticipated the commitment to parochial schools had that effect; it is not evident that Ireland's compromise would have produced a substantially different result.

CITIZENSHIP

The republican ideal, with its emphasis on separation of church and state, led American bishops to distinguish carefully the moral issues in public life from partisan politics. They kept their political view to themselves, save in extreme circumstances, as when Hughes sponsored a slate of candidates in the 1841 New York state assembly elections or when Fitzpatrick allowed the clerical editor of the *Pilot* to proclaim: "We are a Whig." Here again John Ireland broke ranks. Michael Corrigan had clearly cooperated with Tammany Hall Democrats during the McGlynn episode, partly because they had been generous in supporting Catholic charitable institutions with public funds. McQuaid encouraged Corrigan to place a Catholic lobbyist in Albany to watch over Catholic interests, and he even encouraged Catholics to organize in order to make politicians respect their rights on the school question.[45] But Ireland was openly partisan. He was a Republican, he supported Republican candidates and made much of his friendship with party leaders, and he even used his Republican connections to embarrass McQuaid in the New York State election. Other liberals were similarly sympathetic to the Republican party.

From its origin, the Republican party had been considered the party of reform, while the Democrats, rooted in the alliance of northern urban merchants and southern planters, seemed more conservative. In New York reformers like McGlynn, concerned about the corruption of city politics, were drawn to the GOP, while in the West the party was still a symbol of Civil War idealism. But the Democrats remained strong, especially after the southern states were readmitted to national politics. The 1890s were a major turning point. The most severe depression of the century hit the country during the second administration of Grover Cleveland; when that Democratic president responded by protecting the gold standard and using federal troops to put down the Pullman strike in Chicago, his party was badly beaten at the polls in 1894. Two years later, as the Democrats fused with the Populists behind William Jennings Bryan, northern voters flocked to the Republicans, electing William McKinley and establishing a solid national Republican majority that would last until the New Deal years. The shift was economic more than cultural. In Michigan, for example, the party division between Democrats and their Whig and later Republican opponents had been an evangelical and Catholic/ Lutheran split. After 1896 those cultural factors became less severe.

The Republican effort to attract Catholic voters was hampered by its continuing association with nativism and anti-Catholicism. After 1876 every platform endorsed the Blaine amendment until Ireland helped persuade the party to drop it in 1896. But even that step was not enough because of the highly publicized presence of the American Protective Association, which in most places worked within the Republican party. The APA was founded in Clinton, Iowa, in 1887, after the defeat of Arnold Walliker in a mayoral election by what he thought to be Catholic influence. Leadership of the organization soon passed to Henry Bower, who promoted it as a fraternal organization seeking to preserve republican institutions. Members swore an oath denouncing "Roman Catholicism . . . the Pope . . . his priests and emissaries," and pledging themselves to employ Protestants, to refuse to aid the church or vote for a Catholic for public office, or go on strike in a labor dispute with a Catholic. The APA quickly became embroiled in local and state campaigns for compulsory school attendance or abolition of foreign-language instruction in Wisconsin, Illinois, Ohio, and Minnesota. In other states they worked for passage of little Blaine amendments and termination of financial support for charitable institutions sponsored by the church. They fought successfully to end contracts between the federal government and Catholic schools on Indian reservations. Secrecy obscured their exact power and influence, and Catholics made the situation worse by treating anyone who opposed them as a supporter of the APA.[46] This revived the strength and visibility of nativism, and anti-Catholicism made Catholics more self-conscious than ever about demonstrating their patriotism; it also encouraged the emphasis on unity and loyalty characteristic of the immigrant church. Once again conservatives tended to emphasize a group-conscious defense of Catholic rights, and liberals, echoing Brownson, hoped that good citizenship and lay independence would persuade right-minded Americans that they had nothing to fear from the church, at the same time allowing upwardly mobile Catholics to attain the respectability they craved.

The continued presence of anti-Catholic groups like the APA, the concern among middle-class Catholics and liberal bishops about the church's association with political machines, and a growing interest in the social question all led to interest in the role of the laity in the work of the church. Hecker had inspired a vision of militant and energetic lay Catholics winning respect for the church by their work in business, the professions, and politics. From 1866 on Hecker campaigned to hold a Catholic congress, which would bring priests, bishops, and lay people together to discuss the problems of the age and seek means to work together to bring about the "triumph of the church." Such congresses had been held successfully abroad, encouraged as means to unite Catholics against anticlerical governments and support the restoration of the pope's temporal power. Hecker's emphasis on positive evangelization by assisting Americans in solving public problems drew little support, but the need for unity and lay leadership in defense of the church did.

An occasion arose when plans were made to celebrate the centennial of the American hierarchy in Baltimore in 1889. Henry F. Brownson of Detroit took the lead; with the help of William Onahan, the Chicago politician and lay leader, he won the support of John Ireland, who persuaded James Gibbons to give his backing as well. The purpose of the congress, according to Brownson, was to "unite Catholics, giving them an opportunity to see and know one another, of proclaiming to the world that the laity are not priest-ridden, and of ratifying the declarations of the Clergy."[47] Despite this last disclaimer, Brownson fought hard to preserve the independence of the laity, only reluctantly agreeing to have papers submitted for approval beforehand. "If they are only to repeat what is dictated to them, never think for themselves, or dare utter their thoughts, they can have no energy or freedom, and can produce no effect," he wrote. He and other organizers, like Peter Foy of Saint Louis, although they had the backing of Ireland, Gibbons, and other liberals, found even these men overbearing. Foy thought they were fearful that such a united body of Catholics would inspire bigotry, but they also simply distrusted the laity. In fact the sympathetic hierarchy badly wanted to support active middle-class lay people, but they had no thought of reversing the fundamental structures established in the wake of the trustee controversy and now solidly supported by the ultramontane papacy. In his opening speech, Gibbons set the parameters. He called upon the laity to cooperate with the clergy on the great "economic, educational, and social questions." While the clergy were "the divinely appointed channels for instructing the laity in faith and morals, the clergy, on their part, have much to learn from the wisdom and discretion, the experience and worldly sense of the laity." The congress itself featured cogent papers on such subjects as the press, temperance, charity, education, labor (all of which contained strong denunciations of socialism and only one of which, by William L. Richards, attacked laissez-faire and the gospel of wealth), immigration, the race question, and colonization.[48] Plans were made for a second congress, to be held at the Columbian Catholic Congress, preliminary to the World Parliament of Religions in 1893.

An interim committee had been established and William Onahan kept John Ireland informed of its deliberations. Onahan had earlier written a friend: "I believe firmly in the Catholic laity on every question of Catholic principles and I am in favor of trusting them fully and freely in congresses and elsewhere." But his dealing with Ireland was an indication of how far the American church had come in a century since the Carrolls. "I only follow where you lead," he told Ireland, agreeing that bishops should chair all committees in order to exclude "disturbing and intractable elements" and keep the proceedings "within reasonable control." "A little freedom of expression won't hurt," he suggested gently, as "the overwhelming mass of the delegates will be conservative" and "under judicious leadership." Papers and comments would be reviewed beforehand, there would be "a giant banquet" and a "monster" torchlight parade. Ireland's liberalism had little place for the laity within the church, and aside from a few like Brownson and his sister Josephine, most Catholics did not care. What did matter was to demonstrate to other Americans that Catholics were as good as they; beyond that, the clergy were in charge. "The Baltimore Congress," Onahan believed, "had so to say Americanized the era. Before that [Catholics] were looked on as relics— and they had themselves possibly some doubts as to whether in fact they were true Americans." It had demonstrated the "reserved force and possibilities that are (or were) dormant in the Catholic body—a force and a power which ought to be called into exercise for useful works to the general benefit of religion and of society. How this shall be done, in form and method, remains with Bishops and priests to determine."[49] The second congress was held, once again there were excellent papers, and some even introduced a note of self-criticism on Catholic treatment of blacks, the quality of Catholic colleges, and relationships with Protestants. But by the time it ended it was clear that there would be no more congresses. They had fallen victim to the conflicts of the period.

The second congress coincided with the World Parliament of Religions. Catholic participation in that event became yet another source of conflict within the hierarchy. Bishop John Keane had first proposed participation to the archbishops, arguing that the planned event would be an "exposition, not discussion," with each religion granted time and space to present its case. It was going to take place; Keane asked if the Catholic church could afford not to be there. Although there was some opposition, Keane was permitted to proceed with plans. Gibbons, in an opening speech, said that they were there to "present the claims of the Catholic Church to the observation and, if possible, the acceptance of every right minded man." While they differed on religious matters, Gibbons hoped all could unite on a common platform of charity and benevolence. Gibbons and Keane presented additional papers and, while the parliament was meeting, a separate Catholic day allowed presentations and question-and-answer sessions. Keane interpreted the event to the press as a sign of the hunger for Christian reunion. "The oftener such gatherings are held, the better," he said. "We will never come to reunion by standing apart and scowling at one another." Nevertheless there was considerable criticism of this spectacle of Catholics meeting on an equal basis with other religious groups. Satolli spoke at the Catholic congress but let it be known that he disapproved of the World Parliament of Religions. Eventually Rome ruled that, while Catholics could hold meetings and invite Protestants, gatherings such as the parliament were not appropriate. The message was taken as a rebuke to the liberals. It would not be the last.[50]

BLACK CONGRESSES

In 1866 the church turned its back on the freemen, despite urgings from Rome and the pleas of Martin John Spalding, who, as archbishop of Baltimore, presided at the Second Plenary Council held that year. "We have a golden opportunity to reap a harvest of souls, which neglected may not return," Spalding warned, but the bishops turned down a proposal to appoint a vicar apostolic to deal with the problem, for fear this would compromise the authority of local bishops. Yet, left to themselves, the poor and understaffed southern dioceses could do little. When Herbert Vaughn brought Mill Hill Fathers from England to Memphis to begin work among American blacks, he described prevailing attitudes frankly: "Negroes [are] regarded even by priests as so many dogs. . . . I visited the hospital where there were a number of Negroes. . . . Neither the priests with me nor the sisters in the hospital do anything to instruct them. They just smile at them as if they had no souls." Despite the efforts of the Mill Hill priests and several other religious orders of men and women, the absence of pastoral care for black people remained a scandal of the American church. Under Roman pressure the bishops did inaugurate an annual collection for missions among Indians and blacks in 1888, but little more was done.[51]

Daniel A. Rudd was born of slave parents in Kentucky and after the war moved to Cincinnati, where he launched the *Ohio State Tribune* in 1884 and, two years later, the *American Catholic Tribune*, a paper by and for black Catholics. In 1887 he traveled the country to publicize the paper and met a surprising number of well-to-do black Catholics. Having covered the conventions of other black groups, he decided to organize a black Catholic congress, announcing that decision in his paper in May 1888. He also informed John R. Slattery of the Josephites (the former Mill Hill Fathers), a priest known for his work among blacks and his writings on the subject. At Slattery's suggestion, Rudd submitted the agenda for the congress to Bishop William Elder of Natchez. By now he had eleven sponsors from Boston to Saint Louis. The purpose of the meeting was to cooperate with the clergy for the conversion and education of blacks and gather information about black Catholics.

The first congress was held in Washington in January 1889, with eighty-five delegates, three-fourths of whom came from Maryland, Pennsylvania, and the District of Columbia. Mass was celebrated at Saint Augustine's, the largest black parish in the country, by the nation's only black priest, Father Augustus Tolten. After a series of papers and resolutions, in the last speech, Father Michael Walsh of Saint Augustine's stated that "the sacred rights of justice and humanity are still sadly wounded" and appealed for an end to discrimination. The congress was well received, and Rudd was placed on the organizing committee for the general Catholic congress of 1889, where the interest of John Ireland was aroused. In May 1890, Ireland delivered a sensational address at Saint Augustine's, which established him as the champion of black people in the church.

A second congress took place in Cincinnati in July. The mood of optimism was hardly disturbed by an opening sermon of Father John Mackey, in which he declared that nature intended blacks and whites to take separate paths. After a number of hard-hitting talks, the congress resolved to establish an industrial school, but they failed to arouse episcopal interest in the project. A third congress in Philadelphia in 1892 criticized discrimination in Catholic schools and one paper called for "co-education of the races." A fourth took place at the Columbian Exposition, and several papers indicted the church for inaction. The fifth took place in Baltimore a year later; a delegation was sent to present a list of grievances to the archbishops, but no response was forthcoming. No further congresses were held, partly because of internal divisions, partly because of rising frustration after the hopes aroused by the earlier meetings. Not until World War I would there be another effort to organize in the Committee for the Advancement of Colored Catholics, which later folded into the Federation of Colored Catholics.[52]

THE SPANISH-AMERICAN WAR

The Achilles heel of the liberals was a tendency toward uncritical nationalism. Isaac Hecker had promoted the idea of the United States as a providential nation, leading the world to a new era of progress and freedom, and the Americanist bishops picked up this theme, none more enthusiastically than John Ireland. His strident nationalism blended easily into a sense of manifest destiny, irritating not only more conservative bishops but churchmen in Rome, where the pretensions of the United States had always been viewed with a critical eye. Rome was alert to the rising power of the United States, and its attention was drawn particularly to the approaching conflict with Spain. In March 1898, Cardinal Mariano Rampolla, the papal secretary of state, asked Ireland to do what he could to preserve the peace. Ireland went to Washington and consulted with American officials, including President McKinley, and a number of Spanish and other European emissaries. In daily contact with Rome, he urged the Vatican to secure Spanish agreement to American terms and never held out much hope that war could be avoided.[53]

When the war came, of course, Ireland was warmly supportive of the national cause. There are things worse than war, he declared, "the destruction of social security, the disruption of the Nation, its enslavement to foreign power, the robbery of its territory or the possible lowering of its flag through disgrace abetted by cowardice." His friend Denis O'Connell, writing from Rome, was even more enthusiastic: "For me this is not simply a question of Cuba. . . . But for me it is a question . . . of two civilizations. It is a question of all that is old & vile & mean & rotten & cruel & false in Europe against all this [sic] is free & noble & open & true & humane in America. . . . This is God's way of developing the world."[54]

Gibbons, as usual far more restrained, continued the tradition begun by Carroll during the war of 1812 of distinguishing between one's private judgment of the morality of war and the obligations of citizenship once war began. Preaching after the sinking of the *Maine*, Gibbons recommended "calm deliberation and masterly inactivity" for a nation "too brave, too strong, too powerful and too just to engage in an unrighteous or precipitate war." Three months later, however, he declared publicly: "Catholics in the United States have but one sentiment. Whatever may have been their opinions as to the expediency of the war, now that it is on they are united in upholding the government." As John Tracy Ellis commented on these words, Gibbons, like Ireland, had "tacitly, at least . . . accepted the nation as the final arbiter of human affairs."[55]

But others were far less sure of the justice of the war, much less of the almost violent nationalism that accompanied it. William H. O'Connell, who had replaced Denis O'Connell as rector of the North American College in Rome, recalled receiving complaints from Vatican officials because his American students were "causing discord by a too obnoxious flaunting of their national sentiment." He denied that he had criticized the war, but he had told the students that there were differences about whether it was a just war. There is evidence that O'Connell admitted to Roman officials that he had sympathized with Spain and criticized the American war as unjust.[56] Another bishop with reservations was closer to the liberal camp. As early as 1880 John Lancaster Spalding had criticized Irish Catholics for "a tendency to what I call 'ultra-Americanism' "; they were so "intensely American" that they sometimes failed "to recognize the obvious defects of our country and the shortcomings of the American character."[57] Unlike the other bishops in either camp, Spalding accepted the possibility of "double allegiance," and he denounced the Catholic tendency to respond to attacks by anti-Catholic groups such as the American Protective Association with professions of devotion to the nation. "Our record for patriotism is without blot or stain, and it is not necessary for us to hold the flag in our hands when we walk the streets, to wave it when we speak, to fan ourselves with it when we are warm, and to wrap it about us when we are cold".[58] Spalding became a strong opponent of the imperialism that followed the war, joining the Anti-Imperialist League. Holding colonies, he believed, would lead to militarism. Human rights and freedom were not "articles to be exported and thrust down unwilling throats at the point of a bayonet." "If it is our destiny to become an empire," Spalding said, "it is not our destiny to endure as a republic."[59]

As the Philippines were a Catholic country, the American administration had many dealings with the church there, and the Vatican called upon the American hierarchy for help. In addition, the United States planned to establish a public school system, and American Catholics were watchful. Originally a priest was appointed superintendent of schools in Manila, but local opinion was divided between advocates of a Catholic system and advocates of a public system; and church groups in the United States lobbied on both sides. A series of commissions faced the dilemmas posed by the fact that earlier church and state had cooperated and the imposition of separation created many complex problems. Theodore Roosevelt proved more amenable to Catholic interests and, aided by William Howard Taft, he arranged for a more sympathetic superintendent and the appointment of teachers recommended by John Ireland.[60]

THE PUBLIC DIMENSIONS OF AMERICANISM

By the mid-1890s, as the apostolic delegate shifted sides on the school
controversy, it became clear that the liberal group in the American
hierarchy was in trouble. In 1895, Ireland, Keane, and Denis O'Connell
looked forward to a message from Pope Leo XIII, for they believed,
in Keane's words, that the papacy was moving toward an alliance
with France and the United States; "the church and democracy are
fast drawing nearer."[61] When the letter arrived it praised The Catholic
University of Washington, D.C., a liberal project, in glowing terms,
but it also demanded acceptance of the apostolic delegate as a representative of the pope's supreme authority. Leo insisted that he would
keep bishops from interfering in each others' diocese, uphold their
authority over their priests, and "preserve in the multitude a submissive spirit." The letter noted the dangers of associations between
Catholics and non-Catholics and insisted that all Catholics would find
their interests best met "by yielding a hearty and submissive obedience to the church." Even more worrisome were his words on church
and state: "It would be very erroneous to draw the conclusion that
in America is to be sought the type of the most desireable status of
the church, or that it would be universally lawful or expedient for
the State and the Church to be, as in America, dissevered and divorced."[62] A short time later O'Connell was removed as rector of North
American College and Keane was replaced as head of the university.

Now on the defensive, the liberal party turned to Rome, where
they hoped to lobby for a more sympathetic hearing. But their hopes
for the United States soon became caught up in a raging battle in
France and elsewhere between republicans and royalists. When a
somewhat misleading abridgment of a biography of Isaac Hecker appeared in France, the book was praised by liberals as an example of
what was needed for the new democratic era, while conservatives
condemned Hecker and his champions as Americanists who would
minimize doctrine and undercut church authority. Denis O'Connell,
in a public address, attempted to distinguish political from ecclesiastical Americanism, the former implying nothing more than respect
for the constitutional government, common law tradition and popular
participation of the United States, the latter suggesting an independence for the American church that was far from anyone's mind. But
the liberal struggle, already lost in Europe, was doomed in the United
States as well.[63]

In 1899 Leo sent a letter to Cardinal Gibbons condemning a body
of ideas, "Americanism," which he claimed could be reduced to one:
"that in order the more easily to bring over to Catholic doctrine those
who dissent from it, the Church ought to adapt herself somewhat to

our advanced civilization and, relaxing her ancient rigor, show some
indulgence to popular theories and methods." In specifying these
ideas, Leo mentioned what had been taken to be ideas of Hecker:
emphasis on the active over the passive virtues, reduction of the role
of spiritual direction, introduction into the church of a "certain liberty" so that "limiting the exercise and vigilance of its powers, each
one of the faithful may act more freely in pursuance of his own natural
bent or capacity." In contrast, Leo insisted that "the rule of life which
is laid down for Catholics" could be modified only by the supreme
government of the church and not "by the will of private individuals,
who are mostly deceived by the appearance of right." "If anything is
suggested by the infallible teaching of the Church," Leo wrote, "it is
certainly that no one should wish to withdraw from it; nay, that all
should strive to be thoroughly imbued with and be guided by its spirit,
so as to be preserved from any private error." Against the Americanist
affirmation of modern culture the pope set "the license which is commonly confounded with liberty; the passion for saying and reviling
everything; the habit of thinking and expressing everything in print,"
all of which had "cast such deep shadows on men's minds that there
is now greater utility and necessity for this office of teaching than
ever before, lest men should be drawn away from conscience and
duty." In conclusion, the pope tried to soften the blow and offer a
way out by making a distinction common to the liberals themselves:

> We cannot approve the opinions which some comprise under the head
> of Americanism. If, indeed, by that name be designated the characteristic
> qualities which reflect honor on the people of America, just as other na-
> tions have what is special to them; or if it implies the conditions of your
> commonwealths, or the laws and customs which prevail in them, there
> is surely no reason why we should deem that it ought to be discarded.
> But if it is to be used not only to signify, but even to commend, the above
> doctrines, there can be no doubt that our Venerable Brethren the bishops
> of America would be the first to repudiate and condemn it, as being es-
> pecially unjust to them and to the entire nation as well. For it raises the
> suspicion that there are some among you who conceive of and desire a
> church in America different from that which is in the rest of the world.[64]

Writing under a pseudonym, John Ireland told readers of the *North
American Review* that American Catholicism had fallen victim to
antidemocratic forces in the European church. Using O'Connell's distinction between political and religious Americanism, Ireland argued
that the first meant only the frank acceptance of American liberties
and loyalty to the Constitution. Political Americanism, he wrote,
means only "that every good Catholic in America should also be a
good citizen," work to break down bigotry and cooperate with other
Americans in every good cause for the welfare of the American people,

a good statement of the republican tradition regularly repudiated by
Rome. Religious Americanism, which had been condemned, was a
"body of crude heretical opinions . . . foisted on American Catholics
by Europeans hostile to the United States and to the American people," by "heresy hunters" and the Jesuit journal *Civiltà Cattolica*,
which was an "enemy of democracy and democratic institutions."[65]

The opponents of the liberals understood their weaknesses and
capitalized on them after the encyclical. Archbishop Frederick X.
Katzer of Milwaukee said it all:

> Liberalizing opinions [are] always injurious to the true Catholic interest,
> sentimental phrases, closer communion with our separated brethren,
> appeals to a false and unreal American patriotism, lying charges of foreign
> and disloyal nationalism, highflown indiscriminate praise of the public
> school system, together with scornful and unfair criticism of our parochial
> schools, a hypocritical sympathy with the poor, double tax ridden Cath-
> olics, even the silly spectre of a conflict with the political power, all this
> was brought into play to make the Catholics of this country understand
> that parochial schools, Catholic schools, were no longer considered op-
> portune.[66]

Of all, or at least most of this, the liberals were guilty, but what Katzer
and other opponents missed was the most fundamental problem of
modernity, the problem of belief and meaning in a world for which
men and women had become responsible, the problem that the evils
of the twentieth century would expose.

Ireland in another article divided Catholics into three classes: one
primarily interested in the past, a second interested only in their own
piety, and a third eager to spread the influence of the church by using
means appropriate to the age.

> To speak without ceasing in a language understood by those around us
> and in ways that circumstances in which providence has placed us have
> opened to us to make the spirit of the Gospel effectively enter into the
> life of the individual, not the mass; that in a word the Church, representing
> the Divine Absolutism, must oppose every pretence of human absolutism
> and that thus She is essentially and by allocation the Protector of each
> one's personality, the deliverer from all servitude, the safeguard against
> all oppressions; in the light of the doctrine of the Church to recognize in
> the ideas and in the interests which win the hearts of the age, under
> whatever name or whatever veil covers them up, all that which being
> truly living just and progressive is by right a part of the Christian pat-
> rimony.[67]

For Katzer, Corrigan, and to a lesser extent McQuaid, the success of
the American experiment in democratic self-government was not the
problem, or at least not their problem. Ireland and the liberals, not
only in the United States but in Europe, at their best understood the

challenge of democracy. Echoing England's Cardinal Henry Edward Manning, Ireland had told James Gibbons that "the people are the power, and the Church must be with the people." John Lancaster Spalding, speaking at Notre Dame after the encyclical, was even more direct than usual: "What sacredness is there in Europe more than in America? Is not the history of Europe largely a history of wars, tyrannies, oppressions, massacres and persecutions? . . . Why should Europe be an object of awe and admiration for Catholics? Half its population has revolted from the Church, and in the so-called Catholic nations, which are largely governed by atheists, what vital manifestation of religious life and power can we behold?" They were excellent postencyclical questions. Spalding was not finished. In a 1900 visit to Rome he defended Hecker to the pope and preached at the Church of the Gesù on education: "We must think before we can think alike," he told his listeners. "The Church lives in history and must speak to its age." If in the process "we find it necessary to abandon positions which are no longer defensible, to assume new attitudes in the face of new conditions, we must remember that though the Church is a divine institution, it is nonetheless subject to the laws which make human things mutable, that though truth must remain the same it is capable of receiving fresh illustrations, and that if it is to be life giving, it must be wrought anew into the constitution of each individual and each age." Words such as these would rarely be heard in Rome until the advent of a different kind of pope and a new kind of renewal.

CHAPTER
6
Reform Catholicism

⟨ornament⟩

$\mathcal{S}$hortly after the appointment of the apostolic delegate in 1893, John Lancaster Spalding wrote an article in the *North American Review* questioning the wisdom of the appointment. He indicated that the majority of the bishops had opposed the decision, though no others said so publicly. Spalding even asked if Francesco Satolli planned to become a United States citizen. The article caused an uproar in the press and Satolli told Spalding that his open opposition to the pope was "absolutely intolerable" and had caused "a great and monstrous scandal." Spalding told a reporter that, if a problem could not be discussed in public, "rational discussion among Catholics is no longer to be thought of and Catholic universality is but a pretense." Upset with charges of disloyalty, Spalding shot back: "The only manly and American thing is to confront me with arguments and not attempt to frighten me with groanings."[1]

Unfortunately, the appointment of the delegate was only the beginning. The condemnation of Americanism and the decline of liberal Catholicism in the American church opened a gap between Catholic theory and Catholic practice. After the turn of the century, the bishops continued to preach republican ideals of political participation, concern for the public good, and patriotic devotion to the nation, adding a new emphasis on economic justice and social reform. The pope, however, had made it clear that the American church should restrain its enthusiasm for republican ideals and limit its dialogue with Protestantism and secular culture. The condemnation of modernism in 1907, with its related vigilance committees aimed at enforcing orthodox teaching, made the intellectual isolation of the church operative. Bishops were to crack down hard on "those who openly or secretly lend countenance to Modernism . . . by carping at scholasticism, and the Fathers, and the magisterium of the Church, or by refusing obedience to ecclesiastical authority in any of its depositories; and . . . those who show a love of novelty in history, archaeology, biblical exegesis; and finally . . . those who neglect the sacred sciences and appear to prefer to them the secular."[2] Having already made clear that the bishops should encourage Catholics to associate with one another and insure that reform movements remained under episcopal control, the papal influence ran directly counter to professions of Catholic devotion to the public good of the American people and their institutions by making the good of the church the primary criterion for judgment.

Pastoral considerations reinforced internal preoccupations. The needs of the new immigrants, the commitment to Catholic schools, and the problem of retaining the loyalty of the growing middle class all required a degree of cultural and religious segregation. Theoretically the church was fully American, committed to the nation and dedicated to fulfilling its ideals in public life. In practice it remained a voluntary association with a burgeoning array of institutions requiring popular commitment, sacrifice, and energy. This in turn depended upon belief that the church had a distinctive and significant mission. Ultramontane Catholicism and the immigrant church, in different ways, both saw that mission as religious, protecting and preserving the truths of faith and guiding people to an otherworldly salvation. Social, political, and cultural improvement would be possible only when men and women returned to the church; evangelical efforts should be aimed at bringing people into the church and into the subculture it had created.

Liberal Catholics and Americanists, in contrast, saw the church as having a marvelous opportunity to join its eternal truths to the best features of modern civilization, building a Christian commonwealth based on free acknowledgment of Catholic truths. For them the church was never for itself, an alternative culture leading men away from the world, but for everyone, enlightening all aspects of human existence and seeking to embrace all persons. The conservatives, by overemphasizing the gap between the church and the world, risked isolation from the age and irresponsibility regarding its problems. The liberals, by underestimating the dangers posed by individualism, science, and historical consciousness, risked surrendering to the age, jeopardizing Catholic integrity and the very existence of the church. Both groups were unwilling to live with "divided allegiance." Given the demand of the modern state for unswerving obedience and the pressure of modern culture toward conformity, both in the end failed to translate theory into practice. The conservative European church and the immigrant church in the United States both demanded obedience to the state; liberals no more than conservatives offered an alternative theory of public obligation that could allow persons to live with integrity both as church members and as citizens.

In the United States, some Catholic separatism seemed essential to the strength and vitality of the church, but too sharp a separation would bring religious and public obligations into conflict and force Catholics to choose between them. Thus it was necessary to affirm both the superiority of Catholic claims and the obligations of citizenship while avoiding serious reflection on the relationship between the two. The result was a dualism that puzzled contemporaries and later historians. The church articulated comprehensive and universal claims but made little effort to translate these into practice; it spoke like an establishment but showed no inclination to challenge pluralism or even to convert non-Catholics. It acted as though there was no salvation outside the church but insisted that tolerance and good will were essential to the public good. It developed a powerful message of social and political responsibility but concentrated in its schools and parishes on personal and private morality centered on family life and sexuality. At moments of national crisis it adopted the symbols of civil religion, making sacrifice for the nation and obedience to the government a Christian obligation, but it regularly denounced expanding government power, condemned the public schools as godless and decried the rampant secularism of public life, hardly noticing how its own self-interested preoccupations contributed to the separation of religion from public life.[3]

Of course, Catholics after the Americanist crisis were still deeply loyal Americans, but there was no longer any serious effort to make connections between their Catholic and their American experience. Contemporaries and historians attributed this segmentation to the influx of new immigrants, but the more serious problem was retaining the allegiance of the Americanized middle class: how could people no longer bound by ethnic ties be persuaded to continue their commitment to the church, its schools, and its teachings? Historically, wherever Catholics had found themselves in the minority, they had created a subculture, creating bonds among families while seeking a new basis of public life in principles and structures that made religious affiliation irrelevant. From the days of the Maryland exiles, the major task had been the latter, to secure a definition of citizenship that did not exclude Catholics. That struggle had been reawakened in the nineteenth century by nativism and the evangelical crusade, both of which sought, in the public schools if not in the government, to identity American ideals and institutions with evangelical Christianity. In the years before World War I, at least in cities and states where

Catholics were a substantial portion of the population, the nonreligious definition of citizenship and the neutrality of the government were secured. But, when that happened, the first problem, always present, became more visible: how to secure the bonds of religious faith in a distinct people. Put another way, the problem was that the ethnic parish had encouraged both the retention of ethnic identity and assimilation into American life.

As the latter proceeded, the "structural fences" that preserved group integrity against widening contacts outside the group began to disintegrate, and new fences needed to be constructed.[4] As William Kerby put it, the church needed to provide "the natural social reinforcements of the bonds of faith" because "business, locality . . . taste and culture, similar pursuits or ambitions," all of which were "usually final in fixing our associations," no longer fulfilled their function. "There is consequently a tendency to indifference concerning a man's religion." In a pluralistic society, where the right to economic, social, and political participation has been assured, "the interests and sympathies men have in common monopolize conversation, attention, while religion and its particular interests recede from our social intercourse. Hence our own religion tends to become a matter of more personal concern." Kerby thought this process reflected the increase of affiliations outside of the church and that as a result there were fewer positive reinforcements of faith and the church had a shrinking sphere of influence. The church had to "compete and fight for [the] attention" of its own members. To counter this trend, the church needed to develop new associations beyond worship by offering inspirational leadership, a sense of history, evocative symbols, mass demonstrations of group strength, and common experiences of action, both defensive and apostolic.[5]

Gradually, therefore, Catholics created a subculture, a set of mediating institutions, to provide the "natural social reinforcements of the bonds of faith." Professor Milton Gordon has described the phenomenon of acculturation, in which a person can look and act like a member of the host culture without actually being assimilated into it. Such a person may intermarry and join mixed organizations. Secondary associatons in the work place and in politics, can develop; economic interaction can take place, at, for instance, banks, stores, and offices; people can even leave their ethnic neighborhoods or move to a city some distance from their parents and siblings and still organize their primary associations of family, social, recreational, and religious groups among like-hearted and like-minded people. Gordon writes:

> From the cradle in the sectarian hospital to the child's play group, the social clique in high school, the fraternity and religious center in college,

the dating group within which he searches for a spouse, the marriage partner, the neighborhood of his residence, the church affiliation and the church clubs, the men's and women's social and service organizations, the adult clique of 'marrieds,' the vacation resort, and then, as the age cycle nears completion, the rest home for the elderly and, finally, the sectarian cemetery—in all those activities and relationships which are close to the core of personality and selfhood—the member of the ethnic group may if he wishes follow a path that never takes him across the boundaries of his ethnic [or one might add his religious] structural network.[6]

Both as an organization and as a people, Catholicism became a subculture within, not outside of, American culture. From the viewpoint of other Americans that subculture seemed divisive, separatist, too Catholic, not American enough. From the viewpoint of Rome and that of converts or unusually committed Catholics, it seemed narrow, more social than religious, preoccupied with material rather than spiritual measurements of success, too American, not Catholic enough. Voluntary, self-consciously constructed, it was a uniquely American phenomenon.

THE ORGANIZATIONAL REVOLUTION

As American Catholicism entered the twentieth century, the Americanists were chastened, the old battles over, the new ones not yet begun. John Keane returned from exile to become archbishop of Dubuque and Denis O'Connell became the surprisingly conservative rector of Catholic University. The Germans, now satisfied that their interests were assured, rallied to the university's support, raising money for a chair in German literature. They now found common ground with the Irish; in 1910 Peter Paul Cahensley, who had led the fight for German recognition three decades earlier, visited the United States and was well received by Gibbons. The Germans' old nemesis, John Ireland, continuing to give patriotic speeches, used his Republican connections to campaign to be made cardinal, but his national leadership within the church was over. The apostolic delegate now played a crucial role in the selection of new bishops, no more national councils were held, and each bishop was supreme in his diocese, accountable only to Rome. Cardinal Gibbons lived on into the 1920s and continued to hold a kind of primacy of honor among the bishops, but he was no longer the major intermediary between Rome and the American church. After his death there would be no cardinal in Baltimore until after Vatican II. Indeed, American Catholicism after 1900 was more an idea than a fact. There was no authoritative national organization and no symbolic center. American Catholicism was a states' rights church, dominated by the local bishops. The parish was the focal point of Catholic life and apostolic movements had to support the parish and receive approval from the ordinary of each diocese.

Around the country a new breed of episcopal leader appeared, led by Cardinal William H. O'Connell of Boston. Often Roman trained, they combined unquestioning responsiveness to papal authority with an altogether American concern with efficient organization. O'Connell became archbishop of Boston solely on the basis of his Roman connections, and he carried out a thorough reorganization of his diocese. He placed men loyal to himself in key positions; ousted the Sulpicians from his diocesan seminary and replaced them with local priests; drew up a detailed record of his clergy and began regular clergy conferences; required annual reports from the parishes; multiplied the number of pastoral decisions and devotional programs requiring chancery permission; and attempted to require diocesan approval for all building projects and any expenditures over two hundred dollars. He purchased the independent Boston *Pilot* and made it a diocesan house organ, and he established diocesan offices for charities and education to bring greater uniformity, professionalism, and financial stability to these hitherto highly decentralized activities.

When O'Connell received in 1916 a personal bequest of nearly $3 million from the family of theater magnate Benjamin F. Keith, he devoted the money to the construction of a "little Rome" on the hills surrounding Boston. In addition to endowing schools and hospitals, he used the Keith benefaction to erect a new chancery building and a large and elaborate residence. O'Connell had "a remarkably clear vision of what the Church ought to be and how that vision was to be realized. Taking the Holy See as his model, O'Connell worked for the establishment and confirmation in this country of a church in which all authority was centralized at the top and flowed downward from there."[7] As one Boston priest wrote in 1930: "You know the conditions of things in this diocese. . . . We are soldiers under orders."[8]

Cardinal O'Connell had an unusually monarchical style and was unusually conservative in his theology, often acting like a mini-pope, but his basic drive toward centralization, efficiency, and administrative control, which was centered on the disciplined, locally recruited and trained clergy, was repeated in many urban dioceses in the first decades of the century. Chicago's Archbishop George Mundelein, appointed in 1916, engaged in a similar and even more successful centralization of finances, charities, and education, and the seminary and residence he constructed were more elaborate than O'Connell's. One historian characterizes his administration as "going first class" and his building style as "Catholic big."[9] O'Connell, Mundelein, Cardinals Patrick J. Hayes and Francis Spellman of New York, and others who copied their style, rarely succeeded in taking complete control of finances and education away from the pastors, and their centralizing efforts were often stalled by powerful groups of ethnic clergy. However, with the help of a new breed of priest-professional, organized nationally in charities and education, they did create a structure of accountability, they did establish their authority over the clergy, and they did make American Catholicism more Roman in its worship and theology and more bishop-dominated in its administrative procedures than any church in the Western world. In the process they changed the public face of the church as well, as other Americans often identified the church in their local community and in the nation with the powerful personalities who seemed to dominate it.

The theological foundations of the Catholic subculture were solidly in place. The declaration of papal infallibility and papal primacy had firmly established an all but exclusively institutional ecclesiology; as one American bishop expressed it, Christ left behind a "complete organization" that he defined in terms of pope, bishops, and priests. Father Francis Kennedy put the implications of all this in terms that had become common by the 1920s: "The priest is God's representative in our midst. On the altar and in the confessional he is simply omnipotent, simply divine."[10] The condemnation of modernism inhibited the development of scriptural and historical studies that were transforming Christian theology outside the church. What remained was an ahistorical orthodoxy, a sense of a fixed and unchanging body of doctrine and dogma best summarized in the widely used Baltimore catechism. Traditional folk and family devotions were now centered within the church (though the battle for control still raged in newer immigrant communities such as the Italian), where they supplemented the central devotion of the mass, now reinforced by papal encouragement of early and frequent communion. Grace was available primarily through the sacraments, truth primarily through the teaching authority of the hierarchy. The strength of the church, therefore, was the criterion of a healthy society. As Peter C. Yorke, a well-known San Francisco priest and social activist, wrote in a children's textbook in 1904: "The Catholic Church is the Kingdom of God."[11]

Morally the emphasis was increasingly placed on sexual morality. If sermons and pastoral letters were authentic expressions of church concerns, Catholic clerics believed they were living in an era marked by the decline of family life, increasing permissiveness, and approaching sexual hedonism, from all of which the church sought to protect its children, who included adults. According to an editorial in the *Michigan Catholic* in 1913; "By eight or ten years American children, as a rule, are sadly precocious, and too often at that tender age they have lost their baptismal innocence and have made terrible acquaintances with sin and vice."[12] Obviously this meant that parents should send their children to Catholic elementary schools, but by now more of them expected a high school education as well, and those were dangerous years. As the president of a Jesuit high school in New York expressed it in 1899:

> It is simply treason to our Catholic principles to send our children to the public high schools. We cannot state this fact too strongly. The danger to their faith and morals is greater in these schools than in the public grammar schools. . . . Usually it is during the high school years of a boy's life that he makes his first acquaintance with dangerous temptations, and forms habits for good or evil that cling to him for life. Hence the danger of high schools without religion."[13]

Such attitudes were not directed only at the young. Bishop Walter Foery told his people that the church, like a "wise mother," gave her children substitutes for forbidden activities; if she did not "multiply her interests on behalf of her children," adult "impulses" might develop along "unwholesome lines." He went on to specify as substitutes Holy Name societies, women's groups, and charitable and educational apostolates, along with a variety of parish social and recreational activities.[14] Such public activities as the Legion of Decency and the National Office of Decent Literature thus did double duty, protecting against unwholesome activity and providing acceptable substitutes not only in church-sponsored readings and films but in the crusading activities themselves. In the years between the wars fraternal groups like the Knights of Columbus and its feminine counterparts helped keep Catholics together in their social life, while diocesan federations of parish-based men's and women's societies received new vigor by taking on public projects aimed at enhancing Catholic morale and protecting church interests. Similarly Catholic nurses, doctors, lawyers, poets, historians, and many others developed their own organizations to supplement or mediate their participation in the secular professional groups that were growing rapidly during the period.

THE SOCIAL GOSPEL

After the Civil War, American Protestantism changed dramatically. Liberal theology reduced the significance of sin and emphasized the priority of love and benevolence in human affairs. The wealthier classes derived from this comfortable teaching a "gospel of wealth" that affirmed acquistiveness and came dangerously close to identifying the wealthy and successful with the truly Christian and the Dar-

winian "fit." But many more Christians were disturbed by the problems of the city, immigration, labor strife, the evolution of poverty,
and historical criticism. Before accepting a pastorate in a city slum,
the Baptist minister Walter Rauschenbusch recalled, he had "no idea
of social questions." When he tried to apply his "previous religious
ideas" to the problems of his people, he "discovered they didn't fit."
Men and women like Rauschenbusch founded settlement houses in
the cities, organized good government campaigns, joined temperance
and social reform organizations, and often devoted their lives to
proving that Christianity had not been rendered obsolete by urbanization and industrialization. They were moved by Henry George's
Progress and Poverty, and many read Charles Sheldon's *In His Steps*,
a simple story of good people who changed their community by resolving to ask at every decision of their lives, "What would Jesus do?"
The more sophisticated among them discovered the social dimensions
of the gospel and joined it to a millennial sense of American mission.
"The thought of the world is gradually being freed from prejudice
and superstitions," wrote clergyman Washington Gladden. "The social
sentiments are being purified; the customs are slowly changing for
the better; the laws are gradually shaped by finer conceptions of justice. There are reactions and disasters, but, taking the ages together,
the progress is sure." According to Gladden, to contribute to building
the kingdom, "to be a Christian," all that was needed was "to accept
as the ruling axiom of ethical conduct the commandment that a man
shall love his neighbor as himself." Rauschenbusch added social science to the mix and found "the possibility of directing religious energy
by scientific knowledge" to bring about " a comprehensive and continuous reconstruction of social life in the name of God." Together
the social gospel became the religious expression of what Gladden
called "the mighty contagion of social justice" that was the progressive
movement, first in the cities, then, with Theodore Roosevelt and
Woodrow Wilson, a national effort to insure that the "promise of
American life" was realized.[15]

From the earliest days Catholic priests and bishops had avoided
the "contagion" of reform. In a manual of pastoral theology, Bishop
William Stang of Fall River expressed the widely held Catholic view
that social and political problems were not the concern of the good
priest. Stang warned his clerical readers that they should "never speak
about local politics or the political parties of the country" from the
pulpit. "In Church our Catholic people seek rest from the noise and
bustle of everyday life, from the discordant sounds of human strife
and warring politics. They come to church to free their minds from
the disagreeable scenes of the world."[16]

In public life even most liberal of the nineteenth-century bishops were clearly conservative, placing their weight behind modest and orderly reform when that became popular, but avoiding any hint of radicalism. Understanding that government would play an increasingly important role in a complex industrial society, they were alert to developing some influence in public life, if for no other reason than to protect Catholic schools and charities. That influence was better sought through association with business leaders than with labor, although the predominance of Catholics among the laboring classes required that such contacts be discreet and, if public, moderately reformist. John Ireland remained an active Republican, offering private advice to Presidents Roosevelt and Taft and telling a friend he thought candidate Woodrow Wilson was anti-Catholic; Ireland even circulated material to that effect during the 1912 campaign.[17] Gibbons and Ireland joined industrialist Mark Hanna and Samuel Gompers, chief of the American Federation of Labor, in the National Civic Federation to fight socialism by affirming moderate trade unionism and labor management cooperation.

Cardinal Gibbons, the nation's most prominent Catholic leader, was far more conservative than most Protestant spokesmen. For one thing he remained very wary of increasing the role of the federal government to deal with what were now national problems. "The safety and permanence of our Republic largely depends on the autonomy of the several States, without the danger of being absorbed by the General Government."[18] Accordingly, he was particularly worried about any change in the Constitution. He thought the direct election of senators "involves the destruction of a strong bulwark against dangerous popular encroachment," the referendum substituted "mob law for established rule," and the recall of judges would make them "habitual slaves of a capricious multitude." Not every change, whether in politics or religion, was a reformation, Gibbons believed, so it was "better to bear the ills that we know than fly to those we know not of."[19] He was equally conservative in dealing with labor, even though he had endorsed the right to organize and acknowledged that workers had grievances. In 1907 his speeches and statements were collected and published by the American Anti-Boycott Association, one of the most anti-union groups in the country.

Gibbons made these comments from a republican position. Like Carroll, whom he admired greatly, and Ireland, he acknowledged the existence of the two spheres of religion and politics, but having lived through the era of rapid industrial expansion and the response of government intervention to deal with economic and social problems, he recognized how much the republican stance for Catholics required limited government, not just in constitutional theory but in political practice. Gibbons, the premier apologist in dealing with anti-Catholic opinion, never acknowledged, as did Spalding, the likelihood of "double allegiance," of having to choose between the demands of church and state. "I grant that . . . a collision of authorities comes . . . within the horizon of possibility," the cardinal wrote. "But the American concept of government and of liberty puts the hypothesis outside the range of practical affairs. That concept, as I understand it, is that the government should leave as large a liberty as possible to individuals and bodies within the State, only intervening in the interests of morality, justice and the common weal." In the nineteenth century, that limitation depended upon a restricted understanding of "morality, justice and the common weal." The possibility that new readings of those terms could lead to a vast extension of governmental responsibility, and therefore of possible "collision" between contending "authorities," was evident in the Civil War and in the battles over the school question. During the progressive era, Gibbons was well aware of what was happening: "There are forces at work in this country, I know, that tend to paternalism and caesarism in government, but true Americanism recognizes that these forces would bring disaster on American liberties. So long as these liberties, under which we have prospered, are preserved in their fulness, there is, I assert, no danger of a collision between the State and the Catholic Church."[20]

It was, of course, in the church's interests to prevent such a "collision" by avoiding reforms that enhanced federal power. Catholics thus found themselves endorsing ideas from the Jeffersonian tradition, put to conservative uses in the twentieth century. Similar concerns could increasingly lead even liberal Catholics to find virtues in nineteenth-century social and cultural values as well, and to oppose reforms that might endanger family life and orderly relationships between social groups, as well as between the sexes. Catholic leaders strongly opposed women's suffrage, with Gibbons leading the charge. In 1911 he told a reporter he was "unalterably opposed to woman's suffrage, always have been and always will be." In a speech to an antisuffrage group in Maryland, he charged that suffrage supporters spoke "about women's rights and prerogatives, and have not said a word about her duties and responsibilities. They withdraw her from those positions which properly belong to her sex and fill her with ambition to usurp positions for which neither God nor nature ever intended her." In 1916 he told the first National Anti-Suffrage Convention that woman was "queen of the domestic kingdom"; political life would not benefit and domestic life would suffer if the vote were granted. This statement was widely disseminated, as were similar statements by other bishops, some of whom already linked the issue with the danger of birth control and a few of whom ordered their priests to speak against the reform from the pulpit.[21] While at one

point or another both Ireland and McQuaid supported women's suffrage, the majority of the hierarchy were opposed—although they did
encourage women to participate once the vote was granted, in part
to offset the influence of more radical feminists.

Yet such conservatism was inadequate in the years before World
War I. Reform was in the air, with even the most respectable Americans admitting that some changes were needed if the American economy was to continue to expand without bringing about an explosion
from workers and farmers, who had demonstrated their rebellious
potential in the labor disturbances and the Populist movement of the
1890s. Social Gospel Protestants had aroused the national conscience;
middle-class business and professional leaders had been shaken by
the rising power of monopolistic corporations, trusts, and the manifest
corruption of urban politics, the machine; and persons of conservative
interests and temperament had concluded that moderate reform was
needed to alleviate class conflict and preserve respect for government
and law. Bishops and priests still presided over a predominately urban, working-class people and could hardly oppose every effort made
to improve their condition. Thus an ever increasing number of church
leaders were convinced, with Roosevelt and Wilson, that the wisest
conservatism allowed healthy reform.

The most important factor moving the hierarchy toward support
for moderate social reform, however, was the apparent danger of socialism. Before the turn of the century, labor radicalism had usually
taken a uniquely American form, as in the producer-oriented yearning
for cooperation of the Knights of Labor or the land reform proposals
of Henry George, both of which denied the reality of class conflict
and would replace a corporate, banker-dominated economy with a
cooperative commonwealth of middle-class producers. The violence
of corporate and government response to even moderate trade unionism and reform, however, shook confidence in the possibilities of
change through education, cooperation, and moral reform. In 1900
Eugene Victor Debs, a midwestern labor organizer, took the lead of
a new Socialist party that attempted to bring together American socialists, previously confined primarily to foreign-language groups, and
the more radical remnants of the Populist and labor movements of
the previous century. In successive elections Debs expanded the socialist vote for president to a million in 1912, while cities like Milwaukee elected over one thousand socialist candidates to local offices.
At the same time socialists within the American Federation of Labor
were mounting an ever stronger challenge to the conservative leadership of Gompers while a far more radical organization, the Industrial Workers of the World, gave leadership to some spontaneous outbreaks of labor discontent in the lumber camps and mining towns of

the West and in Lawrence, Massachusetts, and Paterson, New Jersey. Some prominent middle-class reformers also endorsed Deb's party. As Cardinal O'Connell, surely one of the most conservative bishops, told President William Howard Taft, "the mental confusion which socialism has engendered seems to affect even many otherwise sane and conservative men. It many be a wave, but I fear it will submerge many."[22] A decade later O'Connell told Archbishop John J. Glennon of Saint Louis: "There are to be undoubtedly many social upheavals affecting society, capital and labor to their foundations. The Church must not be silent but be a directing force in all this."[23]

The problem could be illustrated by the odyssey of Terence Powderly. Even as leader of the Knights of Labor, Powderly had never approved of strikes. In 1900 he appealed to Gibbons to intervene with the clergy of Pennsylvania, where he was trying to persuade mine operators to bargain with their workers: "I abhor strikes at all times but more particularly when those engaged are the poorest of the poor and least able to bear the ills which attend loss of work and money." Gibbons agreed: "I . . . have publicly said and written that strikes are a disaster and a dangerous remedy, often resulting fatally [for] both patients."

Powderly was deeply committed to social change but could find no acceptable means to bring it about, once his earlier hope for co-operatives had proved utopian. He told his friend Father William Kerby that he disagreed with socialist methods but endorsed their goals and could not understand why the church did not work harder to offset the socialists. By now he was bitter: "The church will have to believe Christ's teaching before it can impress others."[24] Toward the end of his life, he wrote Kerby a long angry letter occasioned by a cable of congratulations sent by Pope Pius X to the parents of U. S. Steel executive Charles Schwab:

> The fires of the hell the pope preaches are not more hot than the seething furnaces in the mills before which the image of God is seared and blistered in a struggle for bread. My brothers, the children of God, stand and move, the very marrow in their bones being dissolved in the heat of Charles Schwab's furnaces that their labor may be coined into dollars. 'Six days shalt thou labor' was not heeded by Schwab. The man who preaches 'Keep Holy the Sabbath day' send his blessing to an old man and woman he never saw and would never have heard of did these men not give Charles Schwab the dollars to buy a blessing for his parents.

Powderly recalled that, when the city of New Orleans lost its bid to host the Panama Exposition of 1905, Gibbons had told a reporter the city had benefited, as the event would "have drawn a lot of human driftwood here looking for work." "For fifteen years I held the image of Christ, and Him crucified, before me as my inspiration," Powderly concluded.

> It was the Christ of the toiling poor. It could not be the Christ of Schwab, it could not be the Christ of Pius X, it could not be the Christ of any one who by as much as one cent accepts that which he has not earned. I must have been mistaken. It is unthinkable, from my point of view that these men can believe in Christ and in their daily life and work so utterly differ from Him . . . I think this way all the time but have too long kept still.[25]

Indeed he had. These were sentiments attributed to European workers, not American Catholics; if they should spread, the entire American Catholic project would be in grave danger.

"NOT SOCIALISM BUT SOCIAL REFORM"

There were two elements to the strategy that American Catholic leaders adopted to deal with the discontent expressed by Powderly. One was to support moderate social reform, the other to engage in direct efforts to discredit socialism. The approach had already been foreshadowed in Gibbons's treatment of the Knights of Labor and in the papal letter of 1895, which warned of the danger of socialism and placed reservations on Catholic participation in nondenominational organizations.

In 1891 Leo XIII issued his famous encyclical on labor, *Rerum Novarum*, which endorsed the right of labor to organize and the responsibility of the state to intervene on behalf of justice. Leo argued that labor was not a commodity; workers had a right in justice to the means necessary to sustain life, the "living wage." He condemned the amoral individualism of laissez-faire capitalism and the materialism and state domination of socialism, urging Catholics to stand with their priests and urging priests to go to the workers. Most Catholic commentators praised the encyclical but judged that its concern with the exploitation of workers, class conflict, and state intervention had little application to the United States. When renewed labor strife, the spread of interest in reform, and the threat of socialism spurred the church to action, *Rerum Novarum* provided a convenient platform on which to base a Catholic response that would allow selective support for change without surrendering Catholic distinctiveness.[26]

At first it was not a foregone conclusion that working-class Catholics would be alienated from the socialist movement. In its earliest days it even had some Catholic leadership. Throughout the nineteenth century, radical labor organizations often found support among Irish skilled workers, and Irish nationalist organizations, particuarly the Land League, often adopted radical positions on economic issues—

one reason that the American hierarchy cut its ties with them after 1865. Even the early Socialist party enjoyed some clerical support. Father Thomas McGrady, a colorful, six-foot-three-inch man, served missions in Illinois and Texas before returning to his native Kentucky in 1895. Influenced by the English Christian Socialists, Edward Bellamy and Henry George, he rejected *Rerum Norarum* for its acceptance of the profit motive and taunted Catholic leaders for their accommodation to the capitalist system. After he returned to Kentucky he was ordered by his bishop to recant his praise of Karl Marx, but he refused, although he was a utopian socialist and no Marxist. "I would sacrifice my manhood and my conscience and stultify myself before the public, for every man in the country would say that I should be confined to an insane asylum," he told his congregation. "Therefore I resign to preserve myself from the charge of idiocy and to protect my memory from everlasting infamy." For a year he lectured under party auspices, but his sarcastic replies to priests and bishops made him a liability, his large personal following was divisive, and local organizers thought his fees too high. From 1903 until his death in 1905 he practiced law, lectured, and wrote for the socialist press.[27]

Thomas J. Hagerty, a Texas priest, was a McGrady convert. Intelligent and organizationally sophisticated, he was a leader of the socialist left wing. His radicalism, like that of Bill Haywood, leader of the Western Federation of Miners and later of the Industrial Workers of the World, was formed in the violent atmosphere of the Rocky Mountain mining camps. Hagerty saw the conflict between Marxism and Christianity, and anticipated the problem of bureaucratic centralization that would accompany government ownership of productive enterprise. Instead he favored a form of worker ownership similar to that of European syndicalists. His viewpoint was expressed most directly during a 1902 speech supporting strikers against a particularly repressive coalition of employers and state militia: "That railroad is yours, those large business blocks and office buildings downtown that bring in big rent are yours; if you want them, go and take them."[28] He believed it would be impossible to bring about a socialist society without the support of Catholic workers, so he worked hard to convince his hearers that the antisocialism of the pope and bishops were simply their political opinions. In 1905 he played a major role in drafting the platform of the Industrial Workers of the World. A few weeks later he delivered a speech in Milwaukee, then vanished from the scene.[29]

The isolated efforts of McGrady and Hagerty bore little fruit. Of course, some Catholics were attracted to socialism, and the church knew it. In 1909 the New York Socialist party ran a Catholic for mayor, but he was badly defeated and the party soon lost Catholic support.[30]

At about the same time the secretary of the Socialist party in Massachusetts reported that 70 percent of its members were Catholics. Irish nationalists John Burke and James Connolly were prominent in the socialist cause, and here and there a priest like Father Haire, a populist from Aberdeen, South Dakota, supported the party.[31] But, unfortunately, as one editor put it, good Catholics made bad socialists and good socialists made bad Catholics. On that both sides came to agree.

At first by close votes the Socialist party decided to confine its activities to politics and economics, avoiding religion, but active socialists became increasingly angry at attacks on them by Catholics in the AFL and from the pulpit, attacks many considered unfair. Even the normally tolerant Debs concluded that the Catholic church was "the implacable foe of socialism. . . . It teaches the lowly wage slave to look with mistrust and hatred upon the great working class movement whose mission it is to unlock the economic dungeon in which he is serving a life sentence."[32] This was a mild version of what came to be typical commentary on the church in the Socialist press. What irritated socialists most was that antisocialist churchmen rarely addressed their political and economic arguments. Instead they charged again and again that socialism would undermine family life.

The most popular antisocialist tract was David Goldstein's *Socialism: The Nation of Fatherless Children*. When Father John A. Ryan, the leading advocate of social reform among Catholics, debated socialist leader Morris Hillquit in 1912, the major issue he raised was divorce.[33] Obviously such arguments were intended to deprive the socialists of legitimacy among Catholics, and the behavior of some who were known as socialists or anarchists, like Emma Goldman and George Herron, seemed to lend credence to their arguments. More deeply, American Socialists like Hillquit (though not Debs) were incurably modern. They appealed to reason, claimed that they had discovered a scientific understanding of history and society, and projected into the future a vision of a completed industrialism, efficient, rationally organized, more productive than under capitalism but with its products more equitably distributed. Moreover, their view of history led to an ethical relativism; in the 1912 debate, for example, Hillquit admitted that many forms of traditional morality, and by implication traditional religion, had been rendered outmoded by the inexorable force of historical laws pushing human beings toward an ever greater collectivism. Immigrant Catholic workers did not need popes and bishops to be suspicious of these ideas. From the experience of migration they had forged a family-centered understanding of the world and a political consciousness that reflected family and communal values. They saw their political and union leaders and their pastors within the framework of family and group loyalties, and they expressed in their churches and ethnic associations a larger sense of family, a classless but communal ethic of loyalty and solidarity, realistically hostile to idealistic extravagence, but hostile as well to the social engineering that they sensed in too many liberal reformers and scientific socialists.

Powderly's approach to the labor question was limited and flawed, but he devoted his life to the cause of the workers as he saw it, and his Christian humanism was formed in the early experience of fellowship as an apprentice to a skilled worker. Debs understood the democratic, egalitarian, and fraternal sources of American working-class consciousness, which his Marxist colleagues missed, but neither he nor they ever grasped the family and communal values that were most important to unskilled industrial workers. What James Donnelly has written about the Hillquit-Ryan exchange could be said of the entire conflict:

> Fundamentally, Hillquit could not understand how moral rigidity would be helpful to a human race that would have to struggle to adapt itself and its moral standards of ownership, family structure and social justice to the new demands of the industrial order. Conversely, Ryan was probably incapable of understanding how, when all cultural relationship appeared to have slipped moorings in the storms of the new industrial order, moral flexibility about social, personal and familial relations would help the human race better itself. . . . Their debate revealed the cultural antithesis of Catholicism and socialism in America.[34]

If most Catholic workers in practice took Ryan's side, it was because it best expressed their needs and aspirations, despite the always misleading claims of priests, socialists and historians alike, that they did so because of the influence of "the Church."

But Catholic leaders in 1900 were no more inclined to trust the wisdom of their people than they had been fifty years earlier or would be eighty years later. They launched an energetic anti socialist counterattack that united former liberals and conservatives. In New York Archbishop Michael Corrigan delivered a series of well-publicized sermons between October 1901 and January 1902. A few months later Bishop Spalding published a book on *Socialism and Labor* and Archbishop James E. Quigley of Chicago wrote a strong pastoral letter. Soon the Ancient Order of Hibernians, the American Federation of Catholic Societies, and the Knights of Columbus had made antisocialism part of their platforms. In 1905 Bishop Stang of Fall river wrote *Socialism and Christianity*, one of the most widely circulated Catholic statements. Like almost all Catholics he did not want to belittle the worker's quest for better treatment. "Not all that is put to the credit of Socialists should be termed socialism," he wrote. "There is a deal of solid good in our modern aspirations." He went on to "separate the wheat from the chaff," taking care to "encourage every popular movement which makes for the diffusion of wealth and physical comfort." Socialism was not radical enough, he argued, for it made no provision for "a renovation of men's hearts and minds."[35] The combination of religious influence, which would touch people's hearts, and the reform spirit of the age was sure to make life more just and equitable.

Stang's affirmation of the desire for reform was joined to the consensual conviction of Catholics that socialism was the enemy of traditional morality by two people who turned the debate with socialism into a crusade. Martha Moore Avery had been a Unitarian, a Bellamy nationalist, and a member of the Socialist Labor party before joining the Socialist party in 1901 and opening a socialist school in Boston. Her friend David Goldstein, English-born of Jewish extraction, shared her experience of socialism. Together they tried to give the socialist movement in Boston a more religious and less Marxist tone. They invited Thomas McGrady and Thomas J. Hagerty to speak, and Goldstein wrote the latter in 1902: "Our movement greatly needs the religious elevation which both you and Father McGrady bring to it that it may not fall on all fours as in Europe." Goldstein and Avery were deeply shaken by the divorce and remarriage of the well-known Christian Socialist George Herron, an event heralded by many socialists as a protest against the bourgeois institution of marriage. Reading Engels made Goldstein skeptical of combining socialism and the family; a United States government report on divorce convinced him that the Catholic church was a bulwark of marriage and family life. In 1902 the two presented a resolution to the Massachusetts Socialist party to bar speakers who attacked religion or advocated violence or free love. Defeat of the resolution confirmed their fears; when Avery published her thoughts on these events she was reprimanded by the party and withdrew. Goldstein followed and the two soon published *Socialism: The Nation of Fatherless Children.*

Both Avery and Goldstein entered the Catholic church and began careers as antisocialist speakers and lay evangelists. Avery lectured to Catholic audiences and in 1906 was enlisted by the National Civic Federation to campaign against women's suffrage. She also helped organize the Common Cause Society in Boston to promote the social teachings of Leo XIII. Always she combined her attacks on socialism with support for unions, collective bargaining, and social reform.[36] In 1910 Cardinal O'Connell, alarmed by the spread of socialism in the state, asked Goldstein to join several other priests and laymen to give lectures to workingmen. The following year the German Central Verein hired him as a traveling antisocialist speaker and in 1914 the

Knights of Columbus sponsored a lecture tour by Goldstein and Peter Collins of the electrical workers' union. In later years Goldstein organized the Catholic Truth Guild and evangelized for the church across the country.[37]

Terence Powderly was exasperated by the more heavy-handed assaults on socialism, suspecting that they obscured a lack of concern for social justice. "Socialism, in this country anyway, is an effect, not a cause," he told a friend. The antisocialists attacked those who would "undo the greatest wrong of the age if not of the centuries and would do it peacefully, do it without violating Christ's law."[38] But by the time Powderly wrote those words many were attempting to carry through on Bishop Stang's promise to unite the church to "the reform spirit of the age." The first center of attention was the labor movement.

In 1902, 147,000 coal miners went out on strike, led by John Mitchell, who had become president of the union in 1898 when he was only twenty-eight years old. Faced with a threat to the railroads, and with winter approaching, President Roosevelt appointed an arbitration commission with Bishop Spalding as the "public representative." According to Mitchell, Spalding had helped settle a strike in Illinois in 1900, and his book *Socialism and Labor and Other Arguments* had been well received. After recording fifty-six volumes of testimony and visiting the mines, the commission awarded the miners a ten percent pay increase but denied them recognition of the union and a closed shop. Later, however, Spalding testified before a congressional committee that, while he privately had serious reservations about the closed shop, he believed that the abstract right of anyone to work in the mines should give way when the miners, who had worked for years in the mines and become unsuited for other forms of work, went on strike for just reasons and strikebreakers were brought in. In such cases the idea of the right to work would destroy the unions, and unions had become a necessary means by which the workers could secure a degree of justice.[39]

Cardinal O'Connell was at the other end of the Catholic episcopal spectrum from Spalding but he too claimed to take up the cause of labor. In 1911, during a major IWW-led textile strike in Lawrence, O'Connell sent his closest clerical adviser to investigate conditions and then published a pastoral letter deploring low wages and unhealthy working conditions. In this letter he demanded stronger government supervision of factories and endorsed labor's right to organize, at the same time vigorously condemning the socialists.[40]

Catholics in these years made up at least half the membership of the American Federation of Labor. Most, though not all, of the Catholic leaders of unions within the AFL were strongly antisocialist. Peter Collins of the electrical workers' union, for example, played a major role in the direct assault on socialism launched by the church in New England, and John Mitchell became a Catholic in 1907.[41] Yet little was done to reach or encourage this group, despite the efforts of Father Peter Dietz, the church's strongest advocate for the unions.

Ordained in Cleveland in 1904, Dietz had been impressed during his seminary education in Europe by lay movements for social education and action. More than any other priest of his generation he believed that strong, independent labor unions were the surest means of securing justice and preventing the growth of socialism. He secured a prolabor resolution from the American Federation of Catholic Societies, but, discouraged by that organization's inability to secure funds for national action, he turned to the German Roman Catholic Central Verein, heading its Commission on Social Propaganda and editing the English section of its publication, the first Catholic magazine devoted to social justice. During this period the Verein, under the leadership of Frederick B. Kenkel, attempted to bring to the United States some of the progressive social Catholicism of Germany.[42]

Cranky and opinionated, Dietz tried to overcome the Verein's isolation from other Catholic organizations, which led to clashes with its leadership, so he turned again to the AFCS, becoming secretary of its new Social Service Committee under Bishop Peter J. Muldoon. For a time this organization became a vehicle for Dietz's dream of building a Catholic social movement in America. The commission published pamphlets and a newsletter and attempted to start a national press service. Dietz saw the federation as a "tremendous bulk of unrealized power." He hoped to start a center for Catholic married couples to live together in community while working for social justice, and he dreamed of beginning a school of social service to train lay activists, just as the YMCA trained young people to become local secretaries. With the help of a friendly bishop he launched such a school, for women, in 1914 but it failed for lack of funds. Later, with the endorsement of the AFL, he began a labor college, modeled on the socialist Rand School, but it too failed, this time for lack of support from the hierarchy.[43]

Dietz put his greatest efforts into the Militia of Christ for Social Service, an organization of Catholic leaders of the AFL. Peter Collins explained its purpose to Cardinal O'Connell: "At present there is no bridge between the church in America and the labor movement. The pulpit and the press speak to the individual only and existing Catholic societies are an imperfect medium. It is not possible to *take hold* of the labor movement in these ways. At a critical moment it would be very difficult for the church to influence a given situation. The Militia of Christ would have a disciplined array of responsible Catholic trade unionists prepared to act in concert at a moment's notice."[44] This sounded like a Catholic version of the socialist "boring from within" strategy; the Catholics were thus charged, but the Militia never lived up to its potential.

Formed at the 1909 AFL convention and formally approved by Archbishop Glennon the following year, the Militia eventually numbered 700 members, with Dietz as secretary and with an impressive board of directors. Only one of its local chapters was active; its major work was to meet at the annual AFL convention, hold a labor mass, and pass resolutions. With John Mitchell of the United Mine Workers as its most active leader, the organization strongly supported industrial unionism, resisted by the craft-dominated AFL. It also urged the hierarchy to make a pronouncement applying Leo XIII's teachings to American conditions. Cardinal Gibbons considered this request but failed to act on a draft message prepared by Dietz. Unfortunately, like so many other of Dietz's projects, the Militia did not fulfill its promise. Dietz got more support from the AFL leaders than he did from the hierarchy. Claims by some historians that the Militia played a key role in defeating socialism within the AFL have been exaggerated. Undoubtedly Dietz's presence, the labor masses, and the arranged addresses by clergy to the AFL conventions sustained the sense that the church backed the right to organize, supported legitimate union activity, and opposed socialism, but it was never a major factor in labor politics.[45]

In the period before World War I, Dietz was unusual in his strong support of trade unionism. Most Catholic leaders affirmed the principles of organization and collective bargaining but they went little further; reform interest was directed more at legislation. Locally there are only a few indications of labor activism. The most notable came in San Francisco, where Father Peter C. Yorke gave strong support to labor in the bitter conflicts that wracked the city early in the century. During a 1901 waterfront strike, when employers were using strikebreakers with police protection, Yorke responded to the union's plea for help, persuaded the governor to postpone use of the militia, then helped hammer out a pro-union solution that the governor imposed under threat of martial law. Faced with an anti-union press in the city, Yorke began a prolabor newspaper, through which he worked for labor unity and backed the United Labor Party, which came to dominate local politics. He urged the unions to stay independent and not become submerged in political action, but, at several critical moments in the party's history, Yorke helped keep its various factions united.[46]

If, with the isolated exceptions of Dietz and Yorke, backing for organized labor was general and unspecific during this period, there was growing interest in the broad cause of social reform. Dietz was not alone in dreaming of an American Catholic social movement or in hoping to use the hierarchy's fears of socialism to promote that objective. One of the most effective leaders of this movement was Father William Kerby. Sent to Germany to prepare for a teaching career in the new school of social science at Catholic University, Kerby, like Dietz, was impressed by Catholic efforts in Germany and elsewhere to give the working class an alternative to socialism. Writing from Germany in 1896 to Bishop John Keane, then still rector of the university, Kerby described his assessment of socialism:

> The principle underlying it is a true one, the lines in which men run in applying it are often sadly mistaken, but the principle is of such a character as naturally to arouse any man of mind and heart to enthusiasm. The proper policy for us is to grasp the principle clearly and strongly, to enter heartily into all that is right in it, to head off demagogues by surpassing them in true devotedness to the public welfare, and to captivate the multitude by showing them that we clearly understand their need and the principles by which they shall be met and that we are at heart their best friends.[47]

Kerby was as good as his word. Returning home to the university, he began popularizing the church's social teaching and familiarizing Catholics with European developments. To give expression to these teachings, he turned to Catholic charities at a moment when charitable work in the United States was undergoing a revolution. The history of Catholic charity presented a complex pattern of competition and cooperation. On the one hand, efforts by Protestants to use orphanages and relief programs to win converts, and on the other, the exclusion of the clergy from public institutions, had forced Catholics to develop their own services, especially in the East. In parts of the West and in many smaller cities, however, Catholic hospitals, orphanages and protectories were often the first and perhaps the only such institutions in the area and received broad public support. Even at the height of conflict between nativists and the church, Catholic institutions received public payments for the care of dependent children.

In the late nineteenth century, at the same time that the church was moving into a more clearly separatist direction in education, it was moving toward greater cooperation in charitable work. To cite but one example, after the Civil War Charles Loring Brace of New York, concluding that orphans and abandoned children should be raised in a country setting, established the New York Children's Aid Society, which Catholics accused of placing children in country foster homes without regard for their religious affiliation. As a result, through the Saint Vincent de Paul Society, Catholics established their own Catholic Home Bureau in 1898. A short time later the local branch of the society agreed to place a Catholic representative on the Committee on Dependent Children of the New York Charity Organization Society to clear up problems of duplication and overlap in investigating applications for the commitment of children as public charges. According to the representative this "resulted in creating a better and more intimate relationship between the two societies; cooperation has been more effectively developed."[48] Other forms of cooperation in social services followed rapidly. In 1902 Father Thomas Kinkead became chairman of the Committee on Dependent Children of the New York State Conference of Charities and Correction. By then the rule was to place children in institutions of their own faith. Catholic officials sometimes had to fight to see that this rule was enforced, especially when the children of new immigrants were involved, but the general direction of developments was toward cooperation.

Thomas Mulry, a prominent leader of Saint Vincent de Paul, admitted that Catholics were learning new methods from the professional social workers who were beginning to dominate public and nondenominational programs. Elsewhere Catholic leaders agreed that the church could not hope to meet the needs it confronted, especially in urban areas, so that it should welcome the more systematic approach professionals and reformers were advocating. At the same time Kerby and others at Catholic University were teaching the new social sciences to priests and sisters involved in charitable work, leading them to desire a more professional approach to social problems. The effect of cooperation and a developing professionalism among Catholics was two-fold. On the one hand it suggested the need to broaden the array of services available through the church. As Mulry put it:

> The children of the poor in congested districts are forced to spend more of their lives in the streets under conditions which are most harmful to their moral training, and the lack of nourishing food and sanitary conditions in the home attacks their vitality. To make complete the work inaugurated by our visits to the homes we must follow up the needs of the children by providing for their physical, mental and moral welfare. . . . To do this it will be necessary to establish boy's clubs, summer outings, etc. If we do not do this work the children will be drawn into the non-Catholic institutions of a similar character which now exist in all our large cities and our labors in the homes of these children will be fruitless.[49]

At the same time it drew Catholic leaders into groups like the National Conference of Charities and Corrections and the local branches of the Charity Organization Society, where they learned the new case work techniques of social work and came to share the growing conviction that the primary cause of most social problems was poverty, so that they should seek out its causes and arouse society to its obligations.

All of these efforts led to demands that Catholic charities become better organized. Throughout the nineteenth century there had been the Saint Vincent de Paul Society, with its untrained parish visitors, and a bewildering array of orphanages, hospitals, and protectories, usually run by religious orders, each raising its own money and fighting its own battles, as well as another set of networks of immigrant aid and mutual benefit societies sponsored by ethnic groups. The lay leaders of Saint Vincent de Paul in particular were becoming dissatisfied with this confusion and parochialism.

Mulry, who in 1907 served as president of the National Conference of Social Work, was the primary advocate of the need for trained social workers, for cooperation to avoid hostility and share in public funds, and for coordination to maximize resources. Finally, in 1910, the National Conference of Catholic Charities was born, with Kerby as its principal organizer. In its first fifteen years it struggled to overcome internal conflicts and local disputes, suspicion of non-Catholics and of government agencies, and traditional attitudes toward charity. Gradually more and more dioceses inaugurated central charitable offices to coordinate and professionalize local services, stimulated in part by the movement toward community chest campaigns in local communities. Unfortunately, centralization at the diocesan level meant a shift from lay to clerical leadership, as many believed only priests could persuade pastors and older organizations to cooperate. When John O'Grady succeeded Kerby as national secretary in 1920, the biggest problem was the aloofness of religious orders, who did 75 percent of the charitable work. Nevertheless, unlike education, charities were to be marked in the twentieth century by an ever greater efficiency in utilizing limited resources and by cooperation with other charitable organizations and eventually with government welfare programs.[50] More than any other area of institutional church life, charities reflected the continuing reality of a church called both to express its faith through its own life and to share in building the public life of the nation as a whole, the republican style smothered elsewhere throughout much of the century.

Kerby and others hoped, in the words of the Brooklyn charities leader, that the National Conference of Catholic Charities would "mark the beginning of a Catholic social reform movement on national lines." Its leaders believed that authentic charity presupposed justice, and that the injustices revealed through social services had to be eliminated if the goal of helping people build fully human lives was to be realized. In addition, they believed that the poor could not be expected to respond to the message of faith until they were relieved of suffering and destitution. One step in the direction of building a social movement was to develop a literature on Catholic social teaching, so in 1916 Kerby and his associates launched the *Catholic Charities*

Review. By that time the theoretical basis for a Catholic social movement in the United States had finally been provided by Kerby's Catholic University colleague, Father John A. Ryan.

John A. Ryan, even more than Kerby, was the theorist and organizer of Catholic social action in the twentieth century. Ryan was
born in rural Minnesota in 1869. He grew up in a midwestern Populist
area where he knew Ignatius Donnelly, read about Henry George, and
voted the Populist ticket in 1892. His first published articles, written
before he was ordained, denied an absolute right to private property,
and defended socialist objectives of just distribution. After reading
Rerum Novarum, he decided to devote his career to what he called
the "social gospel." Sent to Catholic University for graduate study,
he worked with Thomas Bouquillon and Kerby, from both of whom
he derived a passion for facts, for the concrete information needed
before making moral judgments. He was a self-taught economist,
drawing heavily on the first generation of American economic thinkers
such as Richard Ely, who were themselves influenced in many cases
by the Protestant Social Gospel movement.[51] For his doctoral disser-
tation, he applied Leo's XIII's doctrine of the living wage to the United
States. He not only determined the amount of income needed for a
person to live at a minimal level of decency, but he concluded that
competitive conditions would not allow that minimum to be reached
unless it was enforced by legislation. As an acknowledged national
expert he helped draft minimum wage laws in Minnesota and several
other states. Ten years later, in 1916, now a professor at Catholic University, he published *Distributive Justice,* a systematic examination
of the American political economy in light of the principles of Catholic
social teaching.[52]

What distinguished Ryan from every major figure in American
Catholic life until the 1950s was that he attempted to articulate a
moral evaluation of the American economy, and to suggest reforms,
in terms that were open to discussion and debate among all American
citizens. Lay people had been reformers, to be sure, but Matthew Carey
and Terence Powderly, when they attempted to connect their religion
with their reform proposals, did so with simple references to Scripture. Ryan rarely referred to Scripture, understanding almost by instinct that to accomplish a reform in society one had to prove it was
reasonable in terms of the norms of public life, whatever further obligations one might feel as a result of religious faith. Other priests
who became interested in social and political questions usually addressed a Catholic audience and spoke in terms of the authority of
the church and of the encyclicals. Ryan did a great deal of that as
well in order to convince Catholics to support reforms in their society.
But more than others he enlisted in the larger public debate, making

a case for a particular reform in light of American conditions and with reference to values shared with other Americans. He joined a variety of progressive organizations, from the Municipal Ownership League to, for a time, the American Civil Liberties Union. He corresponded with non-Catholic economists and social theorists, befriended politicians and reformers, and became a bridge between the church and the larger world of reform politics.

Ryan accepted the competitive economic system as he found it but rejected laissez-faire as an adequate descriptive or normative theory for understanding this system. Instead he developed a kind of welfare economics that made human needs the basis for evaluating the economy as a whole and any particular part of it. Morality itself only made sense in terms of deliberate, purposeful human action. Economic activity was human activity, and therefore subject to moral evaluation in terms of its intention and its effect. From the realistic radicalism of the Populists and Irish radicals he read in his youth, and from the empirical moral philosophy of Bouquillon and the nascent social science of Kerby, he had learned to look beneath the surface to find out exactly what were the purposes and effects of economic policies and institutions. From these sources, as well as from Leo XIII and the reform economists, he had derived a sense of responsibility to propose better ways of realizing morally acceptable objectives that all said they sought, such as meeting human needs and making it possible to put human rights into practice.[53]

The basis of Ryan's philosophy was natural law, the idea that "the laws governing human existence are to be found in the nature of man where the father of all things wrote them." Thus the living-wage argument began with human beings possessing basic rights, of which the most fundamental was the right to life and therefore to the means necessary to sustain life. In an industrial society, that right was only available through the wage system. Therefore the first claim on industry was a wage sufficient to allow a person to live at a minimal standard of decency. The notion of human rights as minimum conditions for life in society linked Catholics to all other Americans and provided common ground for the debate about policy. So did the teaching on private property which, as Ryan saw it, was conditional. The goods of the earth had as their purpose the fulfillment of human needs, so that the common right of use, or access, was absolute and took precedence over private rights of ownership. Private property could insure personal security and protection for family life, therefore there should be greater opportunities for people to own not only their homes but some productive property as well; this right must be exercised in such a way as not to obstruct the prior right of others to the means of sustaining life. There were thus three corollaries: the duties of ownership, the government's right to regulate for the common good, and, in extreme situations, common ownership. *Rerum Novarum* had defined a middle ground between laissez-faire liberalism and socialism, with labor unions and state intervention the basis for reasonable reform, Ryan agreed. Men and women had the right to organize to protect and implement their rights, and the government established to secure human beings in the possession of their rights had the obligation to establish the legal conditions that made justice possible. Justice included commutative justice; equity in exchange; distributive justice; equity in the assignment of burdens and benefits in an organized community; and general justice, the obligation to insure that the system within which men and women carried on their activities was itself just. In the end, good ethics was good economics; natural law led to the conclusion that what was morally right should also be economically practical, at least in the long run. If the ultimate end of human existence was union with God, the proximate end was the fullest development of the human person, and the two must be in harmony. Catholic missionary responsibility, therefore, had less to do with making all persons Catholic than with helping "to bring about the identification of morality and expediency in our industrial system, by persuading all classes that prosperity cannot be maintained unless the receivers of wages and salaries obtain a considerable increase in purchasing power."[54]

Ryan argued that all necessary social reforms were compatible with the teachings of the church. Avoiding the a priori demands of laissez-faire and socialism, Ryan believed that the degree of government intervention and the extent of further organization should be measured by the facts and by basic principles. Thus, granting the idea of the living wage, it was up to opponents to show another way of achieving it if not through legislation. Other forms of necessary state action included insurance against unemployment, accident, sickness and old age, arbitration and conciliation services, public housing, encouragement of migration to the land, regulation of natural monopolies, with public ownership or state competition if needed, a heavy tax on land value increase, and sharply graduated income and inheritance taxes. As for unions, they were indispensable: "No entire class or industrial grade of laborers has ever secured or retained any important economic advantage except by its own aggressiveness and its own powers of resistance, brought to bear upon the employer through the medium of force (economic) or fear." Overall, the distribution of wealth was the most important social question. In the pre–World War I days Ryan argued for a variety of ways to achieve more democratic control of and responsibility for the economy: unions, employer associations and trade agreements, producer and consumer cooperatives, stock and profit-sharing plans. In each case "the supreme aim must be to make the mass of wage earners, in some degree, owners and managers of capital."[55]

Ryan was an activist as well as a scholar. Like Dietz and Kerby, he was anxious to see the church play a more active role in dealing with the social question. Little had been done to apply *Rerum Novarum* in the United States; only a handful of bishops and priests had even made statements on social problems.[56] Simply to be good pastors, to understand the problems their people faced, priests should know more about the economy and about church teaching on social problems. From his post at Catholic University Ryan devoted a lifetime to educating Catholics, supporting social reform groups in the church, and nudging the bishops in progressive directions. His greatest opportunity came at the end of World War I, when the American bishops decided that they must respond to the many programs of social reform being issued by other groups in anticipation of post-war reconstruction. At the request of Father John O'Grady, Ryan turned over a speech he had prepared for delivery to a convention of the Knights of Columbus. With few changes it was published in the name of the hierarchy as "The Bishops' Program of Social Reconstruction."[57]

The "Bishops' Program" of 1919 was the first pronouncement by the American hierarchy on social and economic problems. It proposed continuation of wartime agencies for employment and the adjudication of labor disputes, it endorsed labor's right to organize and bargain collectively, and it called for the establishment of a government-sponsored program of insurance against unemployment, sickness, accident, and old age. The bishops endorsed experiments in stock and profit-sharing, cooperatives, and labor–management councils to share in industrial decision making. In short, it was a very progressive document, containing a summary of Ryan's positions, now given the backing of the American bishops. Ryan wrote his sister in May 1919:

> The Bishops' names are on the Reconstruction program because they made it their own and we all want it to have the authority that it derives from this fact. My name attached to it would defeat this purpose entirely. Most people who are acquainted with these matters know that I am sufficiently radical. What they did not realize is that such doctrines pass muster with the bishops. I think that this action of our bishops has given me more satisfaction than anything that has ever happened in relation to my work. It is a vindication of all the theories that my name has been associated with, and indirectly of all that I have done in this field.[58]

WORLD WAR I AND THE END OF REFORM

When World War I broke out in Europe, most Catholics supported President Woodrow Wilson's hope that the United States could remain neutral. German and Irish Catholics naturally had little sympathy with the Allies, while Catholic leaders were perhaps less inclined than other Americans to be influenced by British propaganda. Catholic newspapers in Indiana and Illinois were anti-British and so leaned toward the Central Powers in their sympathies, as did *America*, the Jesuit weekly, which attempted to evaluate the war from the viewpoint of the European church. The *Catholic World*, still a relatively liberal journal, was the most vocal supporter of the Allied cause. German Catholics strongly resisted suggestions that they would be influenced by ethnic considerations; Irish Catholics were more outspoken in their denunciations of the drift toward the Allies of the Wilson administration. Stung by their charges, Wilson blasted "hyphenates" as disloyal and publicly repudiated Irish nationalist leaders. In fact, most Irish voters continued to support the president in 1916.[59]

When the United States entered the war, however, the same factors that had reinforced neutrality operated to intensify support for the national cause. Fully aware of the divisions that had existed in the country, Wilson and his advisers engaged in a self-conscious policy of winning unanimous and unquestioning backing for the war effort, enlisting public opinion as they would enlist men and resources. Worried about public perceptions of Irish and German antiwar sentiment, the archbishops were unequivocal: "Moved to the very depth of our hearts by the stirring appeal of the President of the United States and by the action of our national congress, we accept wholeheartedly and unreservedly the decree of that legislative authority proclaiming this country to be in a state of war. . . . We stand ready . . . to cooperate in every way possible . . . to the end that the great and holy cause of liberty may triumph." To the national statement, Cardinal Gibbons added an even stronger appeal: "The primary duty of a citizen is loyalty to country. . . . It is exhibited by an absolute and unreserved obedience to his country's call." John Lancaster Spalding's argument about "double allegiance" and his resistance to imperialism were forgotten in the enthusiasm of this war to make the world safe for democracy. "Whatever Congress should decide should be unequivocally complied with by every patriotic citizen," Gibbons wrote. "The members of both Houses of Congress are the instruments of God in guiding us in our civic duty."[60] Paulist John J. Burke expressed the sentiments of many that they indeed wanted to be part of the nation at war: "We have a country—America, which is the land of our first and greatest love. Its interests for us are supreme. . . . We must be all in one, one in Christ, every part of the Church and the country in touch with the whole." In churches across the country "liberty sermons" were preached in churches and liberty bonds sold at the doors, while in a hundred diocesan newspapers the ·

message echoed as stated in Gibbons's *Catholic Review:* "The safety of the world and the preservation of human liberty demand the defeat of what Germany stands for."[61] In New York, where there was concern about the loyalty of the anti-British Irish, the *Catholic News* conveyed a similar message: "The voice of authority in the US is declared for war with Germany, and it is the duty of every American to stand ready to make whatever sacrifice needed in these trying days."[62] For some, at least, there may have been a touch less sincerity, and a bit more realism, than the words indicated. After a passionate attack on the British by an Irish priest in mid-1918, Cardinal Farley's secretary wrote privately: "No matter how true Father Maginness's statements and those of his friends may be, it is a fact that at the present time England is an ally of this country, and every American has got to recognize this. We need her and she needs us, and any agitation which tends to disturb the harmony of our alliance is bad for the country. His eminence cannot and will not permit anyone who represents the church in an official way to impugn the loyalty of American Catholics."[63]

The bishops were as good as their word. Initially the Knights of Columbus took the initiative in providing services for Catholics in the armed forces, but the bishops could not rest content with a lay group representing the church during the national mobilization. Prodded by Father Burke, Gibbons organized a series of meetings that resulted in the establishment of the National Catholic War Council, headed by the archbishops, to organize provision of chaplains, oversee the work of the Knights of Columbus, provide religious, social, and other services for military personnel, and represent the church in dealing with government agencies. When asked to serve as chairman of the committee to oversee war activities, Bishop Peter J. Muldoon wrote in his diary: "I hope we may be able to do something for God and country."[64] To raise money for these programs, the Catholics joined with Protestant and Jewish groups in a national campaign that Muldoon hoped "would do much to bring all classes and creeds together."[65] The drive took place in November 1918 and raised $205 million, of which the NCWC received 17.6 percent, which was spent on vocational rehabilitation, employment services, and Americanization campaigns. The success of the campaign, and the effectiveness of the NCWC's lobbying with government officials, impressed the bishops and gave hope that the new organization would continue after the war.[66]

As the reference to Americanization campaigns indicated, the war for the first time spurred the church to take steps to encourage the assimilation of its immigrant members. But the bishops left little to chance, often taking the initiative to develop citizenship campaigns in parishes and schools in order to forestall interference by public Americanization agencies. Even before the war Bishop Muldoon told the German Catholic Union of Illinois: "You can't be Germans or descendents of Germans in the United States, you must be Americans. The Germans, the Irish, the French, the Bohemians, and all others, must forget that they are anything but children of God and must work for God and their country, America. Good Catholics are good Americans." Wilson's commitment to self-determination provided a bridge for most Irish Catholics to support the war, while wartime hysteria forced some radical Irish nationalists into silence. Others remained active, petitioning Congress and holding a serices of Irish Race conventions to insure that the Irish issue would not be lost sight of. Wilson himself told Irish delegations he would do all he could for their cause, but his secretary of state, Robert Lansing confided to his diary that the issue was "loaded with dynamite."[67]

Irish skepticism about Wilson was confirmed when Wilson refused to force the issue of Ireland onto the agenda at Versailles. The result was an outpouring of Irish anger and a passionate backing of Irish freedom, which forced the hierarchy to join the cause.[68] When Irish leader Eamon de Valera visited in 1919, Catholic leaders flocked to honor him; at Saint Patrick's Church in Chicago he marched up the aisle with a surpliced choir amid the cheers of the congregation. This in turn aroused pro-British groups. Cardinal O'Connell addressed a massive rally of the Friends of Irish Freedom, pariahs during the war, and New York's Cardinal Hayes allowed widespread preaching on the subject in his churches. Bishop Muldoon told an audience in Illinois that British cruelties in Ireland surpassed those of the Germans. He was part of a delegation that met with Wilson and was outraged when the president said that presenting the issue at the peace conference would depend on circumstances.[69] A team of three prominent Irish Catholic laymen, all Democratic party leaders, pursued Wilson to Paris but were rebuffed by the president.[70] Most Catholic newspapers had passionately supported the war, but they turned against Wilson because of the Irish question; almost all Irish party leaders had condemned Wilson by the time the treaty arrived for ratification.[71]

The Irish question broke the church's connection with the Wilson administration but reinforced the determination of the leaders of the National Catholic War Council to continue some type of national organization after the war. Muldoon, who had played such an important role during the war, emphasized the need for some central direction of editors, teachers, even clergy, and for dealing with legislation. Burke, who had been the administrative head of the council, emphasized its use in combating prejudice as signs of a revival of anti-Catholicism appeared.

At the celebration of Cardinal Gibbons's golden jubilee in February

1919, the papal representative urged increased attention to education and social justice. Meeting after that event, the administrative committee voted to continue the organization, with the bishops meeting annually and using standing committees between these sessions. Eventually plans were drawn up for a renamed National Catholic Welfare Council, with permanent departments to deal with the press, social action, education, missions, and lay organizations. Gibbons had actively championed this step and called the decision one of the "measures which I regard as the most important since the Third Plenary Council of Baltimore." He told the bishops: "Our dioceses are well organized. But the Church in America as a whole has been suffering from the lack of unified force that might be directed to the furthering of those general policies which are vital to all."[72]

Cardinal O'Connell and several others had opposed the formation of the National Catholic War Council and they continued to fight the decision in Rome. The result was a ruling in 1922 that directed that the organization be abolished. Supporters rushed to its defense, petitioning the Vatican that "the Catholic Church in this country needs a central organization to promote and defend the interests of the whole Church in America." They pointed out that the NCWC had weight with "public men" because they saw it as "the authoritative voice of the united episcopate" and "the "effective voice also, which would carry with it the solid vote of the Catholic body, if Catholic interests were seriously menaced."[73] The petition was successful, although the Vatican required that the name be changed from "council" to "conference" to make clear its unofficial, noncanonical status. They emphasized the point: "In any case, for the peace of mind of those who have misgivings about united action it should be very well understood that the meeting is entirely voluntary and that Bishops are not in any way bound to attend these meetings, either in person or by representative."[74] Even with those limitations, however, the NCWC was positioned to exert great influence over the public position of the American church

In their petition, the bishops spoke of a desire to "create a united Catholic mind on social questions." They had presumably expressed that mind in their program, published the same year they decided to continue the NCWC, and by their appointment of Ryan to lead its new Social Action Department. But their pastoral letter, published later that year, was far more conservative in tone. It warned of increasing bureaucracy and reliance on government and gave special attention to what it took to be growing materialism and permissiveness, posing dangers to the family. These themes, not those of social reform, would dominate episcopal pronouncements in the decade that followed.[75]

In 1908 Ryan wrote that if the American clergy could not "understand, appreciate and sympathize directly with the aspirations of economic democracy, it will inevitably become more and more unChristian and pervert all too rapidly a larger and larger proportion of our Catholic population."[76] Fear of socialism, then, should spur progressive social action. But Ryan was not optimistic, not because the clergy and hierarchy were opposed to reform, but because most simply ignored the problems that made reform necessary. "There is scarcely any danger that the clergy of America will ever lose sympathy with the desire of the masses for industrial freedom and industrial opportunity," Ryan wrote, "but there is a very real danger that their sympathy will not be equalled by their knowledge. The great majority of our clergy in the United States have not yet begun to study systematically, or take more than superficial interest in, the important social problems of the age and country."[77]

Of course, the problem went deeper than that. The church in the United States had grown at an incredibly rapid rate and only now, with the end of unlimited immigration, would that growth slow down. The burdens of pastoral work were heavy, and the definition of the church's role had made that work heavily sacramental and organizational, the first through the desire to make practicing Catholics, the second by the commitment to schools. At the peak of the progressive movement, Father Joseph Selinger had written that it was the duty of priests "to do all in their power to work for social reform" but few did because "temporalities . . . so occupy them that the care for these unduly detracts their attention from the pressing social problems."[78]

There was another problem—the lack of interest of many middle- and upper-class Catholics. Ryan's brand of liberalism was far more challenging than John Ireland's, and many did not like it. There was widespread cricitism of the bishops' 1919 program, and of Ryan. When the new Social Action Department of the NCWC organized conferences on industrial problems in cities across the country, they invited lay and clerical experts and representatives of labor and management, but businessmen did not attend. Ryan admitted that after twenty years of experience he did not know how to remedy the problem.[79] This situation, of course, resulted from the fact that Ryan and other reformers generally wanted businessmen to pay workers more money and at least share responsibility for the firm with them. But it also stemmed from the same problems that limited the clergy; the thrust of church teaching and pastoral practice identified the church with religion and religious education, located moral responsibility largely around sexuality and family life, and thus made social and political matters at best interesting material for ethical reflection, at worst simply irrelevant to what it meant to be a Catholic Christian. Then and later the marginalized and discontented would look to the church for aid in changing social practices and institutions, but those who had benefited, or had hope to benefit, from those practices and institutions, were not inclined to enter into a dialogue still located at the margins of church life.

Finally, paternalism and elitism were so widespread in the church that they were hardly recognized. Unlike Ryan, Kerby and Dietz, most bishops and priests had become interested in social questions in large part out of fear of radicalism. Even when supporting reform, they did so to pacify society, alleviate discontent, and protect the workers against themselves. Speaking of the need for priests to address social issues, Father George Schmidt wrote in 1919: "The American priest, if he would be true to his calling as good shepherd, must use every legitimate means at his disposal to save society, to save America. The Catholic Church . . . alone can heal the cancerous wounds that must needs sap the life blood of our republic. . . . The duty of the America priest will be to guard his workingmen against the snares of a false society that proposes to heal their wounds and right their wrongs. He must give them the only true remedy, that proposed by the Catholic Church.[80]

Schmidt's self-assured confidence in the church was misplaced. In fact, in its response to the new situation that it confronted in the United States, the church had to a degree isolated itself from public life. It had emphasized an approach to grace, salvation, and meaning that made the organized, institutional church the center of human life and history. The priest who concentrated on "temporalities," and the lay person who believed bishops and priests should not deal with political or economic matters, both of whom were in much evidence in these years, were the products of those pastoral strategies and religious ideologies. So was the increasingly widespread arrogance that the church had all the answers, and all other approaches to life and society were dangerous, even self-destructive. Ireland and Hecker had opened one door to public life by suggesting that Divine Providence had a special mission for America, so that economic and political activity that contributed to the success of the American experiment had religious meaning. That door had been closed. Ryan opened another, more modest, with his use of natural law to offer a distinctive Catholic response to the common problems faced by all Americans. That door remained open, but for the moment too few were ready to walk through it. Not until a pastoral strategy came along that suggested that priests and people, along with workers and those who served them, could walk through together, not until democracy took on Christian significance, would a Catholic affirmation of "economic democracy" make sense.

CHAPTER
7
Social Catholicism

*I*n the two decades between the world wars, American Catholics continued to struggle with the problems of internal diversity, minority status, and uncertain relationships with their society. In the 1920s reformers found it difficult to go beyond the defense of the church and make active efforts to engage public issues. Indeed, there were now a significant number of intellectuals and church leaders who believed such engagement unnecessary, not because American institutions worked so well, but because modern culture was self-destructing and the church had only to wait for a disillusioned world to turn to Catholicism for the order and security that liberalism could not supply. As William Halsey, a scholar of Catholic intellectual life, has argued, American Catholics provided a self-confident remnant of innocence, believing that reality was essentially rational and harmonious, despite the increasing evidence to the contrary. Focusing on the problems of culture, Catholic spokespersons contended that only the church and its wisdom could any longer provide intellectual grounding and institutional support for traditional values of civility, decency, and morality, as well as the political principles of human rights and legitimate authority.

Moving from defense to offense, Catholics ignored what they regarded as an all but moribund Protestantism, concentrating instead on a secularism they thought its logical and historical successor. Insisting that the world left to itself would not be fit for human habitation, that secularism would lead inexorably to communism, they claimed to believe that Americans concerned for traditional values of family life, sexual restraint, social order, and political stability could find a home in the church.

For some the Great Depression seemed to prove the point; they regarded the collapse of the economy, and the rise of dangerous ideologies abroad, with a complacency that amounted to arrogance. But others, realizing that Catholics had to share responsibility for the problems before they could contribute solutions, welcomed the new debate about social justice as an opportunity both to promote Catholic acceptance in America and to contribute a real solution for the nation's problems. Finally, a new voice was heard, one more alert to the depth of the tragedies now plaguing Western civilization. Around a unique movement, the Catholic Worker, some Catholics would face the stark brutality of modernity without the masks of innocence, and offer a response at once prophetic and so Christian as to be outside the normal arena of discourse both in their country and their church. In the process they opened a new door to the ongoing debate about Catholicism and public life in a pluralist democracy.

THE POLITICS OF CULTURE

The population of the United States in 1920 reached 105 million, a tenfold increase in a century. Almost one-third of the American people were immigrants, about half of them Catholics. Americans were becoming city dwellers; slightly more than half the population, and three-quarters of the immigrants, lived in the forty-five American cities with a population of over 100,000. In those same cities 65 percent of the people were immigrants and the children of immigrants. City dwellers were still intensely mobile; only a third of urban households remained in the same residence from one ten-year census to the next.[1]

Rural, small-town Americans, most of them native-born Protestants, had always been wary of the cities. In the 1920s they once again rebelled against the urbanization of American politics and culture. The Klu Klux Klan, revived after the war, spread out of the South through the Midwest and the West, attracting even city dwellers with an appeal against blacks, Jews, and Catholics. The Eighteenth Amendment became a symbol of urban-rural, Catholic-Protestant divisions, despite the efforts of a tiny group of Catholic Prohibitionists. These two issues drove a deep wedge between the two major factions within the Democratic party. Its rural and southern wing, long loyal to William Jennings Bryan, turned its local attention to crusades against evolution, modernism, and Catholic power, and its national energies to checking the new assertiveness of its urban immigrant constituency centered around New York's Catholic governor, Alfred E. Smith. The 1924 Democratic convention was split down the middle by a platform plank condemning the Klan, then exhausted itself with a 103-ballot deadlock between Smith and the Bryanite candidate, William Gibbs McAdoo.

Problems of church and state still revolved around education, long considered a local and state responsibility, but for the first time these problems reached the national courts. In Michigan Catholics joined with Lutherans to beat back an attempt to force all children into public schools, but the Klan persuaded Oregon voters to approve an initiative petition requiring attendance at public schools.[2] Catholics, in alliance with other private school interests, challenged the law. Attorneys for the state argued that the "invidious poison" ruining the nation was "class hatred" that could be overcome by requiring "that the poor and the rich, the people of all classes and distinction and of all the different religious beliefs, shall meet in the common schools, which are the great American melting pot, there to become . . . the typical American of the future." In a landmark decision, the Supreme Court overturned the law, affirming the state's right to regulate and supervise education, but pointing out that

> the fundamental theory of liberty upon which all governments in this Union repose excludes any general power of the state to standardize its children by forcing them to accept instruction from public teachers only. The child is not the mere creature of the state; those who nurture him and direct his destiny have the right, coupled with the high duty, to recognize and prepare him for additional obligations.[3]

The long-standing Catholic contention that parents, not the state, had primary responsibility for the child's education, seemed vindicated, but only the right to conduct independent schools was assured.

The most important effect of the war on the church was to revive the old problem of Americanizing the immigrant. In earlier years Catholic leaders had been satisfied that parishes and schools assisted immigrant adjustment to the new society by strengthening family life, instilling a sense of moral restraint, and directly teaching American ideals of patriotism and good citizenship. During the war, partly to fend off local efforts to pressure immigrants toward conformity, church leaders, who had previously done very little to directly promote Americanization, inaugurated a variety of citizenship programs aimed especially at new immigrant populations.

After the war, fears of radicalism, employer efforts to divide and suppress the labor movement, and the revival of anti-Semitic and anti-Catholic nativism led to immigration restriction biased against southern and eastern Europeans. The church, in response, intensified its Americanization campaigns. Backing for local efforts was a major item on the agenda of the new Social Action Department of the National Catholic Welfare Conference. John Lapp, the director of the campaign, attempted to combine civic education with Catholic social teaching because "no plan short of complete social justice should be held as a goal in programs of good citizenship or Americanization."[4] Within the church the hierarchy once again took steps to limit ethnic divisions; in Chicago, for example, Cardinal Mundulein refused to approve formation of additional national parishes and enforced regulations requiring instruction in English in parochial schools. At a 1920 meeting the hierarchy received a petition requesting appointment of six Polish auxiliary bishops. They decided to reply with firmness "that a racial church would not be tolerated in the United States." Referring to earlier fights, Gibbons reiterated an old theme: "Ours is the American church, and not Irish, German, Italian or Polish—and we will keep it American." Commenting, Bishop Muldoon indicated how important the relation between external attack and internal unity remained: "This unanimous action of the hierarchy will, I think, settle all such tendencies for a long time to come. What a patchwork we would be with national churches. It is against the spirit of the country and would be used against us by non-Catholics."[5]

An American church, that was what restless Poles were to accept, but also a Catholic church, still seeking to build bonds of community and promote an understanding of membership that set clear limits to just how American its members might become. Indeed, since the Americanist crisis Catholic intellectuals had become ever more convinced that there was a fundamental conflict between the church and modern culture. Being a Catholic was more than being a member of one religious denomination among many; it constituted participation in an alternative way of life that encompassed all aspects of a person's existence. Everyone "insisted more emphatically than ever on the organic wholeness of Catholic truth and contrasted it more sharply to the prevailing secularist order that was plunging mankind headlong toward destruction, " historian Philip Gleason writes. In 1933 the College and University Department of the National Catholic Educational Association declared that "because a materialistic attitude and philosophy have dominated secular education, giving it a divided and distorted view of life, from which God and morality have been excluded, the Catholic colleges emphatically assert that their function is to give a totality of view regarding life, in which God and the things of God have their proper place." Two years later one of this organization's committees concluded that "the Catholic college will not be content with presenting Catholicism as a creed, a code, or a cult. Catholicism must be seen as a culture."[6]

For one who absorbed this all-encompassing sense of Catholicism, the give and take of politics and mundane disputes about economics seemed crass evidence of the divisiveness and mediocrity of modern culture. James J. Walsh became famous among Catholics for his best-selling book *The Thirteenth, The Greatest of Centuries*. When he wrote a book about Italy he dedicated it to Mussolini, who had "certainly worked some miracles in transforming the country, and he has done it exactly by suppressing politics and giving Italians a chance to think about other things."[7] This view left little room for Ryan's somewhat detached, objective, and public approach to social problems, which came close to compromising this integral Catholicism. Sociology and social work had to be Christain, examining problems in the light of church teaching, offering solutions aimed first at salvation, which meant union with the church, and acknowledging spiritual means for overcoming social ills. In literature and the arts, like the social sciences, there was a Catholic point of view that included an understanding of human nature, clear stands on a variety of issues, even a program of reform.[8]

Nor was this simply a set of abstract ideas, unrelated to Catholic life. Sulpician provincial John Fenlon told historian Peter Guilday in 1926 that "the greatest recent change in American Catholicism it seems to me is the development of the organization of the church" through such groups as the Catholic Educational Association, the National Conference of Catholic Charities, the Catholic Hospital Association, the still-growing Knights of Columbus, and the diocesan organizations affiliated with the National Councils of Catholic Men and Catholic Women associated with the NCWC.[9] There were now organizations for Catholic philosophers, historians, poets, artists, doctors, nurses, lawyers, and librarians. Liberal Catholics had long desired fuller organization. As early as 1906 John Burke had told William Kerby that the laity lacked "group consciousness and group enthusiasm" because "the organization of the church" had rendered them "complete externs." They needed an inspiring invitation to take "an active, personal part in the organization."[10] In 1924 Ryan still dreamed of "how we Catholics could affect the country had we unity and leadership and judgement."[11] But the organizational drive of the twenties reflected the vision of an organic Catholicism set off against the world, not the apostolic and public-spirited enlistment in national debate for which Burke and Ryan kept working.

Indeed, on the defensive again and told constantly of the need for loyalty and unity, intelligent Catholics felt removed from the central issues of their time. Returning from the Scopes trial, where fundamentalist William Jennings Bryan clashed with the secular rationalism represented by Clarence Darrow, Michael Williams, the editor of a new lay journal, *Commonweal*, felt depressed. "Indeed, to visit Dayton is, for a Catholic, to realize how isolated and remote is the historic tradition and reasoned theology, the age tested philosophy and scholarship of the Catholic Church, in American life today," Williams wrote. "Oh, for a Newman in the United States! Oh, for a really national Catholic voice, or Catholic movement, explanatory of Christianity and competent to meet thoughtful and enquiring minds on a level of intellectual expression commensurate with the needs of the time."[12]

Of course, Catholic isolation was not entirely self-inflicted. Ryan, for example, found his public stance more difficult in the 1920s not only because it was an era of what he called "naked and brazen industrial feudalism" but also because of the hostility to Catholics, not just on the part of the Klan but also of more respectable Americans.[13] When Mexico's anticlerical government closed Catholic schools, suppressed religious orders, and attacked priests and nuns, Ryan thought Americans concerned about religious liberty should rush to their defense. He was outraged when prominent non-Catholic progressives like Norman Thomas and Roger Baldwin of the American Civil Liberties Union made excuses for the Mexican regime, arguing that the church's reactionary role historically made such actions understandable. Ryan resigned in anger from the ACLU after clashing with its leaders not only over this issue but over birth control and extreme definitions of free speech.[14] Ryan insisted that Americans should advocate not their own liberal standards but univeral norms of human needs and human rights. "If this position is given up, liberalism goes with it," he told Thomas. If one condones persecution because one does not like the policies of the victims, you have "simple toryism," for "the quintessence of the tory attitude is the belief that oneself and one's friends should have all the liberty that they desire and that other people should have all the liberty that is good for the other people. How much liberty is good for other people is to be determined, of course, by the tory."[15] Thomas was "amused" to be lectured by a Catholic, although he admitted that if Ryan's ideas represented those of his church, he "would have an entirely different view of things."[16] Caught between Catholic demands for orthodoxy and loyalty and the demand of his liberal friends that he distance himself from unacceptable elements in his church, Ryan was in a difficult position, one not uncommon for twentieth-century Catholics.

Ryan's argument reflected serious problems even among those most determined to lead the church toward public responsibility. He and other liberal Catholics had given strong support to Williams when he launched the *Commonweal* in 1924. Williams had grown up in Canada and was educated by the Jesuits. He left the church, became a sea captain for a time, and later a struggling writer, before returning to the church after reading the autobiography of Saint Theresa of Lisieux, "the Little Flower." He worked for the NCWC during the war, then wrote a book about the Catholic wartime experience. In 1922 he began enlisting support for "a new literary review, a weekly edited by laymen, and quite unattached to official authority, but thoroughly Catholic in its policy and atmosphere, a review aimed at cultivated readers within and without the Church, but particularly without.[17] Fully aware of the internal preoccupations of so many churchmen, Williams hoped the new journal would convey "the Catholic outlook, as distinct from what might be called the Catholic inlook."[18]

With able writers and editors like George Shuster, Richard Dana Skinner, and Carlton J. H. Hayes, *Commonweal* struggled mightily to articulate a Catholic message at the center of American politics and culture. But, like Ryan, *Commonweal* found that too often neither side, Catholics or the general public, appreciated its mediating role and, depending on a Catholic audience, and on friendly bishops and priests, it was forced to regularly assert its faithful adherence to what had become the necessary elements of Catholic loyalty. Commenting on a meeting of the National Council of Catholic Men, the nation's largest lay organization, the editors made it clear that the most vocal lay-people knew their place: "All social and intellectual matters necessarily stem from and are only to be safely guided by the spiritual and moral principles held and guarded by the ecclesiastical authority of the Church" and on "spiritual and moral matters" the clergy are "the sole responsible leaders of the Catholic body."[19]

Historian Peter Guilday backed the *Commonweal* project because he was worried about Catholic isolation. "We are not being strengthened in our Americanism. Even the word has a bad meaning," he told a friend.[20] Guilday and other liberal Catholics understood that to awaken an interest in the public mission of the church required more than a proud sense of Catholic history and a self-rightous assertion of a separate Catholic culture. Catholics must feel at home in their country and consider its problems their own. This meant its own Americanization. Catholics should "keep sacred national ideals by the Americanization of every element within the land," he wrote in 1925.[21] There could be no talk of "double allegiance" when that very charge was used to challenge a Catholic's campaign for the White House. As Frederick Kinsman wrote in 1924: "Catholics are bound to oppose anything contrary to the law of God and were there anything of that sort in the American Constitution they would oppose it. But there neither is, nor is likely to be. Discussion of the attitude of Catholics toward the Constitution is truly academic. . . . It is assumed that American institutions are in conformity with the law of God."[22] More important, for liberal Catholics, the values of Catholic culture were identical with those of authentic Americanism. "Democracy and equality, thus rightly understood, are the ideals of America and the ideals of the Catholic Church," *Commonweal* editoralized. "How wild therefore the idea that Americanism and Catholicism are, or can be, contradictory! They are really the only two conceptions of man which see eye to eye; hence the better Catholic, the better American."[23]

The pressures of the 1928 campaign, however, demonstrated how difficult it was to make this case as long as the definitions of authority and Catholic culture of the Americanist and modernist episodes remained in place. John Ryan was not the only one to have problems with his liberal friends during the decade. When architect and *Commonweal* supporter Ralph Adams Cram challenged John J. Chapman about the latter's criticism of the election of a Catholic to the Harvard Board of Overseers, Chapman responded that Klan violence was unfortunately discrediting a profoundly important cause, for the church was "drilling its adherents into contempt for American institutions."[24] The *Christian Century*, the voice of liberal Protestantism, agreed, leaving *Commonweal's* editors worried.[25] Of course, the bishops continued to deny there was a problem. Cincinnati's Archbishop John T. McNicholas reiterated the long-standing claim: "There never can be a conflict in which American Catholics will be obliged to choose the Pope and reject their own country, so long as the United States is governed by its present constitution and its traditions of religious liberty."[26]

But Ryan was more honest, setting forth the teaching in its most worrisome form:

> But constitutions can be changed, and non-Catholic sects may decline to such a point that the political proscription of them may become feasible and expedient. What protection would they have then against a Catholic State? The latter could logically tolerate only such religious activities as were confined to members of the dissenting groups. It could not permit them to carry on general propaganda nor accord their organizations certain privileges that had formerly been extended to all religious corporations, for example, exemption from taxation.[27]

Ryan wrote these words when he was concerned to demonstrate his orthodoxy; he wanted to avoid the charge of minimizing doctrine made against Hecker and Ireland, and he insisted that the teaching would only apply in an overwhelmingly Catholic country, of which there were few if any left in the world.[28] During the 1928 campaign few Catholics could admit the truth of Ryan's summary of church teaching, but privately many knew he was right.

Charles C. Marshall used Ryan's statement, and the texts on which it was based, in his famous attack on Al Smith. The latter's reply, written by Father Francis P. Duffy, reiterated the many episcopal statements like McNicholas's. Peter Guilday, who told a critical non-Catholic historian that the basic principles of human rights taught by the church were compatible with American institutions,[29] told a friend that Smith's response was a "tissue of heresies."[30] Writing privately to another Catholic who had blasted Marshall in the magazine *Current History*, Guilday said that the debate centered on two questions: did the church teach that "the perfect social and political condition of mankind, living under organized government, is a union of Church and State" and did such a union "implicitly and for all practical purposes place the political government of a State at the mercy of those who represent the Church, namely Churchmen." In Guilday's opinion, there was "only one honest answer to these two questions and that answer corroborates all that Mr. Marshall said, and did not say, out of charity or forethought." As a historian he thought this answer obvious. If it could be shown that "the Church ever avoided the consummation of such a union" or "in a single case" did not where it existed "interfere with the normal processes of free government" then "Catholics would have a right to argue the problem." The only answer was "a vulgar one": that other denominations, when they could, sought the same union.[31] Later he told a young woman who was thinking of writing a biography of Duffy: "No one would dare (in print) to vindicate the theology of that Answer. It is the letter of an opportunist and if you make it a focus, too many theological eyes would find flaws."[32] Given the state of things, one of Guilday's correspondents wondered:

> If this were a Catholic nation, with a long line of Catholic Presidents, I believe that we Catholics would regard with dread the election of a Protestant, and we would take . . . means of preventing his election. Likely we could have a Catholic KKK. Protestantism enthroned in the highest office would constitute a menace for us, as a Catholic enthroned would be a menace for Protestants, and by far a greater menace, on account of Rome (and this I say with all due apologies to Smith's reply to Marshall). May I ask, were you a Protestant, knowing as well as you do the relations of Catholics and the Pope, would you vote for a C. President? Frankly, I would not.[33]

Michael Williams told Cardinal O'Connell after the election that it was a "political disaster" and wrote another correspondent that "my work during the last few weeks has brought a revelation of the depth, strength, extent, force and bitterness and organized character of the anti-Catholic movement for which all my years of experience had not prepared me."[34] Later historians would question whether the race was decided by religion, but contemporaries were not so sure. A few days after the election the great progressive Senator George W. Norris wrote his friend Felix Frankfurter that religion was "the one thing that resulted in the overwhelming victory of Mr. Hoover" and he worried about the results. "In this campaign we have sown the seeds of religious hatred and the fruits will be born generations after we have passed away. We have practically amended the Constitution by saying that no Catholic shall be President of the United States."[35] Many Catholics surely believed that; few, unfortunately, were prepared to face in public the problem so evident in Ryan's book and in Peter Guilday's conscience.

THE EMERGENCE OF SOCIAL CATHOLICISM

The 1930s were the golden age of Catholic social action. With 25 percent of the nation's labor force unemployed, the farmers in revolt, and the banks closing, no further arguments were needed to justify consideration of the social teachings of the church. If a sense of citizenship or pastoral sensitivity were not enough, there was the evident fact that a church that had exanded rapidly, sometimes beyond its resources, in the 1920s, would be badly hurt by declining contributions. Whatever the reasons, Catholics shared with other Americans a profound sense of crisis. The normally conservative James Gillis, editor of the *Catholic World*, reminded his readers in 1931 that people in desperate straits were justified if they stole to feed themselves and their families. "If capitalism, is concerned about perpetuating itself," Gillis warned, "it had better devise an easier and more humane method of distributing the resources of the earth, and it had best be done quickly."[36]

Archbishop McNicholas told his people that the surplus wealth of the rich "belongs to the poor." When one person assisted another who was without the means of subsistence, he was "merely giving him what he has a right to demand." The government, McNicholas wrote, was obliged to see that no one starved; if needed, "a confiscation of excess wealth" was "wholly in harmony with the principles of social justice."[37] Even Cardinal O'Connell, when asked about rich Catholics who had not contributed to charity campaigns, responded that "great numbers of rich men should be flogged."[38]

The sense of crisis peaked during the early days of President Roosevelt's New Deal. "It seems to me we are passing through an almost revolutionary change in points of view and in methods," labor leader John Frey wrote Bishop Francis W. Howard of Covington. "We are attempting the greatest national experiment in government short of dictatorship. . . . If this method of free men working through free institutions fails, then it seems to me that there will be either something in the nature of a dictatorship or of a popular revolt, a revolution . . .

which will result in destroying the governmental mechanism by which free men endeavor to carry on self-government."[39] Howard agreed, writing a few months later that the country was dominated "by a social mentality that sees the market, and not the dignity and welfare of the producer, as the sole end of the production of wealth."[40]

Understandably, Catholic interest in social justice came in a flood compared to what had gone before. Oil executive I. A. O'Shaughnessy founded a League for Social Justice to promote reform among Catholics, and it spread to forty dioceses in two years. By 1938 the NCWC had held seventy Catholic conferences on industrial problems in cities around the country.[41] With the help of the council's Social Action Department many dioceses also sponsored social action days for priests to familiarize them with the social message of the church. The National Catholic Rural Life Conference, founded in the 1920s, led what amounted to an agrarian movement, challenging national agricultural policy and the growth of corporate farming and exploring alternatives in cooperatives, subsistance homesteads, and rural resettlement.[42] Jesuit John LaFarge launched a campaign against racial prejudice and helped found interracial councils to promote understanding and equality.[43] Baroness Catherine de Hueck also joined the interracial apostolate with Friendship House, first in New York, then in other cities. Black Catholics spoke up for themselves through he Federation of Colored Catholics.

The decade also brought the culmination of charities organizations. Boston's Catholic Charities Bureau expanded its relief activity from $85,000 in 1930 to $461,000 in 1940, while Saint Vincent de Paul budgets rose from $155,000 to over $500,000. After a decade of resistance, both joined the Greater Boston Community Fund in 1931.[44] Charity leaders also continued to push for legislation to fight the causes of poverty. First they called for federal assistance to relieve distress, then they pledged their support to Roosevelt in "the titanic effort he is making for the reconstruction and well being of our beloved land."[45] Robert Keegan, president of the National Conference of Catholic Charities (NCCC), said in 1936 that American Catholic charitable work had passed through two periods, the first humanitarian, lasting until 1910, and the second concerned with technique, beginning with the organization of the conference that year; it was now in a third period, that of justice. According to national secretary John O'Grady, the NCCC was calling for a "drastic overhauling of the present economic structure."[46] By joining community-wide fund-raising projects, Catholic charities laid the basis for cooperation in dealing with the crisis of the depression.

Robert Lucey, while serving as director of Catholic Charities in Los Angeles, had been drawn to public service as well. He served on the board of the California State Welfare Department, on the Los Angeles Housing Commission, and on the Committee on Industrial Problems of the American Association of Social Workers. Such experiences enabled social-service professionals not only to lobby more effectively for state and federal action, but also to preserve a role for private and church-sponsored agencies as the American welfare state began to take shape. Welfare programs, now so obviously needed, could be administered by state and local government, with the federal government supplying financial backing where necessary, with the services themselves provided in many cases by private institutions and agencies.[47]

The most common explanation of the depression was a moral one. In 1931, the bishops denounced unemployment as a "moral tragedy" and called for "such a change of heart as will . . . so organize and distribute our work and wealth that no one would lack for any long time the security of being able to earn an adequate living".[48] In a series of editorials, *Commonweal*, for example, denounced the selfishness revealed in the immediate shift of business from the welfare capitalism of the twenties to the jettisoning of workers and closing of plants. "Greed, selfishness, pride . . . these are the evil roots of all economic problems of the world," the editors argued. "Not until the principles taught by religion guide the counsels of men will those counsels issue in the permanent improvement of society."[49]

The crisis provided an opportunity for Catholics to win a hearing if they would live up to their religion and "use some of the dynamite which is inherent in her message."[50] The long task of proving that Catholicism supported all aspects of American life was suspended; few writers doubted that a moral assessment would yield any but negative judgments about the American political economy.

Unlike 1891, in 1931 American Catholics could hear the critical voice of the pope. When Pope Pius XI published his encyclical *Quadragesimo Anno*, Father Paul Blakely of *America* said that "our industrial system repudiates nearly every principle upon which the Pontiff lays emphasis."[51] The encyclical was subtitled *On the Reconstruction of the Social Order*, because the pope proposed as an alternative to capitalism and socialism a corporatist economy modeled on preindustrial guilds. Based on "occupational groups" that included both workers and owners, the system was designed to place the common good above competing interests. The term "social justice" first appeared in Catholic teaching in the 1931 encyclical; it represented that quality of justice that concerns the common good, which should be a governing criterion for individual and corporate decisions. Experience taught that competing interests were not likely to place the good of the community before their own interest, or to recognize the economic rights of workers and consumers, unless the system allowed them to do so without being destroyed by less moral competitiors. More fundamental change was needed if it was to be possible to fulfill basic human needs, eliminate wasteful competition, and subordinate the economy to human purposes, while avoiding the destruction of individual rights under socialism.

Elements of the pope's plan found their way into the policies of various Fascist states, notably Portugal and Austria, but John A. Ryan and other American Catholics adapted it to American conditions. They proposed a plan for a self-governing political economy that Ryan called "economic democracy." Independent trade unions and employer associations would move beyond collective bargaining to jointly determine industrial policy. With other organized agricultural and professional bodies, these industrial councils would determine broader economic policy, including economic planning, with the state playing only an initiating and supervisory role. Unionization, cooperatives, stock and profit-sharing schemes, all were now seen as steps toward a the long-range goal of a self-governing economy. Among its many benefits, this system would give workers a stake in their jobs and their industry, ending the dependency and exclusion from responsibility that came with the loss of control over property and jobs under capitalism. As the bishops put it, the plan looked toward "an organic society in which the individual, through the instrumentality of his group, works for himself, his group and the entire social body." The plan also provided a way of answering the criticism that the pragmatic test, calling in the government when the private sector failed to deliver justice, would inevitably lead to bureaucracy and state control. It provided a way to make social justice more than words; if individuals, unions, corporations, and interest groups were to take the common good into consideration, there had to be a structure that encouraged them to do so, a structure that allowed their participation in economic decisions, now denied to all but owners and the strongest unions and organized interest groups.[52]

Ryan's economic democracy became the centerpiece of offical Catholic social teaching. His assistant at the NCWC's Social Action Department, Raymond McGowan, less interested in policy than Ryan, more interested in education, laid out the parameters. Every worker should belong to a labor union, every employer to a employers' association; wages, hours, and working conditions should be determined by collective bargaining, but each side should work toward partnership, with labor sharing in ownership, control, and responsibility; finally, there should be a system of organization "around separate industries and occupations for the national and regional planning and adminstration of industry by every element of industry, labor included."[53]

This was a long-range goal. In the midst of the depression Catholic leaders adopted a pragmatic approach. Inhibitions about bureaucracy were shelved, at least temporarily. The Catholic press was all but unanimous in calling for positive government action and rejecting as immoral arguments about the autonomy of the marketplace. Most outspoken was Ryan. He had upheld the right to a living wage and now went further. "The workers have a claim upon industry for all the means of living, from the time they begin to work until they die," he wrote in 1931. "When industry does not do it directly . . . then it is the business of government to enforce it upon industry."[54] "Governments should do their best, not least, to look after their stricken people in the time of a famine, and that is what this is," wrote Mayor Frank Murphy of Detroit. "There is a responsibility there, because governments are set up for that purpose because governments represent all the people and when help comes from the government, it comes from those who have given, with their flesh and blood, to make the land just what it is."[55] Or, as *Commonweal* put it, the American government was "dedicated to the people not to a theory," and the future would depend on what use Americans made of their "collective powers."[56]

Catholic journalists and writers greeted the advent of New Deal with universal enthusiasm. The way had been prepared by Ryan, who had argued for a decade that national prosperity was bound to be short lived because of overproduction and lack of consumer purchasing power. The depression proved his case and reinforced his conviction that both moral and economic theory led to the same conclusion: redistribution of income alone could bring prosperity and justice. Denouncing President Hoover as incompetent, he advocated a huge program of public works, lower interest rates, unionization, and national wage and hour legislation.

When Roosevelt became president, Catholics were unanimous in their support. "Practically every act of Mr Roosevelt's has been motivated by a Christian philosophy," wrote editor Partick Scanlan of the normally conservative Brooklyn *Tablet*, and *Sign* praised the president's "forthright and genuine Christian sentiments."[57] Comparisons of the New Deal and papal teaching focused particularly on the government-sanctioned codes of fair competition drawn up under the National Industrial Recovery Act. *Catholic Action*, official organ of the NCWC, thought it "a matter of some congratulations for Catholics that some of the most important proposals in the encyclical have been at least partially incorporated in the law."[58] Putting aside their long-

standing fears of government power, the editors of *America* and the
Catholic World and organizations like the National Catholic Alumni
Federation and the NCCC enthusiastically urged their readers to back
the president. For Ryan, the NRA seemed the culmination of his career. Not only did the program implement his lifelong goal of a living
wage but it involved "a complete break with the system of free enterprise and competition." The codes and the authorities set up to
administer them seemed to Ryan to approximate the papal system.
"With greater representation and authority provided for labor, they
could readily be developed into an industrial system which could be
in complete accord with the social order proposed by the Holy Father."[59]

Ryan became and remained a thorough and consistent New Dealer.
Appointed by Roosevelt to a number of administrative posts, including
the Industrial Appeals Board of NRA, Ryan reciprocated by defending
the New Deal against Catholic criticism. "Never before in our history,"
he insisted, "have government policies been so deliberately, formally
and consciously based upon conceptions and convictions of moral
right and social justice."[60] Father Raymond McGowan, Ryan's assistant, was also enthusiastic about the New Deal but, to a far greater
extent than Ryan, he noticed the very great differences between the
reform legislation and papal teaching. The encyclicals, for McGowan,
provided Catholics with a yardstick against which to measure American practices. By such a standard the NRA was clearly inadequate;
it gave "undue initiative and power" to "organized employers" and
failed to compel union organization and participation in the formulation and administration of the codes. While the NRA drew a
disproportionate share of Catholic attention, other phases of the New
Deal were also examined. Agricultural policy received little attention
in the Catholic press, but comments on the Agricultural Adjustment
Act were generally favorable. The Tennessee Valley Authority was
endorsed by *America*, and *Catholic Action* regarded it as "a vast experiment in Christian sociology." Other journals supported proposals
for public housing and food and drug regulation. Considerable attention was given to subsistence homesteads as a way of providing for
those left out of work by technological changes.[61]

The right of each person to the means of earning a decent livelihood
was a basic principle of Catholic teaching and led to general support
for social insurance. Disagreement arose over the relative roles of federal and state governments and the problem of contribution; some
argued that the entire cost of unemployment insurance should be paid
out of general taxation and others that the cost be borne by industry.
Nevertheless, there was broad and enthusiastic support for the Social
Security Act of 1935. Catholic activist John A. Lapp, for example,

thought social security "the greatest achievement of the present administration, or of any administration in half a century."[62] Throughout the first two years of the New Deal then, American Catholicism spoke with a high degree of unanimity on behalf of social and economic reform. Interested Catholics found in papal teaching ample justification for government action. Applying the principle of subsidiarity, few could see any alternative to stronger intervention by the national government into the nation's economic life. Dean Paul Kiniery of Loyola University in Chicago, for example, argued that the only alternative to government regulation was domination by big business, plutocracy, which would necessarily benefit selfish interests. Catholics, he felt, should present a united front favorable to social legislation, recognizing that the social disruption that would result from continued distress posed a far greater threat to the church than did a stronger federal government.[63] Bishop Bernard Mahoney of Sioux Falls summed up the case. "The Church, the great guardian of human liberties, sees nothing in the recent enactment over which to be alarmed," he wrote. "Despite the possibility of future abuses, a possibility that will always confront us, she can safely place her stamp of approval in the interests of social justice upon the broad and humane philosophy that underlies the national legislation of the changing social order of America today."[64]

By far the most effective Catholic spokesman was the radio priest Charles E. Coughlin, whose weekly sermons on the theme of "want in the midst of plenty" echoed the shock and disillusionment felt by many Americans. A Canadian by birth, Coughlin began religious broadcasts in Detroit in 1926. In the fall of 1930 he dramatically altered the subject matter, telling his listeners that the depression had aroused his concern about the un-Christian character of the nation's political and economic life. He attacked the policies of the Hoover administration, blamed the depression on "international bankers," and, after moving to a national network in 1931, built an audience estimated at ten million. He offered a powerful expression of discontent: "In our country, with its lakes and rivers teeming with fish; its mines heavy with minerals; its banks teeming with money, there are approximately five million unemployed men walking aimlessly through the streets of our cities and the by paths of our country sides seeking not doles but labor."[65] Lashing out at politicians and bankers, Coughlin charged that American democracy had degenerated into "a form of plutocracy and gang rule."[66]

Although Boston's conservative Cardinal O'Connell called Coughlin a "demagogue," most American Catholics shared the radio priest's sense of crisis and even the most respectable publications denounced "plutocracy" and "pagan individualism." Years later Richard Deverall, a self-described Catholic radical in the 1930s, recalled how, Sunday after Sunday, Coughlin "thundered at the evil of overproduction while human beings starved. He hammered at the Republican Party, at President Herbert Hoover, at the classic doctrines of liberalism and the Manchester school which had helped bring America to its knees and capitalism to its doom."[67] When Coughlin told his listeners in 1932 that it was "Roosevelt or ruin," most articulate Catholics appeared to agree. When Al Smith belittled the New Deal's economic policies in 1934, Coughlin attacked him unmercifully, pledging: "I will never change my philosophy that the New Deal is Christ's deal." Coughlin backed the president for two years, but by 1935 he had moved into opposition, angered by Roosevelt's refusal to nationalize the banks or adopt an inflationary monetary policy.[68]

In 1934 Ryan told a Detroit audience that Coughlin was "on the side of the angels," but a year later he told Michael Williams that "the business of stirring up the animals has been sufficiently done." Coughlin had awakened people to the problems, Ryan believed, but he had "no positive and effective remedy to offer them."[69] Of course, in attacking Roosevelt Coughlin was challenging not only Ryan, whom he belittled as "the Right Reverend New Dealer" but the mass of Catholic voters who had now become an important component of the Democratic party's new political majority. Roosevelt had built on the success of Alfred E. Smith in attracting "new immigrants" to the polls and to the party.[70] In 1936 a public opinion poll demonstrated that 66 percent of Catholics favored President Roosevelt, a proportion exceeded only by Jews and Baptists.[71] In part this resulted from the fact that many New Deal programs improved the lot of those classes among whom Catholics were heavily represented. In addition, Roosevelt gave recognition to Catholic political influence by appearing at Catholic ceremonies, consulting Catholic ecclesiastical leaders, appointing Catholic laymen to high administration positions, and inviting some prominent clergy to serve on advisory boards and commissions.

The attraction many Catholics felt toward the New Deal was generally reinforced by their most articulate religious leaders between 1933 and 1936 when the pressures of the depression at least temporarily reduced minority fears and made church leaders receptive to the use of government power to alleviate suffering and unemployment, restore prosperity, and reform American business practices. When those pressures relaxed, however, older fears reemerged.

The most frequent criticism was the old one of federal encroachment on personal liberties and state independence. Growing concern about centralization and the radical tone of some New Dealers was reflected in reaction to the overthrow of NRA by the Supreme Court.

America and the *Catholic World* welcomed the decision. Jesuit Paul Blakely worried about the erosion of constitutional balances, while Father Wilfrid Parsons believed that only the vocational group system could bring economic justice without endangering political freedom. James M. Gillis, the Paulist editor of the *Catholic World*, had become convinced that excessive spending, the leftist leanings of many New Deal officials, and the extension of executive authority endangered fundamental liberties. Patrick Scanlan, editor of the Brooklyn *Tablet*, thought the New Deal should "provide recovery rather than institute vast reforms." Gillis, Scanlan, and others were even more upset by Roosevelt's failure to denounce religious persecution in Mexico, actions that had aroused lay organizations such as the Knights of Columbus. Other Catholic leaders, like Jesuit Edmund A. Walsh of Georgetown, let friends in the administration know of their concern about the radicalism of some New Deal advisers.[72]

The change from support to opposition was even more dramatic in the case of Father Coughlin.[73] In 1934 he had established the National Union for Social Justice as a "people's lobby." Its sixteen-point platform emphasized monetary issues but included as well endorsement of labor's right to organize, "cost of production plus a fair profit for the farmer," government ownership of natural monopolies, "simplified" government, and reduced taxes. Coughlin said this new instrument would overcome the "sham battles" of old party politicians, whom he called "sly rats." In June 1936, Coughlin announced formation of the Union party and its entry into the 1936 presidential race with William Lemke of South Dakota and Thomas C. O'Brien of Boston as its candidates. Coughlin promised to deliver nine million votes for the ticket or retire from the air. He toured the country delivering fiery speeches. In Cleveland he called Roosevelt the "great liar and betrayer" and defined the options of Roosevelt and Republican Alfred Landon of Kansas as a choice between "carbolic acid and rat poison."[74]

Despite rising controversy about the New Deal, however, there remained as late as 1936 a very wide area of agreement among most Catholic social critics. This was illustrated by the publication in January of that year of the pamphlet "Organized Social Justice: An Economic Program for the United States Applying Pius XI's Great Encyclical on Social Life." Among the 131 signers were Ryan, McGowan, Dorothy Day of the Catholic Worker movement, Father James Gillis, George Shuster of *Commonweal*, Fathers Edgar Schmeidler, Howard Bishop, and Robert Lucey of the Catholic rural life movement, and Fathers Joseph Husslein, Wilfred Parsons, and John LaFarge of *America*. The program condemned unregulated competition and urged reenactment of the NRA, by means of constitutional amendment if necessary. It called for wages and hours legislation that would insure "continuous employment, a decent livelihood and adequate security for all workers," and agricultural legislation to bring producers similar benefits. The signers urged the government to provide for the well-being and prosperity of society as a whole, the protection of the poor and the workers, and the enforcement of the obligations of private ownership. Significantly the manifesto concluded that "these and other social obligations of public authority" would have to be performed mainly by the federal government since industry was "national in its scope and effects." The sole alternative to a constitutional amendment broadening the power of the federal government to deal with such matters was inaction; critics who hoped "that the thing can be done by the forty eight states" were in reality upholding the continuation of laissez-faire and unlimited competition. Yet, the program added, legislation itself was inadequate and could lead to totalitarianism. Labor organization was a "right and a necessity," while collective bargaining had to be carried forward to a system of joint organizations of capital and labor into vocational groups. These would maintain standards of wages, hours, prices, and business practices; they would enable labor to share responsibility for industrial policy-making and they would prevent dictatorship by keeping "immediate and day to day control in the hands of the agents of production." The intent of these proposals was "to build an economic order within a government order," an economy of partnership between government at all levels, and "the self-governing, democratically organized membership of the industries, of farming, of trade, and of the professions."[75]

"Organized Social Justice" was part of a Ryan-directed strategy to counter Catholic critics of the New Deal such as Coughlin and Al Smith, who was backing the conservative Liberty League.[76] Ryan had reservations about the New Deal, but he was convinced it offered the only hope for social justice. "American business intelligence is bankrupt," he wrote in 1935. Businessmen had not "learned a thing from the depression. They are as selfish, as credulous, as greedy as they were in the Delirious Twenties."[77] Ryan divided critics of the New Deal into two camps, the "advocates and retainers of plutocracy" and those impatient because progress toward social justice had been too slow. He was especially angry with the second group, because they "turn their backs upon the only existing social force that is likely to bring about any reforms and apparently give their allegiance to a program of inaction."[78] Ryan told the president that he was appalled by the attitudes of Coughlin, Smith, and other Catholic critics. At a key moment in the campaign, he went on the radio under the auspices of the Democratic party to defend Roosevelt against these attacks. Another confidant of the president, Father Maurice S. Sheehy, assistant to the rector at Catholic University, claimed that he had distributed thousands of copies of Ryan's talk.[79] Acknowledging Roosevelt's thanks, Ryan told the president that he took satisfaction from the speech not only because it aided his reelection but because it helped get Coughlin "off the air." Ryan was then invited to deliver the benediction at Roosevelt's 1937 inauguration.[80]

After the election the division between pro- and anti-New Deal Catholics sharpened. Roosevelt's plan to reorganize the Supreme Court upset many bishops; one called Ryan's support for the plan evidence of a "fascist, dictatorial mind." Others saw their fears of federal power confirmed in the 1938 reorganization plan. There had always been a touch of self-interest in this fear of centralization. William Montavon, a lawyer who followed legislation for the bishops, reported in 1933:

> The welfare of religion is closely tied up with the problems of federalism. Because of divergent and conflicting views, the larger the scope of any political authority in our country, the more rigidly must it adhere to a policy of minimum interference in controversial matters. This minimum, so far as religion is concerned, is secularism. Local authorities covering a small scope are less rigidly bound in this respect and can often do things which a Federal agency could not do. This affects especially schools, benevolent institutions, charities, etc. We are in the midst of trends by which the federal system is endangered.[81]

He might have added that Catholic political leverage was much greater in heavily Catholic cities and states than it was at the federal level. Catholic charities, by working in cooperation with other groups, were learning to live with, even benefit from, government intervention at all levels, but the bishops remained drawn to a decentralized philosophy of government as closer to the church's interests.

Cardinal George Mundelein had long been the president's most ardent backer. When Catholics criticized Roosevelt's Mexican policy, the cardinal arranged for him to receive an honorary degree at Notre Dame and introduced him with high praise and claims of personal friendship. He took on Father Coughlin and during the 1936 campaign denounced those who tried to pin a communist label on the New Deal, making it clear that he backed New Deal policies. In 1938 he had a highly publicized visit with Roosevelt after the latter's "quarantine the aggressors" speech in Chicago, and then entered into negotiations with the Vatican aimed at diplomatic relations.[82] Only Bishop Robert Lucey of San Antonio matched the Chicago cardinal's dependable support for the Roosevelt administration.

Then there were well-connected Catholics in the administration, like James A. Farley and Thomas Corcoran. When Frank Murphy was defeated for reelection as governor of Michigan in 1938, Roosevelt named him attorney general; later he would serve on the Supreme Court. Regarded by the acerbic Harold Ickes as "the most strictly religious man I know," Murphy was a devout Catholic, an ardent foe of anti-Semitism, and an idealist who had hoped to devote his life to "undoing those who would make life unnecessarily cruel and burdensome."[83]

But critics were multiplying. Some had disliked the New Deal from the start. German Catholic leader Frederick B. Kenkel, who had long ago abandoned his pre-World War I progressivism, now believed that only moral reform and religious renewal could overcome the nation's problems; he and other German American writers regularly condemned New Deal "experiments." Liberal democracy was finished, Kenkel believed, and the world was "face to face with a new order of things, political and economic." The choice lay "between a totalitarian state on the one hand and the corporative society on the other."[84] Others had always been conservative. Cardinal O'Connell, for example, saw the church as "the very cornerstone of law and order." Liberty was "submission to proper authority" and he warned that temporary grants of power to government required by crisis should be rescinded "when that need ceases." He saw evidence of communism everywhere and blamed it on the decline of respect for authority, abandonment of sound traditions in favor of social reform, and the increasing discontent of the poor. Archbishop McNicholas, unlike O'Connell, believed in moderate social reform, but he shared his blend of moral absolutism and fear of communism. Arguing that society needed a "fixed moral code" that only the church could provide, he deplored the influence of "liberals" who had "no real convictions and no real stamina." A strong supporter of Catholic action to influence public morality, he denounced a local newspaper's defense of divorce, asserting that "liberty of the press can in no sense justify the degradation of the reading public." If Catholics were a majority in the United States, he argued, they would defend the First Amendment; but their influence would bring public opinion into conformity with the "fixed moral code," divorce would no longer be permitted, family life would be strengthened, and the "flippant spirit" and "destructive teachings" of many college professors and intellectuals would not be tolerated. McNicholas, O'Connell, and other bishops of the later 1930s saw the Legion of Decency's campaign against immoral movies as the most significant form of Catholic Action.[85]

But it was foreign policy that soon came to dominate the public debate. Most Catholic leaders actively championed the cause of Franco's Nationalists in the Spanish Civil War, bringing them into sharp conflict with American liberals, many of whom were convinced that Catholic pressure had forced Roosevelt to apply the neutrality act's ban on arms shipments to the Loyalists. Moreover, many liberals believed that the church in Europe had moved into an alliance with fascism, presenting as evidence the church's accommodation with Mussolini, its concordat with Hitler, its support for Franco, and its endorsement of fascist regimes in Portugal and Austria. Few responded to these charges directly; instead they charged their critics with anti-Catholic bias. Francis X. Talbot of *America*, for example, argued that "liberals" were always "Catholic haters."[86] They could justify this response because they saw the Spanish Civil War as a struggle between communism and democracy. One paper compared Franco's forces to "our patriots of 1776"; others repeated over and over again stories of Loyalist atrocities against the church to make the case that the Nationalists were fighting for religious liberty.[87] Once again, as so often happened on an issue close to church interests, dissent became dangerous. The Catholic Worker adopted a pacifist stance, denying that force could ever be used in the Christian cause.[88] *Commonweal*, under the influence of its antifascist editor, George Shuster, attempted to maintain neutrality. The magazine lost 25 percent of its subscribers.[89] Father Coughlin compared the editors to Pontius Pilate and Archbishop McNicholas told the Knights of Columbus that a Catholic could only be neutral by "turning against Christ."[90]

As Europe moved toward war, one powerful group of Catholics became isolationists. At the extreme end of this group was Coughlin, back on the air and concentrating on the danger of communism. His audience was now more limited and more exclusively Catholic, and toward it he directed a steady stream of emotional attacks on Roosevelt, liberals, communists, and Jews.[91] Drawing on traditional anti-Semitic writings, he blamed both communism and capitalism on Jewish conspiracies and charged that American Jews were conspiring to lead the United States into a war against Germany that could only help the Soviet Union. His new superior, Archbishop Edward Mooney, attempted to control his embarrassing activity, but he pulled back out of fear of a Coughlinite backlash. In some sectors of American Catholicism, Coughlin's assault on the Jews struck a responsive chord. Not only did Catholics share with other Americans certain anti-Semitic prejudices, but they had come to resent the way in which their complaints about persecution of the church were ignored and those of the Jews were not. Bishop James E. Cassidy of Fall River, at a rally he organized to support the Spanish embargo, said it directly: "The Jews have made a wailing wall of the world. What about Spain? What about Mexico, where churches and people have suffered? We Catholics have much to learn from the Jews. It is time for us Americans to rise up against these wrongs." In 1938 an unsigned editorial in the family magazine *Ave Maria* made note of this: "The Jew gets a hearing and sympathy, even if he does not get effective help [but] persecuted Catholics get neither a hearing, nor sympathy, nor anything else."[92] The same line of reasoning could be found, sometimes in more subtle form, in other sectors of the Catholic press.[93]

But most Catholic opponents of Roosevelt's foreign policy did not share Coughlin's anti-Semitism. Their problem was communism, the threat of a war with Germany that could only aid the Soviet Union. Intense opposition to communism and Russia began almost immediately after the 1917 revolution. Edmund A. Walsh, S.J., of the Georgetown School of Foreign Service became the Catholic expert and leader of the anti-Soviet campaign.[94] When Roosevelt recognized Russia in 1933, Walsh was not opposed, but a number of Catholic journals and organizations attacked the decision.[95] Fear of communist influence grew through the foreign policy fights and increasing charges made against more radical labor leaders and New Dealers. Bishop John Francis Noll, editor of the widely circulated *Our Sunday Visitor*, wrote a pamphlet called *It is Happening Here* that was widely circulated and contained slanderous labeling of a variety of public figures.

The anticommunist crusade received an infusion of new blood with Fulton J. Sheen, who, after a distinguished academic career in Europe, returned to teach philosophy at the Catholic University of America and achieved fame as speaker on the NBC radio program "The Catholic Hour." In articles, books, and speeches, Sheen sharpened the Catholic argument that modern civilization in the West lacked guiding principles and was in fact chaotic, opening the door to a variety of ideologies promising order, stability, and absolute truth, the most virulent of which was communism. Modern man turns to communism, Sheen argued, "because it replaces the doubt and skepticism of an irresponsible indifference by a certitude of absolute authority embodied in a social institution" that "he believes will save the world." Only Catholicism could adequately oppose it, and the showdown was coming. "The forces are already aligning themselves, preparing for a battle," Sheen wrote. "Men will enlist on one side or the other; we must battle either for brotherhood in Christ or comradeship in the anti-Christ."[96]

Inspired by such a view of the world, confirmed in 1937 by Pius XI's encyclical *Divini Redemptoris*, the American bishops launched a "Catholic Crusade for Christian Democracy" with a pastoral letter marking the golden jubilee of Catholic University. The bishops told their people that they were "seriously alarmed by the spread of subversive teaching and the audacity of subversive action in our country." To defend democratic government and follow the pope's instruction to develop "a constructive program of social action," the bishops turned to what the church did best, education, with an educational program to instruct children in the rights and duties of citizenship. These would be instilled with the conviction "that love of country is a virtue and that disloyalty is a sin." Similar ideas found their way into educational programs at every level of the church, from Holy Name societies to the Knights of Columbus to the colleges and universities. It was little wonder that the barrage of Catholic anti-Communist rhetoric, combined with church actions abroad, convinced many non-Catholics that the church indeed preferred fascism to communism. Given that choice, most Catholics agreed that this was in fact their position. Francis Talbot, arguing with George Shuster, wrote: "But here is a point: a collaboration with Fascism is possible for the Catholic Church; a collaboration with Communism is absolutely impossible for the Catholic Church. Mr. Shuster can be a fascist and a fervent Catholic; he cannot be a Communist and a Catholic."[97]

This led even moderate Catholic leaders to find the most fearsome motives in each Roosevelt initiative. Archbishop McNicholas, for example, called the 1940 proposal for a peacetime draft the "beginning of a totalitarian form of government."[98] The majority of the hierarchy opposed the bill and McNicholas and several other bishops joined the Catholic Worker in calling for conscientious objection. A survey by *America* showed that 36 percent of young Catholics would consider that option.[99]

Yet support for Roosevelt remained strong among Catholic voters. Catholics were only slightly more pro-Franco than Americans as a whole. In addition, Roosevelt could look for support to his friends in the church. Mundelein spoke out against Hitler and lent powerful support to Roosevelt's foreign policy. Mundelein met with Roosevelt after his "quarantine the aggressor" speech in October 1937 and then became an intermediary in discussions with the Vatican. He told the president: "You can count on us here to hold up your hands in this and in all your undertakings for the good of our own country and of humanity."[100] On the eve of his death the cardinal prepared a speech for radio broadcast dealing with the war in Europe. Read by his auxiliary, Bishop Bernard J. Sheil, another Roosevelt supporter, the speech attacked isolationists as "emotional charlatans who have become statesmen overnight" and praised the president's "matchless political leadership in foreign affairs."[101]

Francis Spellman, appointed auxiliary bishop of Boston and later archbishop of New York because of his close friendship with Pope Pius XII, became an intermediary between the president and the Vatican and helped arrange Roosevelt's decision to send a personal ambassador to the Holy See. Ryan, of course, was a strong supporter, and he broke with old friends who opposed the president's policies.

He had the least sympathy with pacifists who supported Republican Wendell Willkie in the 1940 election, but this time he was barred from speaking out for Roosevelt. Father Francis Haas was another active supporter, as was Maurice Sheehy of Catholic University, who kept in close touch with the White House, reporting secret opponents and talking up his own pro-Roosevelt activities. In August 1940, he told Roosevelt's secretary that "We Catholics *who are American* face a real battle this fall. With God's help, and under the President's leadership, we shall win, against all the pro-Nazi, pro-fascist and traditional haters of England."[102] Help also came from the Catholic Association for International Peace. Established a decade earlier to educate American Catholics about world problems, its leaders strongly supported Roosevelt's internationalist initiatives. George Shuster, forced out of *Commonweal* over the Spanish issue, continued to arouse Catholics to the dangers posed by Hitler to the church and to democracy.[103]

Catholic isolationists, whose major concern was communism, were incensed when Roosevelt extended lend-lease to Russia after the German invasion in June 1941. They charged that such cooperation could not be justified in light of the papal condemnations of communism. By this time, however, the Vatican was shifting ground. Archbishop Edward Mooney, then head of the NCWC, made inquiries at the Vatican as to whether the action could be justified by distinguishing between the Russian people and the Soviet state; the Vatican responded in the affirmative but told Mooney to keep its decision private among the bishops. Mooney then arranged for McNicholas, an isolationist but his personal friend, to make this case in a pastoral letter, which was done, with Mooney arranging wide distribution of the letter through the NCWC. When McNicholas wrote Mooney to pass on Senator Robert Taft's reservations about cooperation with Russia, Mooney responded:

> Of course it is easier for a non-Catholic than a Catholic to be an isolationist. They have not the worldview or the world wide spiritual interest that is our heritage of faith. Of course too 'the conflict in Europe is based largely on national interest.' The real question is—on that side—whether or not we have a deep national interest in Hitler's defeat. But the opposition of a sincere and moderate man like Taft may be a providential drag on precipitate action. But—like yourself—'I do not want to get into the arena of politics'—and I hope we can keep the boys out of the arena in Washington the week after next—and still be within the orbit of good Catholic American citizenship.[104]

THE NEW UNIONISM

In 1938 Cardinal Mundelein startled Chicago's annual Holy Name convention.

The trouble with us in the past has been that we were too often allied or drawn into alliance with the wrong side. Selfish employers of labor have flattered the Church by calling it the great conservative force, and then called upon it to act as a police force while they paid but a pittance of a wage to those who worked for them. I hope that day is gone by. Our place is beside the poor, behind the working man. They are our people, they build our churches, they occupy our pews, their children crowd our schools, our priests come from their sons. They look to us for leadership but they look to us too for support.[105]

The cardinal may have exaggerated labor's interest in the church, but his words expressed a new and rather dramatic commitment to the labor movement, more positive and direct than any in the past. As the New Deal got underway there was a spontaneous uprising of organization. Priests in many areas gave their backing, defending the unions against critics, challenging anti-union employers and newspapers, and eventually setting up a network of labor schools to train union members.

The widespread belief that higher wages were essential for recovery led almost all Catholic commentators to support the extension of labor unions early in the depression. Few Catholics, however, found much to admire in the conservative policies of the American Federation of Labor. *America*, for example, regularly blasted union leaders for their failure to organize the organized or adapt their craft union structure to the requirements of the mass-production industry. Francis Haas, a Milwaukee priest trained by Ryan, worked closely with Secretary of Labor Frances Perkins and was appointed to a number of New Deal agencies. He was an outspoken advocate of the unions, but he too called for basic changes in union policy.[106]

The bishops regularly endorsed labor's right to organize and, in 1935, broke their policy of abstaining from supporting particular legislation to back the Wagner Act, which gave government support to the right to organize and established the National Labor Relations Board.[107] When adherents of industrial unionism, led by John L. Lewis, broke with the AFL in 1935, most Catholic spokesmen blamed the split squarely on the old guard leadership of the federation. In the mass organizing drives that followed, the church was warmly supportive, breaking ranks only over the controversial techniques of the sit-down strikes in the auto industry. Yet, once again, as the nation moved into the later 1930s, anti-union and anti-CIO sentiment spread, again spurred in part by the fear of communism.

In defending the CIO against such attacks, many bishops and labor priests drew on the corporatist teaching of the encyclicals to argue that workers had a duty, not just a right, to join independent unions. In the words of Detroit's Archbishop Mooney: "Let there be no doubt about it, labor organization, sound and responsible organization on democratic principles, is not merely something which the Church accepts as an inevitable development of our industrial society, it is something which she wholeheartedly approves ... something which she earnestly commends to worker and management alike as a remedy for the evils of industrial life which press upon us." As Mooney saw it, every worker had a responsibility to join and take an active interest in his or her union, and priests who urged them to stay aloof were derelict in their duty. Even stronger was Bishop Lucey, who denied that good will was enough to secure justice. "There are those who say that if everybody kept the ten commandments all would be well with society," Lucey said. "Nothing could be further from the truth. Industrial and agricultural relations cannot control or manipulate themselves.... Only machinery intelligently constructed can make them work ... and assure a regime of justice and charity." Eventually this would require a system like Ryan's economic democracy, but for the moment labor had the greatest need for the church's assistance. With all the money and power on the side of capital, he said, workers had "a duty to join a labor union for their own good, the welfare of their families, and the peace and security of human society." He rebuked Catholic critics who said they sympathized with labor but could not support the unions, insisting that "devotion to the laboring classes automatically includes the union." Charges of communism leveled against the CIO amounted to a slander of American workers. Lucey even told Lewis that the CIO did not go far enough because it did not demand a share in the management of industry.[108]

Criticism of communism in the CIO unions persisted. John Brophy, one of Lewis's top aides, who had once been a socialist, was regularly attacked for cooperating with communists. He fought back, challenging bishops, priests, Bishop John Noll of *Our Sunday Visitor*, and the Jesuit editors of *America*. One of the latter, Francis X. Talbot, told Brophy that Lewis had let the CIO become a "camping ground of Communists and other subversives." He wanted Catholics to fight them.[109] Bishop Lucey sympathized with Brophy, and few of the critics mentioned the large number of Catholics in leadership positions in the CIO. But others, including Mooney, were in fact worried about communist influence. For this reason they gave strong backing to their own labor priests, to Talbot's fellow Jesuits, launching labor schools around the country, and to a lay organization, the Association of Catholic Trade Unionists.

The ACTU was founded by a group of young men associated with the New York Catholic Worker house. Its goal was to bring the social teachings of the church to Catholic working people, to support the unions and encourage their development toward the vocational group system of the pope.[110] They believed there could be no solution of economic problems until "American employers honestly recognize the natural rights of their workers to organize in bona fide trade unions, to receive a living annual wage and a proportional share in the profits of business, to be assured of job security, a just price, decent hours and working conditions." Eventually they hoped to see "national guilds for the self-regulation and self-government of our economy." As the Michigan *Labor Leader*, an ACTU publication, expressed it in 1939, the church had "a program as complete and well-developed as the 'party line' of the Communists." If its goal could be achieved in Detroit, "the auto industry, now sick unto death with the cancer of class war, would be·one big fraternal unit, dedicated to the public service of making autos."[111] Whatever else they wanted, the ACTU activists were "dedicated to the proposition that to give the workers a meaningful share in control, *power*, over the industrial system, was a Christian and Catholic thing to do, that power should be used with reason and prudence but the main thing right then was to get some for the workers."[112]

In New York the ACTU helped a number of organizing drives and assisted union members to fight corruption in the transport and long-shoremen's unions.[113] The ACTU was strongest among the auto workers, especially in Detroit, where they had the blessing of Mooney, and among the electrical workers, where one of the leaders, James B. Carey, made an anticommunist alliance with the ACTU that would play a major role in ousting the communists from leadership. In fact, anticommunism became a major theme of the ACTU, and it would enjoy its most effective period in the bitter fights against the communists after World War II.[114]

EVANGELICAL CATHOLICISM

For those who are huddling in shelters trying to escape the rain
For those who are walking the streets in the all but futile search for
    work
For those who think that there is no hope for the future, no recognition
    of their plight—this little paper is addressed
It is printed to call attention to the fact that the Catholic Church has a
    social program, to let them know there are men of God who are
    working not only for their spiritual but for their material welfare.[115]

The Protestant Social Gospel movement found its strongest support in evangelical churches and its theme in an early fictional account of men and women attempting to apply the gospel to problems of society in their everyday life, to follow "in his steps," by asking "What would Jesus do?" Emerging contemporaneously with the rise of social science, however, the movement blended eventually with progressive reform and ended by emphasizing changes in social institutions. Starting from a very different Catholic emphasis on papal teaching rather than on Scripture, mainstream Catholic social reformers followed John A. Ryan in the belief that institutional changes that would encourage people to fulfill their needs by cooperation rather than competitive self-interest should take priority. In the words of one writer, "It is useless today to talk of reform in the social, political or perhaps even the religious life of men unless a radical change can be effected in the economic sphere, where most of our present day disorders originate."[116] Ryan and others took the encyclicals' consistent emphasis on moral and spiritual reform as pro forma; when Ryan was challenged on the point, he said that he regarded the natural and supernatural plane as connected by elevator, if at all.

The dilemma, of course, was that religion could become in that case a kind of caboose on the train of social engineering, awaiting the proper readjustment of social arrangements without which authentic spiritual regeneration could not take place. Like the Marxists, whose behaviorist assumptions about the priority of economics forced postponement of spiritual growth until the advent of the classless society, the liberal reformer, Protestant or Catholic, could easily come to regard appeals for religious conversion and individual moral regeneration as ideological mystification designed to distract attention from problems of power and privilege. Yet the lesson seemed to be that again and again, economic reforms led not to the liberation of the human spirit but to further problems of power and privilege requiring continuing struggle.

There was an alternative approach in the West, one that insisted that reformed men would make a better society, and not the reverse, and that only personal conviction and commitment would produce the kind of courage and creativity capable of resisting social evil and keeping open the possibility of an alternative way of life. Such a position went beyond simple charity and benevolence to argue that, while the Christian must always respond first to the person in need, with charity and almsgiving, that very response required as well a personal commitment to live according to the demands of the gospel, to renounce those affiliations that compromised or corrupted Christian ideals, and to attempt to build an alternative way of life based on the word of God. Like Protestant, scriptural, and Jesus-centered evangelicalism, this utopian, perfectionist commitment to a Christian social order had enormous appeal to Christians as Christians, but posed insuperable obstacles when located within a pluralistic society, for it posed the simple proposition that social relations and institutions should be based on the radical, seemingly impractical moral norms of the Sermon on the Mount.

Among American Catholics this evangelical approach had its soft side, as heard in ordinary sermons contending that the quest for reform was futile unless men and women decided to put self-interest aside and live by a creed of love for others. Ordinarily such appeals simply legitimated indifference or opposition to social change or confined social action to church-based programs of charity. But in the 1930s a new and radical version of this appeal appeared in the United States, and it would grow in the years that followed.

Personalism in the United States was stripped of the intellectual refinements that marked that school of thought in Europe. Instead it was activist, emphasizing the responsibility of each individual Christian to live out his faith by assisting his neighbor at a personal sacrifice. It stressed personal sanctity and holiness, a strong grounding in the liturgy, and an apostolic desire to improve the lot of humankind. Perfectionist and unsystematic, it emphasized personal commitment and voluntary action, focused on the giver and not the recipient, on the action itself rather than the social change the action brought about. While others directed attention to legislation, organization, and institutional change, the personalists concentrated on reforming themselves and changing society by the example of Christian love. Their actions were self-consciously Catholic and they were vividly aware of the gap that separated them from other reformers; they stressed the superiority of the Christian way and were not upset at charges of sectarianism. Their exclusivism was the opposite of self-righteousness, for they went out to others, attempting to see in each person, poor or rich, Christian or communist, the image of God, to regard each person, regardless of creed or lack of it, as another Christ. It found its strongest support from sociologist Paul Hanley Furfey, from the liturgical reformer Virgil Michel, and especially from the founders of and participants in the Catholic Worker movement.

Furfey was a diocesan priest who taught at the Catholic University of America. For over half a century, he argued in books and articles that Christian social science needed to be guided by Christian moral norms and oriented always toward the fulfillment of the gospel mandate to serve the poor and build the kingdom of God. He divided reformers into moderates and extremists; the former bargained with the world, they understood the demands of the gospel but consistently compromised those demands, settling for half a loaf in the name of realism. Moderates were prudent, neglecting the black in order to avoid damaging the church, teaching business courses to prepare young Catholics to compete in an unjust social order, later offering

ROTC to assist them to take leadership roles in the military, all at the expense of what seemed to Furfey the clear mandates of Christ. Extremists, on the other hand, saw the fundamental message of the gospel as love, they set impossibly high standards they knew they could not reach without divine assistance, and they relied on grace and the power of good example, witness rather than politics and organization, as methods of reform. Regarding social work as a "poor substitute for Christianity," they argued that the prime Christian method of social reform was through the works of mercy. "If we really love the poor," Furfey wrote, "we shall be forced . . . to share our goods with them until we ourselves have become poor." If voluntary poverty seemed to leave unjust structures intact, Furfey responded that it alone offered the promise of the fundamental change needed to overcome sin and evil and open the imaginations of men and women to a truly different way of life.[117]

What was required of the individual Catholic, the commitment to live entirely under the inspiration of grace, was required of the church as well. Catholics must try "to reproduce in their common life the unearthly beauty of the mystical body of Christ." Thus radical personalism became closely tied to the liturgical movement, which had arisen in Europe and come to the United States through Benedictine priests in the Midwest, led by Dom Virgil Michel. "The liturgy is the perfect expression of the new social Catholicism," Furfey wrote.[118] Michel took this idea further, arguing that the spirit of individualism had infected even the church, and that the Catholic vision of society required a true conversion to human solidarity. "As long as the Christian is in the habit of viewing his religious life from the subjectivist and individualist standpoint," Michel wrote, "he will be able to live his daily life in terms of the prudent individualism and subjectivism without any qualms of conscience." Recognition that all persons are saved through Christ was imperative if Christians were to see in every person the image of God. Only then could one see that, in performing spiritual duties, one contributed to the spiritual welfare of all, and that a failure to live a life of charity and justice was an injury to the whole body. Only the vision of the solidarity of humankind could provide a basis for the corporate and cooperative spirit of the Christian social order. Although the liturgy offered no "detailed scheme of social reconstruction, or anything of the kind" it did supply a model of society, the Mystical Body, and it put the concept into action by inspiring the laity "to live it out in everyday life." Indeed the liturgical movement gave new meaning to the life of the laity, bringing them back into participation and emphasizing their responsibility for the church's mission. "Not paper programs, not highsounding, unfulfilled resolutions once renewed the world," wrote Michel, "but new and living men born out of the depths of Christianity." For this reason Michel, while admiring the work of others, regarded the liturgical movement as "the primary apostolate".[119]

The most important expression of this integral Catholicism came from a new, radical Catholic movement that seemed to turn upside down most of the accepted assumptions of American Catholicism. On May Day 1933, a ragtag group of New York Catholics appeared in Union Square, hawking a new newspaper, the *Catholic Worker*, for a penny a copy. Before long the little monthly was circulating across the country, and small groups were gathering in cities to form houses of hospitality to serve the poor at a personal sacrifice and to discuss the radical ideas they read in the paper. Those ideas came from Peter Maurin, an itinerant French-born "apostle on the bum" and Dorothy Day, a journalist whose spiritual odyssey had led her through the radical counterculture of pre–World War I New York to imprisonment with suffragists and eventually to the Catholic church.

Maurin offered in unique free-verse essays a call for radical renunciation of "bourgoise" culture. In the gospel, the example of the saints and religious orders, and the modern Catholic critique of modernity, Maurin found the outline of a distinctive Catholic approach to the pursuit of justice as radical and as consistent as that of the communists. Maurin believed that society by definition required "unity of thought" and he aimed to provide a new synthesis that eventually would enable Western society to recover its spiritual foundations. In one sense he was a reactionary, for he harked back to a preindustrial ideal of decentralized farming and handicraft production, religious unity expressed in liturgy and prayer, and cultural integration in which religion, art, and community life reflected the dignity of each person and the solidarity of all. Accused of communism, he was in fact a communitarian who despised industry, capitalism, technology, and the impersonal life of the city. Yet there was far more than nostalgia to the peasant-born Maurin. Like so many cultural critics of modernity, he confronted the realities of alienation, the destructive force of an unchecked technology, and the human need for community and a sense of being at home in the world. More than any other American Catholic thinker, he understood the importance of work as the means for personal growth and social interaction. For others, politics or organized social action were primary means for fulfilling social responsibilities. Maurin, however, saw that human work was the major form of each person's participation in a common life, the means whereby people supported themselves and their families and contributed to the common stock, not only of goods and services, but of art and beauty as well. Maurin believed that bourgois society, by tying work to wages and to machines, devalued persons, destroyed community, and endangered the human enterprise. To begin building a new social order, Maurin proposed round-table discussions, a labor paper and constant agitation to spread these ideas, houses of hospitality to express love and solidarity, and farming communes to witness to the possibility of a new way of living.[120]

When Maurin met Dorothy Day in 1932, he persuaded her to support his threefold program. Day blended Maurin's ideas into her own rich experience of American democratic radicalism. She had a deep commitment to the working class, and a democratic instinct for the rich lives of the people around her. Perhaps more than any writer of the century she captured the human and spiritual meaning of the daily lives of ordinary people. More important, she was fearless in confronting injustice, profoundly honest in her use of language, and thoroughly committed to living by her beliefs.

The Catholic Worker remained a movement rather than an organization, bound together by the paper and by the powerful leadership of Day. Catholic Worker houses were centers where young Catholics determined to respond to the depression and the political ferment of the times could meet, discover a Catholic approach to the social question, learn of the new trends in theology, the liturgical movement, or the myriad forms of social action stirring their church. Few would devote their lives to the movement; many would spend a year or two and go on to careers elsewhere, their minds and hearts permanently marked by the experience. But the movement itself went on. In its earliest days bishops and priests were captivated by the direct service to the poor, and moved by the dedication of the workers. But some were worried about what seemed a romantic agrarianism, others were incensed by the Catholic Worker's implicit criticism not only of conservative Catholicism but of other forms of social action. Prolabor activists, including the former Workers who founded the ACTU, were irritated by Maurin's constant criticisms of unions; John Cort, one of them, criticized Day's "attitude of indifference bordering on hostility, [and] the 'conspiracy of silence' that is apparent in every issue of the paper."[121] New Dealers were put off by the founders' mocking references to "our Holy Mother the State." One correspondent told John A. Ryan that Jesuits were backing Day "partly out of an instinct that Dorothy Day's methods, while seemingly more drastic and radical, in a way are less likely to bring to pass at present or in the very proximate future legislation inconvenient to the possessing classes." While he knew Day and distributed her paper at his parish, he thought that "a thoroughly intelligent and subtle communist, understanding well our Catholic people and wishing to undermine completely their confidence in reconstructing the social order, could hardly do better, if he had the means, than to subsidize the Catholic Worker and the Catholic Worker group."[122]

Most controversial was the Catholic Worker's commitment to pacifism. Dorothy Day insisted that the Catholic Worker philosophy could allow no compromise with violence. During the Spanish Civil War the paper adopted a neutral position, praying for the Spanish people. This initial, almost instinctive gospel-centered nonresistance had a brief period of popularity when it corresponded with the opposition of many American Catholic leaders to Roosevelt's foreign policy and the draft, but when the Worker persisted after Pearl Harbor, its circulation and following dwindled. But the movement had introduced a new and critical voice into American Catholic life. The reasonable, careful dualism of the republican tradition and the self-interested realism of the immigrant church had few obvious roots in the gospel. They could appropriately be adapted to the needs of the institutional church, or to the demands of a Catholic people conscious of their unity and their minority status. Each could make reference to papal teaching, but they were rarely explored in terms of the Scripture and the message of Jesus. Yet, as American Protestants had learned, once supportive subcultures erode, American Christians become almost inexorably evangelical, resolving the diversity and conflicts of Christian pluralism by direct, and democratic, encounter with the Gospels. That could lead, as it often did, to comfortable accommodation, but it could also generate enormous energies to challenge sin and injustice, as every American reform movement had demonstrated. Eventually American Catholics too would confront the dilemmas of freedom and pluralism more directly, and when they did so the debate about the public stance of the church would become less papal, more personal, less Catholic and more Christian. The Catholic Worker would be there to welcome, and to shape, that moment.

SOCIAL CATHOLICISM

In 1940, in the midst of the bitter debates over foreign policy, the administrative board of the NCWC issued a major statement on "The Church and the Social Order." It was a progressive document, which affirmed the principles underlying a Ryan-style support for the New Deal, trade unionism, and economic democracy. Yet it also reflected the dilemmas of a still self-conscious immigrant outsider church when it tried to speak, republican-style, to public issues. Sounding the theme of secularism, which had been growing since the 1920s and would dominate episcopal social consciousness for another generation, the bishops drew on the papal motto "to restore all things in Christ." To achieve social justice and world peace, the bishops contended, "we must bring God back into government; we must bring God back into education; we must bring God back into economic life; we must bring God back indeed into all life, private and public, individual and social. The truth of God, the law of God, the justice, mercy, and charity of God must, by conscious effort and willing submission, be made to permeate all our social intercourse and all our public relations." Needing God, society also needed the church, which taught with authority those things contained in the law of God and imposed obligations on all human beings. The bishops asserted their right to speak on public issues as deriving from this authority, for the church is "the teacher of the entire moral law and more particularly as it applies to man's economic and social conduct in business, industry and trade." The church did not offer technical prescriptions for economic problems, the bishops admitted, but it did teach the principles required for any proper solution. After outlining the most comprehensive list of reforms offered since the 1919 program, the bishops acknowledged they did not hold "individual employers as a class . . . responsible for this present state of insecurity but we do claim that a system which tolerates such insecurity is both economically unsound and also inconsistent with the demands of social justice and social charity." A new system of partnership was needed that would give labor a "graduated share in the ownership and profits of business and also some voice in its management." After outlining the vocational group system of economic democracy, they summed up thus:

> Our economic life then must be reorganized not on the disintegrating principles of individualism but on the constructive principle of social and moral unity among the members of human society. In conformity with Christian principles, economic power must be subordinated to human welfare, both individual and social; social incoherence and class conflict must be replaced by corporate unity and organic function; ruthless competition must give way to just and reasonable State regulations; sordid selfishness must be superseded by social justice and charity.[123]

The hierarchy had come a long way in a decade. But the problem remained. A manifesto issued at the end of the first National Catholic Social Action Conference in 1939 contained a similar list of needed reforms, short- and long-term, but concluded as did the bishops' document that real change had to take place "on the basis of a full acceptance of the person and teachings of Jesus Christ." Bishop Aloysius J. Muench told that same conference that "social justice must build the juridical framework within which [men] must pursue their economic aims; and social charity must be the soul of that order, tempering selfishness and greed and lust for power." To gain the juridical framework, Catholics could work with others for laws and institutions that would alleviate suffering and limit injustice. To get more than this, the Christian social order proposed by the pope, they would have to permeate society with "social charity" that would lead people to respect one another's rights and cooperate for the common good. If a Christian people and acceptance of Christ were prerequisites, then Catholics might remain in the ghetto, denounce the foolishness and pride of modern man and await a mass return to the church. In 1935 Charles Bruehl, a long-time leader of German Catholics, argued that they should build up "a rich social life" in order to preserve "the purity of Catholic thinking and the integrity of Catholic practice" and provide "prophylactic measures against the social contagion emanating from our environment." Jesuit Francis Talbot was more optimistic, arguing that amidst the now dominant secularism and materialism, Catholics had become the largest group still upholding "the Constitution and the traditional Americanism that made this country what it was before 1914." "Convinced that they can furnish the answer to every national question," Catholics believed the nation would soon turn to them in its search for "a virile, vigilant and clear eyed American citizenry" needed to "defend our traditional American democracy."[124]

McGowan and Ryan were fully aware of the difficulties. Collective bargaining would inevitably deteriorate into class warfare or the short-run pursuit of self-interest unless men and women on both sides placed the common good before the good of their own group. Thus the labor schools and social-action conferences attempted to develop a Catholic leadership familiar with Catholic teaching and committed to something beyond collective bargaining. But there were two fundamental problems: they did not reach employers and they could not overcome the culture of individualism. In an irritation others would feel over the years, Paul Kiniery of Loyola University told Ryan that "the majority of Catholics are far more affected by their economic environment than by the encyclicals. Certainly many of them reverence the Wall Street Journal far more than they do the new Testament."[125] Archbishop Mooney of Detroit almost a decade later told another bishop that his "friends . . . in big circles at General Motors, who are excellent Catholics in a sacramental sense, are utterly allergic to Catholic social doctrine." He got on well with them but to date could not "boast of having converted them to the views of Pius XI, or even Leo XIII."[126] As for the culture: "We have been so long accustomed to going it alone," McGowan wrote, "that the thought of going it together is hard to swallow." To stimulate reform toward a more organic and cooperative order would require "a people that is

Catholic minded." Beyond human dignity and democracy, a just order required a third element missing in the United States, "brotherhood dedicated to the common good." Ryan and other social activists knew this; the failure of priests to aquire knowledge of the social teaching and of social and economic conditions, and of Catholic businessmen to accept the church's "authority to lay down the moral principles which govern industrial relations" had been a recurrent theme of Ryan's writing for thirty years.[127]

The strategy of supporting legislation and trade unions as steps toward economic democracy had wide appeal in the 1930s, when it provided a rationale for the very actions that Catholics were taking anyway. Where Ryan and McGowan failed was not in the immediate tasks, for Catholics did by and large back the CIO and the domestic policies of the New Deal, and their support for unionism and New Deal-type legislation held firm in the postwar years. Where they failed was in popularizing the occupational group idea, and the concepts of social justice, the common good and solidarity on which it rested, a failure indicted by the lack of social consciousness among Catholics as a whole when the sense of crisis eased in the more affluent decades following the war. Like the New Deal itself, the Catholic social movement and its leaders ran out of ideas in the late thirties. Much of their most pressing legislation was enacted, though inadequately, and the NLRB was backing the right of labor to organize; but when Catholic Philip Murray proposed an industrial council plan to the CIO during the war, it died aborning.[128] Then as in 1940 Catholic leaders would blame secularism and call for a spiritual and religious revival that would bring people back to the church, suggesting that only when Americans became Catholic could their problems be solved. Such an argument, even in the hands of reform-minded bishops and priests, served more to enhance Catholic morale than to forward the public debate.

CHAPTER
8
American Catholicism

$\mathcal{S}$ince the beginnings of the American church under John Carroll, Catholics had struggled to reconcile their religious and national loyalties. Self-conscious awareness that there was a complex problem, requiring deliberate, strategic action, provided a central theme of American Catholic history. For Carroll it was a problem of dealing with the minority status of Catholics in the freedom of the new republic. This problem was resolved by minimizing papal claims, regularly articulating republican principles, and building a disciplined native clergy who would avoid politics and interreligious controversy. Immigrant Catholics, needing to build the church among masses of newcomers, continued to articulate republican principles and seek a native clergy. But the association of religion with traditional culture, the need to clarify the boundaries between Catholicism and other religious and cultural associations, and the hostility of many native Americans led to defensive, separatist strategies of grass roots mobilization. Liberal Catholics attempted to put into practice elements of the republican ideal of full participation in American politics and culture, and in the process emphasized more personal faith and providential understandings of the nation.

Conservative leaders of the immigrant church responded from fear that too rapid or enthusiastic assimilation, especially if combined with an emphasis on personal responsibility and openness to the presence of God outside the church, would undermine the foundations of Catholic identity and loyalty. Instead, while still articulating a republican theory of good citizenship, they worked hard to strengthen the institutions of the Catholic subculture, gradually blending the children and grandchildren of the immigrants into a Catholic people, itself in many respects similar to an ethnic group. They still found it possible to affirm militant patriotism without arousing Roman apprehension because they carefully avoided applying American ideals to Catholic theology, morality, or ecclesiology. They also found it possible to affirm their loyalty to the church, and even to the pope, without risking the animosity of the majority of their fellow citizens, by regularly insisting that Catholic teaching accorded with authentic American values, themselves in danger from creeping secularism.

Sounding a recurrent theme of the postwar years, the bishops declared in 1947 that "secularism, or the practical exclusion of God from human thinking and living, is at the root of the world travail today." Opposition to secularism established a place and role for the church that made its own religious work of public significance, because the "moral regeneration which is recognized as absolutely necessary . . . must begin by bringing the individual back to God and to an awareness of his responsibility to God." Thirteen years later, in 1960, they were still insisting that, despite the tremendous growth in church attendance, there had been "a decline in the force of religious conviction" and "religious influences have been losing their vigor with a delibitating effect . . . on both public and private life."[1]

By the twentieth century, then, American Catholicism presented a puzzling public face. Militant Catholicism, complete with the monarchical papacy, coexisted with an at times almost chauvinistic Americanism. By the 1930s there were enough Catholics, and they had enough influence, to constitute a voting bloc requiring the respect of politicans. The church was so strong in its institituions and its popular support that militant, nativist anti-Catholicism became a phenomenon confined to areas of the country where Catholics remained a tiny minority. Elsewhere a more sophisticated anti-Catholicism might keep Catholics from positions of leadership, but most non-Catholics, however hostile to the church as an institution, had come to accept the fact that Catholics (and Jews) were here to stay; pluralism was a fact, however distasteful. But the old dualism remained. Rome still rejected the principles that lay behind the First Amendment. Most European Catholics still had little use for republican principles or democratic practices, and the relationship between the church and various Fascist regimes was an embarrassment. Rome also continued to insist on Catholic intellectual isolation and to place severe restrictions on interreligious contacts. And at home religion remained largely a private matter, moral emphasis was still placed on personal and sexual morality, despite the valiant efforts of Catholic social activists, and the rich experience of Catholics in political, economic, and social life was not endowed with religious or spiritual meaning. To a great extent faith had become a matter of ritual practice, personal moral behavior, and affirmation of what the church taught. For all the work done to develop Catholic social action, even the most activist leaders rarely called for deeper involvement in politics, nondenominational reform organizations, or mainstream culture. The only exception was the labor movement, and labor activists had to insist that Catholic union members would be protected from contamination by their parish priests, labor schools, or the ACTU. So there was still a problem for the Catholic who would be American; the church may occasionally become a public issue, as it did with Father Coughlin or with local attempts at censorship, for example, but the faith was not a public faith and his church was not a public church.

Isaac Hecker and the nineteenth-century Americanists had hoped to bring Catholicism to public significance by awakening a positive vision of a Catholic future for the nation and the world. Ironically, the biggest step toward engaging the church with the larger culture came not from an evangelical, missionary impulse to convert the world while fulfilling democratic yearnings but from a far more political passion—the passion to save the nation and the world from communism. Anticommunism, in fact, offered the best means yet available for overcoming the pervasive dualism of American Catholic life. For the proud, dedicated Catholic, it provided a way to express loyalty without risking respectability. Here at last was a way to demonstrate the sincerity of one's Americanism. Like the fight against immoral movies and birth control, anticommunism could be justified as defending traditional American values and promoting legitimate national interests. Almost all respectable Americans saw communism as a dire threat. Fighting communism was also excellent Catholicism, for every authority in the church agreed that this movement was the greatest modern enemy of the church. It allowed American Catholics to play a world role, coming to the defense of fellow Catholics abroad, first in Mexico and Spain, later in China and eastern Europe. Mission work to spread the faith was also work to stop the spread of the red menace. The apologist for communism was an enemy of the church and an enemy of the United States; the fighter against communist power and subversion was engaged in a mission for the church in the very act of demonstrating loyalty to democracy. The activities of religion, its prayer, worship, charity, and education, of themselves contributed to the cause. Catholicism could make its finest contribution to America simply by being itself.

Thus in post–World War II America, the long-awaited American Catholicism emerged. Increasingly at home in America, able to respond to new outbreaks of anti-Catholicism from a position of strength, convinced that Catholic religious devotion and Catholic educational efforts contributed directly to sustaining traditional values, republican and democratic ideals, and national institutions, American Catholics could now assert that their religion, in and of itself, was of great public value. At the same time they could engage the larger public, in matters of religion, culture, and politics, without having to make direct reference either to the teachings of the church or the group interests of Catholics. Instead they could speak of human rights and the common good. With the election of the militantly anticommunist John F. Kennedy in 1960, it seemed that at last Catholicism and Americanism had become one and the same.[2]

THE WAR

American Catholics fought a bitter battle over foreign policy before World War II. One faction, probably with a majority among the bishops, were isolationists, some from the same motives of nationalism, hatred of England, and suspicion of the economic interests backing internationalism that inspired other isolationists. But a larger number took this stance from fear of a war that would aid the communists, who were considered a greater menace than the Nazis. A second, smaller group, claimed to be pacifists, convinced that modern war could never be an instrument of justice. As we have seen, leaders of these two factions bitterly opposed Roosevelt's internationalist initiatives and even began organizing conscientious objection to the peacetime draft. A third group, some organized around the Catholic Association for International Peace, some, like Ryan, ardent New Dealers, gave unswerving support to Roosevelt. The help Roosevelt received from Cardinal Mundelein was not accidental but the result of careful cultivation. When Mundelein died, the administration let it be known that it favored Bernard Sheil as his replacement in Chicago. That did not come to pass, and Mundelein's place as administration liaison was taken instead by Francis Spellman, who was named archbishop of New York in 1939. He resumed the discussions launched earlier through Mundelein regarding diplomatic relations between the United States and the Holy See. To avoid a congressional fight, Roosevelt chose to send a personal representative, Myron Taylor, making the announcement at Christmas in 1939.

Strongly anticommunist, Spellman nevertheless came to believe that a Nazi victory would jeopardize both the church and his country. In October 1940 he reported to the president that he had told an American Legion convention: "We really cannot longer afford to be moles who cannot see, or ostriches who will not see. For some solemn agreements are no longer sacred, and vices have become virtues and truth a synonym for falsehood. We Americans want peace and we shall prepare for peace, but not for a peace whose definition is slavery or death."[3] In fact, the major leaders of the hierarchy, undoubtedly influenced by the Vatican, became more supportive of the president after the establishment of the Taylor mission, as the negotiations regarding lend-lease to Russia indicated. But antiwar sentiment remained widespread and enjoyed some episcopal support.

Stung by continuing Catholic attacks on the president, young Father Daniel Cantwell of Chicago, then at Catholic University, wrote to assure Roosevelt that Bishop Noll's *Our Sunday Visitor*, the Brooklyn *Tablet*, and *America* did not represent the best of American Catholic opinion. He told Roosevelt that Mundelein, if he were still alive, would have seen the need to combat totalitarianism in all its forms and protect the world against "tyranny and anarchy."[4] Archbishop Lucey, John A. Ryan, Michael Williams, and others actively recruited Catholic support for Roosevelt and attempted to counter Catholic isolationsts. Feelings were bitter. Michael Williams, for example, pleading with Ryan to find new ways to demonstrate that Catholics were as opposed to "Hitlerism and fascism as they are opposed to Communism," characterized the views of anti-Roosevelt Catholics as "anti-Allied, selfishly isolationist and sometimes downright Nazi and fascist."[5]

Fortunately, the manner in which the United States finally went to war left little room for such divisions. Spellman, who would become most active in visiting troops and assisting the Vatican and the American government, set the tone of total commitment to the national cause after Pearl Harbor: "With fire and brimstone came December 7, America's throat was clutched, her back stabbed, her brain was stunned; but her great heart still throbbed. America clenched the palm of those hands oft-stretched in mercy to the peoples of the nations that struck her. America's brain began to clear. America began the fight to save her life."[6] In sermons and even poems Spellman maintained this rhetorical level throughout the war.

He was not alone. Archbishop Mooney, in words that recalled the millennial optimism of Hecker and Ireland, spoke on behalf of the hierarchy:

> The historic position of the Catholic Church in the United States gives us a tradition of devoted attachment to the ideals and institutions of government we are now called upon to defend. Our predecessors in the Third Plenary Council of Baltimore solemnly declared: 'We believe that our country's heroes were the instruments of God of nations in establishing this home of freedom; to both the Almighty and to his instruments in the work, we look with grateful reverence, and to maintain the inheritance of freedom which they have left us, should it ever—which God forbid—be imperiled, our Catholic citizens will be found to stand for-

ward, as one man, ready to pledge anew their lives, their fortunes and their sacred honor'.[7]

Despite this public enthusiasm, the American hierarchy was more restrained in private. While Spellman played an essentially independent role because of his Vatican contacts, Mooney, McNicholas, and Archbishop Samuel Stritch of Chicago, the leaders of the NCWC, were the hierarchy's official representatives. They worked hard to persuade the administration to avoid destruction of religious centers in Italy. After repeated pleas in this regard, Mooney warned the president that "the judgement of history and the conscience of citizens" would hold the Allies and the American government accountable for failure to spare Rome and the papal domains.[8] Postmaster General Frank Walker, a Catholic, pressured Mooney into silencing Father Coughlin, while historian Carleton J. H. Hayes served as ambassador to Franco's Spain, helping to keep that country neutral but suffering heavy criticism for suspected pro-Franco attitudes.[9] In 1943 Father Francis Haas, who had previously served in several capacities with New Deal labor agencies, was appointed chairman of the Fair Employment Practices Committee established in the aftermath of a threatened march on Washington by black activists led by A. Philip Randolph.[10]

Certainly there was little dissent from the war effort. There were only 135 Catholics among 11,887 conscientious objectors registered by the government, despite the widespread talk of this option before Pearl Harbor. Another small group who refused to register served prison terms. Dorothy Day insisted that the Catholic Worker maintain its pacifist stand, despite opposition within the movement. She wrote with some bitterness of the constant demand that the poor and the exploited working class avoid even the appearance of violence in their struggle for justice, whereas when the state was in danger all limits on violence were removed. She preferred to see men refuse to register rather than accept alternative service, but she supported those who acted within the law. Earlier some Catholic Workers had organized an American branch of the English peace organization, PAX, to arouse interest in conscientious objection. When the war started Arthur Sheehan of the Catholic Worker took charge of a self-appointed committee to follow the peace churches in organizing public service camps for those who refused military service. The cost of the Catholic camp in New Hampshire had to be borne by this committee; there was no support from the church at large and most clergy regarded the presence of Catholic pacifists as an embarrassment. After 1942 the residents began to be placed in hospitals and other social service agencies.[11]

The witness of these pacifists, their very presence, made an enormous contribution. With the more militant isolationists before the war, they had introduced the possibility that a Catholic Christian, and the church as a whole, might be compelled by conscience to resist American government policy. Neither the early republicans nor the later liberals had admitted that possibility; the sole exception was John Lancaster Spalding, who had used the term "double allegiance." By making the case, the pacifists forced at least a few Catholics to discuss the moral teaching on war and to evaluate whether the Allied cause could be justified. The attack on Pearl Harbor seemed to make the American war self-evidently just, and the debate disappeared from the major Catholic papers; but Day and a few associates of the Catholic Worker continued to argue that Christianity could not be reconciled with the use of force. Around her newspaper, and among a few theologians, more subtle arguments took place. One was that while defensive war could in theory be justified, the means used in modern warfare, both weapons technology and the enlistment of entire populations, eliminating the distinction between combatants and noncombatants, meant that no war could be conducted justly. Traditionally, Catholic teaching had argued that certain principles could be applied to determine whether the decision to go to war was proper, but even after war began, it remained a human activity subject to moral evaluation. The two tests of war-making were discrimination, that innocent noncombatants were not directly targeted, and proportionality, that the means used had to bear a reasonable relationship to the end to be achieved. By these tests the policies of saturation bombing and unconditional surrender were at least questionable, while the use of the atomic bomb seemed to a clear violation of the just-war tests. A very few theologians joined the Catholic Worker in raising these questions. All but unknown to the majority of Catholics, they did force other theologians to articulate a defense, launching a debate that would remain restricted to a small circle for almost two decades after the war but that would provide a framework of moral discourse when conditions again arose for wider consideration of the morality of warfare.[12] Never again would the unquestioning support of the state go unchallenged.

Throughout the war the bishops warned the administration about the danger of Soviet power in the postwar years. In the crucial months following the end of the war in Europe, Spellman and other bishops used what influence they could to stiffen American resistance to Soviet control of eastern Europe. When communist regimes began attacking the church, the bishops went public, mobilizing their people behind a strongly anticommunist foreign policy, first in Europe, then in Asia. Eastern European ethnic groups and returning American missionaries provided energetic support to these efforts. Later they would quietly organize political and financial support for anticommunist, Christian Democratic, political groups in Western Europe. Yet the Vatican and the American hierarchy did not always see eye to eye. When Myron Taylor resigned as representative to the Vatican in 1950, Spellman persuaded President Truman to name General Mark Clark as ambassador to the Vatican. This action aroused vigorous protests from non-Catholics; Clark withdrew his name and the issue died. Throughout the dispute other leaders of the American hierarchy were clearly unenthusiastic, both because they anticipated the controvesy and because they did not relish having an ambassador bypass their own role in dealing with relations between the government and the church. On the other hand Spellman got no credit for his efforts in Rome; when Archbishop Giovanni B. Montini criticized the failure of American Catholics to bring about diplomatic recognition, Spellman responded sharply, referring to the millions of dollars sent to the Holy See and the European church by American Catholics.[13]

POSTWAR PROSPERITY

Between the end of World War II and the opening of the Vatican Council in 1962, the American Catholic population rose from twenty-four million to forty-four million. The number of priests and sisters rose even faster. By 1965 four million children were attending Catholic elementary schools, twice as many as in 1940, and high school enrollments had risen by 150 percent. Catholic higher education expanded even more dramatically as young men from working-class families used their benefits under the G.I. Bill of Rights to get the education now considered a ticket into the middle class. They were not disappointed: an expanding economy was opening up numerous opportunities in business and professional life. Even those who remained factory workers shared in the prosperity of the times, thanks to the new industrial unions, which turned their attention in the postwar years to improving wages, benefits, and job security rather than demanding a share in decisionmaking.

Socially and economically, American Catholics from the older European ethnic groups were undergoing an almost revolutionary change, but one that would take several decades to complete. Through the years of the depression, Catholics had been near the bottom of income scales and were underrepresented in the managerial and professional classes. While education and opportunity were changing this situation; the process was only beginning. According to a 1953 study 85 percent of the leaders of the nation's top 200 corporations were Protestant; another study the same year found that in manu-facturing, mining, and finance 93 percent of the executives were Prot-estant. Catholic median income still lagged behind that of other groups, but income, occupational, and educational status were im-proving, and by the end of the 1960s Andrew Greeley and others would demonstrate that although the very highest positions in many areas remained closed, Catholics had surpassed other groups in education and some had even achieved the highest levels of income.[14]

Social mobility meant geographic mobility as the sons and daugh-ters of urban ethnic families raised their "baby boom" families in the new automobile suburbs, where the Catholics among them did not perpetuate the national divisions of the past but constructed the "Catholic and American" parishes that John Carroll had called for at the start. On the surface at least, they were incredibly faithful, attending mass in record numbers, contributing vast amounts of money to build schools, churches, convents, and rectories and at the same time contributing to expanding religious orders and their mis-sionary and educational work. Polls showed that they, like most Americans, believed almost unanimously in the basic doctrines of Christianity, and they seemed not to question such controversial Catholic teachings as the prohibition against birth control and the infallibility of the pope. If the historic goals of the American church were to preserve the faith of the immigrants and their children and to win a secure place in American society, those goals seemed to have finally been achieved.[15]

Intellectually, "the main thrust in those years was toward an or-ganically unified Catholic culture in which religious faith constituted the integrating principle that brought all the dimensions of life and thought together in a comprehensive and tightly articulated synthe-sis."[16] In the 1930s there had been two critical views of American Catholic culture. Mary McCarthy, like so many American writers who had been raised Catholic but who had left the church, admired Ca-tholicism's romantic sense of history and its straining against con-temporary culture, but she found the church in practice narrow, anachronistic, and hypocritical, filled with defensiveness and a preoccupation with its own interests and way of life. For McCarthy, Catholicism was too Catholic in a narrow and parochial sense, and not American or modern enough.[17]

Dorothy Day and Peter Maurin, on the other hand, had the opposite problem. For them, the American church had always been *the* church, but it was also caught up in bourgeois culture, too concerned with institutions, too filled with people, clergy, and laity, measuring success in the material terms of the larger society. Catholicism, for them, was too American, and not Christian enough. Most Catholics in the 1950s felt they had transcended that dichotomy, that Catholicism was the most American of religions, and America the most Christian of nations. Cardinal Spellman earned the admiration of Catholics and the enmity of non-Catholics by regularly insisting that Catholicism more than any other religion affirmed the basic principles of American democracy and offered the firmest support to the nation in its resistance against communism. Dr. Thomas Dooley, the medical missionary in Southeast Asia, symbolized a tremendous outreach to the foreign missions in these years, and always the missionary enterprise was presented as a means for spreading Christianity and American democracy. This synthesis led some to wonder whether these were Catholics who happened to be American, or Americans who happened to be Catholic.

One great worry of conservative Catholic leaders had always been that assimilated and Americanized Catholics would become more casual in their practice, intermarry, and drift into indifference. Certainly, that had not yet happened in the 1950s. One explanation, offered by religious sociologist Will Herberg, was that Catholicism had been one part of a triple melting pot; as people ceased marrying within the same ethnic group, they continued to marry within their religious group. Moreover, Herberg argued, Catholicism, like Protestantism and Judaism, was a way of being American. There was, he pointed out, little militance among Catholics to convert other Americans. Indeed, in one of the most highly publicized episodes of the period, Jesuit Leonard Feeney had been excommunicated for a too vigorous presentation of the doctrine of "no salvation outside the church." Herberg's argument was that Catholicism had become a way of being American, of finding identity and belonging while worshiping not the God of the Scriptures but America itself. Catholicism had purchased organizational success at the price of its soul and fallen victim to what Herberg called the "idolatrous new religion of Americanism."[18]

One other explanation of Catholic loyalty and unity was the pressure of an external enemy. In the postwar years, while "brotherhood" flourished in an atmosphere of outward mutual respect, Catholicism was still a public issue and intergroup conflict was far from dead. Indeed, as in earlier times many Catholics welcomed the external challenge as a way of asserting their loyalty and clarifying the boundaries between themselves and other groups. Most notable was the work of Paul Blanshard, whose best-selling 1950 book, *American Freedom and Catholic Power*, was a classic statement of the incompatibility of the church ("an aristocratic moral monarchy") and democracy. Raymond McGowan had written that Catholics should "think Catholic answers to every problem of life," which Blanshard took as evidence that the hierarchy wanted its people to function "primarily as Catholics in every phase of their activity" and cultivate intolerance of other religions. Extensive evidence for this attitude could be found, in, for example, church support for Franco's Spain; the bloc voting that sustained urban political machines; the indifference or hostility to public schools and the single-minded pursuit of aid for parochial schools; the efforts to impose Catholic views on others by supporting public bans on birth control; and the attempt to limit publication and distribution of films, magazines, and books and to prevent the appearance of supposedly anti-Catholic speakers. Drawing upon Ryan's arguments on church and state, the teachings of Leo XIII, and the examples of Spain and Ireland, Blanshard contended that Catholics, if they became a majority, would be bound to seek three amendments to the Constitution, one recognizing Catholicism as the official religion, a second supporting Catholic education and requiring the teaching of Catholic morality in neutral schools, and a third imposing Catholic teachings on marriage, divorce, and birth control. Like so many earlier opponents of the church, Blanshard attacked the hierarchy, not Catholics themselves. If Catholics "controlled their own church," he argued, "the Catholic problem would soon disappear because, in the atmosphere of American freedom, they would adjust their church's policies to American realities." From an American standpoint, he believed that "acceptance of any form of authoritarian control weakens the democratic spirit."[19] And the church was indeed undemocratic, stressing family control of education, but in fact dictating to parents what should be taught, engaging in devotions designed to place responsibility for belief in the hierarchy and clergy, and sharply limiting intellectual freedom for its teachers, scholars, and people. No dissent was allowed. Such practices could not help but weaken American democracy and only fear of being charged with bigotry kept intelligent Americans from facing the fact that the Catholic hierarchy used American freedom to systematically cultivate separation and intolerance.

Blanshard's was a powerful assault, attractive to many non-Catholics concerned about the great influence Catholics had acquired. A new organization, Protestants and Other Americans United for Separation of Church and State (POAU) attracted many respectable Protestant leaders to the defense of religious liberty and the protection of public policy from "Catholic power." In response Catholic writers marshaled their arguments, drawing once again on the republican tradition's distinctions between religion and politics to contend that religious liberty allowed one to join and support an authoritative church and the church allowed Catholics to support any government, whatever its form, which assured the common good. So convincing were these arguments to Catholics that they believed only bigots could defend Blanshard; but he and his supporters could not understand how people with such undemocratic views of religion could remain good citizens. They also wondered about a political flexibility that could affirm both Franco and the First Amendment.

There was another problem area. Catholics saw Blanshard as a militant secularist, and they regarded Jews as among the most militant backers of such secularism. Like other Americans, Catholics no longer accepted the stereotypes of Jews that were widespread in the 1930s, but they reflected little on the fact of the Holocaust beyond ritual moralizing about totalitarianism and liberal Catholic support for the new state of Israel, a support that contrasted with the position of the Vatican. At home, tensions arose because Catholics and Jews had taken separate paths on some public issues, most notably the school question. When Catholics were clearly a minority, they had often found themselves allied with Jews in opposing the use of Christian texts and prayers in schools. For the Jews, secularization seemed a requirement for their full participation in public institutions, but for Catholics exclusion of religion was a tactic required by fear of Protestant proselytization; in fact, they had always agreed that religion, morality, and education were inseparable. In the postwar years, Catholics, now more secure, mounted regular campaigns for aid to Catholic schools and more generally contended that secularism was the enemy of American democracy.

In an outwardly friendly warning, *America* admonished "our Jewish friends" that they were in danger of painting themselves into a corner with their militant support of secularism. Even as intelligent and humane a Catholic spokesman as John Tracy Ellis warned a Jewish audience against "using the numerous high and influential posts to which their superb talents have brought them in American society, whether these be in the press, the fine arts, the drama, or the communications media, in a way that gives justified offense to their gentile neighbors, to say nothing of offering a handle to their enemies." While Jews had benefited from secularism, Ellis argued, they should not attempt to make it the national philosophy of America's pluralistic society. These signs of the times led Rabbi Arthur Gilbert to issue his own warning: "We tear away the defenses that our Christian neighbors have built up to handle their anxieties. Out spills the anger and fear that these defenses have held in check and the anger touches us. The Jews are identified with those who are against these holy symbols. They are identified with the Communist and secularist, with persons blind to the real problems that confront the American community."[20]

Once again it was clear that the coexistence of diverse faiths was not a task resolved by a policy of live and let live. Each religious group learned that official neutrality was necessary for their own equality; they would have to depend upon their own voluntary institutions, their own subculture, to express and promote their distinctive values and beliefs. But if religion is the heart of culture, this combination can leave serious believers divided and uneasy, and tension can become severe when they are required to do things together. In fact the complex problems of industrial society, and even more the requirements imposed by war, and now by a universal campaign to defend the West against communism, meant that Americans were called upon to act together as one people. At points of crisis, when sacrifice was required, public officals almost always made reference to religion, seeking to enlist personal commitment for the common good. Americans should be united, and religious pluralism, unless checked by mutual restraint and subordination of particular interests to the national interest, was a threat to that unity. Never was this more true than in the post–World War II period.

George Kennan, the architect of the postwar containment policy, expressed a widespread concern with national unity when he argued that "the thoughtful observer would welcome the Kremlin's challenge" because it would force Americans to join together to accept "the responsibilities history plainly intended they should bear." The great Protestant theologian Reinhold Niebuhr, another shaper of Cold War consciousness, regretted the separation of religion from education but argued that "however steep the price, such a separation . . . represents a gain for our public life, since organized religion is bound to be divisive, and it is a divisiveness we simply cannot afford."[21] If Americans could not be made one around a common religion, as the older evangelicals had hoped (and Herberg argued they in fact were), or around a seemingly neutral, nonreligious secular ideal, as Niebuhr, Blanshard, and others upheld, how were they in fact to have a common life?

These anxieties found their focus in specific issues, what Monsignor Francis Lally called "points of abrasion." Lally thought the most important of these was continuing suspicion about the sincerity of Catholic acceptance of religious liberty and church–state separation. Another was Catholic opposition to federal aid to education unless Catholic schools were included in the form of assistance for "auxiliary services" such as bus transportation, health services, and textbooks. Another area of conflict involved birth control, sterilization, and abortion, as exemplified in Catholic opposition to efforts to repeal laws in Massachusetts and Connecticut that banned sale of birth control devices. He also noted suspicion that the church favored censorship, as, for example, in the continuing work of the Legion of Decency and the National Office for Decent Literature. A 1957 statement of the hierarchy limited public intervention on such matters to "those things which plainly subvert the good order of society," but of course the definition of "good order" was precisely the issue. Lally saw these disputes as part of the growing pains of pluralism and, in the public piety characteristic of the period that persuaded Herberg that religious groups were not serious, Lally thought conflicts could be limited because all participants had a "shared confidence" in the American future.[22]

THE LAITY

Since the Civil War Catholic leaders concerned about the church's public image and impact had also been forced to discuss the role of the laity. Isaac Hecker had argued that the model of modern holiness would not be found in monasteries but in marketplaces, and John Ireland had spoken of "a church of energetic individuals" bringing the faith into the centers of modern life. In the twentieth century, John J. Burke, C.S.P., had spoken of the laity as mere "externs," with no responsibility within the church and no invitation to work with their priests to Christianize society. John A. Ryan and other social-action leaders found in the banner of Catholic Action a central theme of the pontificate of Pope Pius XI, a mandate to issue that invitation to lay people to work for the welfare of the church and the good of society. In the aftermath of Americanism, what was needed was lay action that would not undermine the subordinate role of the laity within the church. The pope had made it clear, and it was endlessly repeated, that Catholic Action was the "participation of the laity in the hierarchical apostolate, . . . something obviously which cannot be assumed at will by those not in orders."[23] The mission of spreading the message of the gospel and "restoring all things in Christ" had been given by Jesus to the apostles and their successors, the bishops and priests. Only under their direction was lay action officially Catholic. Thus the Legion of Decency was Catholic Action, but the Catholic Worker was not. Furthermore, the best defense was a good offense; the most popular forms of Catholic Action had to do with defending the church or promoting its specific ideals, and only through such indirect means aiding the common good. The lay person leading the Holy Name Society in a campaign for school aid was involved in Catholic Action; the Catholic politician serving on the school committee was not.

For Ryan, McGowan, and others, Catholic Action provided a vehicle, as well as a rationale, for pointing the church outward toward public life. But for most bishops, it was a mandate to enlist the laity in assisting the clergy in the work of the church itself. In a widely read summary of postwar lay activism, Father Leo Ward, C.S.C, found a more positive tone than had been characteristic of lay activism in earlier years. In the past, he noted, the American church had been preoccupied with its domestic and theological enemies, but now it was "much too busy living its own creative life and living it with what must seem to outsiders as an almost disconcerting confidence." At the heart of that new life was "the layman" (sometimes "the laity"; among women's groups, "the laywoman"). The big question was how to achieve sanctity while living in "the world." Quoting French theologian Yves Congar, O.P., Ward argued that the danger was to regard the laity as an "appendage," too often the case in recent centuries; he thought American Catholics were "just beginning to crush that serpent."[24] He then went on to examine in detail the liturgical movement, strongest in the Midwest, emphasizing now less Virgil Michel's ideas of the liturgy as a school of social justice than the participation of the laity in the mass through congregational singing and the dialogue mass. The Confraternity of Christian Doctrine, parish-based, drew lay people into discussion classes, outreach to fallen-away Catholics, convert work, and religious instruction of public school children, either as teachers or more often aides. Ward and others worried, however, that parish-based lay societies no longer met the needs of better-educated Catholics.[25]

At the end of the period *Commonweal* noted over 300 Catholic organizations, including the Catholic Accountants Guild, the Catholic Aviation League of Our Lady of Loretto and the International Federation of Middle Class Catholics. The paper regarded these "Catholic occupational groups" as of questionable value. They were "rooted in defensiveness" and designed to insulate Catholics, generating a "clannishness designed to prevent attrition from the church." The same applied to Catholic versions of nonreligious groups like the Boy Scouts and Catholic organizations that existed for fraternizing, allowing "Catholics to drink and play cards only with other Catholics." All of them perpetuated "the tight dependence of laymen on priests" and prevented the development of mature faith needed by a now mature church. *Commonweal* thought the church no longer needed to bolster Catholic loyalty, which should be taken for granted, but "to develop fully aware Christians who will ... work on their own to create a more Christian environment."[26]

Such in fact was the aim of a small but vigorous network of Catholic Action groups centered in the Midwest. To the standard Catholic Action ideal of multiplying the priest's hands, Monsignor Reynold Hillenbrand and Father Louis Putz added the social-action orientation and formation of laypersons for work in the secular world of the European Catholic youth movement. The church had for too long asked

people to seek salvation against their society by creating a separate
environment, the French theologian M.D. Chenu, O.P., argued. The
new movements called them to "incarnate the life of grace in their
social milieux and in . . . their social institutions."[27] Young Catholic
Students, Young Catholic Workers, and the native-born Christian
Family Movement attempted to provide religious and spiritual formation for laypersons seeking to live a fuller Christian life while promoting Catholic and democratic values in society. In the process they
came to understand the need for autonomy. Seeking in the first instance neither the conversion of individuals to Catholicism nor a
merely personal commitment to social justice but changes in social
institutions, lay people had to become more, not less, involved in secular professions and in nondenominational efforts for reform. "There
is a profound paradox about the layman's handling of papal social
doctrines," Ed Marciniak, a national figure in lay movements, wrote.
"Only by withdrawing from the Pope," by incorporating the "general
principles" of papal teaching "into the meat and potatoes immediacy
of human existence" could the goals of justice and harmony be realized.[28] A decade earlier Father McGowan had urged Catholics "to
think Catholic answers to every problem of their lives" (the phrase
that had so disturbed Blanshard) because, as they became no longer
outsiders in America but "flesh of its flesh," they would otherwise
live "disjointed lives," separating their religion and their temporal
existence.[29]

As the new lay movements helped lay activists to do that, forming
them around those Catholic answers, laymen like Marciniak were
often finding that those answers did not work, or if they did, they
needed to be translated into the concrete circumstances and ordinary
language of everyday life. To accomplish this, it would be necessary
to recognize the independence of the laity and to listen to the experience of lay Catholics. The Christian Family Movement enjoyed the
greatest success, spreading around the country and eventually
achieving international scope. Couples, with a priest chaplain, studied
Scripture and addressed a particular social problem under the meth-
odology of "observe, judge, and act." Providing reinforcement for
marriage and family life, introducing predominantly college-educated
couples to advanced theology, and instilling a sense of social responsibility as an integral dimension of faith, the Christian Family Movement succeeded in forming the lay leaders that *Commonweal* thought
necessary, leaders who increasingly saw their responsibilities in public
terms. They would play a major role in shaping American response
to the Second Vatican Council.

Other groups with a similar orientation included the Grail, a laywomen's movement that combined a deep formation in Catholic culture with outreach to the poor and needy, the still small but vibrant Catholic interracial councils, and the rural life movement, increasingly addressing public problems of food and agriculture while encouraging Catholic farmers to stay on the land. Finally, there was still a more radical version of lay activism. The Catholic Worker movement, somewhat marginalized by its pacifism during the war, developed a more sophisticated commitment to active nonviolence under the inspiration of Gandhi and, later, Martin Luther King, Jr. Aided now by Ammon Hennacy, a native American anarchist, Dorothy Day and her friends acted publicly to oppose the arms race, the draft, and civil defense while continuing their work among the poor.[30]

From the Catholic Worker movement came another form of personalism, centered on *Integrity* magazine, edited by Ed Willock and Carol Jackson. This movement was an expression of the desire for a completely Catholic culture, lived close to the land, with an integration of family life, work, and religion. As Willock put it, "Catholic radicalism" returned "to a more literal interpretation of the Gospels" to offer an alternative way of life to "the massed victims of industrial society." The challenge this radicalism presented to the church, as well as society, arose from the fact that its adherents located "Christ as Victim" not among "the elect" or in the "closed parish" but among "the outcasts, the strangers, the ostracized and the unemployable." Each person was "much more sacred than ecclesiastical pots and pans."[31]

Dorothy Day and *Integrity* called the laity to step out from a corrupt society. Marciniak and the JOCists called them deeper into it, both for the sake of personal integrity and social transformation. For the minority of lay Catholics who entered into these lay movements, usually for a short time, it was an exciting experience, far different from the conventional practice and anticommunist rhetoric of so many parishes. Among the strongest supporters of all this lay activism was Bishop John Wright, who championed development of lay spirituality, the liturgical movement, and an intellectual apostolate. Like many of those associated with this more activist Catholic Action, Wright felt that the problem now facing American Catholics was that they had become too American, having adapted too completely and uncritically to American culture. Thus, even among the best leaders of Catholic life in the postwar years, the emphasis was placed less on their public role as Americans and once again more on their deeper commitment to and involvement with the church, on learning to think Catholic answers to every problem of life. In the words of one of the best-known laymen of the day, John Cogley: "We content ourselves with standing in judgement on our age as if its problems were not our problems, as if its failures were not our own, as if the challenges confronting it were not confronting us."[32]

CHARITY AND EDUCATION

In the postwar years the impact on Catholic charities of the New Deal's modest introduction of the welfare state and, to a lesser degree, its impact on Catholic education, highlighted the contrasting public role of these two important elements of Catholic life. Since at least the turn of the century, charities had avoided the sharp separatism that characterized education; during the 1930s necessity and a legitimate concern with human need accelerated the process of engagement with non-Catholic agencies and with government at all levels. One result was the decline of some institutions as Catholic professionals adapted to new ideas and new policies. Juvenile protective institutions, for example, no longer reflected prevailing theories about handling delinquency, and public assumption of responsibility exerted pressure toward private-sector cooperation and eventually integration. There were 163 such protective institutions in 1945, with a total of 20,623 residents; by 1950 the number had dropped to 129 and in 1984 there were only 99, with 8,792 residents.

A similar process took place with orphanages as foster care and new adoption policies reduced the role of institutions. From 373 orphanages with over 48,000 children in 1945 the number dropped to 257 and 23,379 in 1965, and to 174 and 10,860 by 1984. On the other hand, government support and new forms of insurance meant that Catholic health-care institutions grew enormously while their role as both Catholic and semipublic institutions became far more complex. With consolidations and mergers there were actually fewer Catholic hospitals in the 1980s than there had been in 1945, but the number of patients treated in general hospitals rose from 3.2 to 36.5 million; special-service hospitals, also fewer in number, experienced comparable growth. The particular concern of the church, together with public-funding possibilities, also resulted in a multiplication of nursing homes and residences for the aged, especially in the 1970s.

By now Catholic charity agencies, courts, hospitals, community chests, and other local fund-raising and planning systems were all interlocked with city, state, and federal welfare agencies. Occasionally intergroup tensions would jeopardize this complex social and constitutional arrangement, as when the New York Health and Welfare Council broke up because of Catholic opposition to aid for Planned

Parenthood, but protests and constitutional challenges from religious and civil liberties groups were surprisingly few.[33]

During all these developments Catholic spokesmen regularly stressed the differences between their own approach to charitable work and that of public institutions, and most dioceses had regular charitable appeals that were responded to generously; nevertheless outsiders noticed the similarities between the services offered and the increasingly heavy proportion of charities budgets that came from public sources. Through cooperation not only charities personnel but bishops as well experienced public responsibility, they were drawn of necessity to consideration of public policy, and the church remained tied to the poor, even those who were not Catholic. The public perspective and the perspective of the poor were somewhat different from the institutionally centered consciousness formed by the immigrant church, and these perspectives insured that public responsibility would be an important element in the life of the organized church in years to come.

The situation with education was very different. Here the church was deeply committed to its own institutions, and the dynamics of that commitment had led to continuing criticism of non-Catholic education, lack of attention to public education and the educational needs of non-Catholics, and an adversary relationship with the government. As already noted, Catholic schools had grown dramatically after the war. In 1945 there were 7,493 parochial schools, 537 private elementary schools, 1,599 diocesan high schools, and 762 private high schools, with a total enrollment of 2.6 million. By 1965 the number of parochial schools had risen to 11,000, with 4.5 million students, and high schools to 2,400 with just under 1.1 million students. Yet the proportion of parishes with schools had changed little since the turn of the century. In 1900, 3,812 parishes, 63 percent of the total, had parochial schools; in 1959 there were 9,814 schools in 16,753 parishes, or 58 percent. At the end of the decade one study found that 57 percent of the adults in selected parishes had attended parochial schools, while 63 percent would send their children if they had the opportunity. There were wide ethnic variations. Only 12 percent of adult Italians had attended Catholic schools, but half wished such an education for their children. The comparable figures for French Canadians were 72 percent and 74 percent. Studies also found that parochial students were more, not less, oriented toward success in their work and they were more identified with the church and more faithful to its rules; but there was no discernible difference between parochial and public school graduates in their attitudes toward public issues.

Education was becoming increasingly expensive. Religious orders could not keep up with the demand for their services, so already there were more lay teachers; heightened educational expectations required specialized training and equipment. The teaching sisters also were gradually demanding more professional recognition, which meant increased training and, again, increased cost. Catholic leaders still gloried in their educational self-reliance, but, convinced that their schools provided a major public service, they found the "double taxation" of supporting both public and parochial schools increasingly burdensome. Catholics had vigorously opposed federal aid to education before and after World War I and they continued to argue vigorously against federal control. But attitudes had begun to change in the 1930s, occasioned by the experience of federal relief efforts and the distribution of some services to schools through the National Youth Administration and other agencies. The possibility existed that education could follow the path set by charities of at least moderate participation in federal efforts to deliver educational services.

In 1938 Roosevelt's Advisory Committee on Education, which included George Johnson of the National Catholic Educational Association, recommended federal aid to education, with services such as reading materials, transportation, and scholarships made available to both public and private school students. After World War II church leaders were prepared to offer qualified backing of federal aid if Catholics shared in its provisions under the "child benefit" theory upheld by the Supreme Court. Bills introduced were permissive, allowing states to determine distribution of benefits and decide what was a public school under the law, but these provisions were opposed by many Protestants. Similar fights took place in several states.[34]

In 1949 the U.S. Senate passed a bill allocating $300 million to equalize opportunities, with a proviso that states decide whether to allocate funds to private and parochial schools. An amendment to limit benefits to public schools was defeated 71–3, but in the House, Representative Graham Barden reported a bill from committee containing that limitation. The bishops were aroused. Cardinal Spellman attacked Barden's "craven crusade of religious prejudice against Catholic children" and the Catholic chairman of the House Education and Labor Committee agreed in equally harsh language. When Eleanor Roosevelt defended the Barden bill, Spellman wrote her a long, bitter letter, concluding with the words: "Your record of anti-Catholicism stands for all to see—a record which you yourself wrote on the pages of history which cannot be recalled—documents of discrimination unworthy of an American mother."[35] Not surprisingly Spellman's letter fueled the controversy. Compromise efforts to limit aid to areas such as transportation failed, and federal aid to education died.

The charge that Catholic leaders would fight any form of federal aid to education that did not include Catholic schools reinforced the conviction that the church placed its own interests before the public good. The problem would surface regularly until the mid-1960s, when President Lyndon B. Johnson won approval of a federal aid bill with limited benefits available to Catholic school children. Throughout that period, the issue regularly was debated, with Catholics caught between the argument that religion must permeate the school that they used with their own people and their demand for public assistance for the nonreligous areas of education.[36]

THE SURVIVAL OF SOCIAL LIBERALISM

In 1945 John A. Ryan, in his last speech, denounced the "authentic Bourbons of our time," conservative economic interests he feared would return to power after the war, having "learned nothing and forgotten nothing." He hoped that Americans in general and Catholics in particular would not be "fooled by the old claptrap concerning 'rugged individualism' 'American opportunity' or 'American equality' " into restoring "an economy dominated by the philosophy of 'free enterprise.' "[37]

In fact a Republican Congress was elected in 1946 and, among other things, it enacted the antilabor Taft-Hartley bill. Most bishops opposed the bill, and throughout the next two decades they would oppose right-to-work laws in the states and strongly defend labor's right to organize and bargain collectively.[38] But their support for the unions had always been conditioned on opposition to labor radicalism, and a number of CIO unions were in fact under communist control. Led by labor priests like Charles Owen Rice of Pittsburgh and by the ACTU, which was strong in the automobile, electrical, and transit unions, the Catholic labor network became an important factor in the fight to oust the communists. Although the Catholic activists had strongly opposed red-baiting in the 1930s, the Cold War and the behavior of the communists themselves had made it imperative to break any links between the labor movement and the party.

Philip Murray, leader of the CIO, was an active Catholic close to the labor priests; so was James Carey, chosen to lead the new International Union of Electrical Workers against the communist-dominated United Electrical Workers, which itself included among its leaders several men raised as Catholics and some active laymen.[39] In the end the CIO purged from its ranks not only communists but also many militant radicals. The labor priests, labor schools, and lay activists could take a portion of the credit. Later, some, like Rice, would regret their actions, which included close cooperation with the FBI, reflecting that in fighting the communists they might also have contributed to the conservative drift of union policy and public attitudes in the postwar years.

In fact, faced with rising inflation and increasingly anti-union public opinion, labor put aside what had always been a minimal interest in industrial reform and liberal politics to fight for union benefits. Lack of interest in Ryan's economic democracy, despite Murray's wartime endorsement of industrial councils, led to a more modest emphasis on labor-management cooperation.[40] As Bishop John Wright told an AFL-CIO convention in 1960, in the United States, labor–management disputes were "differences of groups with equal honor and equal rights, groups which made different, perhaps, but equal contributions to the national common good," so that the church did not take sides but worked to reconcile them.[41]

Priests involved with the labor movement found themselves serving as arbitrators and mediators and only a few, like George Higgins, a Chicago priest serving under Father McGowan in the NCWC Social Action office, reminded labor and the church of the vast number of workers who remained unorganized. As late as 1960 Higgins, by then the nation's leading labor priest, was still hoping that the unions would broaden their agenda to include joint labor-management committees that would share responsibility for industrial decisions. Echoing his predecessors, he also insisted on the need for more militant organizing in the South among minorities and white-collar workers, for he believed it still possible for the unions to go beyond their negative function of protecting workers to their positive role of providing their members with a way to carry out their responsibilities to one another and to the community.[42] In addition, Higgins regularly pointed out that no major piece of social legislation had been adopted in the quarter-century following the war that did not enjoy labor support.

But it was not until the new organizing drives among predominantly Hispanic farm workers in California, clothing workers in Texas, and textile workers in North Carolina and elsewhere in the South in the late 1960s and 1970s that the bishops and clergy were again aroused to militant championing of the labor movement. This organizing, reflecting as it did the experience of grassroots mobilization of Catholic parishes, ethnic groups, and political machines, seems to have provided a powerful link between the church and business unionism. Once the organizing had been accomplished and the issues had become more structural and political, the church backed off, both because labor was unreceptive and because involvement of clergy in such matters was less appropriate once the basic right to organize had been achieved.

The problem was well laid out in 1976 by Thomas Donahue, himself a product of the Catholic labor network and then executive assistant to the president of the AFL-CIO. Donahue reminded Catholic social activists that "unions are, of course, special interest organizations whose first and principal function is to organize workers and represent these workers in an effort to improve job conditions." "People don't join American unions because they want to express a particular social or political attitude," Donahue continued, referring to a photograph of a striking black sanitation worker who was holding up a sign reading "I AM A MAN." "They join because they want to express their human dignity on the job and have it recognized in the job." They were reluctant to pursue schemes of partnership with management, as the church had long advocated, because they suspected labor would be "most likely the junior partner in success and the senior partner in failure." Participation of that sort would compromise union independence and divert energy and attention from the concrete benefits workers needed.[43]

From the 1880s, when the carpenters' union had been taken over by its business agents, American trade unions had frustrated reformers. Workers sought from their unions improvement in wages, hours, and working conditions, which required recognition and collective bargaining. Once those were achieved, successful negotiation and avoidance of costly strikes required stable relationships with employers. In times of depression workers and union leaders might broaden the agenda to include wider demands, but in prosperity and periods of inflation concrete economic goals, together with job security, took precedence. Joseph Ettor, an agitator for the radical Industrial Workers of the World, in 1914 had learned the lesson that Catholic labor activists were to relearn after the war. He and his fellow radicals had tried to take over the AFL to fight capitalism, Ettor wrote, "but the more we fooled with the beast, the more it *captured us*." When they lost a strike, the members left; when they won, they had to bargain, sign a contract, and enforce its provisions. In either case the socialist goal was as distant as ever. Something of the same could be said of the Catholic hope for a corporatist collaboration in a self-governing economy.[44]

Labor was not the only area in which the Catholic social movement of the 1930s lost ground after the war. Prosperity dulled the sense of urgency of the depression era, while the enormous growth in population led to the tremendous expansion of the church and of its schools in the suburbs, turning episcopal and clerical energies in more parochial directions. Among Catholics as among other Americans, there was a revival of conservative attitudes, including a championing of laissez-faire hitherto little evident in Catholic circles. As in the 1920s, the bishops' pastoral statements tended to emphasize cultural issues, particularly the danger of secularism, the erosion of family life, which the bishops called "a present danger, more fearsome than the atom bomb," and the problems of education.[45]

Economic justice issues were less clearcut than they had been since the 1890s. Writing in 1951 Higgins noted that the United States now had a mixed and highly collectivized economy that still lacked a principle of unity and authority. The "American dilemma" remained: "how to establish effective social controls over a predominantly private but already highly collectivized economy without becoming totalitarian in the process." The answer, of course, was the vocational group system as modified by Ryan; Higgins still hoped to see unions and management come together on the basis of natural law, but he recognized that the pragmatic, Keynesian policies offered the path of least resistance, and, for the moment, they worked.[46]

George Higgins was not alone in hoping that business concentration might be a blessing in disguise. Benjamin Masse, the editor of the *Catholic Mind*, felt that large corporations and trade unions expressed interdependence and raised consciousness of social responsibility; if that sense of concern for the common good did not express itself in deeds, the reason was the absence of social institutions that would allow it to do so. The need for cooperation between the public and private sectors to control inflation raised the possibility that eventually new institutions of government, business, and labor collaboration would appear. As Father John Cronin, S.S., argued in a widely used textbook on social Catholicism, the present institutions of the American political economy could provide the basis for an organic, self-governing economy, free of the twin dangers of selfish individualism and the bureaucratic state if "they progressed into functional rather than mere interest and pressure groups" and developed new forms to deal with matters of mutual interest.[47]

To accomplish this goal Cronin called for a long-range educational and pastoral strategy aimed at forming Catholic lay leaders who could help move American culture away from competitive individualism. Social justice "imposes the obligation of *group action* to reform the *framework* and *institutions* of society so that the *common good* will be served," Cronin wrote. This was the church's task to be carried out within the framework of Catholic action. He compared the church to an army, with the pope as commander-in-chief, the bishops as generals, the clergy as officers, and the laity as noncommissioned officers and privates. The laity, he wrote, "do not make policy or give orders in their own name" but work "under minute and detailed guidance." If the church could be organized for the work, with well-trained lay leaders, the vocational group system could be established and the goal, "to restore all things in Christ," could be achieved.[48]

There were a few places, and a few people, who broke out of the straitjacket of papal corporatism and faced new issues, including those affecting people outside the church. One of the few centers of vigorous social action during the period was in San Antonio, where Robert E. Lucey had become archbishop in 1941. Lucey argued that racial discrimination was a sin. During the war he testified in favor of the Fair Employment Practices Commission and in 1954 he abolished school segregation in his diocese, soon after aiding the smooth desegregation of local public schools. His diocese joined the local community chest and Lucey championed federal housing and health care programs before community and civic groups and the state legislature. Named to the Bishops' Committee on the Spanish-Speaking, he soon controlled it and used it as a platform to defend farm workers. He vigorously backed American efforts to assist the development of catechetical instruction in Latin America as well.

But overall the continuing preoccupation with the internal discipline of a clerically dominated church, and the persistent fascination with the corporatist views of the encyclical reflected the poverty of Catholic social thought and the lack of imagination among leaders of the Catholic social movement. In fact even the most basic principles of Catholic social teaching remained almost unknown to most Catholics. "The American Catholic community as a whole has not been much affected by Catholic social thought," wrote Jesuit Edward Duff, editor of *Social Order*, one of the few bright lights of the period. "The idea that our social and economic institutions need reform does not occur to the average American Catholic." Duff worried that, "enjoying a tolerable level of economic justice and political freedom, the average Catholic [was] content." Like Bishop Wright, he thought Catholics were overidentifying with American culture, confusing "the American Way of Life" with "the Kingdom of God." Linking his criticism to that of John Tracy Ellis, who had ignited a firestorm with an essay decrying the weakness of American Catholic intellectual life, Duff charged that Catholic education was "more apologetic than intellectual"; the church encouraged the spiritual and corporal works of mercy, but "speculation about economic structures was a luxury beyond the scope of the Catholic minority." Ten times more people had attended a recent anticommunist meeting in Milwaukee than had attended the annual National Catholic Social Action Conference. The bishops were doing little to promote the church's own social teaching. In short, Duff concluded, the American church had to "face up to the arduous task of analysing contemporary American society from a Christian perspective. It must do this as the price of the providential favors it has enjoyed under the American political system and at the peril of being socially futile."[49]

CATHOLICISM AND ANTICOMMUNISM

For most of their history in the United States, Catholics had walked
a tightrope between America's dominant culture, which they perceived to be in one way or another hostile to their faith, and Roman
leadership, which was in many ways implicitly anti-American. Catholics regularly affirmed their loyalty to the nation that seemed to
reject their church and to a church that seemed to reject many of the
ideals of their nation. The result was an ambivalence in Catholic
thought about their country, an ambivalence raised to a dualistic
clarity by their philosophers and theologians. Whatever the reservations of their ecclesiastical leaders abroad, American Catholics loved
their country, and with good reason. But at the same time, they often
felt considerable suspicion of the government, they distrusted many
of the nation's political and cultural leaders, and they were deeply
antagonistic toward the public schools. In 1928 James Gillis of the
Catholic World had argued that Catholics were in fact more American
than those who denied their right to be American. In 1938 the bishops
launched their "Catholic Crusade for Christian Democracy" to "re-
Americanize America" by teaching youngsters proper interpretations
of American values. Years later John Courtney Murray would clinch
the argument when he proposed, to the evident satisfaction of his
most sophisticated fellow Catholics, that they were the last defenders
of the authentic American consensus. Catholics were thus intense nationalists but were convinced that they, more than the nation's elites,
were the carriers of authentic Americanism.

Father Coughlin in the 1930s and Senator Joseph R. McCarthy in
the 1950s both expressed this combination of patriotism and suspicion. So did Cardinal Francis Spellman. No prelate ever surpassed
Spellman's profession of love of country or his belief that the United
States was in grave danger from enemies foreign and domestic. In
1946 he told a graduating class of FBI agents: "To help save America
you must constantly and loyally labor to unmask traitors who give
lip service to democracy while anarchy and tyranny nestle in their
hearts." At a Polo Grounds rally later that year he warned that communists were "digging deep inroads into our own nation." In a famous
sermon from the pulpit of Saint Patrick's Cathedral in New York, he
began with the suffering of Cardinal Mindszenty of Hungary and ended describing the rags to riches story of his country, "the America I
beg Americans to save." More than most rabid anticommunists, however, Spellman backed his government. In 1948 he broke ranks with
other bishops and joined *Commonweal* and *America* in endorsing universal military training. "I hate war," he said. "And it is because I
hate war that I must put my trust in men who know better than I

the dangers that beset America, and if these men, chosen by the vote and confidence of the American people, believe that preparedness will prevent war, then I, who love my country better than I love my life, cast my vote, as a private American citizen, for universal military training."[50]

Throughout the 1950s anticommunism like Spellman's became intimately intertwined with many elements of Catholic life. Missionary appeals featured dramatic descriptions of communist atrocities; American missionaries combined conversions with provision of food, clothing, and medical care, building democracy while building barriers against communism as well. Marian devotions flourished during the period, especially devotion to Our Lady of Fatima, and invariably these devotions were linked to the danger from Russia.[51]

The bishops commissioned John Cronin to produce a report on the threat of foreign and domestic communism in 1945, and one result was a questionnaire asking local bishops to identify suspected local communists. Yet the hierarchy appears never to have discussed the controversy aroused by Senator McCarthy after he launched his campaign against communist subversion in 1950. At the time, most observers believed that Catholics backed McCarthy wholeheartedly, but in fact there were deep divisions. In November 1951 the NCWC administrative committee, probably at the urging of Cardinal Mooney of Detroit, issued a statement condemning dishonesty, slander, and defamation of character that some took as a slap at the Wisconsin senator. Spellman made no public comment until August 1953, when he told reporters that "[McCarthy] is against communism and he has done and is doing something about it. He is making America aware of the dangers of communism." Two months later he said: "Anguished cries and protests against McCarthyism will not deter America" from trying to root communists out of government. During the Army-McCarthy hearings Spellman attended a New York police communion breakfast where McCarthy was honored. When the senator had finished speaking, the cardinal addressed the policemen: "Senator McCarthy has told us about the Communists and about the Communist methods. I want to say I'm not only against Communism— but I'm against the methods of the communists."

Five days later Auxiliary Bishop Bernard Sheil denounced McCarthy before a convention of the United Auto Workers in a speech written by *Commonweal* editor John Cogley. Sheil contended that McCarthy's brand of anticommunism "mocks our way of life, flouts our traditions and democratic procedures . . . feeds on the meat of suspicion and grows great on the dissension among Americans which it creates and keeps alive in its mad pursuit of headlines." Sheil insisted that he spoke only for himself, and Catholics could disagree on

the subject, and they did. *Commonweal* and *America* consistently criticized the senator, while many diocesan papers championed his cause.
Historian Vincent de Santis found that, of forty-six Catholic weekly
papers, twenty-four, including that of Chicago, ignored Sheil's speech,
twenty-four carried news stories, only two on page one, and only four
commented editorially.[52]

After the fall of McCarthy, the split within the Catholic community
remained, though it rarely surfaced in the hierarchy. In the early
1960s, when the John Birch Society and other extremist groups were
appealing to the continuing fear of communism, the bishops once
again called upon Cronin, their resident expert. His widely used pamphlet, *Communism: Threat to Freedom*, stressed the themes used earlier
by the liberal press and by Sheil, that communism was primarily an
external danger, that the threat required national unity, and that the
best method of combating it was military strength combined with
economic and military assistance to countries struggling to retain
their freedom against subversion.[53]

The pamphlet aroused almost as much controversy as the earlier
Sheil speech. Critics were set back, however, by Pope John XXIII's
endorsement of dialogue based on a distinction between the ideas,
which the church condemned, and the people who held them, who
deserved respect. Guided by Cronin, the hierarchy rejected a secret
invitation to official dialogue from the American Communist party,
but many liberal Catholics welcomed this new opportunity to defuse
Catholic anticommunism, which they felt supported a wider conservative drift among Catholics.[54]

Throughout the period, however, differences about domestic subversion were minor compared to the all but unanimous belief, outside
the Catholic Worker community, that communism was the major enemy of the nation and the world, that it required a strong, superior
military posture, and that Catholics had a religious obligation to support a militant foreign policy. Another voice was beginning to be heard
but had not yet made a major impact. In 1964 Dom Helder Camara
of Recife in Brazil told *Commonweal* readers that the military approach to combating communism, contained even in liberal American
assistance polcies, was self-defeating. In northeast Brazil the church
was trying "to awaken the people's conscience, to develop their political consciousness . . . to make them realize their condition of poverty, the value of team work and the duty to struggle against injustice
and oppression." If communism did not exist, he reminded American
Catholics, "the Christian would still be obliged to arouse the political
self-awareness of the masses that live in subhuman conditions." For
taking that position, he told them gently, he and others were charged
with subversion. Most American Catholics, including the readers of

Commonweal, were not yet ready to hear that message.[55] Similarly, even liberal Catholics still took a view of the international system that placed the United States at the center of the world struggle of democracy against communism. Through the Catholic Association for International Peace they supported foreign aid, the United Nations, and international cooperation, but like most American liberals, they interpreted those positions through a lens of American leadership; as one scholar puts it, "in the end the CAIP's Americanism controlled its internationalism.[56]

As *Commonweal* editor William Clancy noted, the political debate was part of a larger effort of a growing, educated Catholic laity to articulate a self-conscious liberal Catholicism despite the "historical antipathy" between the two words. These Catholics enthusiastically accepted "certain ideals for which liberalism has waged its great battles—maximum human freedom under law, social progress and democratic equality." In doing so they found that liberals doubted their Catholicism, Catholics their loyalty. "The beleaguered 'liberal Catholic' thus stands between two worlds which view each other with mutual distrust and which, according to their proper lights, exclude each other," Clancy wrote. "Those whose theology he shares frequently distrust him because of his politics, and those with whom he feels at home politically may doubt him because of his theology." In defense against Catholic critics, Clancy argued that "the very things for which Pius IX had condemned liberalism, its belief in inevitable progress, its overly optimistic view of human nature and its dogmatic rationalism were the very things which had now given liberalism a bad name." Yet defense against the "absolutism of the east" required revival, "not of the philosophy but surely of many of the values for which liberalism had fought in shaping the modern world." Liberal Catholics therefore worked for a "synthesis of the Church's unchanging truths with whatever good is to be found in the modern City of man." Taking up the call of Cardinal Emmanuel C. Suhard of Paris to "discard whatever of non-essential method and outlook had been carried over from a society that can never return," the liberal Catholics were attempting to promote ideas not yet learned by many Catholics, such as the repudiation of claims of special privilege, the refusal to engage in censorship, the repudiation of coercion in religious and cultural matters, the need for tolerance and civility in public debates, and the need to support freedom and democracy, not just to oppose communism.[57]

Liberal Catholics were little concerned with the critical view of the Catholic Worker, whose pacifism, critique of just-war teaching and American foreign policy, and quite different reading of problems of economic development did not yet enjoy their attention. They were

far more worried about a new conservatism that had appeared after
the war and grown slowly during the Eisenhower years. Its centerpiece
was the *National Review*, a lively, iconoclastic magazine published
and edited by William F. Buckley, Jr., a wealthy Catholic and a graduate of Yale. While still in college he had written a stinging conservative critique of his university education, and of modern liberalism,
and after graduation he had begun gathering a stable of conservative
writers, only some of whom were Catholic, to combat what he considered the reigning intellectual, cultural, and political liberalism in
American society, while taking an occasional swipe at church leaders.
A warm supporter of Senator McCarthy, Buckley was not afraid to
take on church leaders. When Pope John XXIII's *Mater et Magistra*
appeared in 1961, giving a more democratic, almost socialist interpretation of economic issues, Buckley reported hearing in "Catholic
circles" some saying "Mater si, Magistra no." Intended to be hu-
morous, the remark drew bitter rebukes from liberal Catholics, who,
on matters of social justice and international peace, had become used
to relying on papal authority to combat their conservative opposition.

Buckley rejected the basic premise of liberal anticommunism, the
argument that communism was the product of injustice and could
be combated by working for social reform. "It is theologically wrong,
historically naive and strategically suicidal to assume that the forces
of communism, like those of the devil, are routed by personal or even
corporate acts of justice and love," he wrote. In the fight against communism, the relevant discussion should be over effective and inef-
fective ways of combating the evil. Every penny of foreign aid should
be evaluated in terms of its contribution to the anticommunist struggle. Free-market economies, not socialist ones, were most promising
for bringing about economic development. Disarmament negotiations
were futile unless backed by superior military power. And at its heart
the struggle was a spiritual one, between different conceptions of human nature, so that all religious people should oppose the secularism
and humanism which, by reducing human beings to material objects,
played into the hands of the communists.[58]

In 1960 Clancy and Buckley met three times in debates that demonstrated the wide area of consensus that still existed. Clancy admitted that every Catholic was "in a certain sense a conservative . . .
by definition" because the idea of a doctrinally liberal Catholicism
had been "disposed of once and for all" by Pius IX and Pius X. What
liberals and conservatives differed over was the modern world. Conservative rejection of modern culture risked "utter transcendence,"
while the temptation of the liberal was modernism, an accommodation to the world that betrayed the vocation of the Christian. The
conservative attitude of rejection since the French Revolution pre-

vented people from seeing the church as a community of "creative love and salvation." The liberal fought for freedom of the press, freedom of conscience, for racial justice and against anti-Semitism, and within the church contended for an adaptation that would allow Catholicism to bring its saving message to men and women in the modern world. Conservatives and liberals shared responsibility to defend the church and preserve its inheritance, but Clancy thought "the tragedy of conservative Catholicism [was] that it had so polarized itself, and built such thick walls around itself, that it has foresaken the Christian's second vocation, which is to adapt the truths he conserves to the unique needs of the present."[59]

But the most important contribution to clarifying the public responsibilities of the American church since the work of John A. Ryan was made by a Jesuit theologian, John Courtney Murray. Born in New York City in 1904, Murray entered the Jesuit seminary at sixteen and received the usual extensive education before his ordination in 1933. He then taught at the Jesuit theologate at Woodstock, Maryland, for thirty years, becoming editor of the newly established *Theological Studies* in 1941 and religion editor of *America* soon after. In addition to his academic work in systematic theology, Murray wrote and lectured on a wide variety of topics. Essays on interfaith cooperation written during World War II embroiled him in his first controversy. While upholding Catholic exclusivism, Murray argued that failure to cooperate with non-Catholics could not be justified if it endangered human life or social justice. He was attacked by a number of critics, including Father Joseph Fenton of Catholic University, all of whom warned of the danger of religious indifference among Catholics if barriers between the churches were lowered; they did not hesitate then or after to cite the warnings of Pope Leo XIII in the Americanist crisis. Fenton, like so many modern theologians, devoted his career to helping the church insulate itself from the dangers of modern thought. Murray, in contrast, saw himself as a missionary to the intellectual and spiritual milieu around him. Like Clancy and Clancy's hero, Bishop John Wright, and like the Americanists of an earlier era, Murray believed it necessary to engage modern culture if the spread of secularism, which so worried church leaders, was to be reversed.[60]

It was hardly surprising, therefore, that Murray's major interest became the relationship between church and state. He began by placing the teaching of Leo XIII in its historical context. Leo, dealing with a militant, anticlerical liberalism, resisted separation because he believed it would in fact subordinate the church to the state. The pope's major concern was the freedom of the church, until now guaranteed only when Catholicism was the state religion. Murray believed conditions had changed, allowing other constitutional forms to insure the church's freedom. His work drew warnings from conservative churchmen, but bishops sought his advice on church-state cases and he was now recognized as a first-rate speculative theologian. John Tracy Ellis supported Murray's work with historical accounts of the positions taken by the Amerian bishops. They had of course always affirmed separation; as Ellis wrote, "no variation from this theme has been heard from an American Catholic bishop."[61] Murray was grateful, telling Ellis he hoped the American bishops would overcome their fear of Rome to defend the American situation not as an ideal, but as legitimate, standing on an equal basis with that of Spain, where the church was established.

Murray's thought engendered warnings from Rome, forcing his Jesuit superiors to come to his defense. Murray interpreted a speech by Pope Pius XII as a rebuke to Cardinal Alfredo Ottaviani, who had become Murray's major Roman critic. When he stated this view publicly, pressure from Rome escalated; a book published at Notre Dame containing a Murray essay was withdrawn from circulation, Ellis was denied permission to give a paper on church and state, and in July 1955 Jesuit authorities denied Murray permission to publish the last of his papers on Leo XIII. An American on the Jesuit general's staff told Murray: "It seems to me a mistake to wish to carry on that controverted question under present circumstances." Murray was crushed; he canceled a contract for a book on church and state and symbolically removed books on the subject from his room. To another Jesuit he made clear that his work was aimed at clearing up what had always been the American Catholic problem. The "emotional aspects of the matter" were "external to the problem as such, which concerns the inner integrity of the Catholic conscience as such, and the legitimate terms on which it can affirm Catholic existence within the American constitutional commonwealth," Murray wrote. "It is we who need the theory for our own sakes."[62]

For several years Murray concentrated on other issues, including the school question and the ethics of national security policy. In 1958, with another Catholic clearly running for president, he submitted an article to his Roman superiors hoping it could be published in Rome. The answer was negative, but a few months later there was a new pope, John XXIII, and Murray sent his book to be published. Coming out as John F. Kennedy's campaign began to heat up, the book, *We Hold The Truth*, earned Murray considerable attention, including his picture on the cover of his friend Henry Luce's *Time* magazine.

Murray's position arose from the philosophy of natural law, given a historical dimension that emphasized concrete realities rather than abstractions. He combined his historical intepretation of previous teaching with Anglo-American political philosophy, from which he drew the distinction between state and society, the latter aimed at the common good, the former at public order. This provided the basis for an argument that it was possible to have a unified state without religious unity. Finally, like Ryan, he offered a natural law understanding of "the American proposition" of equality, inalienable rights, and limited government. Murray argued that a nation required a constitutional consensus to provide the means whereby people might aquire an identity and society might be given a vital form. That consensus was "not simply a set of working hypotheses whose value is pragmatic. It is an ensemble of substantive truths, a structure of basic knowledge, an order of elementary affirmations that reflect realities inherent in the order of existence." He believed, as did most Catholics, including his critics, that the truths of the American proposition were in danger. They could be sustained only by civil dialogue among citizens, a dialogue he believed only possible on the basis of natural law. Thus the public discussion was philosophical, not theological, preoccupied with natural ethics more than religious meaning. Just as the state, with its limited powers and jurisdiction, could not resolve religious questions, so the church could not claim to resolve political problems; it could only present its case on the basis of reason, seeking to form the consciences of its own members and influence the consciences of others. Such a position, Murray admitted, did "not promise to transform society into the City of God" but only to prescribe "that minimum of morality which must be observed by the members of society if a social environment is to be human and habitable."[63]

Murray, it should be clear, was arguing for Catholic participation in the American constitutional arrangement in the context of religious pluralism, not for democracy. He was pessimistic about human nature and convinced that most people were unsuited for civil dialogue. For the masses, it was important that everything not be in doubt. "It is a Christian theological intuition, confirmed by all historical experience, that man lives both his personal and social life always more or less close to the brink of barbarism," Murray wrote. "Society is rescued from chaos only by a few men, not by the many. . . . It is only the few who understand the disciplines of civility and are able to sustain them in being and thus hold in check the forces of barbarism that are always threatening to force the gates of the city." He directed his sharpest barbs at modern philosophy, which treated the very notion of natural law with skepticism. The modern "barbarian," he argued, "goes busily and happily about his work, a domestic and law abiding man," unwittingly undermining the "inherited intuitive wisdom by which the people have always lived" not by spreading new beliefs "but by creating a climate of doubt and bewilderment in which clarity about the larger aims of life is dimmed and the self-confidence of the people is destroyed." He had little use for the revolutions in the understanding of human consciousness that for others had made such firm assertions of absolute truth impossible. "One is, I take it, on the brink of impotence and nihilism when one begins to be aware of one's own awareness of what one is doing, saying, thinking." Such awareness, for Murray, meant "rejection of the traditional role of reason and logic in human affairs" and the reduction of "all spiritual and moral questions to the test of practical results and the analysis of language and to decision in terms of individual subjective feeling."[64]

Catholics affirmed that the American proposition was based upon "principles and doctrines of western constitutionalism, classic and Christian." They held "these truths" because they were true. Their "participation in the American consensus has been full and free, unreserved and unembarrassed, because the contents of this consensus—the ethical and political principles drawn from the natural law tradition—approve themselves to the Catholic intelligence and conscience." Elsewhere the claims of the liberal state had overridden all others, and the church had resisted. But in the United States the rallying of the church to the republic had been "original, spontaneous and universal. It had been a matter of conscience and conviction, because its motive was not expediency in the narrow sense—the need to accept what one is powerless to change. Its motive was the evident coincidence of the principles which inspired the American republic with the principles that are structural to the Western Christian political tradition." Now, in the midst of the Cold War crisis, amid the collapse of philosophical realism elsewhere, Murray could present the paradox that "the guardianship of the original American consensus . . . would have passed to the Catholic community."[65] Here was a tour de force; according to the most highly sophisticated, and most respected, theologian the American church had ever known, Catholics really were the most American of all. It could not have come at a better time.

The 1960 campaign for the presidency of John Fitzgerald Kennedy marked a major turning point in American Catholic history. The new pope, John XXIII, was immensely popular, and the Jesuit theologian's careful arguments were available to anyone who cared to look, not simply in the complex writings of Murray but in the columns and articles of innumerable translators. Politically the question was whether enough Catholics in the large industrial states would return to the Democratic party after their brief flirtation with President Eisenhower to offset the hard-to-predict anti-Catholic vote. Early indications were that about 20 percent of the electorate would not vote for a Catholic, but Kennedy swept to victory in the key West Virginia primary, apparently demonstrating that the issue was dead in a state with very few Catholics.[66] Once the general election got underway, however, popular outbreaks of suspicion appeared among some fundamentalist and evangelical churches, and a few well-known Protestant leaders rehearsed some of the traditional arguments, with special reference to the school question. Facing the issue head on, Kennedy delivered a major address to a group of ministers in Houston, Texas. The speech, prepared with the help of John Cogley, went beyond Murray. Kennedy affirmed that his belief in the separation of church and state was absolute; that he would not allow the hierarchy to dictate his response to any issue; that his first responsibility was to his oath to uphold the Constitution; and that if he was faced with a conflict between his duty and his conscience, which any man of principle could face, he would resign.[67]

Kennedy's election, close as it was, came about in part because about 8 to 10 percent of the Catholics who had voted Republican in 1956 came home to the Democrats. During his too-brief presidency, Kennedy steered clear of Catholic issues like education, irritating some bishops, but a milestone had clearly been passed. The process of Catholic Americanization had come to some kind of climax. Pope John's impact on public opinion added to the erosion of Catholic minority consciousness as well. No event of those first years of the 1960s shook the broad anticommunist consensus, though Pope John's 1963 encyclical on peace, *Pacem in Terris*, while it angered some conservatives, gave support to the tiny Catholic peace community. Coming as it did in the wake of the Cuban missile crisis of 1962, it also attracted wide notice in the press and in international organizations. More important, the public interest in Catholicism sparked by the now popular president and the genial pope was given added impetus by the ecumenical council that opened in the fall of 1962. Informed Catholics expected little from the council, but by now things Catholic had become most public; this church event was regarded with curiosity by many Americans and with eager anticipation by some Protestants. In fact, the 1960 election had marked the end of an era and, in Rome, a new one was about to begin.

CHAPTER
9
Styles of Public Catholicism

❦

*I*n the years from the election in November 1960 of John Fitzgerald Kennedy as the first Catholic president of the United States to the visit to the United States in October 1965 of Pope Paul VI, American Catholicism reached a new climax in its history. The historic goals of the church in the United States, to retain the faith of its European immigrant people and secure a respected place for the church in American society, had been achieved. At least three-quarters of the church's more than forty million people attended mass regularly; four million children attended Catholic schools; and the rich endowment of parishes, schools, colleges and universities, hospitals, seminaries, missionary societies, and religious orders of men and women were the envy of the world's other churches.

The Vatican Council just ending had removed the long-standing problem of religious liberty by effectively reversing the church's teaching and doing so with a ringing endorsement of human dignity, human equality, and human rights. The liturgy was well on its way to being offered in the vernacular language, rules of fasting were being relaxed, Marian devotions were being subordinated to a more christological piety, there was widespread conviction that the church would modify its teaching on birth control, and Pope Paul was respected, as Pope John XXIII had been loved, by millions of non-Catholics. The assassinated President Kennedy was revered as a national hero; his solemn funeral in the Catholic rite had been an experience for the entire nation as Catholic symbols helped unify, and heal, the

American people. Ecumenical dialogue was taking place from small-town churches to theological conferences; in that exchange the numbers, organization, discipline, and unity of the Catholic party made it the senior partner. In major cities the local Catholic bishop was seen as the key religious figure; newspapers sought out his views of local affairs, and gatherings of religious leaders were considered successful and deserving of front-page attention only when he took part. Even divisions among Catholics over the character and pace of renewal were taken as signs of new openness and vigorous health. In short, here was a magnificently successful church, whether measured by the Catholic standards of unity, orthodoxy, and practice, or by American standards of numbers, good works, and public clout. American Catholicism had arrived.

A "REVOLUTIONARY MOMENT"

The moment was euphoric but short. Only a few years after Pope Paul's visit, newspapers were filled with reports of deep divisions and bitter dissent; sisters and priests were leaving the active ministry, and not quietly; and parochial school enrollments were dropping dramatically. Some lay Catholics were angry at church leaders for their failure to challenge racism and the Vietnam War; others were equally angry at priests and bishops who did so. Catholics seemed as divided about belief, authority, and worship as American Protestants. Now the headlines and television reports spoke of nervous shepherds and restless sheep, radical priests and conservative laity in political matters, conservative bishops and radical priests and lay people in religious affairs.

Theories of what had happened abounded. Some thought the people had finally become Americanized but the hierarchy had failed to follow suit. Others thought the hierarchy had become too American, too bureaucratic, too wedded to corporate and military power. Old-guard conservatives said "we told you so," arguing that Pope John's theory of changing the church's outward forms while preserving its inner essence of faith had always been impossible. If the church tampered with any part of its teaching, its organization, or its ritual, the entire package would unravel. Liberals responded that the institutional church had failed to follow through on Pope John's promise. The pope and the bishops clung to outmoded language, structures, and privileges, fearing that a more open, honest, and democratic church would expose the church's theological, pastoral, administrative, even financial, failures. And every analysis seemed to come with a prescription, pleasing some and angering others.[1]

One thing was clear. The American church, like its sister churches in the world, had reached a "revolutionary moment," as historian James Hennesey called it.[2] That moment was made revolutionary by the convergence of three profound streams of historical change. First, there was the measurable fact of what everyone persisted in calling Americanization. Two generations earlier, the United States had closed the golden door, not entirely but enough to drastically reduce European immigration. Spurred by postwar educational and economic opportunities, millions of second- and third-generation Catholics had entered the middle class and moved to the suburbs.

To say they were more American than their grandparents is to have a standard of "American" that is unavailable. But, by the mid-1960s, Catholics were as well educated as other Americans, more likely than most to go to college and on to graduate and professional schools. The once blue-collar Catholic population was now spread through the class structure of the country; the day was fast approaching, as Hispanic newcomers supplemented the upwardly mobile, when in class terms Catholics as a group would be indistinguishable from Americans as a whole. And finally, and more subjectively, with the experience of President Kennedy and Pope John behind them, Catholics seemed to feel more at home; they were Americanized because they felt they were. That was one stream of change. If the experience of American Protestantism was any signal, the erosion of the supportive subcultures of neighborhood and small town, the scattering of individuals through the social structure, and the decline of minority consciousness would mean a more voluntary church, one in which membership, belief, and moral decisions would become more matters of personal decision, less matters of family decision or community conformity. If there had never been a Vatican Council, this first stream would have created enormous pressure for change.[3]

But there was a second stream, the Vatican Council, which surprised almost everyone involved, from the pope to the people in the pews. Going far beyond the expectations of even the most optimistic reformer, the council changed the liturgy, directed attention away from doctrinal formulas to Christ and the gospel, and subordinated institutional and hierarchical understandings of the church to its life as a community, "the people of God," and to its mission, the Kingdom yet to come, so that, whatever its form, the church would always need reform and renewal. The Council Fathers denounced no people and condemned no ideas; they initiated dialogue with non-Catholic Christians, "separated brethren," and told its people to do the same. They explored respectfully the experience of Jews and other non-Christians. They made their own Pope John's optimistic sense of human history, abandoning the rhetoric of decline and fall that had begun with the

Reformation. The Council affirmed religious liberty and separation of church and state, condemned total war, and acknowledged the possibility of Catholic pacifism. It called upon religious orders to undertake deep renewal, reexamining their life and work in terms of the gospel, the charism of their founders, and the needs of the church. It told lay people to speak up, share their faith with one another and with their pastors, and share responsibility for the life and mission of the Mystical Body. Looking upon human culture as the creation of human beings, the Council affirmed the role of the laity in forwarding all those works that led to peace, justice, and the unity of the human family. Most important, it shattered the dualism of the church and the world, opting instead for Pope John's vision of a church "truly and intimately linked with mankind and its history." In conscious rejection of a siege mentality of opposition to a world gone wrong, and of a privatized faith irrelevant to a secular age, the council located the church and the Christian faith at the very center of human experience: "The joys and the hopes, the griefs and anxieties, of the men (and women) of this age, especially those who are poor or in any way afflicted, these too are the joys and the hopes, the griefs and anxieties of the followers of Christ."[4]

These two streams of change, the startling success of American Catholicism and the astonishing renewal of its church, might have seemed for a moment to fit easily together. At the very moment American Catholics had become comfortable with their Americanness, it seemed, their church had become itself more American, more open, more flexible, more tolerant, more accommodating and democratic. The tone of conciliar commentary was incredibly optimistic, pointing to an American age in the worldwide church and a Catholic era in American culture. American Catholics would show the universal church how to live with democracy, pluralism, and technology, how to be more democratic, more efficient, more humane. Catholics would simultaneously show other Americans how to combine freedom and authority, how to fight communism in a positive, constructive way, how to achieve new levels of unity and understanding while respecting differences. There was a "new generation, American and Catholic," who would show in their lives that the historic antagonism could be overcome to the enduring benefit of a nation and a church they loved.[5]

But things did not work out as expected. A third stream intersected the others, and disrupted the church as it was shaking the country. The first Catholic president had been murdered. The popular Pope John had ended his pontificate with a ringing appeal for peace, and the first pope to visit the United States, at the most dramatic moment of his visit, cried out "no more war, war never again." Those words were spoken at the United Nations while the United States was going to war in Vietnam. Three years later, in 1968, that war reached its shattering climax in the Tet offensive as the year began; Martin Luther King, Jr., was killed in April and cities exploded in violence; Robert Kennedy was shot in June; and the next month students battled police in the streets of Chicago during the Democratic National Convention. One Catholic, Mayor Richard Daley, directed the police; another, Eugene McCarthy, was the leader of the peace forces inside the convention, and across the continent a group of nine other Catholics, led by two Catholic priests, Daniel and Philip Berrigan, awaited trial for the destruction of selective service records at Catonsville, Maryland. All, it should be noted, considered themselves faithful Catholics and loyal Americans. In July as well, Pope Paul announced that the church would not, after all, change its teaching on birth control. A large number of theologians publicly stated their dissent from the pope, some lay people were angry, and more made it clear that they would ignore the decision. All considered themselves faithful Catholics and normal Americans.

In short, the three streams converged. The promising renewal of a successful American church was undertaken amid dramatic changes in American culture. Everything seemed to be changing at once: youth rebellion and sexual revolution as controversy over birth control raged; powerful religious denunciation of American racism and militarism at a time of liturgical and devotional changes; long hair, drugs, and a "counterculture" while schools were closing and children were studying the gospel and Dr. King instead of the catechism and the Sixth Commandment. American Catholicism had been shaped by the three factors of the conservative, dogmatic, and authoritative ultramontane church, the fluid social structure and stable democracy of the United States, and its own experience as an immigrant people. Now the immigrant era was over, the ultramontane church was in disarray, and blacks, priests, and one's own children were challenging the very values of America Catholics had made their own. Historian Philip Gleason refers to his experience of the period as one of "disintegration"; in his words, "the strongest sense I had was of a church, a religious tradition, that was coming undone, breaking apart, losing its coherence." Gleason was not alone.[6]

VATICAN II

From the point of view of the church and public life, Vatican II brought some profound changes. Most important was the "Declaration on Religious Freedom," written in part by John Courtney Murray. Excluded from the first session, Murray joined the Council advisors in 1963 through the influence of Cardinal Spellman and saw his ideas vindicated.[7] For the first time the church accepted the separation of church and state and religious liberty and it went further, affirming that everyone had "the duty, and therefore the right, to seek the truth in religious matters."[8] Basing its teaching on the dignity of the human person and the necessary freedom of the act of faith, the Council enabled the church to catch up to the modern world and American Catholics to abandon equivocation in speaking about the First Amendment. It also, and inadvertently, opened the door to the possibility that individual Catholics might apply its principles to their own relationship to ecclesiastical authority.

The dignity of the human person ran like a thread through another major Council document, "The Pastoral Constitution on the Church and the Modern World." Here the Council summed up Catholic social teaching, expanding the idea of human dignity to encompass a broad range of civil and political rights, with which Americans were comfortable, and social and economic rights, less clearly defined in American traditions. While the church has no political agenda of its own, the Council taught, it has the duty of engaging the political order to defend human dignity, promote human rights, and contribute to building the unity of the human family. The Council acknowledged the need to address the problem of modern war with "an entirely new attitude." Over significant American objections, the bishops affirmed the possibility that a Catholic could renounce the use of force and they urged governments to make legal provision for conscientious objection. In the only specific condemnation of the entire Council, it denounced total war: "any act of war aimed indiscriminately at the destruction of entire cities or of extensive areas along with their population is a crime against God and man himself. It merits unequivocal and unhesitating condemnation."[9] On the other hand, the bishops also reaffirmed traditional just-war teaching, praised those who served conscientiously in the military, recognized the right to self-defense, including deterrence, and called for disarmament through negotiation. In the discussion of this section of the document, American bishops, led by Philip Hannan, worked hard to assure that its language did not undercut American strategic policy or embarrass the American president.

For the American hierarchy, the council was a learning experience. Most were uncomfortable with the theological debates, but they had great faith in Pope John. Most joined the progressive element of the Council and they made religious liberty their special concern. Many were personally transformed by the Council, returning different men, determined to build a more community-oriented, open and mission-centered church. They moved quickly to implement reforms in the

liturgy and to initiate ecumenical dialogue, less quickly to share responsibility with priests and lay people. The debates over the pastoral
constitution had opened their eyes to problems in Catholic teaching
on family life and birth control, and awakened in some a sense of the
need for independent moral judgment on foreign and military policy.
But few anticipated that their greatest challenges would come not
from the demand for renewal but from public issues that called into
question the very integrity of the church.[10]

THE SIXTIES

Three complex sets of issues—race and poverty, the Vietnam War,
and abortion—would test the leadership of the bishops and the integrity of the community. Despite the efforts of black Catholics, sisters
and priests working in the black community, and the Catholic interracial councils and friendship houses, Catholics had not been prominent in movements for civil rights. The American bishops stated their
opposition to racial discrimination after the war, and Saint Louis
and some other dioceses, often over considerable opposition, moved
to desegregate schools. Growing numbers of priests, religious, and
lay people were moved by the nonviolent action and Christian appeals
of Dr. King. In 1963 many participated in the March on Washington,
and Catholics played a key role in the National Conference on Religion
and Race held in Chicago. From that point on, the weight of the hierarchy was thrown behind civil rights legislation. Priests and religious joined Dr. King at Selma in 1965 and back home joined with
other religious leaders to promote desegregation. Early moderate efforts proved inadequate to the growing pressure for change, especially
after black anger led to a growing number of violent urban disorders.
In many cities heavily Catholic ethnic neighborhoods stood directly
in the way of expanding black ghettos.

In Milwaukee, an Italian-American priest, James Groppi, gained
national prominence by his militant assistance to the local civil rights
movement, which focused its attention on open housing and clashed
with the city's heavily Polish working class. When Dr. King came to
Chicago, once again Catholic neighborhoods responded negatively,
sometimes violently; people were shocked to see Catholics shouting
at priests and sisters participating in civil rights marches. Coming
as it did in the midst of the changes in the church initiated from the
top and imposed on the people, the race crisis exposed some deep
divisions between urban and suburban Catholics. More important, it
revealed disunity between church professionals—not only activists
but many bishops and religious educators—and the rank and file.

The roots of later public divisions in the church and of such surprising events as the appearance of a Catholic pentecostal movement, lie in the experience of new feeling of distrust and division between the institutional church and at least some of its members.

The race crisis drew the church into public life to deal with a problem that had its most serious impact on a group who were for the most part non-Catholic. Indeed, the issue sometimes placed the church in conflict with its own members, first in desegregating areas of the South such as Louisiana, later in northern and midwestern cities. The organization responded in three ways. First, if there had once been doubt as to where the church stood on racial equality, this doubt was removed by 1965. In a series of powerful statements the bishops made clear their unanimous and unequivocal support for civil rights, desegregation, and racial justice, and these national statements were repeated in local communities. Both nationally and locally the issue provided an important occasion for Catholic leaders to work with their Protestant, and sometimes Jewish, counterparts, giving concrete expression to new ideas about ecumenism and new experiences of shared responsibility for community well-being. Second, the bishops now encouraged priests and sisters to work with the black community and gave a new prominence to social ministry. Through Catholic Charities agencies and offices the church was deeply involved with local social service delivery systems challenged by the black poor. Moreover, they had the expertise and experience to organize effective programs in housing, emergency services, and community development. In addition, the shifts in urban populations left parishes and schools holding on in the inner city, creating a presence that activists hoped could be placed at the service of the now often non-Catholic residents of the neighborhood.

The bishops supported the war on poverty launched by Congress and President Johnson in 1965, and in many local communities Catholic Charities officials and social action leaders helped organize interreligious and interracial coalitions to organize head start programs, housing corporations, neighborhood centers, and antipoverty agencies. When the cities again exploded after Dr. King's assassination in April 1968, the bishops issued a statement on the church and the urban crisis that acknowledged the structural character of racial and economic injustice and endorsed programs aimed not simply at helping the poor but empowering them to deal with their own problems. Challenged to give concrete expression to that belief, the following year the bishops launched their own antipoverty crusade, the Campaign for Human Development. With an annual national collection, funds were directed at self-help organizing efforts controlled by the poor themselves.

The combination of national civil rights and antipoverty legislation and local, grass roots organizing constituted the Catholic response to economic and social injustice that persisted after the crisis years of the sixties. Finally, the church could not ignore the fact that white working-class Catholics, often still close to their ethnic roots, often opposed initiatives in housing, employment, and education designed to redress racial injustices. Monsignor Geno Baroni, a diocesan priest long active in the civil rights movement, spearheaded a drive to awaken a sense of pride and responsibility among such groups while seeking eventual coalitions between the black and white poor and the urban working class. Baroni campaigned among bishops, social action leaders, and public officials, pointing out that low- and moderate-income Americans were asked to bear a disproportionate burden of social change. Through the National Center for Urban Ethnic Affairs, Baroni spearheaded what became known as the ethnic revival, which found expression in a new sense of pride among ethnic groups, new attention to such groups by scholars and journalists, and organizing efforts to enable ethnic neighborhoods to gain some control over the process of urban development. For Baroni, reflecting on the long history of trade unions and political machines, it seemed that only when blacks and whites were both fully organized could dialogue and negotiation free from fear and prejudice take place. Baroni's support for community development won a wide audience; eventually he would serve as assistant secretary of Housing and Urban Development in the Carter administration.

The Catholic church came to grips with racism best when it translated the problem into economic terms and applied its experience in the form of grassroots community organizing and improved social services. The broader moral problems of racism remained for Catholics and other Americans, and church leaders knew it. To provide representation for blacks within the church structure, the bishops founded the National Office of Black Catholics, and in the 1970s a growing number of black priests were appointed to the episcopate. A major pastoral letter on racism by all the bishops pledged the church to a continuing struggle against discrimination and injustice; it was followed in 1985 by another pastoral by the black bishops themselves, pointing toward stronger efforts at evangelization on the part of black Catholics. But the number of black Catholics remained small, and in many areas the burgeoning Hispanic population required attention and resources.

No group had seemed more reliable in support of American foreign policy after World War II than Catholics. The American church clearly favored containment policies in Europe and more than other groups had a continuing concern about communist expansion in Asia. Americans had participated actively in missionary work in China before World War II; the victory of communism in that country had left a powerful Catholic anticommunist lobby in the United States. As for Vietnam, when the French withdrew in 1954, they left behind in South Vietnam a noncommunist government dominated by Catholics led by Ngo Diem, who had spent part of his exile with the Maryknoll missionaries in the United States. Cardinal Spellman and Catholics such as Senators Kennedy and Mike Mansfield of Montana were supporters of an active pro-Diem lobby in the United States. Medical missionary Tom Dooley popularized a view of Indochina as a battleground between communism and democracy, the latter associated with Diem and the Catholics. Thus there was among Catholics as other Americans an initial sympathy with American efforts to counter communist attacks on South Vietnam and an understanding of the situation colored by Catholic Cold War ideology.

In 1963 Diem was overthrown amid reports that his family and their Catholic followers were hardly democratic and commanded limited popular support. Two years later the supportive American presence became a full-scale war. Catholic attitudes toward the war mirrored those of the country at large, initially supportive, turning critical after the Tet offensive, and heavily opposed by 1970. More surprisingly, the American hierarchy was cautious in its public statements on the war and, most shocking of all, Catholics took an active and highly visible role in the growing resistance to the war, creating a distinctive Catholic peace movement. For the bishops and many priests and religious, Vietnam, coming with the race crisis, occasioned a new sense of distance from the nation, and forced new questions about the relationship between religious integrity and public responsibility.

To explain this experience there was, first of all, the war itself. The length of the war, the levels of bombing, the numbers of American troops, the seemingly futile efforts at pacification, and the absence of a stable government all made it difficult to preserve national unity, while raising unavoidable moral questions. Second, the Vatican Council had made the American hierarchy more internationally conscious and more theologically sophisticated. Once the council had spoken, it was necessary to give some endorsement to sincere conscientious objectors. The bishops did so, acknowledging the legitimacy of a Catholic objecting to participation in war, as the law allowed, but also recognizing that, in Catholic teaching of the just war, provision should be made for selective conscientious objection, which refused service in a particular war. Eventually these national statements were translated in many places into educational and draft counseling programs. In addition, the Council's condemnation of total war, so clear and well-publicized, made evident what had long been known: that Catholic teaching allowed only defensive wars and set limits on the conduct of war once undertaken. Bishops familiar with church teaching had to admit the possibility, perhaps the responsibility, of continually measuring war policy against the standards set by the teaching. When Cardinal Spellman, in traditional fashion, called Vietnam a "war for civilization" and demanded unequivocal support, other bishops rushed to explain that the church could never give governments a blank check.[11] Pushed by the peace movement, the bishops individually, and eventually collectively, applied these teachings, first arguing on balance that the war could be justified, then admitting that people of good will could differ, and eventually, in 1971, judging that the levels of violence had become disproportionate to the end sought, and that the war should be ended. For the first time in modern history a body of national bishops, during a war, had publicly judged their government's actions unjust.[12]

The bishops' actions would not have developed as they did without the pressure created by the Catholic peace movement. At the center of the movement in the beginning was Dorothy Day and her Catholic Worker movement, marginalized in the 1950s but now once again a center for exploring nonviolence and organizing for action against the war. Gordon C. Zahn, a World War II conscientious objector and sociologist, also helped lay the ground by dissecting the just-war teachings and publishing challenging studies of the church's complicity with the wars of Nazi Germany. His study of the Austrian World War II conscientious objector Franz Jaeggerstadter was particularly influential. Just-war teaching, Zahn argued, had "elevated a civil obligation . . . to the status of a morally binding religious obligation" but Pope John's *Pacem in Terris* and the spirit of the conciliar teaching had forced churchmen to be attentive to the roots of religious obligation.[13]

Josephite priest Philip Berrigan was a well-known activist on behalf of racial justice. He and his brother Daniel, a Jesuit poet and teacher, also came early to oppose the war, under the influence of Dorothy Day, Martin Luther King, Jr., and the Trappist monk Thomas Merton. Merton, whose best-selling spiritual autobiography, *The Seven Storey Mountain*, had established him as the nation's best-known Catholic spiritual writer, turned his attention to public issues in the 1960s and gave the Catholic peace movement depth and sophistication. Never an unequivocal pacifist, Merton challenged the church at the very heart of its beliefs, raising the question of integrity in terms that made it difficult to put aside. Together with several leaders of the Catholic Worker, notably James Forrest and Thomas Cornell, both of whom eventually served prison terms, these men established the

Catholic Peace Fellowship, (CPF) as a branch of the interdenominational Fellowship of Reconciliation. In addition to organizing antiwar demonstrations, the CPF publicized church teaching and led draft counseling programs around the country.

The Berrigans and Merton also joined with Protestant and Jewish leaders to establish Clergy (later Clergy and Laity) Concerned About Vietnam, another major effort to move the churches and public opinion into opposition to the war. In 1968, at Catonsville, the Berrigans escalated antiwar militance in the first of a series of raids on draft boards, most led by Catholic priests, nuns, and lay people, a movement that became known as the Catholic resistance. Although never involving more than a handful of people, these direct actions challenged the consciences of informed Catholics, especially religious; they popularized basic Catholic teaching and opened up discussion of an evangelical, scriptural assessment of moral responsibility. The Catholic peace movement they led would survive Vietnam. While the Berrigans and others continued to engage in civil disobedience against arms production, a handful of committed bishops, the Catholic Worker movement, and Pax Christi (an American branch of the international Catholic peace organization) would keep the hierarchy alert to the moral problems of the arms race and contribute to the formulation of a dramatic pastoral letter on nuclear weapons in 1983.

Finally there was the context in which all of this took place. At one end of that experience was the council, with its refocusing of attention on the Christ of the Scriptures. This more evangelical emphasis called upon the church to assess its deepest beliefs and required more than the careful calculations of traditional social ethics, whether the issue was race, war, or poverty. At the other end of the experience was the national crisis, touching all areas of life from the family to the federal government, making insistence on submission, unequivocal praise for national institutions, or mindless repetition of patriotic slogans simply inadequate. People expected more from religious leaders, and most expected more of themselves. They had been forced to take a moral stand on race, they could hardly avoid facing the moral issue of the war, and if their neighborhood or city was shaken by it all, they were forced to take notice. They were public figures, whether they liked it or not. And when they did address the issues of the day, the terms of the discussion had changed. They felt compelled to speak not in terms of traditional papal teaching, addressed to Catholics and familiar only to a minority of them, but in terms of the message of the gospel, affirmed by all Christians, and the values of human dignity and human rights accepted by all Americans. By the 1970s, not only in public statements but in prayer and piety, the issue was no longer the compatibility of Catholicism and Americanism, but of serious Christian discipleship and responsible American citizenship, evangelical faith and republican ideals and practice.

As if all this were not enough, there was another blow to come. In 1973 the Supreme Court overturned the nation's laws limiting abortion. The decision was not a surprise, for the hierarchy had faced challenges to these laws in many states. But the broadly stated decision opened the door to "abortion on demand" and marked yet another collapse of the national moral consensus. Here was an issue on which church teaching was clear, and one that sharply separated Catholics from their government and from many of their fellow citizens. In marked contrast to their statements on war and peace, where even committed bishops simply laid out the teaching and encouraged Catholics to make up their own minds, the hierarchy treated abortion as a direct violation of church teaching. They undertook a massive educational campaign to mobilize their people, and they skirted the borders of church–state separation by backing lobbying and even partisan political activities. In contrast to their stands on war and race, they also argued for a specific solution, a constitutional amendment banning abortion.

Many bishops, priests, and lay people who had supported the Vietnam War and who regarded the civil rights movement with suspicion were shocked by the abortion decision. Some ignored the other issues and concentrated on abortion, attempting to use Catholic power to force politicians to respond in an approach that reflected the immigrant style. Others were drawn to reflect on the relationship between abortion, racism, poverty, and violence, becoming active on all these issues under the banner of "the right to life," an approach that would eventually be articulated by Cardinal Joseph Bernardin as "the seamless garment" of prolife teaching and witness of the Catholic community.[14] In any event, abortion more than any other issue ensured that the public turn the church had taken in the 1960s would not be reversed in the 1970s, as it had been in the 1920s and 1950s.

CONCLUSION: CONTEMPORARY PUBLIC CATHOLICISM

By the 1980s, the Catholic church had become more than ever a public church. Its internal problems were matters of public discussion, with more Catholics able to participate, while its relationships with other institutions were matters of public significance. Both were now matters of self-conscious reflection and more than a little controversy. Internally the new voluntarism left in the wake of renewal forced the exploration of new pastoral strategies. Top-down educational programs designed to reeducate Catholics after Vatican II foundered on ideological conflicts and lay indifference. Radical strategies spawned by groups as diverse as traditionalists, charismatics emerging from the surprising pentecostal movement, and peace and social justice radicals called the church to recover its integrity and coherence by committing itself to clear beliefs defined in opposition to a larger society seen, in one way or another, as incurably corrupt. While such sectarian zeal had considerable attraction for people committed to full-time work in the church, and while it touched a wider need for Christian and Catholic identity, it made unrealistic demands on lay people and ignored the web of personal and family needs that had always underpinned American congregational life.

In addition to those mentioned, a variety of movements—Marriage Encounter, divorced Catholics, Cursillo, Christian feminism, even Catholic homosexuals—indicated the range of unmet needs within the church and the diversity of responses required. Shrinking numbers of priests and religious reinforced the sense that something more would be needed to attract individuals to church service, especially as women expressed growing discontent with their exclusion from positions of responsibility and leadership. The result was the development of a bottom-up, rather loose, pastoral style, seeking to encourage men and women to define their needs and find the resources to meet them, while providing training and support for a variety of new forms of ministry. In dioceses, parishes, apostolic movements, and church-based institutions, the need to generate voluntary support, lay leadership, and human and financial resources also led to a greater sharing of responsibility evident in team ministry, lay-dominated advisory boards, and pastoral planning based on widespread participation.

All of this drew individuals, whether full-time church workers, volunteers, or simply members, to the kind of participation once hinted at among nineteenth-century lay trustees. It also made the church more public, as its actions and decisions, subject to debate and various forms of deliberation, achieved legitimacy through participation. Authority, it seemed, would require some degree of consent, and it would have to be based on pastoral skill and service, whatever the church might teach. This direction could also, once again, create problems between the American church and Rome.[15]

The church had also become public in another sense. The bishops were now heavily involved in public debates about government policy, and the relationship between the church and public life was a matter of serious debate within the community. In 1976, attempting to enlist broad support for the social mission of the church, the bishops sponsored a program of national consultation in celebration of the bicentennial of the American Revolution. Hearings on social problems were held across the country and in October 1976, dioceses and movements sent delegates to the first national Catholic convention, the Call to Action conference. Given the grass roots, bottom-up nature of the process, internal church issues came up for discussion along with issues of peace, social justice, and political responsibility. The 1,300 delegates, a majority of whom were employed by church agencies, passed a large number of resolutions covering everything from birth control, homosexuality, and women in the church to world hunger and the arms race. The democratic process, which saw a lay person having the same vote as a bishop, and the progressive nature of the resolutions made many members of the hierarchy nervous, so that its results were more or less shelved. But the program signaled changes that could not be reversed. Both the church's internal vitality and external integrity depended upon participation and consent. From the preparation of pastoral letters to the determination of parish and diocesan priorities, the consultative process would in fact be consistently broadened in the decade that followed.

In the debates that took place during and after the Call to Action program, three distinctive approaches to the public presence of the church emerged, each rooted in the history of American Catholicism.[16] The first approach, and in many ways the most dynamic and influential, was evangelical. Catholic faith and piety, like that of other American Christians, was increasingly centered on the Scriptures and the person of Jesus. Pastoral approaches to baptism, confirmation, marriage, and adult education increasingly featured invitations to personal commitment and decision. While public debates continued to feature discussion of papal teaching and doctrinal formulas, church documents and catechetical materials were less significant than the Scriptures and works of piety that emphasized Christian discipleship. Emphasis on community and ministry increasingly redefined parish life in more voluntary, even covenant, terms. And, as had happened among Protestants, social responsibility came to be seen in more personal terms. The question was less "What does the church teach?" than "What would Jesus do?" Naturally enough the demands of religious faith and church membership were seen as challenging conventional values and practices, establishing new boundaries for the church not so different from the old.

Whether it was a charismatic-oriented lay person worried about drugs, sexual promiscuity, and abortion or a Catholic Worker worried about militarism and poverty, the response was similar: personal conversion, detachment from a corrupt society, and commitment to the community of faith. Touching the heart of faith and establishing the distinctive ground of the church, this approach had enormous appeal and moral force.

In their 1983 pastoral on nuclear weapons the bishops came close to affirming this position by emphasizing the dramatic demands of the gospel, affirming nonviolence as an option for individuals, and calling their people to discipleship in a "society increasingly estranged from Christian values," indeed, a society in which they might expect persecution and martyrdom to become normal.[17] In their later pastoral letter on economics, they referred to the phrase popular in Latin America, "the fundamental option for the poor," as reflective of the demands of discipleship and the priorities for the church, once again set over against a society seen as materialistic and selfish.[18]

The reason for the resurgence of this more radical language is clear. In 1961 *America* magazine published an article justifying the use of force to keep neighbors from invading one's fallout shelter in the event of nuclear war. Writing to peace movement leader James Forrest, Thomas Merton exclaimed: "Are we going to minimize, and fix our eyes on the lowest level of natural ethics, or are we going to be Christians and take the Gospel seriously?"[19] John Courtney Murray's advanced version of the republican tradition had been modest; he had pointed out that natural law ethics provided no leverage for bringing about the kingdom of God, only for establishing minimal levels of decency. Neither did it provide an emotionally compelling ground for resistance to evil. Indeed Murray himself had argued that because limited nuclear war might be necessary, it must be justified. Merton posed this question about such natural ethics, and about the gospel, in 1962. In the years that followed he and others would ask similar questions about racism, about the Vietnam War, about world and domestic poverty, and finally about the nuclear problem. In the face of such issues, the republican style, for all its strengths, seemed inadequate for religious leaders; even more inadequate was the self-interested group-oriented style of the immigrant church.

The strength of the evangelical approach is its appeal for integrity, calling the church and its members to live out their faith and thus witness to the demands, and the truths, of Christianity. Like the Catholic Worker movement it exposes the impersonal character of the state; condemns a spiritually empty pursuit of material self-interest; opens up prospects for spiritual and social renewal; and expands the social imagination to embrace all human persons, including society's outcasts and unfortunates, conveying a vision of a world of personal responsibility and mutual self-help.[20]

Like all radical movements, the Catholic Worker has been marked by "a fierce adherence to a fixed set of ideas, a focus on final ends rather than changing conditions, and a willingness to endure political failure and to stand alone of necessary."[21] It presents a necessary challenge to the concern of other movements with effectiveness. "We believe that success, as the world determines it, is not the criterion by which a movement should be judged," the Worker maintains. "We must be prepared and ready to face seeming failure. The important thing is that we adhere to there values which transcend time and for which we will be asked a personal accounting, not as to whether they succeeded . . . but as to whether we remained true to them even though the world go otherwise."[22] Such evangelical Catholicism inspires dedication and sacrifice as evidenced in the tremendous variety of projects serving poor, homeless, and powerless people, the challenging of the arms race, and the opposition to American policy in Central America and the Third World.

The weakness of evangelical Catholicism lies in the fact that, by defining issues and responses in Christians terms, its advocates become marginalized in the larger public debate. Respected, even admired, they are not seen as offering an appropriate or reasonable way in which the American public as a whole can evaluate problems and formulate solutions. Only part of the problem is church and state. Rather, it is a problem of responsible citizenship. If social problems are at least in part problems of power, organization, and institutions, and if they almost always intersect with government policy, a pluralistic society simply cannot deal with those problems in specifically Christian terms. Nor can the individual citizen effectively participate in the public debate, persuade non-Christians or indifferent ones to the need for change, or influence the larger culture by appealing to the authority of the gospel.

Evangelical Catholicism taken alone, then, challenges the church but limits the audience, restricts the language and short-circuits responsibility, tending toward a perfectionism, even an apocalyptic sectarianism, that, by always questioning the legitimacy of secular institutions and policies, devalues the demands of citizenship and reduces the moral significance of work, politics, and wider community life. At its worst, as has been seen so often, it slips into a soft sentimentality that excuses inaction on public issues by arguing that until people decide to be good, reform will not work. "That one should work first for the moral reform of individuals before seeking political and economic reform is altogether too simple and superficial," John A. Ryan told a friend who was discouraged by economic and racial injustice. "Those who advocate this course are . . . persons who haven't taken the trouble to analyze the possibilities and implications of the moral reform proposal."[23]

The second approach to the public church is an immigrant style rooted in the church's experience in the United States. The immigrant style did not disappear with the assimilation of European immigrants. In fact it has experienced a revival among newer immigrants, most notably Hispanics, but is also reaching a growing number of Asians. Echoes of older church battles are heard in demands for foreign-language parishes, while older forms of grass roots mobilization take place around parish-based community organizations. Community organizing, that is, grassroots empowerment of poor people and minorities through self-help organizations built upon neighborhood, ethnic, and racial groups or people suffering a specific form of powerlessness, is the major form of Catholic social action and reflects the legacy of Catholic experience in parishes, political machines, and trade unions. Unfortunately, there has been little theological reflection on this uniquely American form of social action or on the business unionism and bread-and-butter liberalism so strong in the American Catholic tradition. Church teaching on social issues is caught between evangelical and republican approaches; from both of those perspectives, community organizing, like self-interest politics and conflict-oriented unionism, seem to unduly compromise either Christian or civic ideals.

There is another, more visible expression of the immigrant style, one that also continues to persist in the American church. John Hughes was the first to mobilize Catholics for public goals, and later church leaders, while professing to be aloof from politics, occasionally used their implied political influence to seek aid for parochial schools, to resist changes in legislation regarding birth control, or to insure that Catholic interests were respected in welfare and education legislation. While opposition to abortion attracted considerable non-Catholic support, the strategies used by activists reflected this approach. In 1968 Cardinal John Krol of Philadelphia seemed to favor the election of Richard Nixon because of his support for aid to private schools; four years later he and several other bishops leaned in Nixon's direction because of his professed opposition to abortion. Four years later, despite public statements that insisted on a multi-issue approach to the election, the bishops aroused widespread criticism by appearing to test candidates Gerald Ford and Jimmy Carter on the basis of their view of abortion.[24] In 1984 several bishops similarly challenged the abortion views of vice-presidential candidate Geraldine Ferraro and New York Governor Mario Cuomo, both Catholics. In the states, abortion, homosexuality, and the school issue continue to arouse Catholic leaders and pose the threat of a Catholic vote. Conservative writers like James Hitchcock even contend that Catholics should develop and promote their own agenda of family and sexual issues and demand respect for these specifically Catholic concerns in the political arena.

The strength of the immigrant style is its recognition of how often the moral dimension of an issue is irrelevant in practice. When Americans differ over the morality of a problem, that problem cannot be resolved by government; only when a widespread national consensus was developed was civil rights legislation possible. In the absence of such a consensus, issues are resolved by the relative power that groups can exert in the legislative and administrative process and on public opinion, which shapes the parameters of institutional behavior. This was the wisdom of the Legion of Decency; recognizing that officially imposed censorship would be unacceptable, the movement mobilized Catholics and used boycotts and publicity to influence decisions within the film industry. In the economic sphere, the problem of unionization was not resolved by a moral decision of the government to recognize the right to organize, but by labor mobilization, posing a threat to labor peace, community order, and successful antidepression policy, while taking advantage of an antibusiness climate to influence public opinion in a pro-union direction. Neither the evangelical emphasis on gospel fidelity nor the republican emphasis on civic-mindedness faces the problem of power in a pluralistic society, nor does either have an evident strategy to bring about changes in policy. The best strategy of the immigrant tradition had included a role for the laity in the secular order; at the boundaries between the immigrant and republican style was the method of the Catholic youth movement and lay activism of the 1950s. By the 1970s those movements and organizations had virtually disappeared.[25]

The weakness of the immigrant style is also self-evident. To the faithful evangelical, it seems cynical: what would Jesus have to do with organizing, conflict, and confrontation, or with hard negotiation about competing interests? To the republican, the immigrant style seems divisive and self-interested. Madison's factions expanded beyond property to include social, cultural, and moral interest groups. The labor or community organizer and the lobbyist for business seem equally abhorrent to the citizen concerned with the public good. When the church acts from this perspective, therefore, it is compelled to escalate the moral language, making the issue it promotes seem to be directly related to Christian belief, and therefore to brand opponents as anti-Catholic or anti-Christian. It also must argue that its position corresponds with the public interest, that what is good for the church is good for the community. In either case it risks appearing self-righteous and authoritarian and often appears more concerned with vindicating its own rights and commanding recognition than with doing something about the issue itself. On an issue like abortion, when it becomes defined as a Catholic issue and a test for the Catholic politician, the church ends up in the same position as the evangelicals, marginalizing its voice and restricting its potential influence by the sectarian strategy of loyal witness whatever the cost.

Finally, there is the republican approach, extending from John Carroll and John England to John Courtney Murray and to the present-day Cardinal Joseph L. Bernardin. Acknowledging as always the sharp separation of the religious and political order, the bishops use the Vatican II formula that the church has no specific agenda of its own but seeks to defend human dignity, promote human rights, and contribute to the unity of the human family. Drawing on its own experience of poverty, its strong teaching on race, and its sense of responsibility within the worldwide church, the bishops, acting through their national episcopal conference established after Vatican II, have been extraordinarily active. They have spoken out on a wide variety of foreign and domestic issues, in some cases even testifying on behalf of specific legislation. Major statements have dealt with welfare reform (1970), the environment (1971), correctional reform (1973), the world food crisis (1974), domestic food policy and gun control (1975), aged and the new immigrants (1976), Native Americans (1977), the handicapped (1978), and the energy crisis (1980). Because their first priority has been the poor, they have campaigned for more humane food policies, more equitable welfare benefits, adequate housing, and budgets that give priority to those most in need. In economics they have championed full employment while calling for greater collaboration between the public and private sectors, and within the private sector. These statements in the two decades after Vatican II constitute a large volume, climaxing with the major pastoral letters on nuclear arms and the economy of the mid-1980s. In presidential election years the bishops have offered testimony to the platform committees of both parties and issued "political responsibility" statements to the faithful setting forth their views on a broad range of issues, listed without priority among them.

In the peace pastoral of 1983, the bishops came closest to clarifying the role of the public church. In that letter they distinguished two styles of teaching that had developed since the council. One, addressed to members of the church, begins with the message of Jesus and explores the responsibility of Christians and of the church. The second, aimed at the general public, is intended to contribute to the development of the public moral consensus, to influence public opinion, and to help shape the public debate about policy by clarifying its moral dimension. Here the language is that of natural law, human dignity, and human rights. In other words, within the church the evangelical style is dominant, in the public debate the republican style is required. The tone of the theological and pastoral discussion is radical and demanding, tending toward nonviolence and calling for a separation from those values and practices in society that contradict the gospel. The bishops again endorse conscientious objection, including selective objection; they warn military officials against committing immoral acts; and they challenge employees of defense firms to question whether their work can be reconciled with the demands of faith. The public sections of the document, in contrast, are carefully nuanced, their conclusions tentative, their language guarded, most dramatically in the "strictly conditioned moral acceptance of deterrence." As the bishops put it, their "no" to nuclear war is clear and unequivocal, but deciding on the next step becomes complex and difficult. Thus the problem is clarified but not resolved. By arguing that nonviolence is an option for individuals, but states have the obligation to defend their citizens, the bishops further separate the two discussions. The pastoral contains no ringing call for political action and no exploration of the role of the lay Catholic in business, government, the media, or education in forwarding the work of peacemaking. The public dialogue and public responsibility are affirmed, but there is no scriptural or theological ground for that affirmation, no religious symbols to give meaning to public life. Meaning and spiritual energy instead concentrate on the community of disciples, the church.

In similar fashion, the economics pastoral three years later, in its several drafts, moved from a Vatican II emphasis on work in everyday occupations as the locus for the pursuit of holiness by enhancing human dignity to a more evangelical emphasis on family and church as repositories of countercultural values standing in opposition to the dominant values of American society. Once again there are serious policy proposals and appeals for ethical behavior, but the religious language and symbols are confined largely to the church.[26]

While church teaching struggles between the evangelical approach of Dorothy Day and the republican approach of John Courtney Murray and John A. Ryan, more than a few bishops forget both when they deal with what they regard as a Catholic issue, such as abortion, further confusing the church's witness. Often disputes about these approaches appear irrelevant to the experience of most Catholics. As in the past, the level of educational and pastoral commitment to public Christianity is far less than the moral intensity of episcopal and papal messages would seem to demand. Lay Catholics remain largely unfamiliar with church teaching. Pastors are only slightly more conversant with the teaching and are often sadly lacking in the knowledge of public issues that Ryan thought so necessary. Lay Catholics tend toward an evangelical sense that personal conversion and personal morality are at the heart of the Christian community, and its fruits are measured by being as decent as one can in a hard, amoral world.

Most important, the problems posed by the lay movements of the 1950s have not been faced in the postconciliar years. The tendency of evangelical Catholicism is to devalue everyday life to the extent that it is lived amid contemporary institutions; if one does not join a radical community, renouncing ordinary secular existence, then the church tends to become a refuge, an alternative, a counterculture standing in negative judgment on the world and therefore on the worldly part of the lay person's life. In another way, the immigrant style, with its emphasis on loyalty to the Catholic church and community, does the same. The republican style tends toward another kind of separation between the church and everyday life; by looking upon Christian existence in evangelical terms and public life in terms of natural law ethics, and not religious meaning, it can contribute to the very separation of religion and life it seeks to overcome and thus plays into the hands of those who regard the intrusion of the church into public matters as inappropriate. All the styles are impaired by a separation of the church and the world, ignoring the religious dimensions of human existence outside the church, and the worldliness of the church itself.[27] Not until the layperson, seeking to live with integrity as a Christian and responsibly as a citizen, (the Catholic member of the school board, the Catholic executive, the labor leader or social worker, rather than the Catholic Worker or the lay director of religious education) becomes the center of pastoral attention and theoretical reflection will this dichotomy, so self-serving for the church and so counterproductive for its public mission, be overcome.

One suspects, on the basis of the historical record, that in the future public Catholicism will not be contained exclusively in any of these three approaches. The force of evangelical Catholicism will undoubtedly grow as the realities of voluntarism assert themselves more fully among Catholics. Republican ideals, with their separation of religion and politics, have always dominated episcopal political thought; they seem inseparable from the experience of pluralism. The immigrant style will persist as long as there are groups in need of power and recognition, and as long as the church feels insecure about the integrity of its witness to its specific values. Furthermore, when republican ideals of democracy and human rights are carried into the church, they threaten ecclesiastical authority and risk the unity and discipline of the church, as the bishops learned in the trustee dispute. Evangelical ideals, testing everything in the church by gospel standards, also threaten to undermine episcopal power and open the door to an egalitarian church rooted in baptism and calling forth the gifts of the community. The immigrant style tends to affirm grassroots organizing and empowerment of the poor while maintaining the internal structures of the church; it poses no threat. Thus bishops like George Mundelein and Robert Lucey were highly authoritarian in dealing with their priests and in their theological and moral teachings. At the same time they were powerful champions of the working class in one instance and of Mexican Americans in the other.[28] The combination of ecclesiastical conservatism and social progressivism is in greater continuity with the past than the other positions and could receive strong reinforcement as Hispanic Catholics become a more significant element within the church. In the tension between these three, between integrity, responsibility, and effectiveness, a potentially creative dialogue might emerge. If the laity, standing at the center of attention within both church and society, becomes the paradigm of the good Catholic, a better, richer theoretical framework and a more effective pastoral style might emerge. There can be no escape from public Catholicism, for even a religion that professes to confine itself to spiritual matters by that very stance influences the larger society. Whether the development of public Catholicism is constructive, making a substantial contribution to the nation and the universal church, or simply further fragments the American church and weakens its witness and influence, depends, in the end, on attitudes toward history, toward the human community, and, most important, toward American society and culture. If Catholics and their church can learn to understand and appreciate their history; if they can come to feel that this land in which they live is their own and that they are responsible for it, if they can come to see themselves as part of an American as well as a Christian people, then they may indeed help enliven public life and restore a sense of public responsibility in American institutions. The story of American Catholicism is not yet finished. The next chapter remains to be written.

Notes

Chapter 1. Public Leadership and American Catholicism

1. *The Challenge of Peace: God's Promise and Our Response* (Washington, D.C., 1983), par. 16, 17.
2. Bernard Bailyn, *Education and the Formation of American Society* (Chapel Hill, N.C., 1960).
3. Martin Marty, *The Modern Schism* (London and New York, 1969).
4. I have discussed this idea in a number of places, most recently in *Public Theology, Civil Religion, and American Catholicism* (pamphlet), The George Dana Boardman Lecture in Christian Ethics, 26 (Philadelphia, 1987).

Chapter 2. Republican Catholicism

1. Thomas O'Brien Hanley, S.J., *The John Carroll Papers*, vol. 1 (Notre Dame, Ind., 1976), pp. 80–81.
2. Quoted in James Hennesey, S.J., *American Catholics* (New York, 1980), 37.
3. *Ibid.*, p. 39. See also Hennesey, "Roman Catholicism: The Maryland Tradition," *Thought* (September 1976):282–95.
4. John D. Krugler, "Lord Baltimore, Roman Catholics and Toleration: Religious Policy in Maryland during the Early Catholic Years, 1634–1647," *Catholic Historical Review* 65 (January 1979):554.
5. Hennesey, *American Catholics*, p. 42.
6. Thomas O'Brien Hanley, S.J., "Church and State in the Maryland Ordinance of 1639," *Church History* 26 (April 1956):325–41.
7. For a detailed examination of the calculated and self-conscious approach of Maryland Catholic leaders to public life, see Ronald Hoffman, "Charles Carroll of Carrollton: The Formative Years, 1748–1764," Working Papers Series 12, Cushwa Center for American Catholic Studies, Fall, 1982. Quotation is from pp. 60–61.
8. Gerald P. Fogarty, S.J., "Property and Religious Liberty in Colonial

Maryland Catholic Thought," *Catholic Historical Review* 72 (October 1986):573–600.

9. Adams quoted in Hennesey, *American Catholics*, p. 58. See also Charles H. Metzger, S.J., *Catholics and the American Revolution* (Chicago, 1962).

10. Father Joseph Mosley to Mrs. Dunn, 4 October 1784, quoted in John Tracy Ellis, "Religious Freedom and American Catholicism," *Cross Currents* 13 (Winter 1963):5. For Madison, see Edwin S. Gaustadt, ed., *A Documentary History of Religion in America to the Civil War* (Grand Rapids, Mich., 1982), pp. 262–64.

11. Thomas O'Brien Hanley, "The Catholic Tradition of Freedom in America," *American Ecclesiastical Review* 145 (November 1961):309.

12. *John Carroll Papers* 1:81.

13. John Tracy Ellis, ed., *Documents of American Catholic History*, vol. 1 (Chicago, 1967), pp. 146–47.

14. Hanley, "The Emergence of Pluralism in the United States," *Theological Studies* 23 (June 1962):229.

15. Hennesey, *American Catholics*, p. 21.

16. Annabelle Melville, *Jean Lefebvre de Cheverus, 1768–1836* (Milwaukee, Wisc., 1958).

17. Joseph Chinnici, "American Catholics and Religious Pluralism 1775–1820," *Journal of Ecumenical Studies* 16 (Fall 1977):727–41.

18. *John Carroll Papers* 1:46.

19. Quoted in Gerald Fogarty, S.J., "Public Patriotism and Private Piety: The Tradition of American Catholicism," *U.S. Catholic Historian* 4 (1982):2. See also Thomas O'Brien Hanley, S.J., "Archbishop Carroll and the French Revolution," *Records of the American Catholic Historical Society* (hereafter *Records* 71 (September-December 1960):67–72.

20. *John Carroll Papers* 3:173.

21. Fogarty, "Public Patriotism," p. 2. John Tracy Ellis argued, in a similar fashion, that the concern for the precarious new freedom of the church that led Carroll to insist that Catholics demonstrate their attachment to the new government "expressed the principal motivation that lay behind Catholic acceptance of national policy, whether it be for war or peace, during the nearly two centuries that followed." See "American Catholics and Peace," originally published in James S. Rausch, ed., *The Family of Nations* (Huntington, Ind., 1970) and reprinted as a pamphlet by the United States Catholic Conference in 1971.

22. James Hennesey has shown how the need to establish the relative autonomy of the American church developed into an authentic tradition of episcopal collegiality best seen in the seven provincial and three plenary councils of Baltimore held between 1829 and 1884. See "Papacy and Episcopacy in Eighteenth and Nineteenth Century American Catholic Thought," *Records* 77 (September 1966):175–89; "The Baltimore Conciliar Tradition," *Annuarium Historiae Conciliorum* 3 (1971–1972):71–88.

23. *John Carroll Papers* 2:202. For an extended discussion of this subject see James Hennesey, S.J., "The Vision of John Carroll," *Thought* 54 (September 1979):323–33.

24. *John Carroll Papers* 1:105–106.

25. Quoted in Hennesey, *American Catholics*, p. 71.

26. *John Carroll Papers*, 1:155; Peter Guilday, *The Life and Times of John*

Carroll, Archbishop of Baltimore (1735–1815) (Westminister, Md., 1954), p. 770.

27. Report in Ellis, *Documents* 1:147–50.
28. David O'Brien, *Faith and Friendship: Catholicism in the Diocese of Syracuse, 1886–1986* (Syracuse, N.Y., 1987), chap. 2.
29. Quoted in Hennesey, *American Catholics*, p. 75.
30. *John Carroll Papers* 1:87.
31. Timothy L. Smith, "Congregation, State and Denomination: The Forming of the American Religious Structure," *William and Mary Quarterly*, 3rd ser., 25 (April 1968):176.
32. Joanne Manfra, "The Catholic Episcopacy in America, 1789–1852" (Ph.D. diss., University of Iowa, 1975), chap. 5.
33. *John Carroll Papers* 1:204.
34. Ellis, *Documents*, 1:214.
35. O'Brien, *Faith and Friendship*, p. 33.
36. Peter Guilday, *The Life of John England*, vol. 1 (New York, 1927), p. 225.
37. Patrick Carey, "American Catholic Trustees' Views of the papacy, 1785–1860" (unpublished).
38. Patrick Carey, *People, Priests and Prelates: Ecclesiastical Democracy and the Tensions of Trusteeism* (Notre Dame, Ind., 1986), p. 156.
39. Guilday, *England* 1:227.
40. Patrick Carey, "A National Church: The Catholic Search for Identity, 1820–1829," Working Paper Number 3, Cushwa Center for American Catholic Studies, Fall 1977, p. 9.
41. Patrick Carey, *An Immigrant Bishop: John England's Adaptation of Irish Catholicism to American Republicanism* (Yonkers, N.Y., 1982), pp. 114–28.
42. Patrick Carey, "Two Views of Lay-Clerical Conflicts, 1785–1860," *Records* 92 (March-December 1981):85–98.
43. Patrick Carey, "Voluntaryism: An Irish Catholic Tradition," *Church History* 48 (March 1979:59).
44. Jules A. Baisnee, "The Early Years of Gabriel Richard," *Records* 62 (December 1952):233–52.
45. Constance Green, *American Cities in the Growth of the Nation* (London, 1957), p. 56.
46. O'Brien, *Faith and Friendship*, chaps. 2–3.
47. *Miscellaneous Essays* (Philadelphia, 1830), cited in R. Emmett Curran, S.J., "Confronting 'The Social Question': American Catholic Thought and the Socio-Economic Order in the Nineteenth Century," *U.S. Catholic Historian* 5 (1986):176.
48. Kenneth Wyer Rowe, *Mathew Carey: A Study in American Economic Development* (Baltimore, 1933), p. 66.
49. Rowe, *Carey*, pp. 24–27.
50. Dora Guerrieri, "Catholic Thought in the Age of Jackson: Equal Rights and Freedom of Religion," *Records* 87 (March–December 1976):85–98.
51. Quoted in Ellis, "Religious Freedom," p. 7.
52. Guilday, *England* 2:498–501.
53. Peter Guilday, ed., *The Pastoral Letter of the American Hierarchy, 1782–1919* (Westminister, Md., 1929), pp. 36–37, 85.
54. Sr. Mary McGreal, O.P., "Samuel Mazzuchelli, Participant in Frontier Democracy," *Records* 87 (March 1976):99–114.

55. *John Carroll Papers* 2:219.
56. Walter Abbott, ed., *The Documents of Vatican II* (New York, 1966), p. 715.

Chapter 3. Immigrant Catholicism

1. Hennesey, *American Catholics*, p. 89.
2. "Some Early Letters of James F. Wood from Rome, Cincinnati and Philadelphia," *Records* 83 (March 1972):39, 47.
3. Alexis de Tocqueville, *Democracy in America*, ed. J. P. Mayer (New York, 1969), pp. 291–92.
4. Emmett Larkin, "The Devotional Revolution," *American Historical Review* 77 (October 1972):636–52.
5. Jay P. Dolan, *Catholic Revivalism* (Notre Dame, Ind., 1979); Joseph Chinnici, O.F.M., "Organization of the Spiritual Life: American Catholic Devotional Works, 1791–1866," *Theological Studies* 40 (June 1979):229–53.
6. Jay P. Dolan, *The Immigrant Church* (Baltimore, 1976).
7. "Ethnic Factors in Social Mobility," in *Explorations in Entrepreneurial History* 9 (1956):1; Oscar Handlin, *The Uprooted* (Boston, 1954).
8. Dolan, *Immigrant Church*, p. 199.
9. *John Carroll Papers* 1:441.
10. Dolan, *Immigrant Church*, p. 238.
11. *Ibid.*, p. 241.
12. Henry B. Leonard, "Ethnic Conflict and Episcopal Power: The Diocese of Cleveland, 1847–1870." *Catholic Historical Review* 62 (June 1976):388–407.
13. Timothy Walch, "Catholic Social Institutions and Urban Development: The View from Nineteenth Century Chicago and Milwaukee," *Catholic Historical Review* 64 (January 1978):16–32. See also O'Brien, *Faith and Friendship*, chaps. 2–3; Leslie Tentler, "Detroit" (manuscript history of the archdiocese of Detroit, forthcoming).
14. Quoted in Edith Abbott, *Historical Aspects of the Immigration Problem, Selected Documents* (Chicago, 1926), pp. 16, 18, 20.
15. *Ibid.*, pp. 336–37.
16. Hasia Diner, *Erin's Daughters in America* (Baltimore, 1985).
17. Roger Lane, *The Roots of Violence in Black Philadelphia, 1860–1900* (Philadelphia, 1986), pp. 140–42.
18. Robert D. Cross, "The Changing Image of Catholicism in the United States," *Yale Review* 47 (June 1959):562–75.
19. The standard history of nativism in this period is Ray Alan Billington, *The Protestant Crusade* (New York, 1954).
20. John Higham, "Another Look at Nativism," *Catholic Historical Review* 44 (July 1958):147–58.
21. David B. Davis, "Some Themes of Counter-Subversion: An Analysis of Anti-Masonic, Anti-Catholic and Anti-Mormon Literature," *Mississippi Valley Historical Review* 47 (September 1960):205–224.
22. *Ibid.* 209.
23. *Ibid.* 220.
24. Clyde S. Griffin, "Converting the Catholic: American Benevolent So-

cieties and the Ante-Bellum Crusade against the Church," *Catholic Historical Review* 47 (October 1961):324–41.

25. William O. Bourne, *History of the Public School Society of the City of New York* (New York, 1870), p. vii; Edward M. Connors, *Church-State Relationships in Education in the State of New York* (Washington, D.C., 1951), p. 8.

26. *Truth Teller*, 14 September 1839, cited in Henry J. Browne, "Public Support for Catholic Education in New York: Some New Aspects," *Catholic Historical Review* 39 (April 1953):1.

27. George Baker, ed., *The Works of William Henry Seward*, vol. 2 (Boston, 1884), pp. 215–16.

28. *Ibid.* 3:214–15.

29. Frederick W. Seward, ed., *The Autobiography of William Henry Seward* (New York, 1877), p. 53; Seward to Mrs. M. P. Mann, 5 May 1842, Seward Papers, University of Rochester.

30. Seward to Herman Westervelt, 25 March 1840, Seward papers.

31. Joseph McCadden, "Bishop Hughes versus the Public School Society of New York," *Catholic Historical Review* 50 (July 1964):1949–95.

32. McCadden, "Public School Society," p. 195.

33. John R. G. Hassard, *Life of Bishop Hughes* (New York, 1966), pp. 243–47.

34. New York *Tribune*, 1 November 1841 and 5 November 1841.

35. Seward, *Works*, 309 and Seward to Christopher Morgan, 10 June 1841, Seward Papers.

36. Seward to H. V. R. Schermerhorn, 20 February 1849, quoted in McCadden, "Public School Society," pp. 188–207. On the entire episode see Vincent P. Lannie, *Public Money and Parochial Education* (Cleveland, 1968).

37. Hughes to Anthony Blanc, 3 January 1852, cited in Lannie, *Public Money*, p. 253.

38. This is clear in Hughes's report to Rome in 1858, reprinted in Henry J. Browne, ed., "The Archdiocese of New York a Century Ago: A Memoir of Archbishop Hughes," *Records* 39–40 (1952):129–90.

39. Lannie, *Public Money*, pp. 255–56.

40. Quoted in *ibid.*, p. 249.

41. Quoted in Robert Michaelsen, "Common School, Common Religion? A Case Study in Church-State Relations, Cincinnati, 1869–1870," *Church History* 38 (June 1969):213.

42. Kathleen Gavigan, "The Rise and Fall of Parish Cohesiveness in Philadelphia," *Records* 86 (March–December 1975):107–130.

43. Coleman J. Barry, *The Catholic Church and the German Americans* (Milwaukee, Wisc., 1953), p. 37.

44. Peter Guilday, *The National Pastorals of the American Hierarchy, 1782–1919* (Westminister, Md., 1927), pp. 36–37, 83, 144, 152.

45. Raymond H. Schmandt, comp., "A Selection of Sources Dealing with the Nativist Riots of 1844," *Records* 58 (June-September 1969):68–200.

46. Daniel P. Moynihan and Nathan Glazer, *Beyond the Melting Pot* (Cambridge, Mass., 1963), p. 221.

47. See, for example, Samuel P. Hays, "The Social Analysis of Political History, 1880–1920," *Political Science Quarterly* 90 (September 1965):373–94.

48. Lee Benson, *The Concept of Jacksonian Democracy: New York as a Test Case* (Princeton, N.J., 1961), pp. 323–27.

49. See Paul Kleppner, *The Cross of Culture: A Social Analysis of Midwestern Politics, 1850–1900*, 2nd ed. (New York, 1970).

50. Charles P. Connor, "Archbishop Hughes and Mid Century Politics, 1844–1860," *U.S. Catholic Historian* 3 (Fall and Winter 1983):70.

51. The card is quoted in Charles P. Connor, "The American Catholic Political Position at Mid Century: Archbishop Hughes as a Test Case," (Ph.D. diss., Fordham University, 1979), p. 203. The *Freeman's Journal* and *Tribune* quotes are from Benson, *Jacksonian Democracy*, pp. 189–91.

52. Connor, "Mid Century Politics," p. 168.

53. George Barany, "A Note on the Prehistory of American Diplomatic Relations with the Papal States," *Catholic Historical Review* 47 (January 1962):508–513.

54. Connor, "Mid Century Politics," p. 172.

55. Blanche Marie McEnery, *American Catholics in the War with Mexico* (Washington, D.C., 1937), pp. 18–23. See also Ellis, "American Catholics and Peace," pp. 7–8.

56. Ted C. Hinckley, "American Anti-Catholicism during the Mexican War," *Pacific Historical Review* 31 (May 1962):121–38.

57. Peter Guilday, "Gaetano Bedini," *Historical Records and Studies* 23 (1933):87–170.

58. Frederick J. Zwierlein, *The Life and Letters of Bishop McQuaid*, vol. 1 (Rochester, N.Y., 1927), pp. 164.

59. Thomas O'Connor, *Fitzpatrick's Boston, 1846–1866* (Boston, 1984), p. 97.

60. *Ibid.*, p. 141.

61. Ronald P. Formisano, *The Transformation of Political Culture: Massachusetts Parties, 1790s–1840s* (New York, 1983), pp. 329–36.

62. O'Connor, *Fitzpatrick's Boston*, chaps. 5–6.

63. Thomas M. Keefe, "Chicago's Flirtation with Political Nativism, 1854–1856," *Records* 82 (September 1971):131–58.

64. Patrick Blessing, "Culture, Religion and the Activities of the Committee of Vigilance, San Francisco, 1856", Working Paper Series Number 3, Cushwa Center for American Catholic Studies, Fall 1980.

65. Thomas W. Spalding, *Martin John Spalding: American Churchman* (Washington, D.C., 1973), p. 122.

66. Guilday, *National Pastorals*, pp. 109, 142–43.

67. Quoted in Guilday, *England* 2:498.

68. Thomas N. Brown, "Nationalism and Irish Peasant 1800–1848," *Review of Politics* 15 (October 1953):431; Thomas F. Moriarty, "The Irish American Response to Catholic Emancipation," *Catholic Historical Review* 66 (July 1980):353–73.

69. The *Citizen*, 28 October 1854.

70. Thomas R. Ryan, C.P.P.S., "Orestes Brownson's Lectures in St Louis, Missouri, in 1852 and 1854," *Records* 89 (March-December 1978):45–58.

71. Henry F. Brownson, ed., *The Works of Orestes Brownson*, vol. 18 (Detroit, 1882–1907), p. 286.

72. Brownson, *Works* 18:289.

73. *Ibid.* 293.

74. *Ibid.* 291, 314.
75. Henry F. Brownson, *The Life of Orestes Brownson* (Detroit, 1898–1900), vol. 2, p. 585.
76. *Ibid.*, p. 528.
77. Isaac McDaniel, O.S.B., "Orestes A. Brownson on Irish Immigrants and American Nativism," *American Benedictine Review* 32 (June 1981):122–39.
78. David O'Brien, *The Promised Land: Isaac Hecker and American Catholicism* (forthcoming), chap. 19.
79. *Miscellanea* (Louisville, KY., 1852), in Spalding, *Spalding*, pp. 472–74.

Chapter 4.   Industrial Catholicism

1. Quoted in Eric Goldman, *Rendezvous with Destiny* (New York, 1965), p. 8.
2. Quoted in Sylvester L. Malone, *Dr. Edward McGlynn* (New York, 1918), p. 4.
3. Quoted in Goldman, *Rendezvous*, p. 27.
4. W. E. B. DuBois, *The Souls of Black Folk* (1904; reprint, New York, 1961), pp. 15–17, 45–47.
5. Quoted in Timothy L. Smith, *Revivalism and Social Reform* (New York, 1957), p. 225.
6. O'Connor, *Fitzpatrick's Boston*, p. 96.
7. Quoted in Walter Sharrow, "John Hughes and a Catholic Response to Slavery in Antebellum America," *Journal of New York History* (Fall 1972):11
8. Gilbert Osofsky, "Abolitionists, Irish Immigrants, and the Dilemmas of Romantic Nationalism," *American Historical Review* 80 (October 1975):900–902.
9. Hugh J. Nolan, *The Most Reverend Francis Patrick Kenrick, Third Bishop of Philadelphia, 1830–1851* (Washington, D.C., 1948), p. 242. The entire issue is examined in Madeleine Hooks Rice, *American Catholic Opinion in the Slavery Controversy* (Gloucester, Mass., 1964).
10. Hughes, *Works* 2:222.
11. O'Connor, *Fitzpatrick's Boston*, p. 167.
12. *Ibid.*, p. 178.
13. James J. Pillar, "Catholicism in the Lower South," in L. F. Ellsworth, ed., *The Americanization of the Gulf Coast* (Pensacola, Fla., 1972); Randall M. Miller, "Catholics in the Old South: Some Speculations on Catholic Identities," Working Paper Series 9, Cushwa Center for American Catholic Studies, Spring 1981.
14. Randall M. Miller, "Black Catholics in the Slave South: Some Needs and Opportunities for Study," *Records* 86 (March-December 1975):93–106.
15. Guilday, *England* 2:152–53.
16. *Ibid.* 471–72.
17. Quoted in John Tracy Ellis, *American Catholicism*, 2nd ed. (Chicago, 1969) p. 94.
18. Quoted in Dorothy Dohen, *Nationalism and American Catholicism* (New York, 1960), p. 140.

19. Leonard R. Riforgiato, "Bishop Timon, Buffalo, and the Civil War," *Catholic Historical Review* 73 (January 1986):73.
20. Connor, "Hughes as a Test Case," p. 358; Rice, *Slavery Controversy*, p. 123.
21. O'Connor, *Fitzpatrick's Boston*, p. 209. See also James McCague, *The Second Rebellion: The New York City Draft Riots of 1863.*
22. Spalding, *Spalding*, pp. 135–60.
23. Oscar Hugh Lipscomb, "The Administration of John Quinlan: Second Bishop of Mobile, 1859–1883," *Records* 78 (March-December 1967):30–38; Miller, "Catholics in Old South", pp. 6–9.
24. McGreal, "Mazzuchelli," pp. 112–13.
25. Guilday, *Pastorals*, pp. 205–206.
26. *John Carroll Papers* 2:48–49.
27. The quotes in this paragraph are taken from Joseph Chinnici, "Spiritual Capitalism and the Culture of American Catholicism," *U.S. Catholic Historian* 5 (1986):131–64.
28. Jeffrey M. Burns, "The Ideal Catholic Child: Images from Catholic Textbooks, 1875–1912," Working Paper Series Number 2, Cushwa Center for American Catholic Studies, Spring, 1978.
29. A. A. Lambing, *The Orphan's Friend: A Series of Plain Instructions for the Use of Orphans after Leaving the Asylum, and for Persons of the Same Class Living in the World* (New York, 1875), pp. 20, 32–33, 43–44.
30. Quoted in Goldman, *Rendezvous*, p. 7.
31. "To Do the Duty of Lowell: The Struggle for Power behind the Formation of St. Patrick's Lowell, 1827–1847," paper delivered at Conference on Perspectives on American Catholicism, Notre Dame, Ind.; 1982.
32. Stephen Thernstrom, *Poverty and Progress* (Cambridge, Mass., 1973).
33. Timothy L. Smith, "Religion and Ethnicity in America," *American Historical Review* 83 (December 1978), p. 1181.
34. Smith, "Religion and Ethnicity," pp. 1165–66.
35. Diner, *Erin's Daughters*, chaps. 2–3; Timothy L. Smith, "Immigrant Social Aspirations and American Education, 1880–1930," *American Quarterly* 21 (Summer 1969):539–42.
36. Mary Cygan, "Ethnic Parish as Compromise: The Sphere of Clerical and Lay Authority in a Polish American Parish, 1911–1930," Working Paper Series Number 13, Cushwa Center for American Catholic Studies, Spring 1983. The Bodnar quote cited by Cygan (p. 23) is taken from "Immigration and Modernization: The Case of Slavic Peasants in Industrial America," *Journal of Social History* 10 (February 1976):44–71.
37. Robert E. Park and Herbert A. Miller, *Old World Traits Transplanted* (New York and London 1921), p. 286.
38. Robert A. Slayton, *Back of the Yards: The Making of a Local Democracy* (Chicago, 1986), chap. 1.
39. Robert H. Lord, John E. Sexton, and Edward T. Harrington, *History of the Archdiocese of Boston*, vol. 3 (New York, 1944), pp. 47, 238; Jay P. Dolan, "Catholic Ethnics Past and Present" (unpublished).
40. John M. Farley to Bernard McQuaid, 5 May 1907, McQuaid Papers, Saint Bernard's Seminary, Rochester, N.Y. See also Richard M. Llinkh, *American Catholicism and European Immigrants, 1900–1924* (Staten Island, 1975), pp. 177–78.

41. Barry, *Catholic Church and German Americans* and Anthony J. Kuzniewski, *Faith and Fatherland: The Polish Church War in Wisconsin* (Notre Dame, Ind., 1980).

42. Aaron Abell, *American Catholics and Social Action* (Garden City, N.Y., 1960), pp. 30–31.

43. Park and Miller, *Old World Traits*, pp. 212–21; Daniel S. Buczek, *Immigrant Pastor: The Life of Right Reverend Monsignor Lucyan Bojnowski of New Britain, Connecticut* (Waterbury, Conn., 1974).

44. Joseph Parot, "Sources of Community Conflict in Chicago Polonia: A Comparative Analysis and Historiographic Appraisal," *Ethnicity* 7 (1980):333–48; Timothy L. Smith, "Lay Initiative in the Religious Life of American Immigrants, 1880–1950," in Tamara Harevan, ed., *Anonymous Americans* (Englewood Cliffs, N.J., 1971), p. 243.

45. Quoted in Lawrence McCaffrey, "Catholicism and Irish American Identity in the mid Nineteenth Century" (unpublished).

46. Parot, "Sources of Community Conflict," p. 357; William Galush, "Both Polish and Catholic: Immigrant Clergy in the American Church," *Catholic Historical Review* 70 (July 1984):407–27.

47. Park and Miller, *Old World Traits*, p. 290.

48. Joseph Parot, "Steelmills, Stockyards, Sweatshops, and Slums: The Social Fabric of the Polish Catholic Working Class in Chicago, 1870–1900," paper delivered at Conference on Perspectives on American Catholicism, Notre Dame, Ind., 1982.

49. Dolan, *Immigrant Church;* O'Brien, *Faith and Friendship*, pp. 132–39; Timothy L. Smith, "New Approaches to the History of Immigration in Twentieth Century America," *American Historical Review* 71 (July 1966):126–27.

50. Rudolph Vecoli, "Prelates and Peasants: Italian Immigrants and the Catholic Church," *Journal of Social History* 2 (Spring 1969):209–229.

51. John T. Cumbler, *Working Class Community in Industrial America: Work, Leisure and Struggle in Two Industrial Cities, 1880–1930* (Westport, Conn., 1977), p. 272; Judith E. Smith, "The Transformation of Family and Community Life in Immigrant Neighborhoods, 1900–1940," in Herbert Gutman and Donald H. Bell, eds., *The New England Working Class and the New Labor History* (Urbana, Ill., 1987), p. 171.

52. Guilday, ed., *National Pastorals*, p. 85.

53. Susan E. Hirsch, *Roots of the American Working Class: The Industrial Crafts in Newark, 1800–1860* (Philadelphia, 1978), esp. pp. 106–107; Roy Rosenzweig, *Eight Hours for What We Will: Workers and Leisure in an Industrial City* (New York and London, 1983); James R. Barrett, "Unity and Fragmentation: Class, Race and Ethnicity on Chicago's South Side, 1900–1922," *Journal of Social History* 18 (Fall 1984):37–55.

54. David Montgomery, *Beyond Equality* (New York, 1972), pp. 124–28.

55. Victor C. Greene, *The Slavic Community on Strike: Immigrant Labor in Pennsylvania Anthracite* (Notre Dame, Ind., 1968), p. 32.

56. Robert C. Reinders, "T. Wharton Collens: Catholic and Christian Socialist," *Catholic Historical Review* 52 (July 1966):212–33.

57. Bayley quoted in Aaron Abell, "The Catholic Church and the American Social Question," in Waldemar Gurian and M. A. Fitzsimons, eds., *The Catholic Church in World Affairs* (Notre Dame, Ind., 1954), p. 382.

58. Francis G. McManamin, *The American Years of John Boyle O'Reilly,*

1870–1890 (Washington, D.C., 1959); Augustine Hewit "The Duties of the Rich in Christian Society," 6 pts.; *Catholic World* 14 (February 1872) to 15 (July 1872).

59. Spalding, *Spalding*, p. 252.
60. John Gilmary Shea, "Labor Discontent," *American Catholic Quarterly Review* 7 (October 1882):712.
61. Charlotte Erickson, *American Industry and European Immigrants 1860–1885* (Cambridge, Mass., 1957), p. 113.
62. Autobiographical fragment, Powderly Papers, Catholic University of America.
63. James E. Roohan, "American Catholics and the Social Question, 1865–1900" (Ph.D. Diss., Yale University, 1952).
64. Sylvester L. Malone, *Dr. Edward McGlynn* (New York, 1918), p. 4.
65. Steven B. Cord, *Henry George: Dreamer or Realist?* (Philadelphia, 1965), p. 118.
66. Frederick Zwierlein, *The Life and Letters of Bishop McQuaid*, vol. 3 (Rochester, 1925), pp. 6–7.
67. McQuaid to Corrigan, 28 December 1892, in Zwierlein transcripts, Archives, Saint Bernard's Seminary, Rochester, N.Y.
68. Gilmour to Elder, 17 April 1888 in Cincinnati Papers, University of Notre Dame.
69. The entire episode is well described in Robert Emmett Curran, S.J., "The McGlynn Affair and the Shaping of the New Conservatism in American Catholicism, 1886–1894," *Catholic Historical Review* 66 (April, 1980):184–204. See also Curran, *Michael Augustine Corrigan and the Shaping of Conservative Catholicism in America, 1878–1902* (New York, 1978).
70. Letter to Mr. Wingate, 28 February 1887, in Americanism Papers, Notre Dame.
71. Text printed in Malone, *McGlynn*, pp. 18–26.
72. Corrigan to McQuaid, 28 December 1892, McQuaid Papers.
73. John Tracy Ellis, *The Life of James Cardinal Gibbons*, vol. 1 (Milwaukee, 1952), pp 214–15, 496.
74. Aaron Abell, "American Catholic Reaction to Industrial Conflict: The Arbitral Process, 1885–1900," *Catholic Historical Review* 41 (January 1956):385–407.
75. Ellis, *Gibbons* 1:532.
76. Quoted in Sister Joan de Lourdes Leonard, "Catholic Attitudes toward American Labor, 1884–1919" (M.A. thesis, Columbia University, 1940), pp. 32–34.
77. *Ibid.*, pp. 33–34.
78. Quoted in Leonard, "Catholic Attitudes," p. 48.
79. M. Servina Pahoreski, O.S.F., *The Social and Political Activities of William James Onahan* (Washington, D.C., 1942).
80. Moynihan and Glazer, *Beyond the Melting Pot*, pp. 217–87; Croker quote, p. 227.
81. Daniel P. Moynihan, "When the Irish Ran New York," *Reporter*, 8 June 1969.
82. Lord, Sexton, and Harrington, *Boston* 3:87.
83. Humbert S. Nelli, "John Powers and the Italians: Politics in a Chicago Ward, 1896–1921," *Journal of American History* 57 (June 1970):67.
84. Montgomery, *Beyond Equality*, pp. 212–13.

85. Brian Greenberg, *Workers and Community: The Response to Industrialization in a Nineteenth Century American City, Albany, New York, 1850–1884* (Albany, N.Y., 1985), pp. 120–38.
86. Alan Dawley, *Class and Community* (Cambridge, Mass., 1976).
87. Joseph P. O'Grady, "Anthony M. Keiley (1832–1905): Virginia's Catholic Politician," *Catholic Historical Review* 54 (January 1969):613–35.
88. Powderly to Sister Rose Mary, 1 December 1915, Kerby Papers, Archives of the Catholic University of America, hereafter cited as ACUA.
89. Charles Beard, *The Rise of American Civilization*, vol. 2 (New York, 1927), p. 409.
90. Philip Foner, *History of the Labor Movement in the United States*, vol. 3 (New York, 1947), p. 135.
91. Daniel Walkowitz, *Worker City, Company Town* (Urbana, Ill., 1978), p. 257.
92. Robert Ernst, *Immigrant Life In New York City, 1825–1865* (New York, 1949), p. 184.
93. James F. Donnelly, "Catholic New Yorkers and New York Socialists, 1870–1920" (Ph.D. diss., New York University, 1982), p. 177.
94. Tentler, "Detroit."

Chapter 5. Liberal Catholicism

1. Joseph F. Gower and Richard M. Leliaert, eds., *The Brownson–Hecker Correspondence* (Notre Dame, Ind., 1979), p. 105.
2. "The Future Triumph of the Church," typescript, Paulist Fathers Archives, Saint Paul's College, Washington, D.C.
3. Quoted in David Sweeney, *the Life of John Lancaster Spalding* (New York, 1967), pp. 182–83.
4. Quoted in Sweeney, *Spalding*, p. 230.
5. James Cardinal Gibbons, *A Retrospect of Fifty Years* vol. 1 (New York, 1916), pp. 230–34.
6. *Ibid.*, p. 219.
7. *Ibid.* 1:234 and 2:152 and James Moynihan, *The Life of Archbishop John Ireland* (New York, 1953), p. 136.
8. Barry, *Catholic Church and German Americans*, p. 235.
9. Moynihan, *Ireland*, p. 58.
10. *Ibid.*, p. 134 and Gibbons, *Retrospect* 1:308.
11. Joan Bland, *The Catholic Total Abstinence Union of America* (Washington, 1951), p. 22.
12. See, for example, Rosenzweig, *Eight Hours for What We Will.*
13. Dorothy Ross, "The Irish Catholic Immigrant 1880–1900: A Study in Social Mobility" (M.A. thesis, Columbia University, n.d.).
14. Quoted in R. Emmett Curran, "Prelude to 'Americanism': The New York Accademia and Clerical Radicalism in the Late Nineteenth Century," *Church History* 47 (January 1978):51.
15. *Ibid.*, 48–65.
16. *Ibid.*, 62.
17. James Hennesey, S.J., "The Baltimore Council of 1866: An American Syllabus," *Records* vol. 76 (1965), p. 6; Spalding, *Spalding*, pp. 240–41.
18. John Tracy Ellis, "The Formation of the American Priest: An Historical

Perspective," in Ellis, *The Catholic Priest in the United States: Historical Investigations* (Collegeville, Minn., 1971), p. 39.

19. Spalding, *Spalding*, p. 242.
20. Paul K. Hennessy, "Infallibility in the Thought of Peter Richard Kenrick," *Theological Studies* 45 (December 1982):702–714.
21. Robert D. Cross, *The Emergence of Liberal Catholicism in the United States* (Cambridge, Mass., 1958), pp. 85–86.
22. Thomas T. McAvoy, "Public Schools vs. Catholic Schools and James McMaster," *Review of Politics* 28 (January 1966):19–46; 1877 Instruction in Ellis, *Documents* 2:405–408.
23. "Pastoral Letter of 1884," in Peter Guilday, *National Pastorals*, pp. 243–47.
24. Robert Michaelsen, "Common School, Common Religion? A Case Study in Church-State Relations, Cincinnati, 1869–1870," *Church History* 38 (June 1969):201–217.
25. David Tyack, "The Kingdom of God and the Common School: Protestant Ministers and the Educational Awakening in the West," *Harvard Education Review* 36 (Fall 1966):9.
26. *Ibid.*
27. New York *Tribune*, 9 October 1875.
28. Tyack, "Kingdom of God," pp. 8, 10.
29. John Whitney Evans, "Catholics and the Blair Education Bill," *Catholic Historical Review* 46 (October 1960):273–98.
30. Patrick H. Ahearn, *The Life of John J. Keane, Priest, Educator, Archbishop, 1883–1918* (Washington, D.C., 1953).
31. Edward McSweeney, *Rt. Rev. Patrick Francis McSweeney* (Philadelphia, 1908), pp. 16–17.
32. Norlene M. Kunkel, "Christian Free Schools: A Nineteenth Century Plan," *Notre Dame Journal of Education* 7 (Spring 1976):18–27.
33. Joseph F. Gower, "A 'Test Question' for Religious Liberty: Isaac Hecker on Education," *Notre Dame Journal of Education* 7 (Spring 1976):28–43; Edward J. Langlois, C.S.P., "Isaac Hecker's Political Thought," in John Farina, ed., *Hecker Studies* (New York, 1983), pp. 49–86.
34. Zwierlein, *McQuaid*, pp. 136–47.
35. Timothy H. Morrissey, "A Controversial Reformer: Archbishop John Ireland and His Educational Belief," *Notre Dame Journal of Education* 7 (Spring 1976):63–75.
36. Daniel F. Reilly, *The School Controversy, 1891–1893* (Washington, D.C., 1943), p. 280.
37. William E. Akin, "The War of the Bishops: Catholic Controversy on the School Question in New York State in 1984," *New York State Historical Society Quarterly* 50 (January 1966):41–61.
38. Thomas J. Bouquillon, *Education: To Whom Does It Belong?* (Baltimore, 1891).
39. McQuaid to Denis O'Connell, 16 January 1892, quoted in C. J. Nuesse, "Thomas Joseph Bouquillon (1840–1902), Moral Theologian and Precursor of the Social Sciences in the Catholic University of America," *Catholic Historical Review* 72 (October 1972):601–619. McQuaid to Pope Leo XIII, 16 January 1893, in Edward Hanna Papers, Saint Bernard's Seminary, Rochester, N.Y.
40. Quoted in R. Cross, *Emergence of Liberal Catholicism*, p. 15.
41. Quoted in Frederick Zwierlein, "Triumph of the Conservative Pro-

gressives in the Catholic Church in the United States," *Social Justice Review* 51 (July-September 1958):119–20.

42. McQuaid to Pope Leo XIII, 16 January 1893, in Edward Hanna Papers, Saint Bernard's Seminary, Rochester, N.Y.

43. Zwierlein, *McQuaid*, p. 305.

44. Thomas S. Byrne to McQuaid, 10 February 1897, McQuaid Papers, Saint Bernard's Seminary, Rochester, N.Y.

45. Zwierlein, *McQuaid*, p, 141; Frederick W. Zwierlein, *Letters of Archbishop Corrigan to Bishop McQuaid and Allied Documents* (Rochester, N.Y., 1946), p. 75.

46. Donald L. Kinzer, *An Episode in Anti-Catholicism: The American Protective Assocation* (Seattle, 1964).

47. Thomas P. Ryan, C.P.P.S., "A Memoir of Henry Francis Brownson," *Records*, 51–62.

48. Brownson to Onahan, 22 March 1889; Foy to Brownson, 22 August 1889 and 9 September 1889, H. F. Brownson Papers, Archives of the University of Notre Dame.

49. Onahan to Mr. Hyde, 21 February 1892, Onahan Papers, Archives of the University of Notre Dame; Onahan to Ireland, 25 August 1890, Onahan Papers.

50. Ahearn, *Keane*, p. 598; James F. Cleary, "Catholic Participation in the World's Parliament of Religions, Chicago, 1893," *Catholic Historical Review* 55 (January 1970):585–609. See also John R. Betts, "The Laity and the Ecumenical Spirit, 1889–1893," *Review of Politics* 26 (January 1964):3–19.

51. John T. Gillard, S.S.J., *The Catholic Church and the American Negro* (Baltimore, 1929), p. 37.

52. David Spalding, C.F.X., "The Negro Catholic Congresses, 1889–1894," *Catholic Historical Review* 55 (October 1969):337–57. See also Cyprian Davis, O.S.B., "Black Catholics in Nineteenth Century America," *U.S. Catholic Historian* 5 (1986):1–18.

53. Moynihan, *Ireland*, chap. 8.

54. Quoted in Gerald Fogarty, *The Vatican and the Americanist Crisis: Denis J. O'Connell, Americanist Agent in Rome* (Rome, 1974), p. 280.

55. Quoted in Ellis, "American Catholics and Peace," pp. 9–10.

56. William O'Connell to Denis O'Connell, 23 February 1904, copy in transcripts of the Portland Papers in Boston Archdiocesan Archives. Years later Cardinal Montini told Dorothy Wayman that O'Connell had written Leo XIII on 20 April 1903, discussing the proposal that he be sent to Manila: "Inasmuch as he had not concealed from the beginning of the Spanish American war his sympathy for Spain and had openly stated the war was unjust, he had been openly criticized for lacking in patriotism." Montini's letter of 26 June 1953, in Wayman manuscripts, Archives of the Archdiocese of Boston.

57. Sweeney, *Spalding*, p. 124.

58. Quoted in Ellis, "American Catholics and Peace," p. 6.

59. Sweeney, *Spalding*, pp. 255–56.

60. Frank T. Reuter, "American Catholics and the Establishment of the Philippine Public School System," *Catholic Historical Review* 49 (October 1963):365–81. See also Reuter, *Catholic Influence on American Colonial Policy, 1898–1904* (Austin and London, 1967).

61. Keane to Gibbons, 31 July 1894, photostat in Ireland Papers (film), Saint Thomas College, Saint Paul, Minn.

62. Leo XIII, "Longinqua Oceani" in Ellis, *Documents* 2:499–511.

63. On the Americanist crisis see Gerald Fogarty. *The Vatican and the American Hierarchy from 1870 to 1965* (Wilmington, Del., 1985), pp. 115–95.

64. Leo XIII, "Testem Benevolentiae," in Ellis, *Documents* 2:538–47.

65. J. St. Claire Ethridge [pseudonym], "The Sources of Americanism," *North American Review* (May 1900), copy in Ireland Papers.

66. Thomas T. McAvoy, C.S.C., *The Great Crisis in American Catholic History* (Chicago, 1957), pp. 296–97.

67. Moynihan, *Ireland*, pp. 134–35.

68. Ellis, *Gibbons* 1:524.

69. Sweeney, *Spalding*, pp. 266–70.

Chapter 6.   Reform Catholicism

1. Sweeney, *Spalding*, pp. 230–34.

2. Ellis, "Formation," p. 62; Michael Gannon, "Before and After Modernism: The Intellectual Isolation of the American Priest," in Ellis, ed., *Historical Investigations*, pp. 293–384.

3. Helpful here is Peter W. Williams, "Catholicism Militant: The Public Face of the Archdiocese of Cincinnati, 1900–1960," Working Paper Series 8, Cushwa Center for American Catholic Studies. See also Christopher J. Kauffman, *Faith and Fraternalism: The History of the Knights of Columbus, 1882–1982* (New York, 1982).

4. C. J. Nuesse, "Empirical Problems for Sociological Research in the Parish," in *Sociology of the Parish*, (Washington, D.C., 1954), pp. 217–18.

5. William Kerby, "Reinforcement of the Bonds of Faith," *Catholic World* 84 (January 1907):591–606; my attention was drawn to this article by Beth McKeown, "Catholic Identity in America," in Thomas M. McFadden, ed., *America in Theological Perspective* (New York, 1976), pp. 56–67.

6. Milton Gordon, "Assimlation in America: Theory and Reality," *Daedalus* 90 (Spring 1961):280.

7. James M. O'Toole, " 'That Fabulous Churchman': Toward a Biography of Cardinal O'Connell," *Catholic Historical Review* 70 (January 1984):28–44.

8. Robert Lord to Peter Guilday, 29 April 1930, Guilday Papers, ACUA.

9. Edward Kantowitz, *Corporation Sole* (Notre Dame, Ind., 1981).

10. O'Brien, *Faith and Friendship*, 192–93; Tentler, "Detroit."

11. Burns, "Textbooks," p. 5.

12. Tentler, "Detroit."

13. Christa Ressmeyer Klein, "Catholic Institutions for Adolescants in 19th century New York City: Comparative Histories," paper given at Conference on the Reinterpretation of American Catholic History, Notre Dame, Ind., October 1974.

14. O'Brien, *Faith and Friendship*, pp. 313–14.

15. Quotes are taken from selections in Robert Handy, ed., *The Social Gospel in America, 1870–1920* (New York, 1966), passim.

16. Rt. Rev. William Stang, *Pastoral Theology* (New York, 1867), p. 39.

17. Ireland to Father Daniel Hudson, 14 September, 30 September, and

9 October 1912, Hudson Papers, Archives of the University of Notre Dame.

18. Gibbons, *Retrospect* 1:209.
19. *Ibid.* 145–46.
20. *Ibid.* 230.
21. Antoinette Iadorala, "The American Catholic Bishops and Woman: From the Nineteenth Amendment to ERA," in Yvonne Haddad and Ellison Findly, *Women, Religion and Social Change* (Albany, 1985), pp. 458–60.
22. O'Connell to Taft, 11 March 1914 in O'Connell Papers, Archives of the Archdiocese of Boston.
23. O'Connell to Glennon, 20 March 1918, copy, O'Connell Papers.
24. Powderly to Gibbons, 29 August 1900; Gibbons to Powderly, 31 August 1900, in Powderly Papers, ACUA; Powderly to Kerby, 15 August 1904, Kerby Papers, ACUA.
25. Powderly to Kerby, 29 May 1911, Kerby Papers, ACUA.
26. The text of *Rerum Novarum* is found in Etienne Gilson, ed., *The Church Speaks to the Modern World* (New York, 1954).
27. Robert E. Doherty, "The American Socialist Party and the Roman Catholic Church, 1901–1917" (D.Ed. diss, Teachers College, Columbia University, 1959), chap. 5; Toby Terrar, "Thomas McGrady, American Catholic Socialist," *Ecumenist* 21 (November and December 1982):14–16.
28. Robert E. Doherty, "Thomas J. Hagerty, the Church and Socialism," *Labor History* 3 (Winter 1962):43.
29. Doherty, "Socialist Party," chap. 6.
30. James F. Donnelly, "Catholic New Yorkers and New York Socialists, 1870–1920" (Ph.D. diss., New York University, 1982)
31. *Ibid.*
32. Donnelly, "New York Socialists," p. 97.
33. Text of Ryan-Hillquit debate in Albert Fried, ed., *Socialism in America: From the Shakers to the Third International* (Garden City, N.Y., 1970), pp. 471–95.
34. Donnelly, "New York Socialists," pp. 241–42.
35. Leonard, "Church and Labor," pp. 48–50.
36. Owen Carrigan, "Martha Moore Avery: Crusader for Social Justice," *Catholic Historical Review* 54 (April 1968):17–38.
37. Debra Campbell, "David Goldstein and the Rise of the Catholic Campaigners for Christ," *Catholic Historical Review* 72 (January 1986):33–50.
38. Powderly to Kerby, 4 August 1904, Kerby Papers, ACUA.
39. Sweeney, *Spalding*, pp. 316–26; Paul Stroh. *The Catholic Clergy and American Labor Disputes, 1900–1937* (Washington, D.C., 1939), chap. 2.
40. Stroh, *Catholic Clergy*, chap. 3.
41. Marc Karson, *American Labor Unions and Politics, 1900–1918*, pp. 212–84.
42. Philip Gleason, *The Conservative Reformers: German American Catholics and the Social Order* (Notre Dame, Ind., 1968) and Mary Elizabeth Dye, *By Their Fruits: A Social Biography of Frederick B. Kenkel* (New York, 1960).
43. Mary Harrita Fox, *Peter E. Dietz, Labor Priest* (Notre Dame, Ind., 1953);

Henry J. Browne, "Peter E. Dietz: Pioneer Planner of Catholic Social Action," *Catholic Historical Review* 30 (January 1948):448–56.

44. Collins to O'Connell, 15 March 1913, O'Connell Papers, Archives of the Archdiocese of Boston.

45. Karson's argument is rejected by Philip Taft, *The A. F. of L. in the Time of Gompers* (New York, 1957), pp. 334–41.

46. Bernard C. Cronin, *Father Yorke and the Labor Movement in San Francisco, 1900–1910* (Washington, D.C., 1943).

47. Kerby to Keane, 17 January 1896, Kerby Papers, ACUA.

48. Dorothy Mohler, "The Advocate Role of the St. Vincent de Paul Society," *Records* 86 (March–December 1975):80–81.

49. Mohler, "St. Vincent de Paul," p. 86.

50. Donald P. Gavin, *The National Conference of Catholic Charities 1910–1960* (Milwaukee, Wisc., 1962), chap. 1–4.

51. John A. Ryan, *Social Doctrine in Action: A Personal History* (New York, 1941).

52. John A. Ryan, *A Living Wage* (New York, 1906); *Distributive Justice: The Right and Wrong of Our Present Distribution of Wealth* (New York, 1916). On Ryan, see Francis L. Broderick, *Right Reverend New Dealer* (New York, 1963) and David O'Brien, *American Catholics and Social Reform: the New Deal Years (New York, 1968)*, chap. 6.

53. Karl H. Cerny, "Monsignor John A. Ryan and the Social Action Department" (Ph.D. diss., Yale University, 1954), p. 234.

54. Charles Curran, "American and Catholic: American Catholic Social Ethics 1880–1965," *Thought* 52 (March 1977):50–74. Quote is from *Seven Troubled Years* (Ann Arbor, Mich., 1937), p. 59.

55. Cerny, "Social Action Department," pp. 104–105.

56. Patrick W. Gearty, *The Economic Thought of Monsignor John A. Ryan* (Washington, D.C., 1953).

57. Joseph M. McShane, S.J., *'Sufficiently Radical,' Catholicism, Progressivism and the Bishops' Program of 1919* (Washington, D.C., 1986).

58. Ryan to Sister Mary John, 12 May 1919, copy made available by Monsignor George G. Higgins.

59. Dean R. Esslinger, "American German and Irish Attitudes Toward Neutrality, 1914–1917: A Study of Catholic Minorities," *Catholic Historical Review* 53 (July 1967):194–216. But statistical evidence shows no decline of the Irish vote for Wilson in 1916: Edward Cuddy, "Irish Americans and the 1916 Election," *American Quarterly* 21 (Summer 1969):288–43. Most historians see ethnic rather than religious considerations influencing responses to World War I: Joseph P. O'Grady, *Immigrant Influence on Wilson's Peace Policies* (Lexington, Ky., 1967).

60. Quoted in Dohen, *Nationalism*, pp. 147, 148 and Fogarty, "Public Patriotism," p. 28.

61. Burke quoted in John B. Sheerin, *Never Look Back: The Career and Concerns of John J. Burke* (New York, 1975), p. 29; Sr. Teresa Maria Helldorfer, "The Editorial Opinion of the Catholic Review on Contemporary Domestic and Foreign Affairs 1913–1923" (M.A. thesis, Catholic University, 1961).

62. Quoted in John Patrick Buckley, "The New York Irish: Their View of American Policy, 1914–1921" (Ph.D. diss., New York University, 1974), p. 121.

63. Quoted in *ibid.*, p. 160

64. Muldoon Diary, 26 December 1917, microfilm, ACUA.

65. *Ibid.*, 15 August 1918.

66. Beth McKeown, "The National Bishops Conference: An Analysis of Its Origins," *Catholic Historical Review* 66 (October 1980):565–74.

67. Edward Cuddy, "Pro-Germanism and American Catholicism, 1914–1917," *Catholic Historical Review* 54 (October 1968):427–54. The Lansing quote is taken from John B. Duff, "The Versailles Treaty and the Irish Americans," *Journal of American History* 55 (December 1968):586.

68. "Woodrow Wilson and Self-Determination: A Re-Evaluation," *Records* 74 (March-December 1963):159–73.

69. See Muldoon Diary, 16 March 1919, for meeting with Wilson.

70. Buckley, "The New York Irish," p. 147.

71. John B. Duff, "The Versailles Treaty and the Irish-Americans," *Journal of American History* 55 (December 1968):582–98; Sister Mary M. Zacharewicz, C.S.F.N., "The Attitude of the Catholic Press toward the League of Nations," *Records* 68 (March-June 1957):46–50.

72. Quoted in McKeown, "Origins of Bishops Conference," p. 526.

73. McKeown, "Apologia for an American Catholicism: The Petition and Report of the National Catholic Welfare Council to Pius XI, April 25, 1922," *Church History* 43 (December 1974):514–28.

74. *Catholic Standard and Times* (Philadelphia), 19 August 1922.

75. Hugh J. Nolan, ed., *Pastoral Letters of the United States Catholic Bishops*, I (Washington, D.C., 1984):272–333.

76. *The Church and Socialism and Other Essays* (Washington, D.C., 1917), p. 159.

77. "The Study of Social Problems in the Seminary," *American Ecclesiastical Review* 39 (August 1908):117.

78. "Is Social Reform Work a Duty of the Parish Clergy?" *American Ecclesiastical Review* 42 (April 1910):453–58.

79. Ryan to Bishop John F. Noll, 8 March 1938, Ryan Papers, Catholic University.

80. *The American Priest* (New York, 1919), pp. 84–85.

Chapter 7. Social Catholicism

1. David Ward, *Immigrants and Cities* (New York, 1969), pp. 121–49.

2. Timothy Mark Pies, "The Parochial School Campaigns in Michigan, 1920–1924: The Lutheran and Catholic Involvement," *Catholic Historical Review* 71 (April 1986):222–38.

3. David Tyack, "The Perils of Pluralism: The Background of the Pierce Case," *American Historical Review* 72 (October 1968):74–98.

4. Aaron I. Abell, ed., *American Catholic Thought on Social Questions* (Indianapolis, 1969), p. 393.

5. Muldoon Diary, 23 September 1920.

6. Philip Gleason," In Search of Unity," *Catholic Historical Review* 65 (April 1979):198–99.

7. James J. Walsh to Peter Guilday, 14 August 1929, Guilday Papers, ACUA.

8. See "The Goal of Christian Sociology," *Christian Front* 1 (December 1936):179–80; Charles A. Hart, "The Philosophy of Society," *Commonweal* 19 (23 February 1934):455–57; John O. Reidl, "Philosophy and Social Science," American Catholic Philosophy Association *Proceedings*, vol. 11 (1935), pp. 1–12; Clarence Enzler, "Wanted: Christian Social Science," *Catholic World* 142 (March 1936):687; Enzler, "Sociology in the Catholic College," *Catholic World* 143 (July 1936):422–29; and Frank Cavanaugh, "Modern Sociology," *Commonweal* 17 (9 June 1933).

9. John Fenlon to Peter Guilday, 16 January 1926, Guilday Papers, ACUA.
10. John Burke to William Kerby, 7 November 1906, Kerby Papers, ACUA.
11. Ryan to Kerby, 12 July 1924, Kerby Papers; ACUA.
12. Michael Williams, "At Dayton, Tennessee," *Commonweal* 2 (22 July 1925):262–65.
13. Letter to the *Nation* 113 (27 July 1921):99–100; see also *Declining Liberty and Other Papers* (New York, 1927), p. 236.
14. Ryan to Roger Baldwin, 5 November 1931, Ryan Papers, ACUA.
15. Thomas to Ryan, 10 February 1927; Ryan to Thomas, 15 February 17, 1927; and Thomas to Ryan, 25 February 1927, in Ryan Papers, ACUA.
16. Thomas to Ryan, 25 March 1927, Ryan Papers, ACUA.
17. Williams to Guilday, 16 October 1922, Guilday Papers, ACUA.
18. "An Introduction," *Commonweal* 1 (12 November 1924) and "From the First Year," *Commonweal* 1 (18 November 1924).
19. "What Shall the Layman Do?" *Commonweal* 2 (23 September 1925):463.
20. Guilday to James J. Walsh, 4 January 1923, Guilday Papers, ACUA.
21. Guilday to Thomas J. Meagher, 10 March 1925, Guilday Papers, ACUA.
22. Frederick J. Kinsman, *Americanism and Catholicism* (New York, 1924).
23. "Democracy and Equality," *Commonweal* 2 (27 May 1925):63–66.
24. Followed in "Week by Week" column of *Commonweal* (26 November to 10 December 1924).
25. "Are Catholics Christian?" *Commonweal* 1 (24 February 1925):333–34.
26. McNicholas, *Mosaic*, pp. 17–22 and pp. 37–43 from 1928 columns.
27. John A. Ryan and Moorhouse F. X. Millar, *The State and the Church* (New York, 1922), pp. 30–35.
28. Francis L. Broderick, "But Constitutions can Be Changed . . .," *Catholic Historical Review* 49 (October 1963):390–93.
29. Peter Guilday to Joseph Schaeffer, 23 February 1928, Guilday Papers, ACUA.
30. Guilday to Christopher Perotta, 27 March 1928, Guilday Papers, ACUA.
31. Guilday to William Franklin Sands, 26 May 1927, Guilday Papers, ACUA.
32. Guilday to Ellen Flick, 5 April·1933, Guilday Papers, ACUA.
33. Christopher Percotta to Guilday, 22 March 1928, Guilday Papers, ACUA.
34. Williams to Mrs. Nelson O'Shaughnessy, 3 October 1928, copy in Ryan papers, ACUA.
35. Norris to Frankfurter, 13 November 1928, in Frankfurter Papers, Library of Congress.
36. Editorial and "This Our Day," *Catholic World* 133 (May 1931):225–34 and 261–75.
37. McNicholas, "Pastoral Letter," *Catholic Mind* 29 (22 August 1929):464 and "Pastoral Letter on Charity," *Catholic Charities Review* 15 (October 1931):268–69.

38. *Tablet*, 9 December 1931.
39. John P. Frey to Bishop Francis W. Howard of Covington, 9 October 1933, Frey Papers, ACUA.
40. Bishop Howard to W. A. Appleton, 1 February 1934, copy, in Frey Papers, ACUA.
41. Donald R. Campion, S.J., "Survey of American Social Catholicism, 1930–1940" (M.A. thesis, Saint Louis University, 1949), pp. 25–26; I.A. O'Shaughnessy, *Man or Money* (New York, 1932). On Catholics and the Roosevelt administration, see George Q. Flynn, *American Catholics and the Roosevelt Presidency, 1932–1936* (Lexington, Ky., 1968) and *Roosevelt and Romanism: Catholics and American Diplomacy, 1937–1945* (Westport, Conn., 1976). On Catholic social thought and action, see O'Brien, *American Catholics and Social Reform: The New Deal Years* (New York, 1968).
42. Edward S. Shapiro, "Catholic Agrarian Thought and the New Deal," *Catholic Historical Review* 65 (October 1979):583–99.
43. John LaFarge, "The Interracial Apostolate", *America* 53 (8 June 1935):198–200; Edward S. Stanton, "The Manner was Extraordinary," *America* 103 (24 November 1975):397–99.
44. Lord and Sexton, *Boston* 3:657.
45. Introduction of president, *Catholic Charities Review* 17 (October 1933):5–6.
46. Gavin, *Charities*, p. 130.
47. John O'Grady, "Catholic Social Work," *Commonweal* 25 (19 March 1937) and "The Charities Conference Takes Stock," *Catholic Action* 14 (March 1932):5–6.
48. "Unemployment," in Raphael M. Huber, ed., *Our Bishops Speak* (Washington, D.C., 1959), 191–93.
49. "Sursum Corda," *Commonweal* 16 (8 April 1931):619.
50. "The Catholic Revival," *Commonweal* 13 (4 March 1931):477–78.
51. "The School and *Rerum Novarum*," *America* 45 (9 May 1931):111–12.
52. Karl H. Cerny, "Monsignor John A. Ryan and the Social Action Department," (Ph.D. diss., Yale University, 1954).
53. "Industrial Organization in the Light of the Encyclical," *Salesianum* 27 (January 1932):19–22.
54. "The Necessity of Federal Relief for the Unemployed," *Catholic Charitis Review* 15 (November 1931):290.
55. *Tablet*, 26 January 1932; Frank Murphy, "The Moral Law in Government," *Commonweal* 18 (19 May 1933):63–64.
56. "Two Times Two," *Commonweal* 16 (7 September 1932):442.
57. *Tablet*, 15 May 1933; *Sign* 13 (July 1934):13.
58. "Catholic Principles Reflected in Industrial Recovery Act," *Catholic Action* 15 (July 1933):6.
59. Ryan to P. J. Connolly, 30 September 1933, copy, in Ryan Papers; *Seven Troubled Years 1930–1936* (Ann Arbor, Mich., 1937), pp. 130.
60. "Are We on the Right Road?" *Commonweal* 20 (12 October 1934):548.
61. Raymond McGowan, "The Yardstick," *Tablet*, 24 June 1933, 8 July 1933 and 30 March 1935; Ernest P. Ament, *Industrial Recovery Legislation in Light of Catholic Principles* (Washington, D.C., 1936), pp. 88, 93. On responses to early New Deal legislation, see O'Brien, *Social Reform*, pp. 53–54.
62. Lapp, "Social Security and the Forgotten Man," *Catholic Charities Review* 18 (September 1935):204–206.

63. "Catholics and the New Deal," *Catholic World* 141 (April 1935):10–20.

64. "The Mind of the Church on Social Legislation," *Catholic Mind* 32 (22 November 1934).

65. *Father Coughlin's Radio Sermons, October, 1930–April, 1931* (Baltimore, 1931), p. 16.

66. *Father Coughlin's Radio Discourses, 1931–1932* (Royal Oak, Mich., 1932), p. 218.

67. Richard L.-G. Deverall, "The Way it Was", *Social Order* 2 (May 1961):197.

68. Arthur M. Schlesinger, Jr., *The Politics of Upheaval* (New York, 1959), p. 23; Coughlin, *The New Deal In Money* (Royal Oak, Mich., 1933), pp. 84–89.

69. Ryan to Williams, 13 April 1935, Ryan Papers, ACUA.

70. See J. Joseph Hutmacher, *Massachusetts, People and Politics, 1919–1933* (Cambridge, Mass., 193), chap. 9 and William E. Leuchtenburg, *Franklin D. Roosevelt and the New Deal* (New York, 1963), pp. 184, 272.

71. Hadley Cantril, ed., *Public Opinion, 1935–1946* (Princeton, N.J., 1951), p. 755.

72. In December 1935 Father Edmund A. Walsh of Georgetown wrote Secretary of Commerce Daniel C. Roper a letter, "personal and confidential," intended for the president, protesting the class language of Rexford Tugwell. "While fully in sympathy with the high purpose of social justice and the reform of capitalism inherent in much recent legislation, I deplore any attempt from high government sources to drive a wedge between the various groups of our citizenry, who more than ever should now march with solidarity and in a spirit of union toward the accomplishment of national recovery and stability.... Without associating myself in any way with party politics, and mindful of my spiritual obligations, I consider it a duty of conscience to resist now and always any attempt to divide our people by exhortations to hatred and other vengeful attitudes.... The abuses of capitalism, which no one has condemned more openly than I have, will be cured only by the Christian principles of persuasion and an enlightened social conscience. All attempts to do it by compulsion run counter to the experience of psychology and those familiar with the stubborn instincts of human nature." Walsh to Roper, 13 December 1935, included in Roper to president, same date, Roosevelt Papers, Hyde Park, OF36.

73. *Series of Lectures on Social Justice* (Royal Oak, Mich., 1936), p. 41; see also *Series of Lectures 1935* (Royal Oak, Mich., 1935), pp. 155, 191, 193–96, 197–99.

74. *Social Justice*, 27 July 1936 and 5 June 1936.

75. *Organized Social Justice* (New York, n.d.).

76. Jordan A. Schwarz, "Al Smith in the Thirties," *New York History* 45 (October 1964):316–330.

77. Ryan to William Hard, 7 January 1935, Ryan Papers; "What About Industrial Recovery," *Catholic Action* 17 (March 1935):7–8.

78. Ryan to editors of *Christian Front*, 22 January 1936, Ryan Papers, ACUA.

79. Sheehy to LeHand, 8 October 1936, Roosevelt Papers, PPF4996.

80. Ryan to president, 12 November 1936 and Roosevelt to Ryan, 7 January 1937, Roosevelt Papers, PPF 2406.

81. William F. Montavon, Report of the Legal Department of the National Catholic Welfare Conference for the Six Month Period Ending April 20, 1933, in Montavon Papers, Catholic University of America. For a case study of this problem see William J. Sweeney, "Opinions on Proposals for National Health Insurance in American Catholic Periodicals, 1919–1950" (M.A. thesis, Catholic University of America, 1950).

82. The Roosevelt papers are filled with correspondence between the two; see, for example, Mundelein to Roosevelt, 23 October 1936. See also Edward Kantowitz, *Corporation Sole* (Notre Dame, Ind., 1983).

83. Murphy to Felix Frankfurter, 21 February 1945, in Frankfurter Papers, Library of Congress. See also J. Woodford Howard, "Frank Murphy: A Liberal's Creed" (Ph.D. diss., Princeton University, 1959).

84. "On the Threshold of a New Order," *Central Blatt and Social Justice* 31 (January 1939):299–301 and "Economic Inequality under Political Democracy," *CBSJ* 31 (February 1939):335–37. See series "New Deals Past and Present," in *CBSJ* for 1935 and 1936; quote from November 1935, p. 242.

85. Francis J. Weber, "John J. Cantwell and the Legion of Decency," *American Ecclesiastical Review* 151 (October 1964):237–47.

86. "Clarifying the Issues of the Spanish Civil War," *America* 52; Allan Gutmann, *The Wound in the Heart* (New York, 1962).

87. *Tablet*, 22 August 1936.

88. Dorothy Day, "On the Use of Force," *Catholic Worker* 6 (September 1938).

89. J. David Valaik, "Catholics, Neutrality and the Spanish Embargo, 1937–1939," *Journal of American History* 54 (June 1967):73–85.

90. Valaik, "American Catholic Dissenters and the Spanish Civil War," *Catholic Historical Review* 53 (January 1968):537–55. Donald F. Crosby, "Boston Catholics and the Spanish Civil War, 1936–1939," *New England Quarterly* 44 (March 1971):82–100; Valaik, "Catholics, Neutrality and the Spanish Embargo, 1937–1939," *Journal of American History* 54 (1967 June):73–85.

91. In 1938 less than 10 percent admitted to listening regularly, although 30 percent said they had done so before the 1936 election: Cantril, *Public Opinion*, 147–48.

92. "A Letter from Austria," *Ave Maria* 48 (9 July 1938):52.

93. Polls of 1939–1940 showed that 53 percent of Catholics thought Jewish businessmen less honest than others, 42 percent thought the Jews more radical, 54 percent thought they had too much power, and 61 percent thought they had "objectionable qualities." Edwin H. Stembler, et al., *Jews in the Mind of America* (New York, 1966), p. 289.

94. Peter Filene, "American Attitudes Toward Soviet Russia, 1917–1933," vol. 1 (Ph.D. diss., Harvard University), pp. 155–57.

95. Filene, "Soviet Russia," pp. 492–518.

96. *The Cross and the Crisis* (Milwaukee, 1938), pp. 45–55.

97. Huber, *Our Bishops Speak*, pp. 98–101; *America* (1 May 1937).

98. Reported in Edward T. Delaney to Ryan, 15 August 1940, Ryan Papers; ACUA.

99. "National Catholic College Poll," *America* 62 (11 November 1939:144.

100. Mundelein to Cicognani, 6 October 1937, enclosed in Mundelein to Roosevelt, same date, in Roosevelt Papers.

101. Congressional record, 9 October 1939, in Roosevelt Papers, Hyde Park.
102. Ryan to LeHand, 12 September 1940, Roosevelt Papers.
103. F. K. Wentz, "American Catholic Periodicals React to Nazism," *Church History*, pp. 400–420.
104. Fogarty, "Public Patriotism," p. 37; Fogarty, *Vatican and U. S. Hierarchy*, pp. 315–32.
105. Quoted in Kantowitz, *Corporation Sole*, pp. 207–208.
106. Thomas Blantz, *A Priest in Public Service: Francis J. Haas and the New Deal* (Notre Dame, Ind., 1982).
107. Huber, *Our Bishops Speak*, pp. 272–300.
108. Edward A Mooney, "Industry's Great Need: Cooperation, not Competition," *Catholic Action* 19 (January 1937):9–10; Mooney, "The Duty of the Catholic Worker to Join Organized Labor," *Catholic Mind* 38 (8 March 1939):569–71; Edward Mooney, "Rethinking Economics," *Christian Front* 3 (May 1939):9–11; Robert Lucey, "Economic Disorder and *Quadragesimo Anno*," *Homiletic and Pastoral Review* 35 (June 1935):858–64; Robert Lucey, "Apathy: Our Scourge," *Homiletic and Pastoral Review* 36 (June 1936):468–77; Lucey, "Are We Fair to the Church?" *Commonweal* 28 (9 September and 16 September 1938):490–92 and 521–23; Lucey, "Labor in the Recession," *Commonweal* 28 (6 May 1938):47. See also *Time* 37 (7 April 1941):73–74.
109. Talbot to Brophy, 24 September 1938, Brophy Papers, ACUA.
110. *Labor Leader*, (Navyor) 23 January 1938 and 30 April 1938.
111. *Michigan Labor Leader*, 17 November 1939.
112. John Cort, "The Evolution of the Catholic Worker," *Commonweal* 93 (8 January 1971):343.
113. Neil Betten, *Catholicism and the Industrial Worker* (Gainesville, Fla., 1976).
114. Richard Ward, "The Role of the ACTU in the American Labor Movement" (Ph.D. diss., University of Michigan, 1958).
115. *Catholic Worker* 1 (May 1933).
116. Thomas E. Davitt, "Labor and Ownership," *Christian Front 3 (February 1938):23–25*.
117. O'Brien, *Social Reform*, pp. 185–89.
118. O'Brien, *Social Reform*, pp. 189–92; Paul Hanley Furfey, "The New Social Catholicism," *Christian Front* 1 (December 1936):181–84.
119. Quoted in Paul Marx, *Virgil Michel and the Liturgical Movement* (Collegeville, Md., 1957), p. 208.
120. Marc Ellis, *Peter Maurin: Prophet in the Twentieth Century* (New York, 1981). On the Catholic Worker movement, see William Miller, *A Harsh and Dreadful Love: Dorothy Day and the Catholic Worker Movement* (New York, 1973) and *Dorothy Day: A Biography* (New York, 1981).
121. Cort to Day, 29 November 1939, Day Papers, Archives of Marquette University.
122. Wilbur to Ryan, 14 September 1935, Ryan Papers.
123. "Statement on the Church and the Social Order," in Nolan, *Pastoral Letters of the United States Catholic Bishops*, 1:436–53.
124. Charles Bruehl, "Influence of the Social Environment," *Central Blatt and Social Justice* 28 (April 1935):3–4; Talbot in Harold Stearns, ed.,

America Now: An Inquiry into Civilization in the United States (New York, 1938), pp. 528–42.

125. Kiniery to Ryan, 8 March 1937, Ryan Papers.
126. Mooney to Bishop Walter Foery, 3 December 1945, quoted in Tentler, "Detroit."
127. See for example *Declining Liberty and Other Papers* (New York, 1927), pp. 183–85.
128. Edward Duff, "Catholic Social Action in the American Environment," *Social Order* 12 (Septmber 1962):300–314.

Chapter 8.   American Catholicism

1. Statement "On Secularism," 16 November 1947, and "Personal responsibility," 20 November 1960, in LaSalle Woefel, *Catholic Thought in Business and Economics*, vol. 2 (Austin 1961), pp. 5–8, 110–113.
2. For a more extended treatment of Catholic anti communism, see O'Brien, *American Catholics and Social Reform*, chap. 9
3. Spellman to Roosevelt, 1 October 1940, Roosevelt Papers, President's Personal File 4404, Hyde Park, N.Y.
4. Cantwell to Roosevelt, 27 April 1941; Roosevelt to Cantwell, 30 April 1941 in Roosevelt Papers, PPF 7522.
5. Broderick, *Right Reverend New Dealer*, pp. 256–59.
6. Quoted in Lawrence Wittner, *Rebels against War* (New York, 1969), p. 36.
7. Nolan, *Pastoral Letters* 2:36–37.
8. Mooney to Roosevelt, 23 February 1944, Roosevelt Papers, PPF 4727.
9. Thomas T. McAvoy, "American Catholics and the Second World War," *Review of Politics* 6 (1944):131–50.
10. Blantz,*Haas*, chap. 10.
11. Patricia McNeal, "Catholic Conscientious Objection during World War II," *Catholic Historical Review* 61 (April 1975):220–42; Gordon C. Zahn, *Another Side of the War* (Amherst, Mass., 1977).
12. Hennesey, *American Catholics*, pp. 281–82.
13. Gerald Fogarty, "Vatican-American Relations, 1940–1984," Working Paper Series (Fall 1984), Cushwa Center for American Catholic Studies.
14. Liston Pope, "Religion and the Class Structure, in Reinhard Bendix and Seymour Martin Lipset, eds., *Class Status and Power* (New York, 1953), pp. 316–23; R. Schneider, *Religion in Twentieth Century America* (New York, 1945), p. 228; Charles Anderson, *White Protestant Americans* (Englewood Cliffs, N.J., 1970), pp. 140–49: Andrew M. Greeley, *Religion and Career* (New York, 1968) and *American Catholics: A Social Portrait* (New York, 1980).
15. David O'Brien, *The Renewal of American Catholicism* (New York, 1972), chap. 4; Will Herberg, *Protestant, Catholic, Jew* (Garden City, N.Y., 1960).
16. Gleason, "In Search of Unity," p. 189.
17. Mary McCarthy, *Memories of a Catholic Girlhood* (London, 1957).
18. Herberg, *Protestant, Catholic, Jew.*
19. Paul Blanshard, *American Freedom and Catholic Power* (Boston, 1950), p. 5.

20. John Tracy Ellis, "American Jewish-Catholic Relations: Past and Prospect," *American Benedictine Review* 18 (March 1967):55.
21. Reinhold Niebuhr, "A Note on Pluralism," in John Cogley, ed., *Religion in America* (New York, 1958), pp. 47, 49.
22. Francis Lally, "Points of Abrasion," *Atlantic* 210 (August 1962):78–81.
23. Stanley B. James, "The Priesthood in Catholic Action," *Homiletic and Pastoral Review* 38 (January 1938):356.
24. Leo Ward, ed., *Catholic Life, USA: Contemporary Lay Movements* (Saint Louis, Mo., 1959), p. 3.
25. Ward, *Catholic Life*, pp. 200–202.
26. "Catholic Organizations," *Commonweal* 62 (20 March 1964).
27. M. D. Chenu, "Catholic Action and the Mystical Body of Christ," in John Fitzsimons and Paul McGuire, eds., *Restoring All Things: A Guide to Catholic Action* (New York, 1938), p. 15.
28. Edward Marciniak, "Catholics and Social Reform," in *Catholicism in American* ed. *Commonweal* (New York, 1953), pp. 123–32; Marciniak, "Catholic Social Doctrine and the Layman," in Woelfel, *Catholic Thought* 2:4. On the Christian Family Movement see John Kotre, *Simple Gifts: The Lives of Pat and Patty Crowley* (Kansas City, Mo., 1979).
29. Brooklyn *Tablet*, 1 February, 1936.
30. Mel Piehl, *Breaking Bread: The Catholic Worker and the Origins of American Catholic Radicalism* (Philadelphia, 1983).
31. Ed Willock, "Catholic Radicalism in America," in *Catholicism in America*, pp. 133–42.
32. John Cogley, "The Catholic and the Liberal Society," *America* 101 (4 July 1959):495; on lay activism and Wright see Louis Putz, C.S.C., ed., *The Catholic Church USA* (Chicago, 1956).
33. Robert D. Cross, "Catholic Charities," *Atlantic* 210 (August 1962):114. Statistics are taken from the annual *National Catholic Directories*.
34. Ambrose A. Clegg, Jr., "Church Groups and Federal Aid to Education, 1933–1939," *History of Education Quarterly* 4 (September 1964):137–54.
35. Philip A. Grant, "Catholic Congressmen, Cardinal Spellman, Eleanor Roosevelt and the 1949–1950 Federal Aid to Education Controversy," *Records* 90 (March–December 1979):3–13.
36. Stanley Rothman, "The Politics of Parochial Schools: An Historical and Comparative Analysis," *Journal of Politics* 25 (February 1963):49–71.
37. John A. Ryan, "Labor and Economic Construction after the War," *Vital Speeches* 66 (15 February 1943):266–69; *Time*, 11 January 1943.
38. Roger M. Larson, "Trends in the Economic Pronouncements of American Church Bodies, 1908–1948" (Ph.D. diss., University of California, 1950), pp. 37–38.
39. Ronald Schatz, *The Electrical Workers* (Urbana, Ill., 1984), pp. 96–120, 181–83.
40. John F. Cronin, *Catholic Social Action* (Milwaukee, Wisc., 1952), pp. 75–89.
41. Speech in Woelfel, *Catholic Thought* 2:69–72.
42. Donald McDonald, *Catholics in Conversation* (New York, 1960), pp. 121–34.
43. *A Conversation among Friends* (Notre Dame, Ind., 1976). Privately circulated.

44. David Brody, "Career Leadership in American Trade Unionism" in Jaher ed., pp. 283–94.

45. "Christian Family," in Huber, *Our Bishops Speak*, p. 159.

46. George Higgins, "After Sixty Years," *Catholic Mind* (October 1951), in Benjamin Masse, S.J., ed., *The Catholic Mind through Fifty Years* (New York, 1952), pp. 498–510.

47. George Higgins, "American Contributions to the Implementation of the Industry Council Plan, *American Catholic Sociological Review* 13 (March 1952):10–24; Higgins, "Twenty Five Years of *Quadragesimo Anno*," *America* 95 (5 May 1956):130–33; John F. Cronin, "Quadragesimo Anno: An American Symposium," *Social Order* 6 (January 1956):2–13.

48. John F. Cronin, *Catholic Social Action* (Milwaukee, Wisc., 1948), pp. 39, 70, 200–205.

49. Saul Bonder, *Social Justice and Church Authority: The Public Life of Archbishop Robert E. Lucey* (Philadelphia, 1982), chaps. 4, 5; Edward Duff, S.J., "Catholic Social Action in the American Environment," *Social Order* 12 (September 1962):300–314.

50. *Catholic News*, 6 July 1946 and 12 February, 1949; *New York Times*, 7 October 1946 and 18 March 1948.

51. Thomas A. Kselman, "Our Lady of Necedah: Marian Piety and the Cold War," Working Paper Series 12, Fall 1982, Cushwa Center for American Catholic Studies and Kselman and Steven Avella, "Marian Piety and the Cold War in the United States," *Catholic Historical Review* 72 (July 1986):403–424. Kselman points out that references to Fatima in the *Catholic Periodical Index* rose steadily between 1930 and 1959, with fourteen references in the period from 1930 to 1944, thirty-five between 1945 and 1949, fifty-one between 1950 and 1954, and forty-nine in the period from 1955 to 1959. For discussion of the phenomenon at a local level, see O'Brien, *Faith and Friendship*, pp. 287–94.

52. Donald F. Crosby, *God, Church and Flag: Senator Joseph R. McCarthy and the Catholic Church, 1950–1957* (Chapel Hill, N.C., 1978); Vincent P. De Santis, "American Catholics and McCarthyism," *Catholic Historical Review* 51 (April 1965):1–30. The quotations from Spellman and Sheil are taken from the Crosby volume.

53. John F. Cronin, *Communism: Threat to Freedom* (New York, 1962).

54. Father Cronin some years ago kindly gave me copies of correspondence related to the party initiative and the bishops' response. On liberal calls for dialogue, see "The Church and Communism," *Commonweal* 53 (27 September 1963) and Peter Riga, "Beyond Anti-Communism," *Catholic Worker* 33 (January 1966).

55. "Conscience and Anti-Communism," *Commonweal* 54 (18 December 1964) and Dom Helder Camara, "Marxism without Atheism," *Commonweal* 55 (7 May 1965).

56. William A. Au, "American Catholics and the Dilemma of War, 1960–1980," *U.S. Catholic Historian* 4 (1984):49–79; Patricia McNeal, *The American Catholic Peace Movement, 1928–1972* (New York, 1978).

57. William Clancy, "The Liberal Catholic," *Commonweal* (11 July 1952).

58. William F. Buckley, Jr., "Catholic Liberals, Catholic Conservatives, and the Requirements of Unity," in *Rumbles Left and Right* (New York, 1963), pp. 142–52.

59. William Clancy, "A Liberal View," *Commonweal* (16 December 1960).
60. Donald Pellotte, *John Courtney Murray: Theologian in Conflict* (New York, 1977), pp. 1–70.
61. John Tracy Ellis, *Perspectives on American Catholicism* (Baltimore, 1963), p. 8. The essay originally appeared in *Harper's* in November 1953.
62. Fogarty, *Vatican and U. S. Hierarchy*, pp. 368–86.
63. John Courtney Murray, S.J., *We Hold These Truths* (New York, 1960), pp. ix–xi 12, 41, 43.
64. Ibid., pp. 11–12.
65. Ibid., pp. 42–43.
66. Elmo Roper, "The Myth of the Catholic Vote," *Saturday Review of Literature* (31 October 1959), pp. 151–54. See also John H. Fenton, *The Catholic Vote* (New Orleans, 1960).
67. Kennedy's Houston address is in John Wilson and Donald L. Perkiman, ed., *Church and State in American History* (Boston, 1987), pp. 190–92.

Chapter 9.   Styles of Public Catholicism

1. See David O'Brien, *The Renewal of American Catholicism* (New York, 1972), chap. 6. Written in the midst of it all, this book combined interpretation with advocacy, but its explanation of the sources of change still seems valid.
2. Hennesey, *American Catholics*, p. 307.
3. Thomas O'Dea, "The Catholic Immigrant and the American Scene," *Thought* 31 (Summer 1956):251–70 and O'Brien, *Renewal*, passim.
4. Both quotes are from "The Pastoral Constitution on the Church and the Modern World," in Walter Abbott, S.J., *The Documents of Vatican II* (New York, 1966), pp. 199–200.
5. See, for example, Michael Novak, *A New Generation: American and Catholic* (New York, 1964).
6. Gleason, "In Search of Unity," pp. 184–205.
7. Pelotte, *John Courtney Murray*, pp. 124–126.
8. "Declaration on Religious Freedom," in Abbott, *Documents*, p. 680.
9. "Pastoral Constitution," in Abbott, *Documents*, p. 294.
10. For a case study of a bishop changed by the council, and the conflicting pressures of the 1960s in one local church, see *Faith and Friendship*, chaps. 16–21.
11. See O'Brien, *Renewal* and Charles A. Fracchia, *Second Spring: The Coming of Age of U.S. Catholicism* (New York, 1980). Quotation from Ellis," American Catholics and Peace," p. 17.
12. David O'Brien, "American Catholics and the Vietnam War: A Preliminary Assessment," in Thomas Shannon, ed., *War or Peace: The Search for New Answers* (Maryknoll, N.Y., 1981), pp. 119–51.
13. Gordon Zahn, "The Catholic Upheaval," *Saturday Review of Literature* (1971 September 11; Francine du Plessix Gray, *Divine Disobedience* (New York, 1970).
14. Cardinal Joseph Bernardin, *The Seamless Garment*, (Kansas City, Mo., 1984), is a collection of Bernadin's speeches on this matter.
15. David O'Brien, "The Future of Ministry: Historical Context," in Joseph P. Sinwell and Billie Poon, eds., *The Future of Ministry* (New York,

1985), pp. 33–66. See also O'Brien, "American Catholicism's Precarious Prospects," College Theology Society *Proceedings* (1984).

16. For documentation on the Call to Action, see *A Call to Action* (Washington, D.C., 1977) and a series of retrospective articles on the program issued as a "special supplement" by *Commonweal* in October 1986. For another approach to the three styles, see David O'Brien, "Social Teaching, Social Action, Social Gospel," *U.S. Catholic Historian* 4 (1986):195–224.

17. *The Challenge of Peace: God's Promise and Our Response* (Washington, D.C., 1983), par. 276–77.

18. *Economic Justice for All* (Washington, D.C., 1986).

19. Merton to Forrest, 21 October 1961 in William H. Shannon, ed., *The Hidden Ground of Love: The Letters of Thomas Merton on Religious Experience and Social Concerns* (New York, 1985), p. 256.

20. Wayne Lobue, "Public Theology and the Catholic Worker," *Cross Currents* (Fall 1976):270–85; Mary C. Segers, "Equality and Christian Anarchism: The Political and Social Ideas of the Catholic Worker Movement," *Review of Politics* 40 (Summer 1978):196–230.

21. Mel Piehl, *Breaking Bread*, p. 194.

22. "Catholic Worker Positions," *Catholic Worker* 52 (May 1985):31. See also William Miller, "The Radical Idea of the Catholic Worker," *A Harsh and Dreadful Love*, chap. 2.

23. Ryan to Jerome A. Drolet, 4 February 1936, Ryan Papers, ACUA.

24. David O'Brien, "The Catholic Vote," *Commonweal* (10 October 1980):542–46.

25. Ed Marciniak, "Catholic Social Action: Where Do We Go From Here?" *America* 123 (12 December 1970).

26. I have evaluated the teaching of the pastoral letters, with special reference to the problem of the public, in "American Catholics and American Society," in Philip Murnion, ed., *Catholics and Nuclear War* (New York, 1983), pp. 16–29 and in *Public Theology, Civil Religion and American Catholicism*, Boardman Lectureship in Christian Ethics, University of Pennsylvania (Philadelphia, 1987). For a critical view, see J. Brian Benestad, *The Pursuit of a Just Social Order* (Washington, D.C., 1982). The essays in Robin Lovin, ed., *Religion and American Public Life* (New York, 1986) set out the tensions between ecclesiastical and religious integrity and public responsibility.

27. Joseph A. Komonchak, "Clergy, Laity and the Church's Mission to the World," *The Jurist* 41 (Fall 1981):425–47.

28. See Kantowitz, *Corporation Sole* and Saul Bonder, *Social Justice and Church Authority* (Philadelphia, 1983).

Index